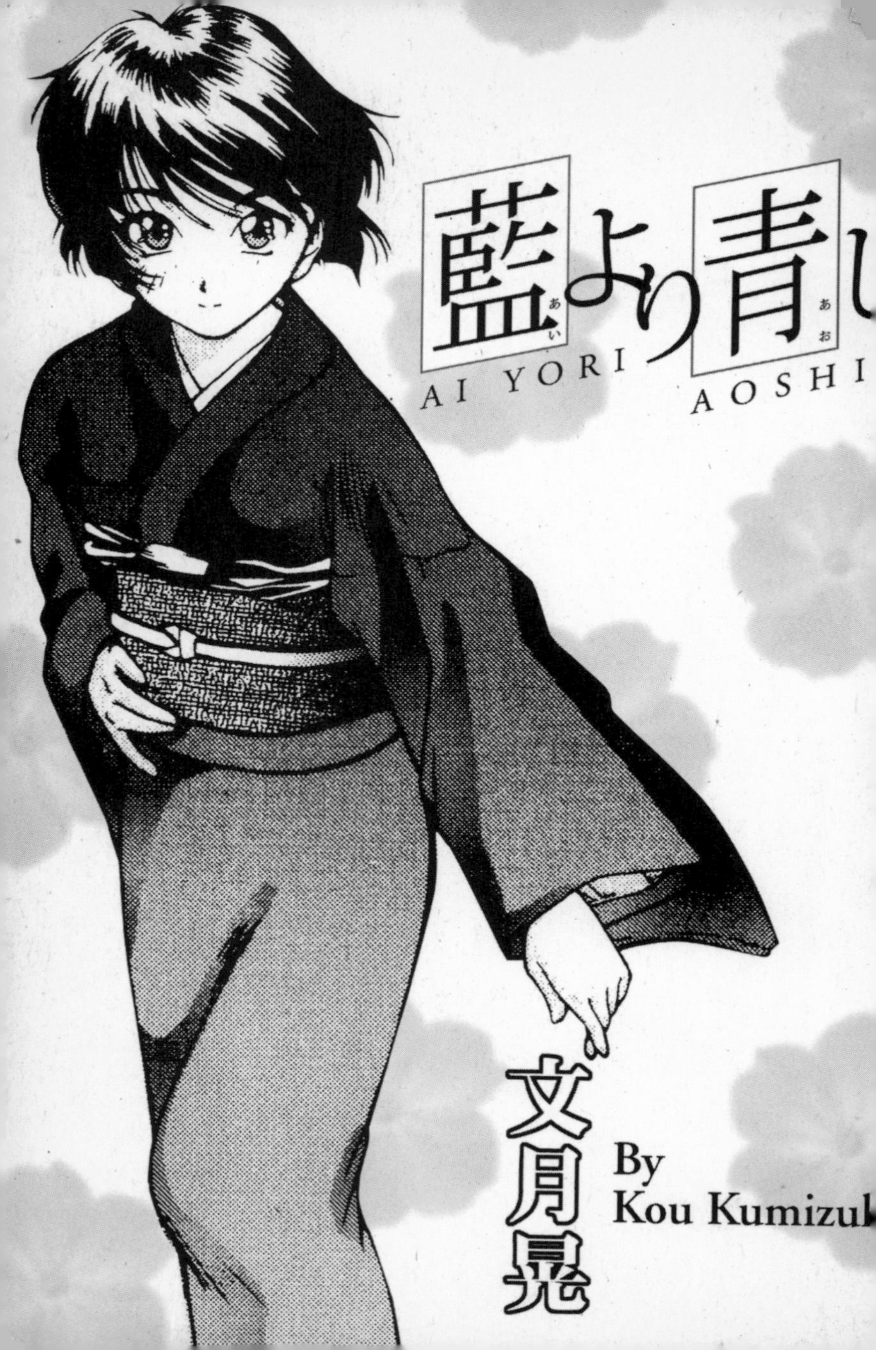

藍(あい)より青(あお)し
AI YORI AOSHI
文月晃
By
Kou Kumizuk

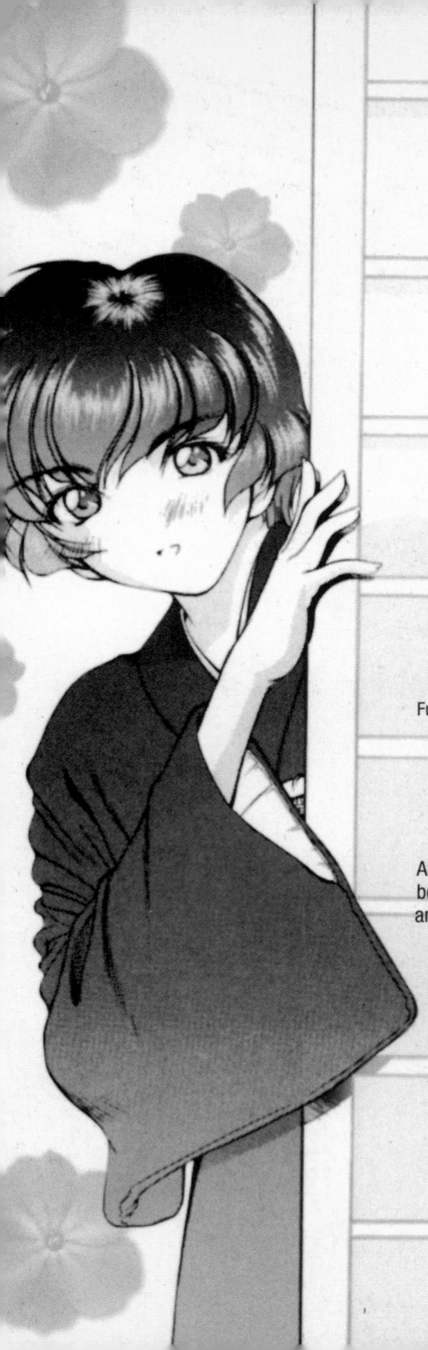



TOKYOPOP Inc.
5900 Wilshire Blvd. Suite 2000
Los Angeles, CA 90036

*Ai Yori Aoshi Vol. 1*



ISBN: 978-1-59182-645-3

First TOKYOPOP printing: January 2004

10 9 8 7 6 5 4 3

Printed in the USA

# AI YORI AOSHI™

### VOLUME 1

## STORY & ART
## BY
## KOU FUMIZUKI

# Irasshaimase!

Welcome to the first volume of Kou Fumizuki's *Ai Yori Aoshi!*
The title literally translates to "Bluer than Indigo," but it is also a
play on "ai," the Japanese word for love. So in a sense, you could
say that this is a tale of "true blue love."

The manga was first serialized in Hakusensha's *Young Animal*
magazine, a seinin (young men) anthology that is also home to the
dark fantasy epic *Berserk.* As of 2003, *Ai Yori Aoshi* has run for 12
volumes and is as strong as ever. The manga inspired a 24 episode
anime series and a 12 episode sequel series called *Ai Yori Aoshi—
Enishi* (fate), both produced by Geneon Entertainment (formerly
Pioneer).

For the English translation of *Ai Yori Aoshi,* the original right-to-
left orientation has been retained, as have Japanese naming con-
ventions and honorifics, so you'll see characters listed last name
first with suffixes after their names. Formality and etiquette play
an enormous role in Japanese culture, and we believe that retain-
ing these honorifics provides a greater understanding of the work.
Honorifics you'll encounter in *Ai Yori Aoshi* include:

san—The default suffix. Equivalent to Mr. or Mrs.
chan—Indicates friendly affection.
sama—Indicates great respect or reverence. Very polite.

At the back of the book, you'll find a glossary of Japanese clothing
and culture pertaining to this volume.

Now, please enjoy the manga!

# 藍(あい)より青(あお)し

# AI YORI AOSHI™

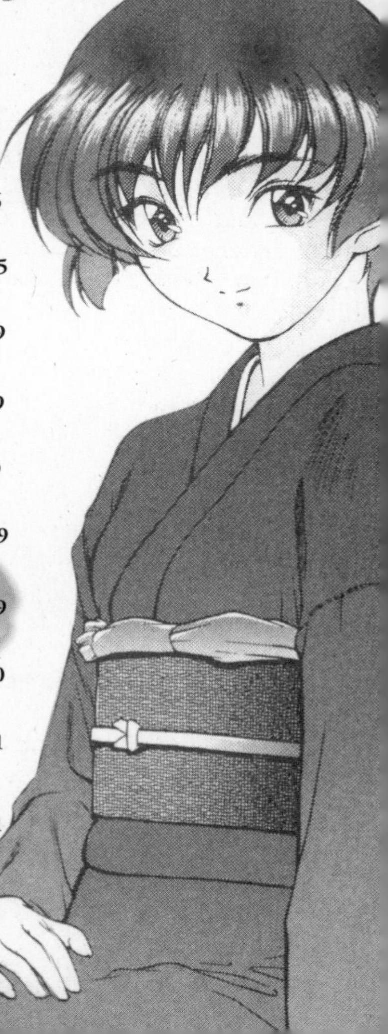

## CONTENTS

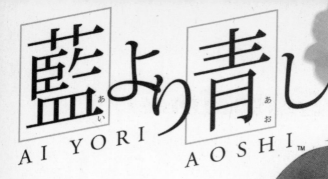

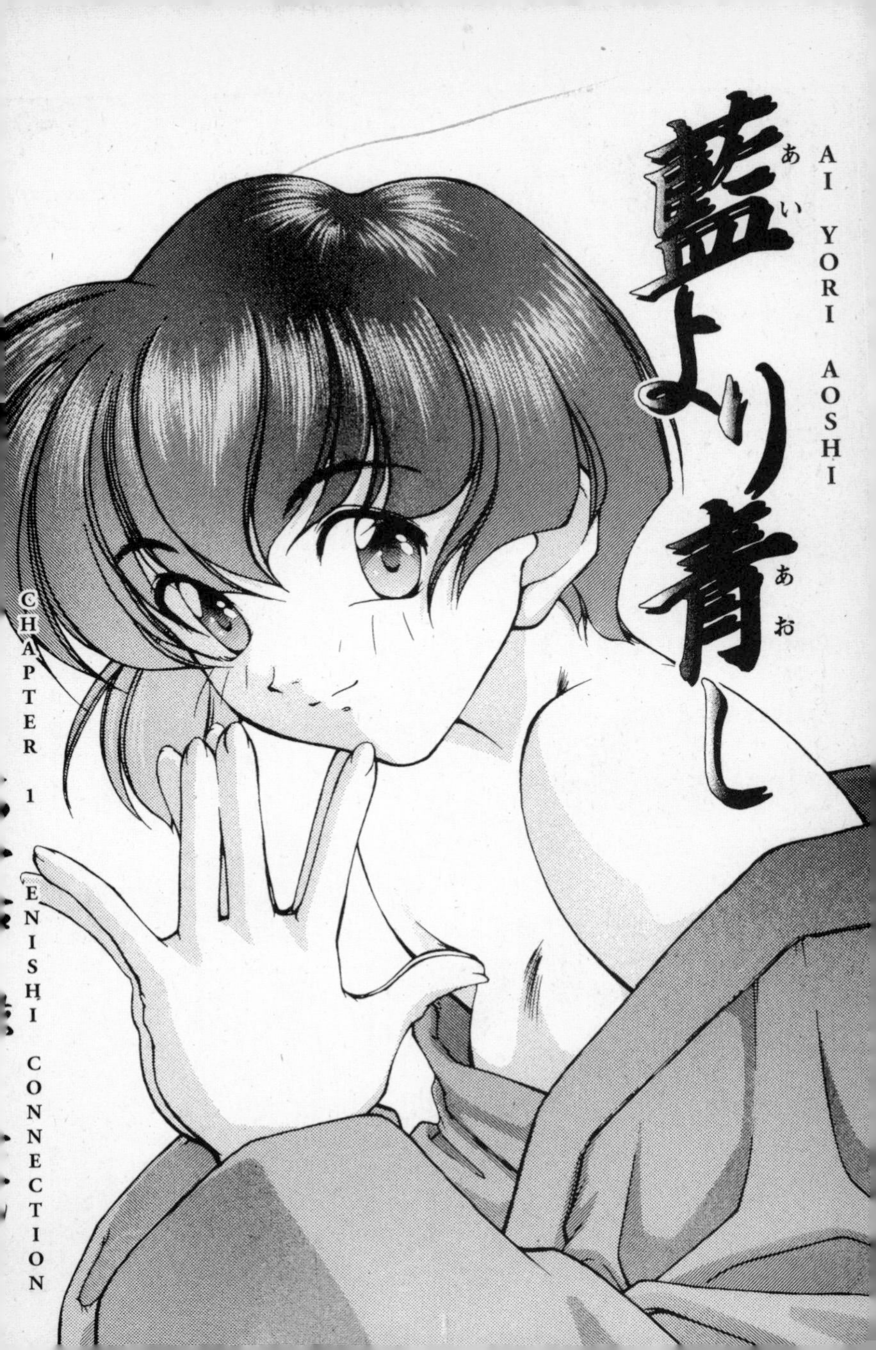
藍より青し
あい
あお
AI YORI AOSHI
CHAPTER 1 ENISHI CONNECTION

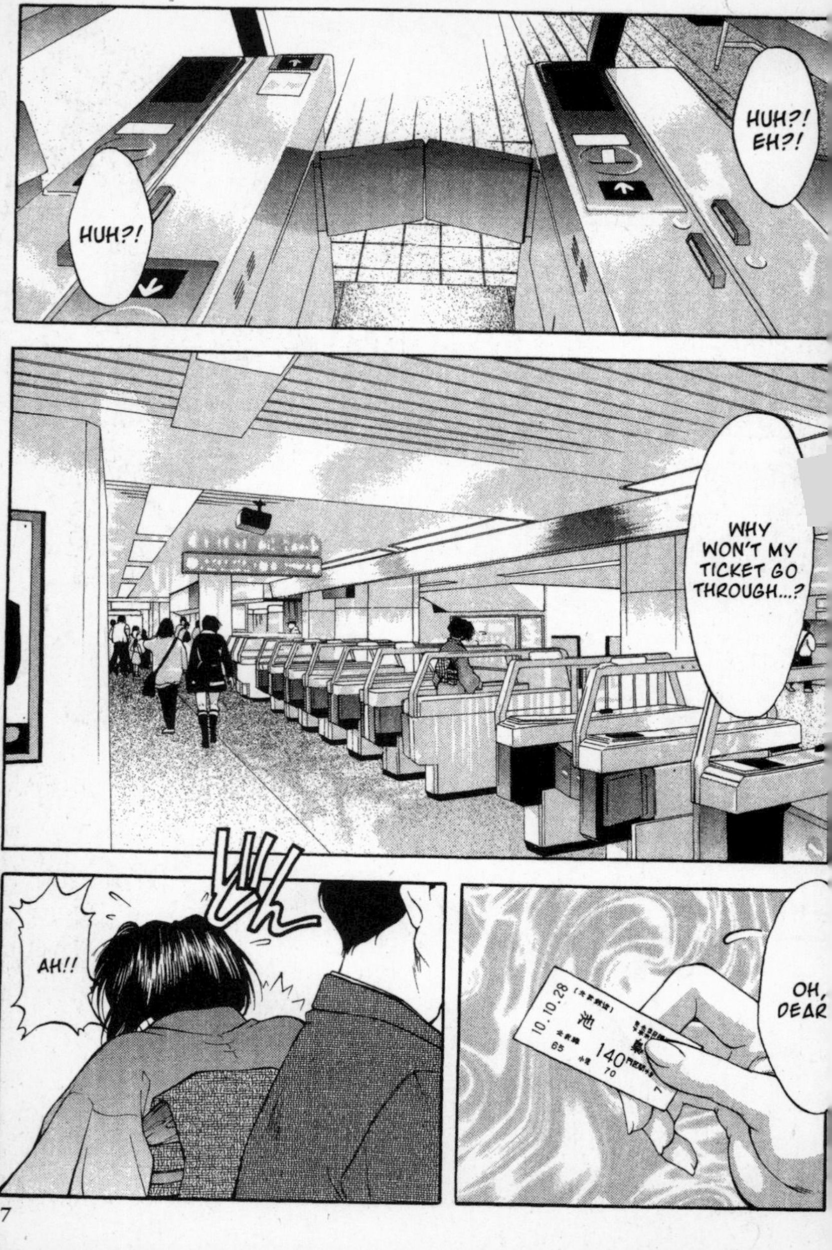
HUH?! EH?!
HUH?!
WHY WON'T MY TICKET GO THROUGH...?
OH, DEAR
10.10.28
140
AH!!

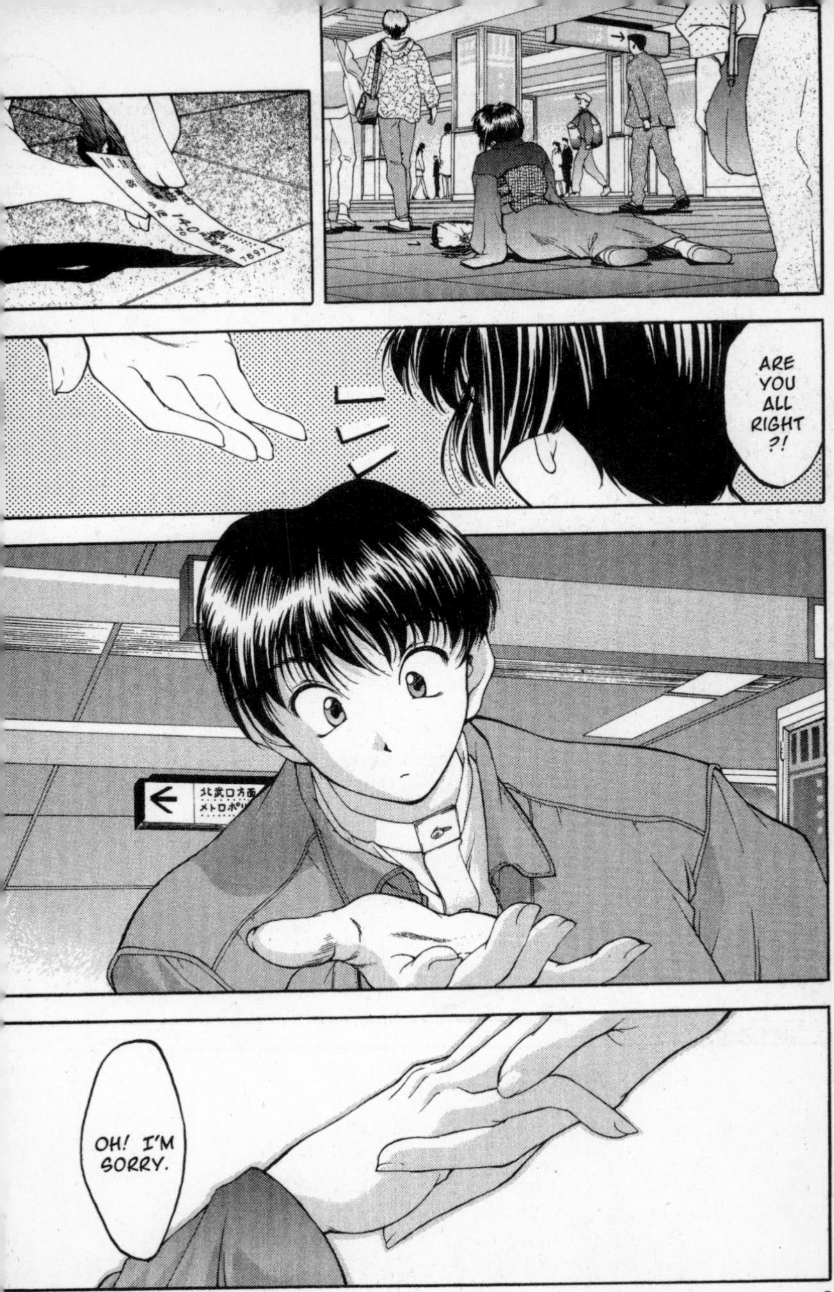
ARE YOU ALL RIGHT?!
北武口方面
OH! I'M SORRY.

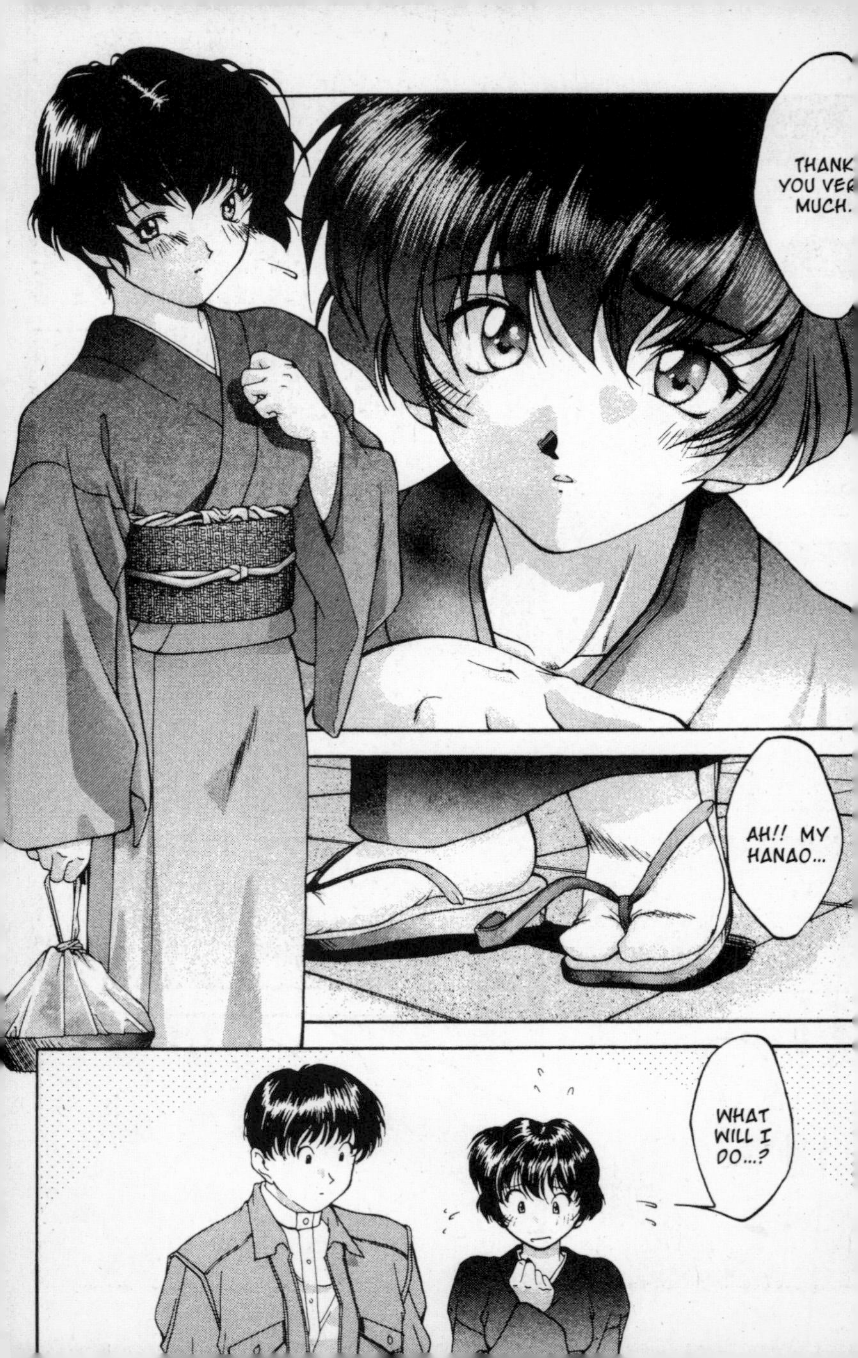
THANK YOU VER MUCH.
AH!! MY HANAO...
WHAT WILL I DO...?

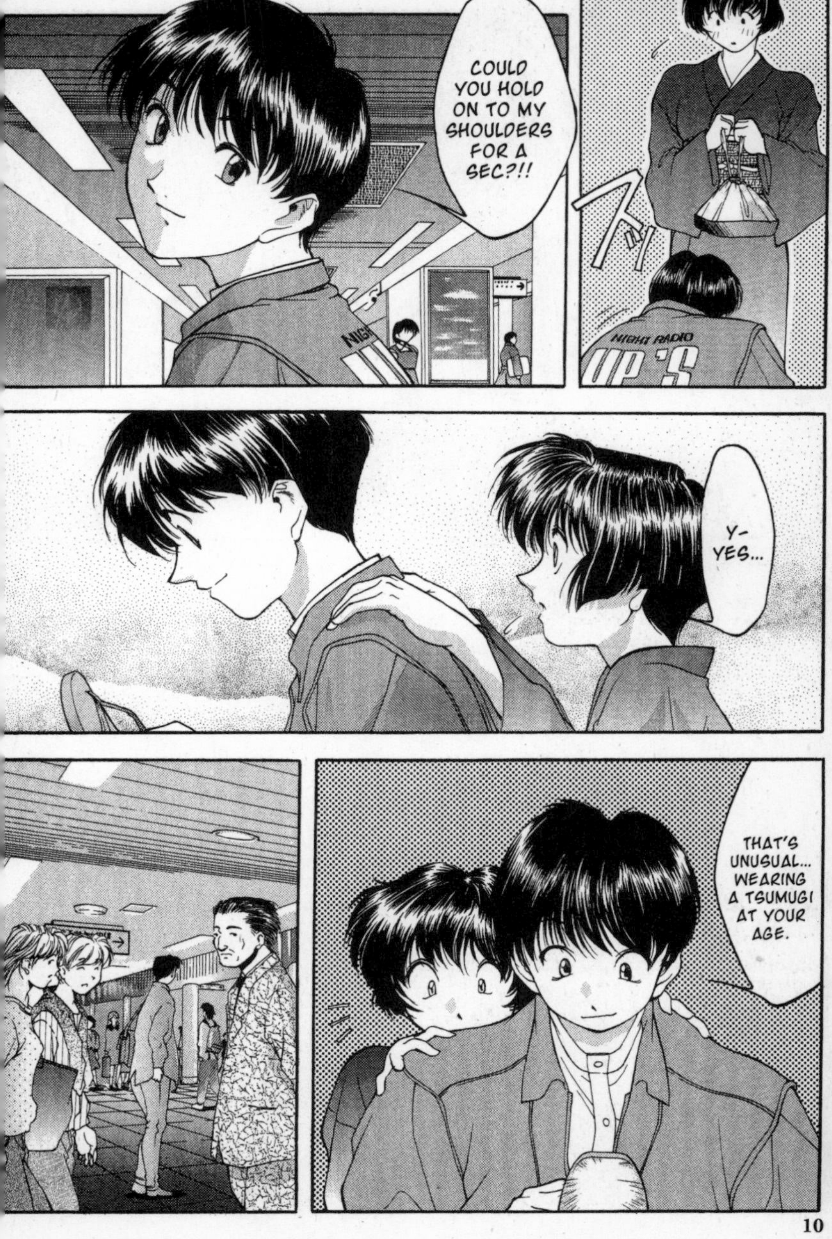
COULD YOU HOLD ON TO MY SHOULDERS FOR A SEC?!!
Y- YES...
THAT'S UNUSUAL... WEARING A TSUMUGI AT YOUR AGE.

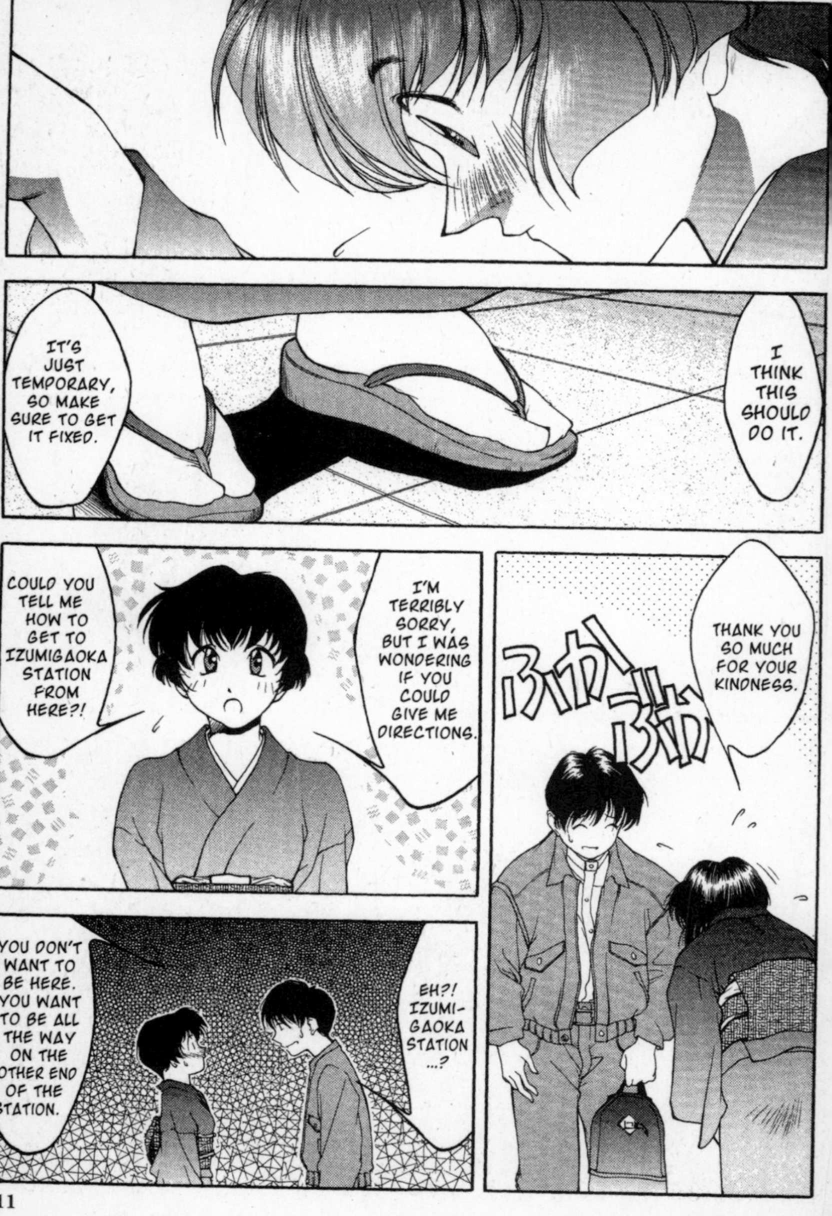
I THINK THIS SHOULD DO IT.
IT'S JUST TEMPORARY, SO MAKE SURE TO GET IT FIXED.
THANK YOU SO MUCH FOR YOUR KINDNESS.
ふか〜っ ふか
I'M TERRIBLY SORRY, BUT I WAS WONDERING IF YOU COULD GIVE ME DIRECTIONS.
COULD YOU TELL ME HOW TO GET TO IZUMIGAOKA STATION FROM HERE?!
EH?! IZUMI-GAOKA STATION ...?
YOU DON'T WANT TO BE HERE. YOU WANT TO BE ALL THE WAY ON THE OTHER END OF THE STATION.

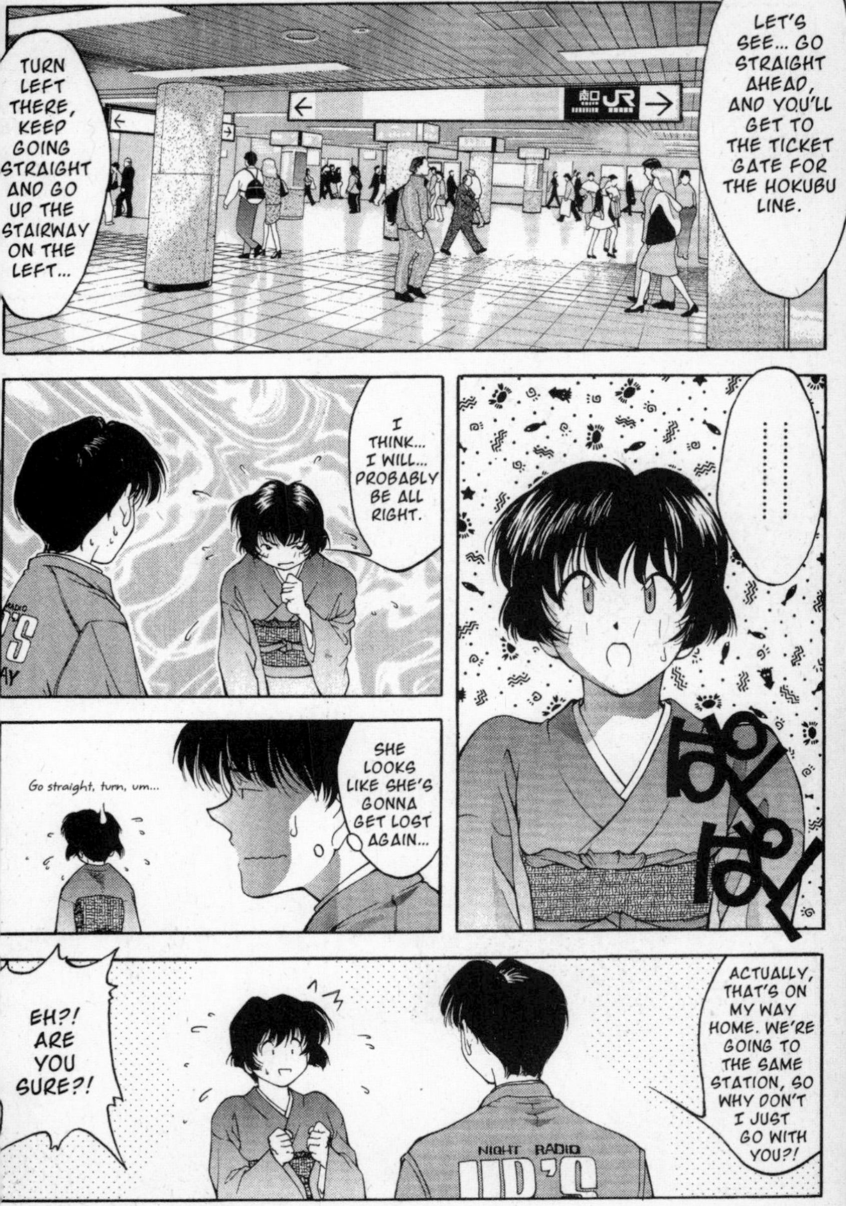
LET'S SEE... GO STRAIGHT AHEAD, AND YOU'LL GET TO THE TICKET GATE FOR THE HOKUBU LINE.
TURN LEFT THERE, KEEP GOING STRAIGHT AND GO UP THE STAIRWAY ON THE LEFT...
......
I THINK... I WILL... PROBABLY BE ALL RIGHT.
SHE LOOKS LIKE SHE'S GONNA GET LOST AGAIN...
Go straight, turn, um...
ACTUALLY, THAT'S ON MY WAY HOME. WE'RE GOING TO THE SAME STATION, SO WHY DON'T I JUST GO WITH YOU?!
EH?! ARE YOU SURE?!
NIGHT RADIO

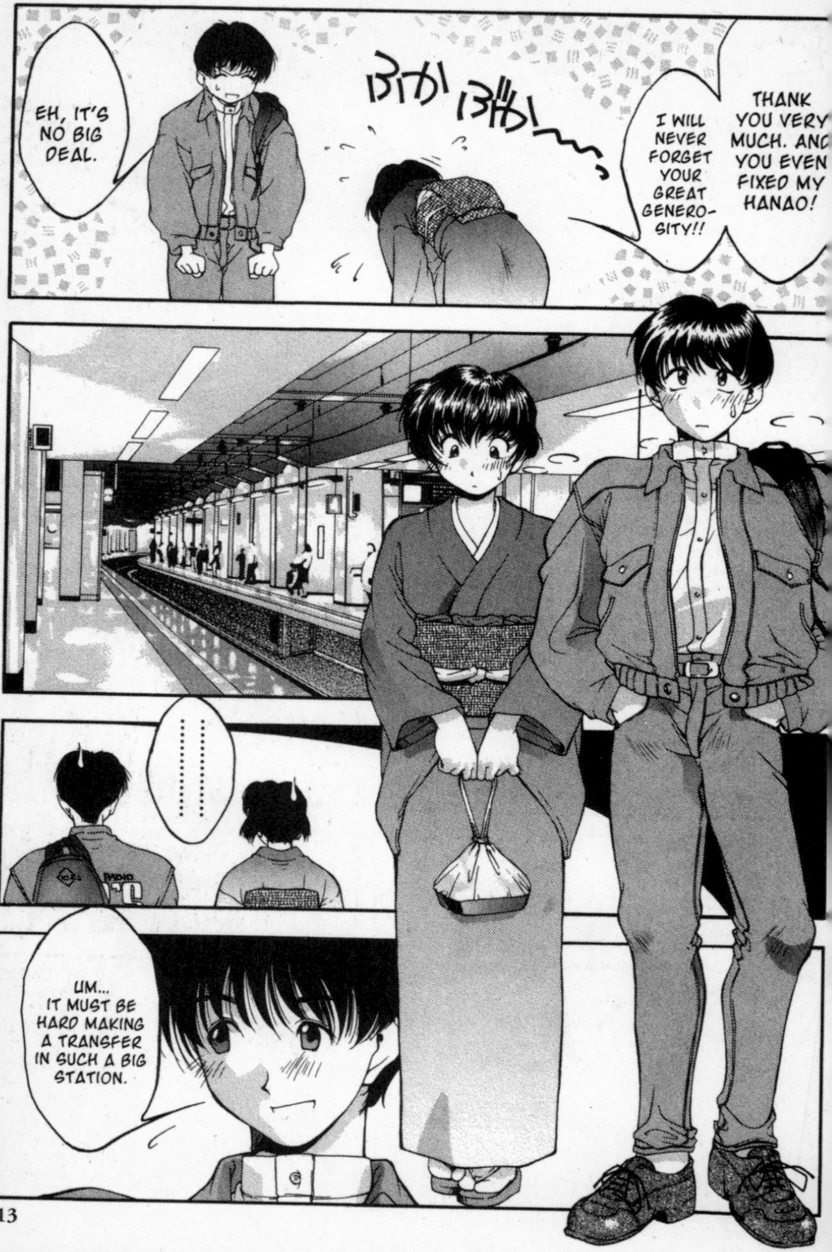
THANK YOU VERY MUCH. AND YOU EVEN FIXED MY HANAO!
I WILL NEVER FORGET YOUR GREAT GENEROSITY!!
EH, IT'S NO BIG DEAL.
......
UM... IT MUST BE HARD MAKING A TRANSFER IN SUCH A BIG STATION.

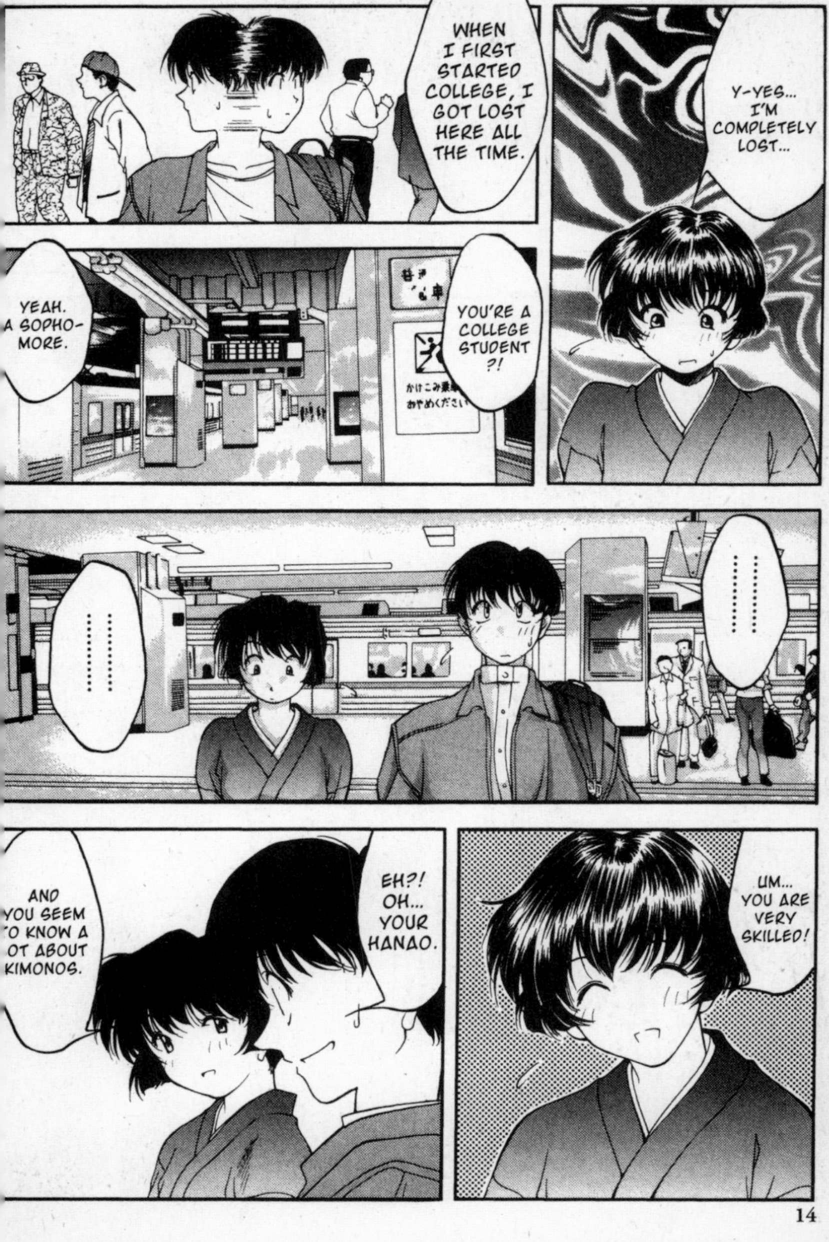
WHEN I FIRST STARTED COLLEGE, I GOT LOST HERE ALL THE TIME.
Y-YES... I'M COMPLETELY LOST...
YOU'RE A COLLEGE STUDENT?!
YEAH. A SOPHO-MORE.
..........
..........
UM... YOU ARE VERY SKILLED!
EH?! OH... YOUR HANAO.
AND YOU SEEM TO KNOW A LOT ABOUT KIMONOS.

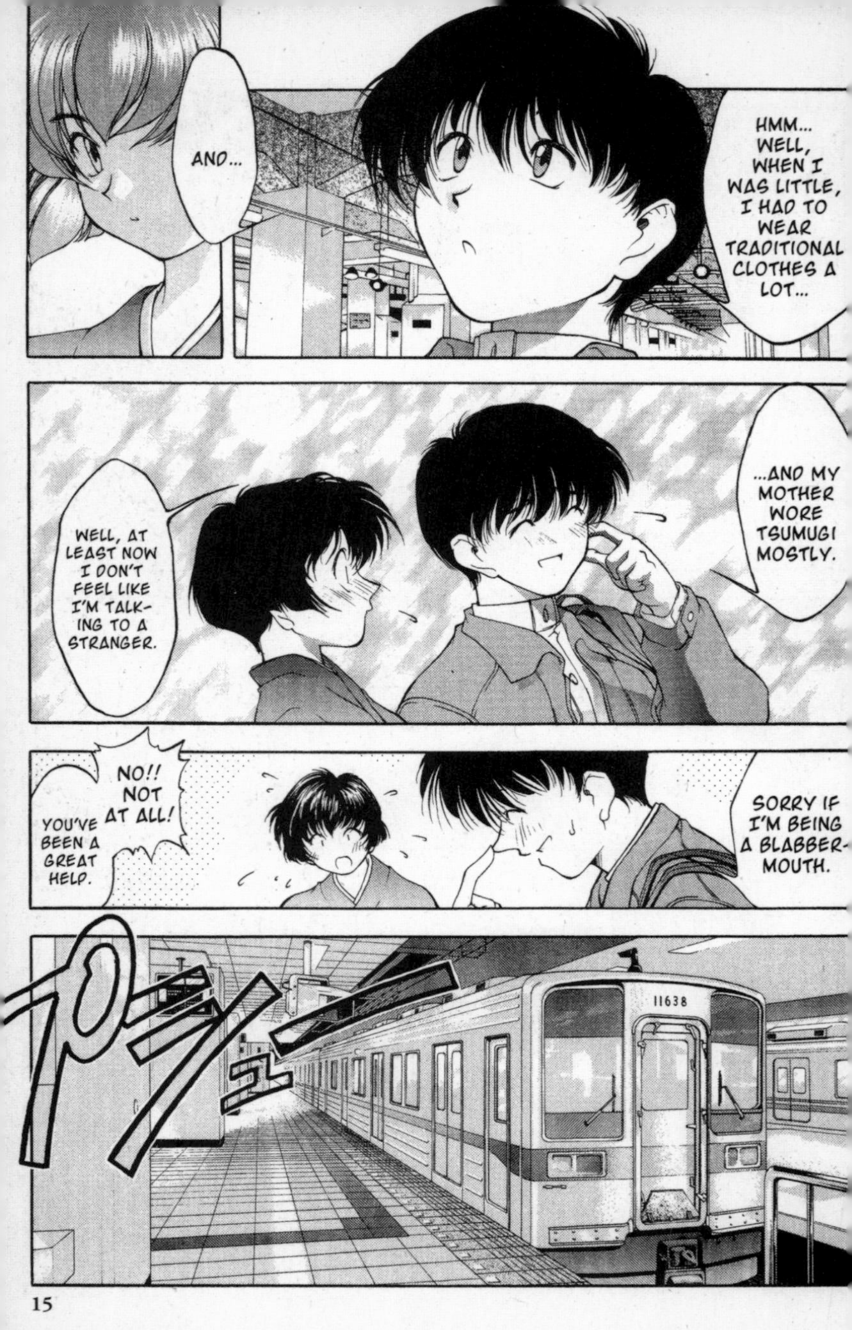
HMM... WELL, WHEN I WAS LITTLE, I HAD TO WEAR TRADITIONAL CLOTHES A LOT...
AND...
...AND MY MOTHER WORE TSUMUGI MOSTLY.
WELL, AT LEAST NOW I DON'T FEEL LIKE I'M TALKING TO A STRANGER.
SORRY IF I'M BEING A BLABBERMOUTH.
NO!! NOT AT ALL!
YOU'VE BEEN A GREAT HELP.

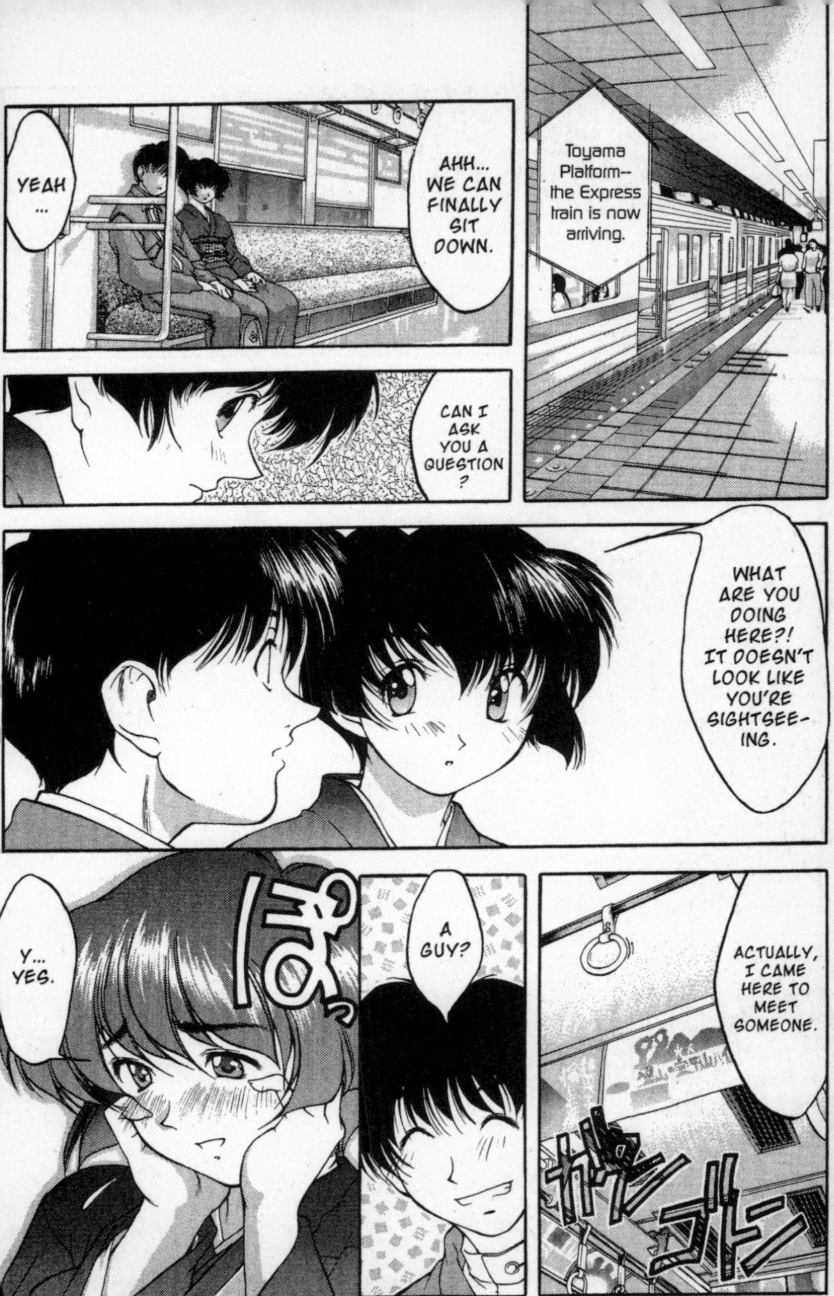
Toyama Platform-- the Express train is now arriving.
AHH... WE CAN FINALLY SIT DOWN.
YEAH ...
CAN I ASK YOU A QUESTION ?
WHAT ARE YOU DOING HERE?! IT DOESN'T LOOK LIKE YOU'RE SIGHTSEE-ING.
ACTUALLY, I CAME HERE TO MEET SOMEONE.
A GUY?
Y... YES.

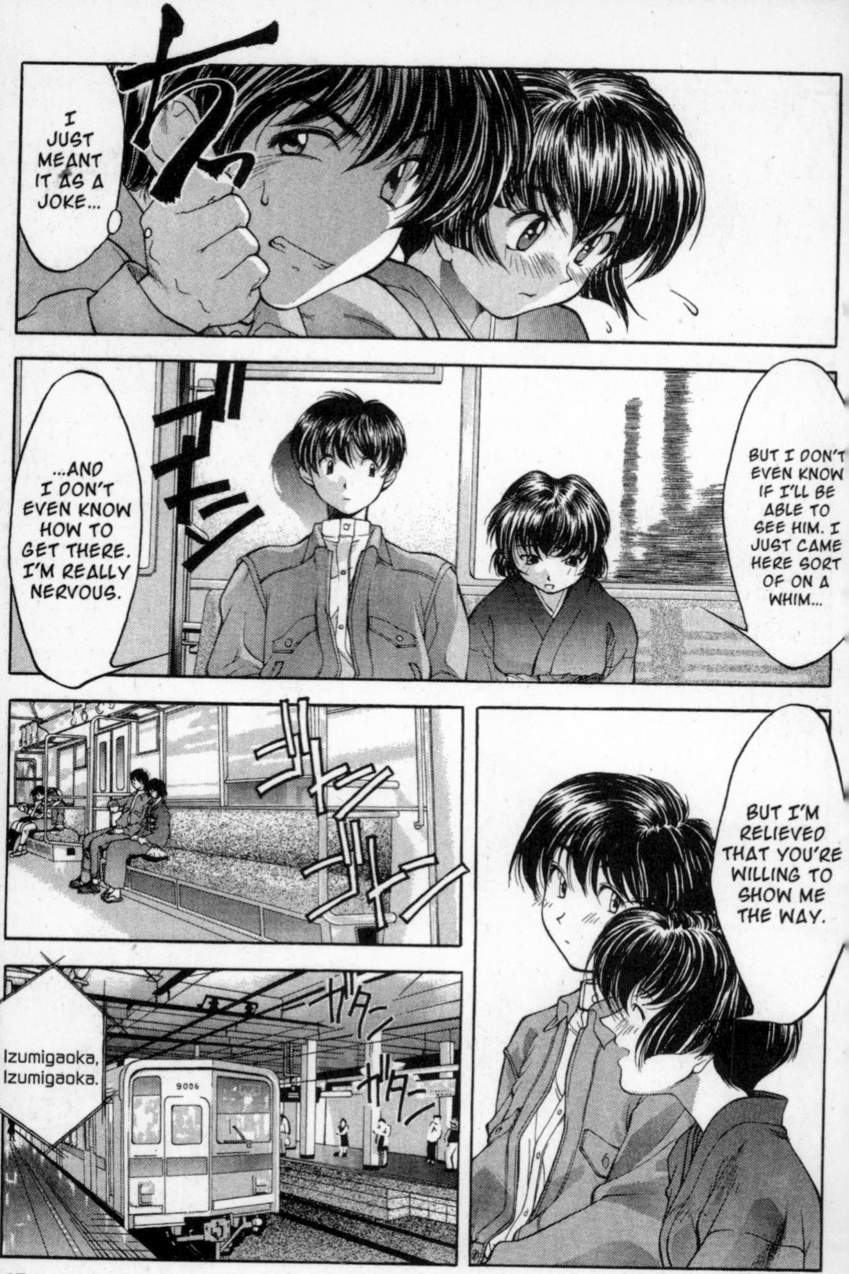
I JUST MEANT IT AS A JOKE...
BUT I DON'T EVEN KNOW IF I'LL BE ABLE TO SEE HIM. I JUST CAME HERE SORT OF ON A WHIM...
...AND I DON'T EVEN KNOW HOW TO GET THERE. I'M REALLY NERVOUS.
BUT I'M RELIEVED THAT YOU'RE WILLING TO SHOW ME THE WAY.
Izumigaoka, Izumigaoka.

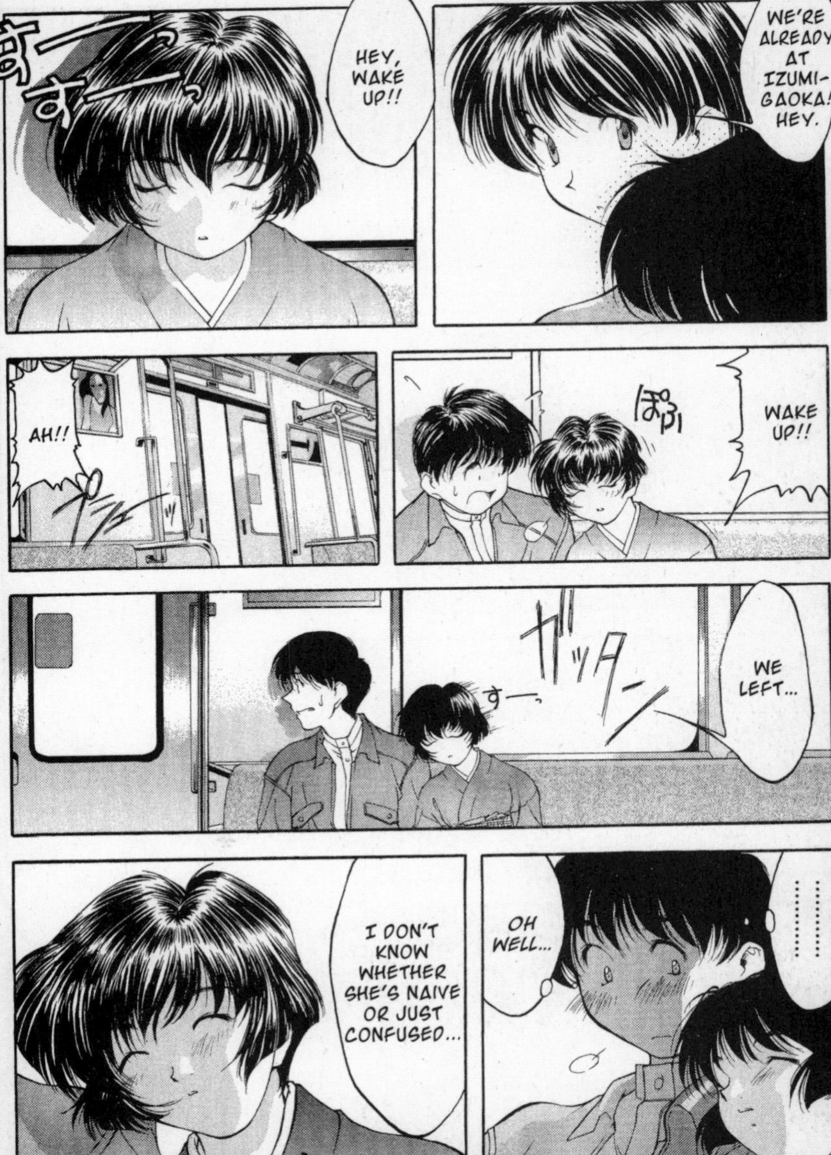

WE'RE ALREADY AT IZUMI-GAOKA! HEY.
HEY, WAKE UP!!
WAKE UP!!
ぽふ
AH!!
WE LEFT...
すー
......
OH WELL...
I DON'T KNOW WHETHER SHE'S NAIVE OR JUST CONFUSED...

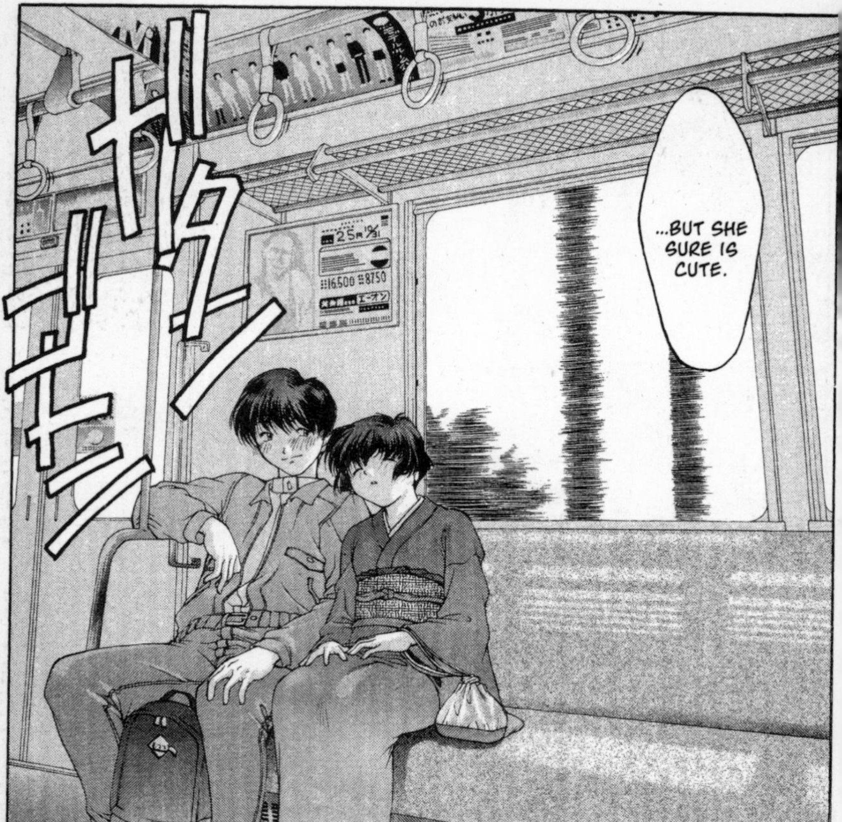
...BUT SHE SURE IS CUTE.

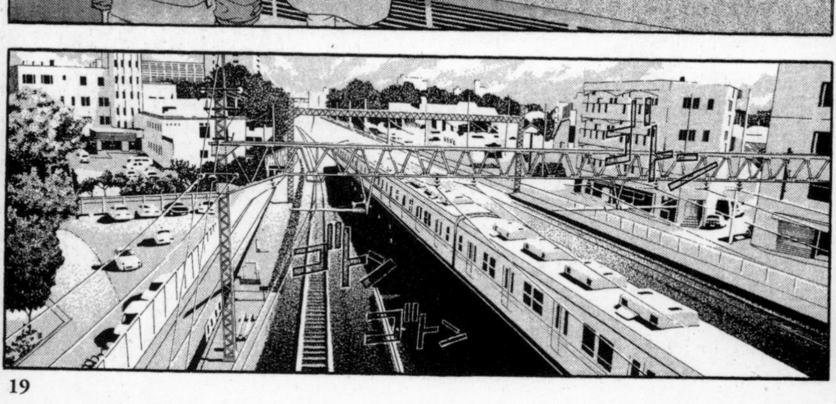

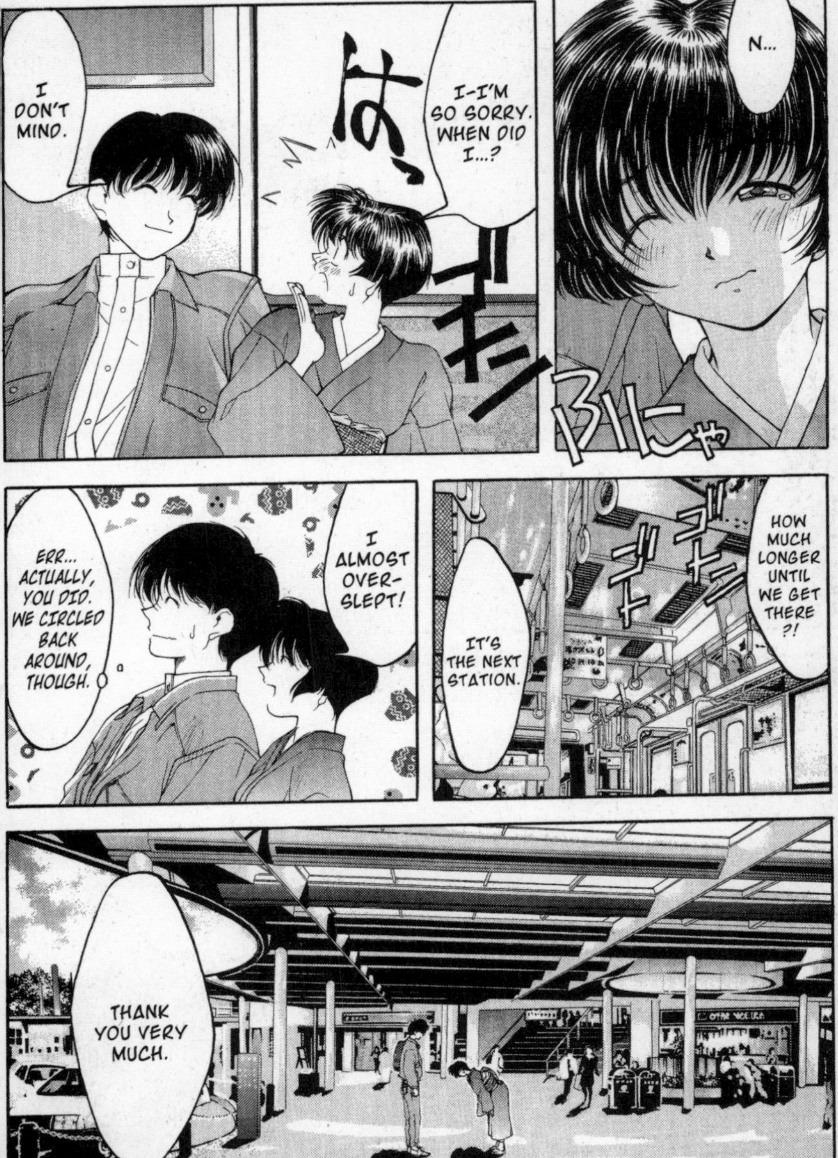
N...
ふにゃ
は
I-I'M SO SORRY. WHEN DID I...?
I DON'T MIND.
HOW MUCH LONGER UNTIL WE GET THERE?!
IT'S THE NEXT STATION.
I ALMOST OVER-SLEPT!
ERR... ACTUALLY, YOU DID. WE CIRCLED BACK AROUND, THOUGH.
THANK YOU VERY MUCH.

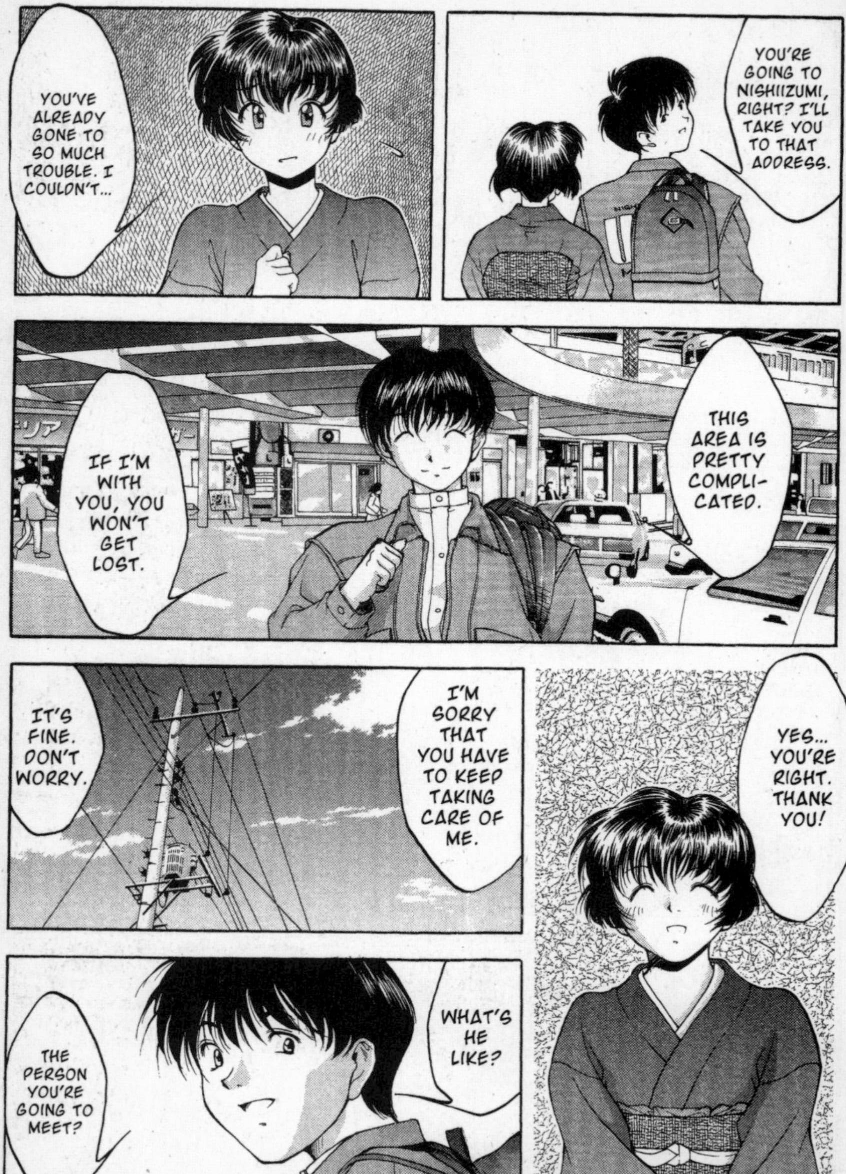
YOU'RE GOING TO NISHIIZUMI, RIGHT? I'LL TAKE YOU TO THAT ADDRESS.
YOU'VE ALREADY GONE TO SO MUCH TROUBLE. I COULDN'T...
THIS AREA IS PRETTY COMPLICATED.
IF I'M WITH YOU, YOU WON'T GET LOST.
YES... YOU'RE RIGHT. THANK YOU!
I'M SORRY THAT YOU HAVE TO KEEP TAKING CARE OF ME.
IT'S FINE. DON'T WORRY.
WHAT'S HE LIKE?
THE PERSON YOU'RE GOING TO MEET?

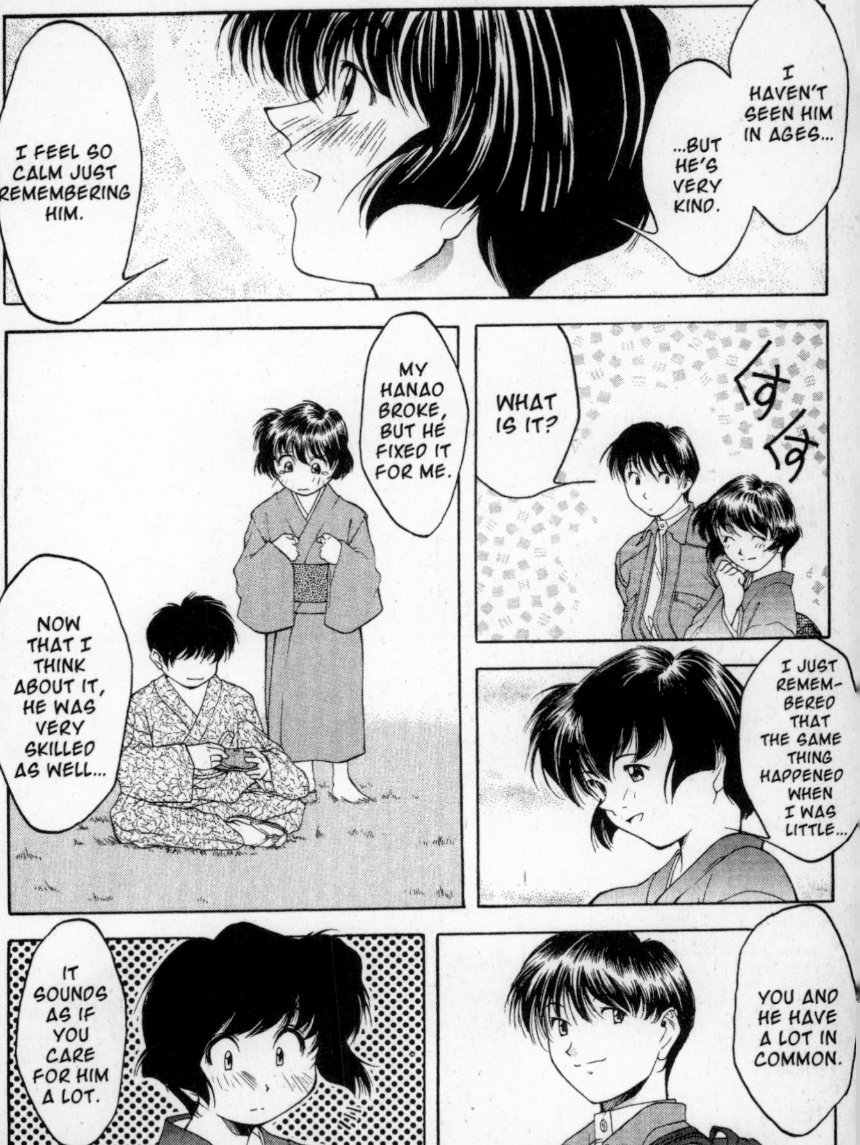
I HAVEN'T SEEN HIM IN AGES...
...BUT HE'S VERY KIND.
I FEEL SO CALM JUST REMEMBERING HIM.
くすくす
WHAT IS IT?
I JUST REMEM-BERED THAT THE SAME THING HAPPENED WHEN I WAS LITTLE...
MY HANAO BROKE, BUT HE FIXED IT FOR ME.
NOW THAT I THINK ABOUT IT, HE WAS VERY SKILLED AS WELL...
YOU AND HE HAVE A LOT IN COMMON.
IT SOUNDS AS IF YOU CARE FOR HIM A LOT.

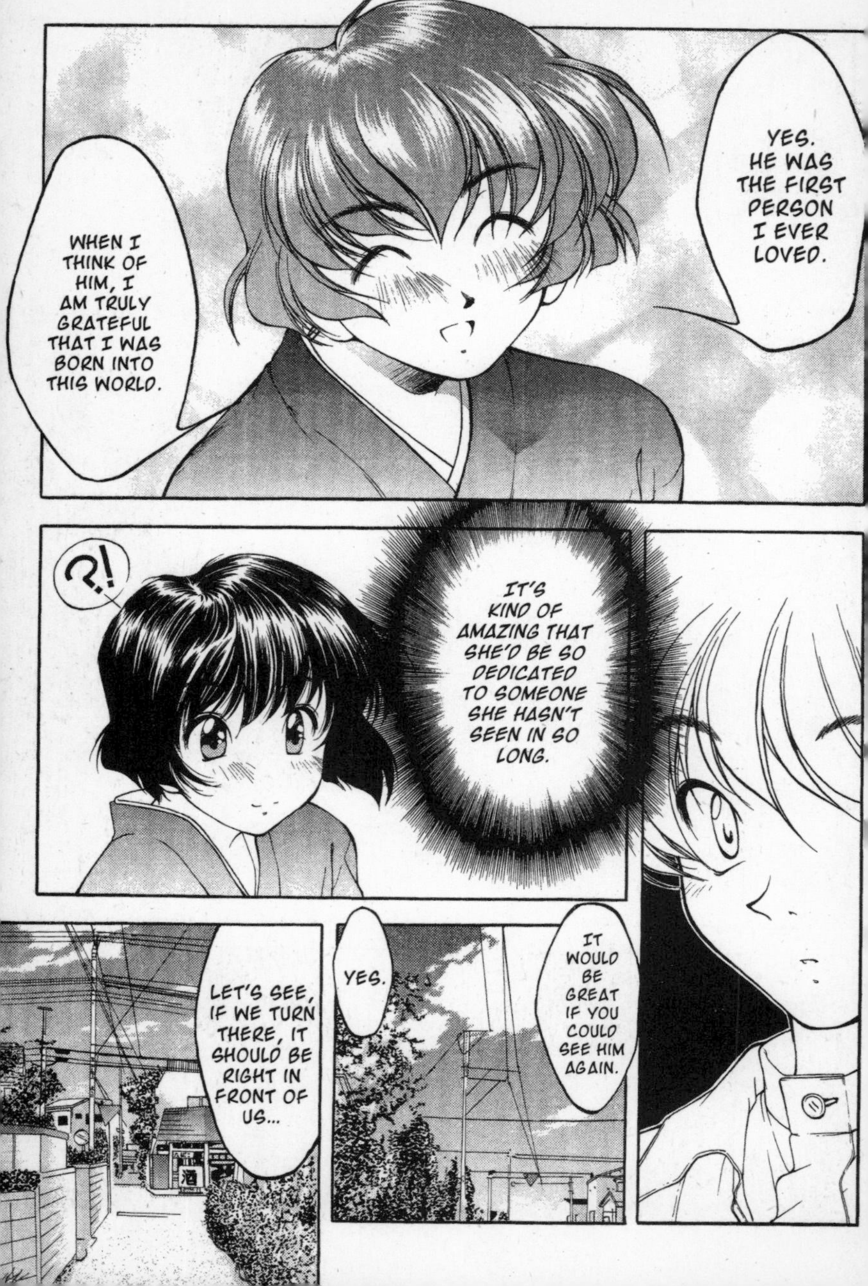
YES. HE WAS THE FIRST PERSON I EVER LOVED.
WHEN I THINK OF HIM, I AM TRULY GRATEFUL THAT I WAS BORN INTO THIS WORLD.
IT'S KIND OF AMAZING THAT SHE'D BE SO DEDICATED TO SOMEONE SHE HASN'T SEEN IN SO LONG.
IT WOULD BE GREAT IF YOU COULD SEE HIM AGAIN.
?!
YES.
LET'S SEE, IF WE TURN THERE, IT SHOULD BE RIGHT IN FRONT OF US...

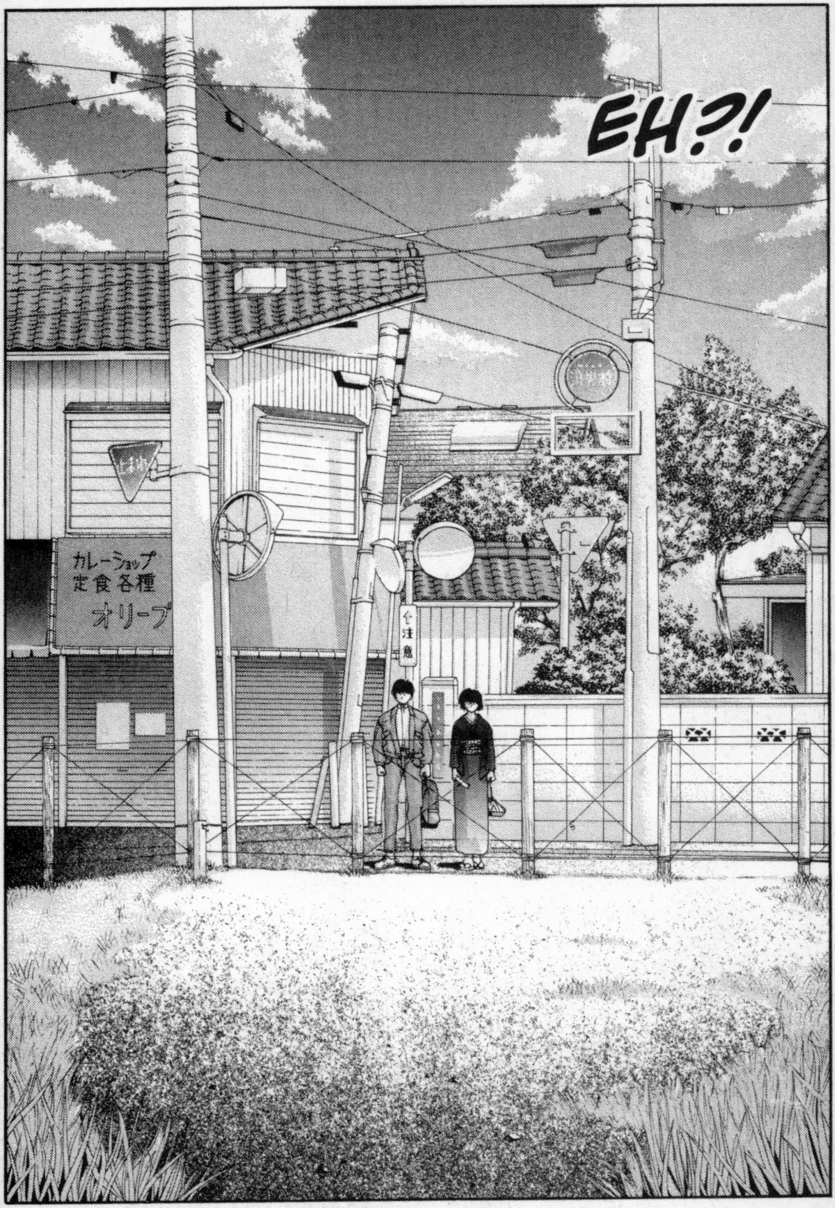
EH?!
カレーショップ
定食各種
オリーブ
注意

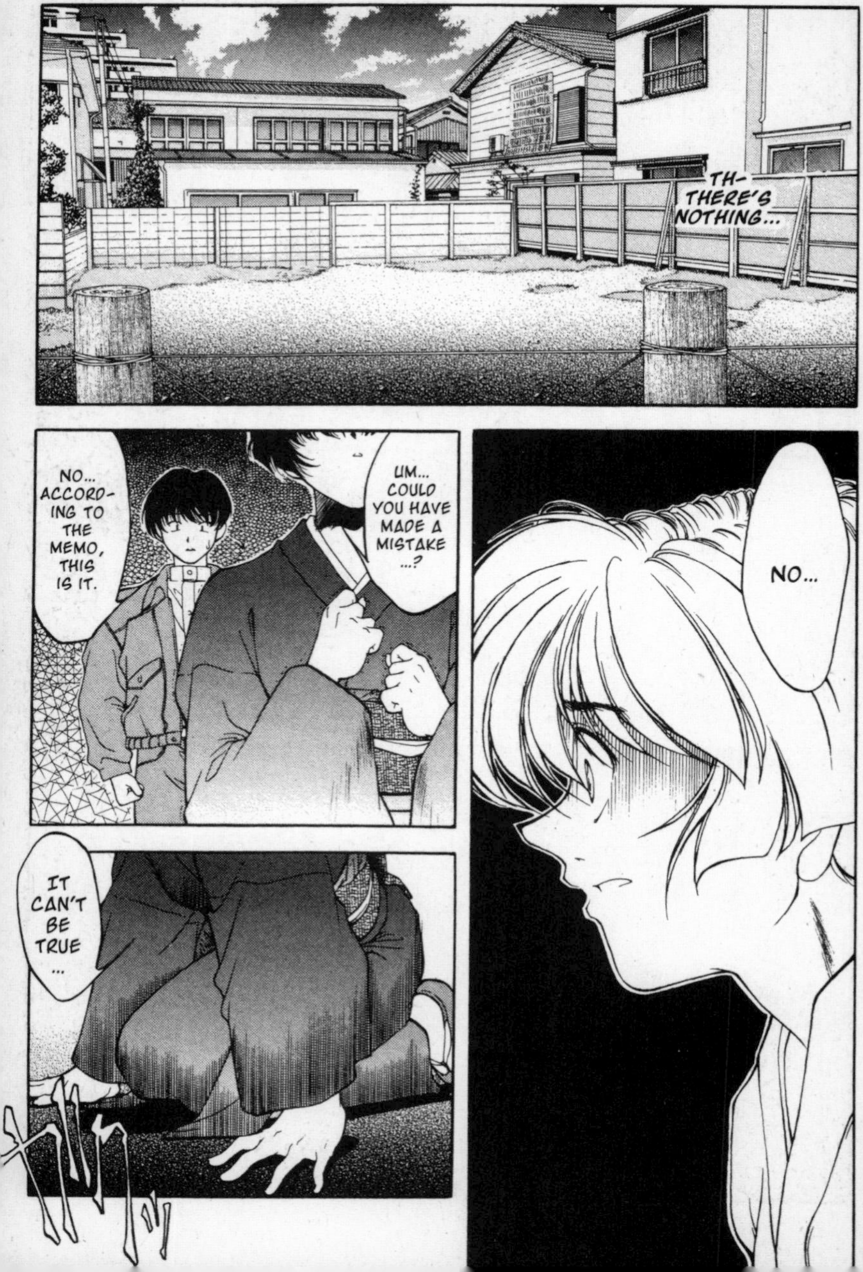
TH- THERE'S NOTHING...
UM... COULD YOU HAVE MADE A MISTAKE ...?
NO... ACCORDING TO THE MEMO, THIS IS IT.
NO...
IT CAN'T BE TRUE ...

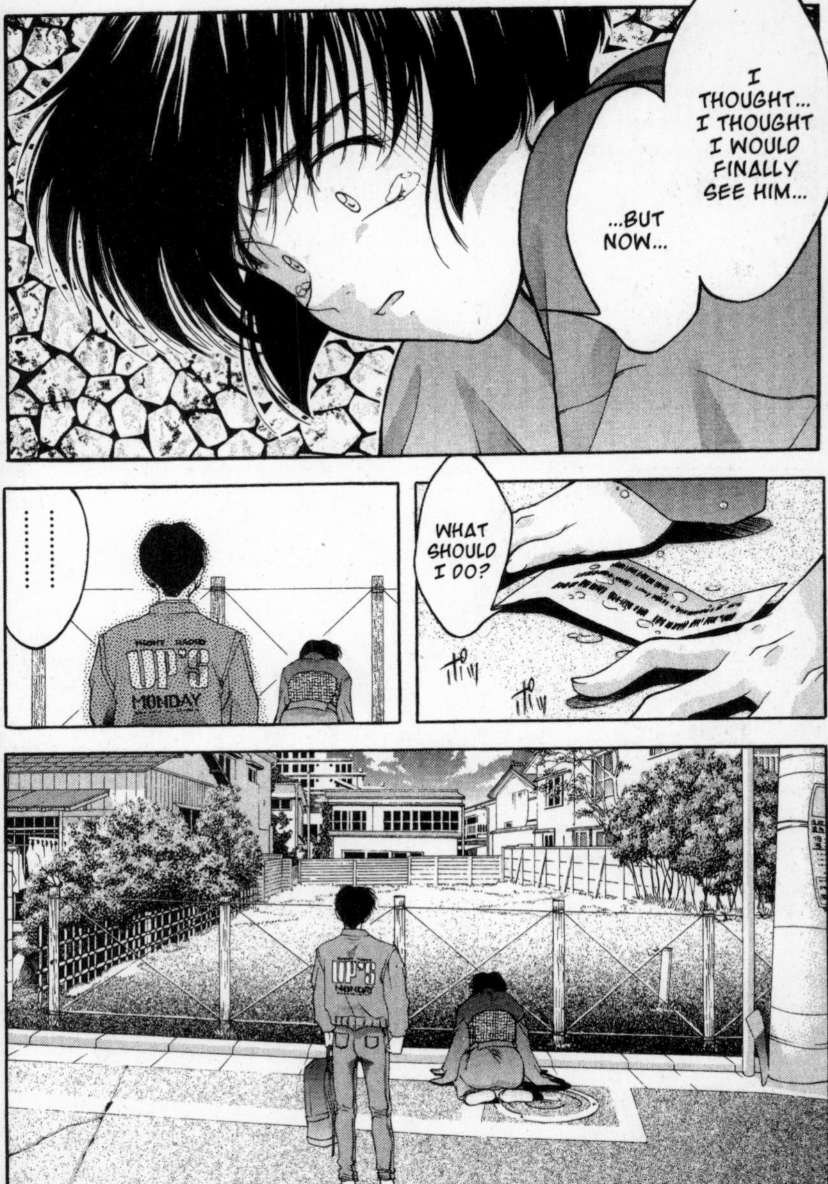
I THOUGHT... I THOUGHT I WOULD FINALLY SEE HIM...
...BUT NOW...
WHAT SHOULD I DO?
......

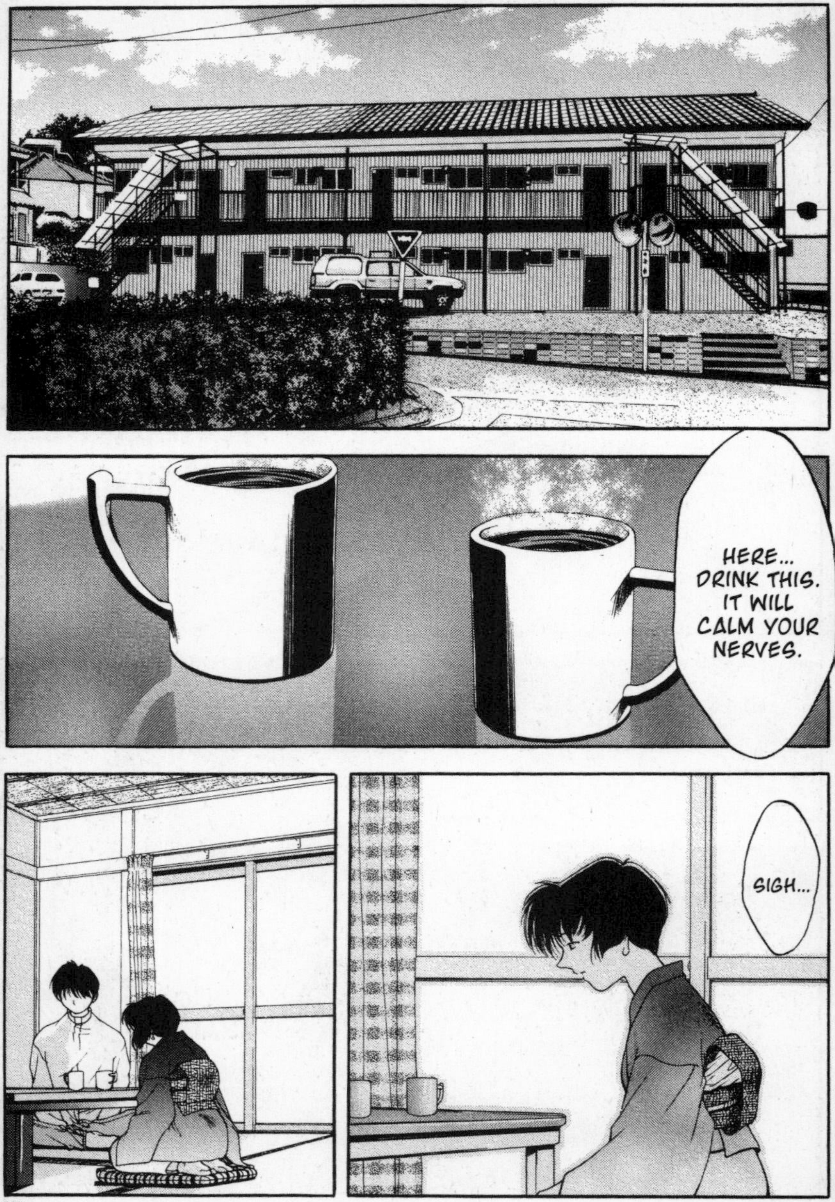
HERE... DRINK THIS. IT WILL CALM YOUR NERVES.
SIGH...

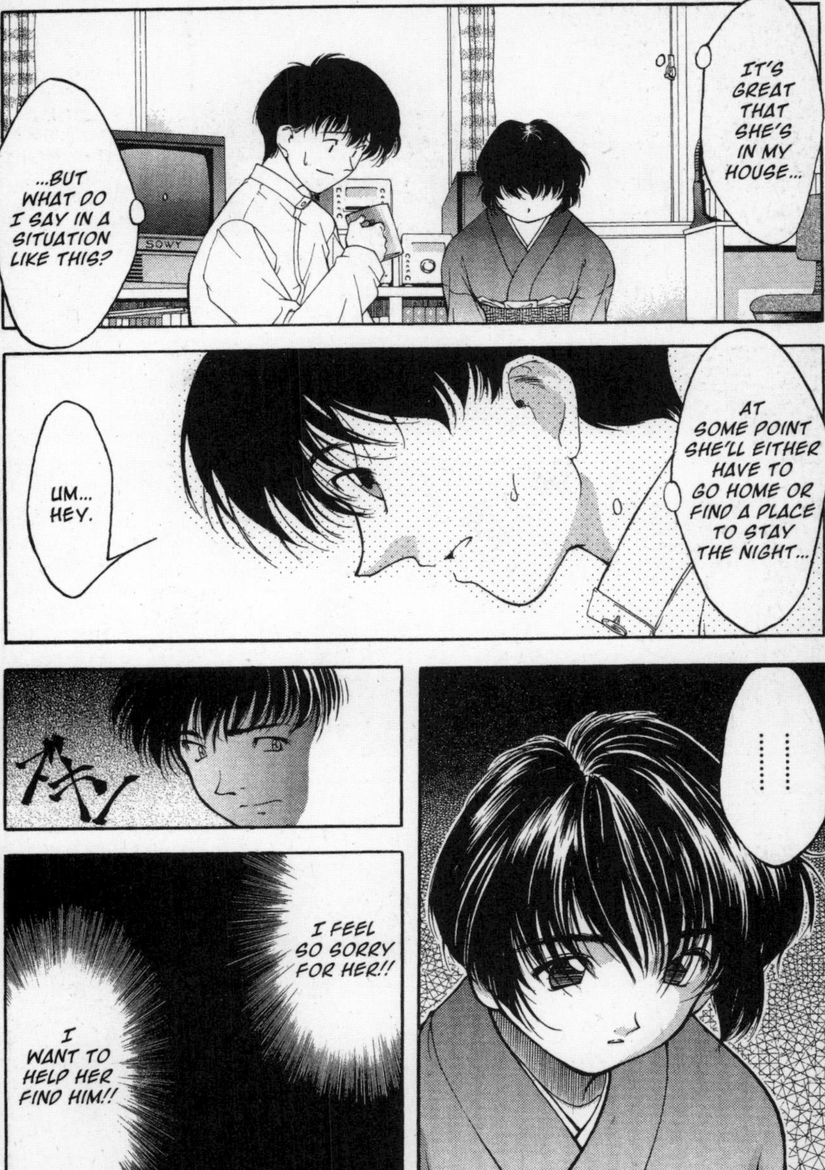

IT'S GREAT THAT SHE'S IN MY HOUSE...
...BUT WHAT DO I SAY IN A SITUATION LIKE THIS?
AT SOME POINT SHE'LL EITHER HAVE TO GO HOME OR FIND A PLACE TO STAY THE NIGHT...
UM... HEY.
......
I FEEL SO SORRY FOR HER!!
I WANT TO HELP HER FIND HIM!!

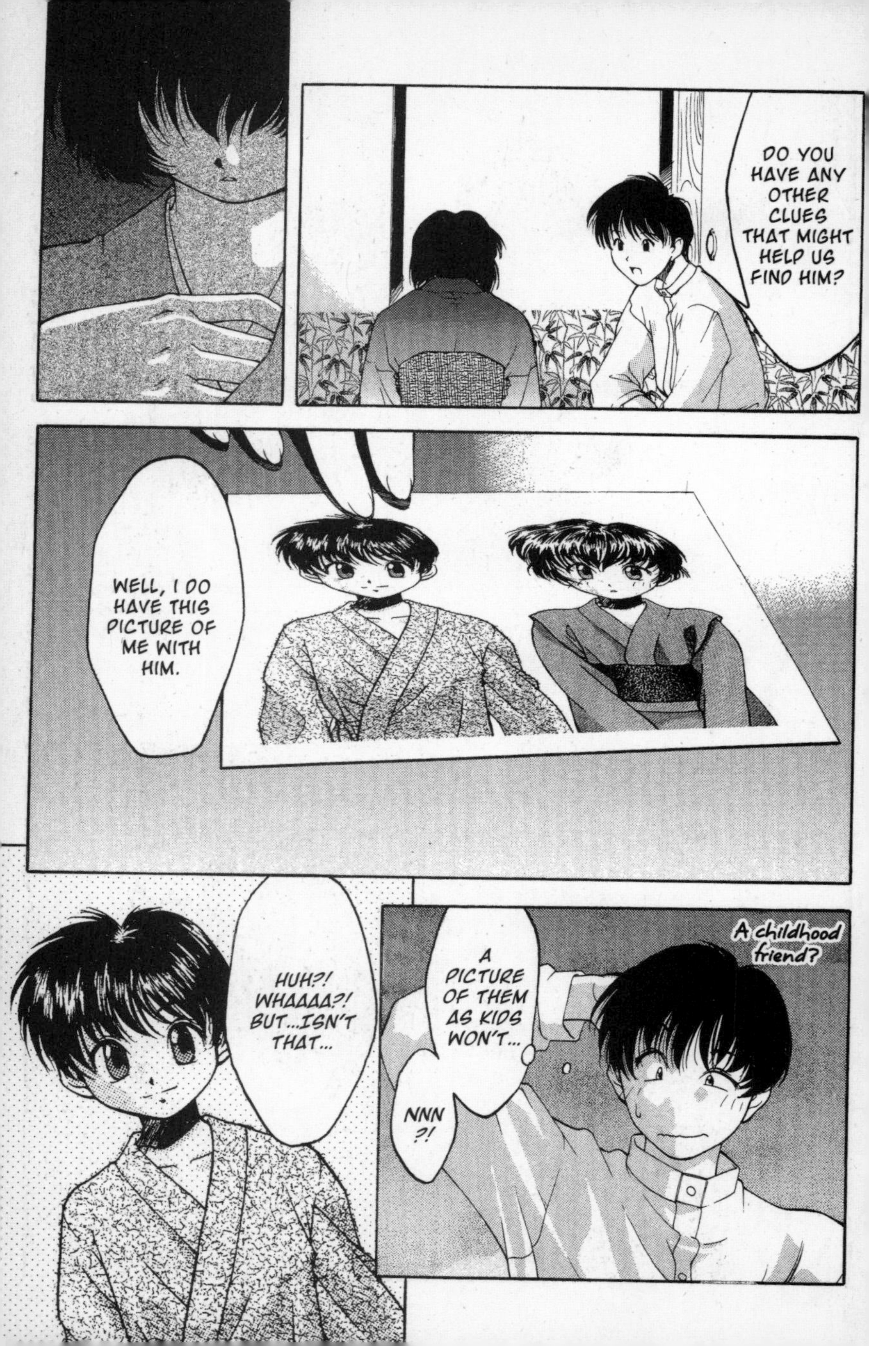
DO YOU HAVE ANY OTHER CLUES THAT MIGHT HELP US FIND HIM?
WELL, I DO HAVE THIS PICTURE OF ME WITH HIM.
A childhood friend?
A PICTURE OF THEM AS KIDS WON'T...
NNN ?!
HUH?! WHAAAA?! BUT...ISN'T THAT...

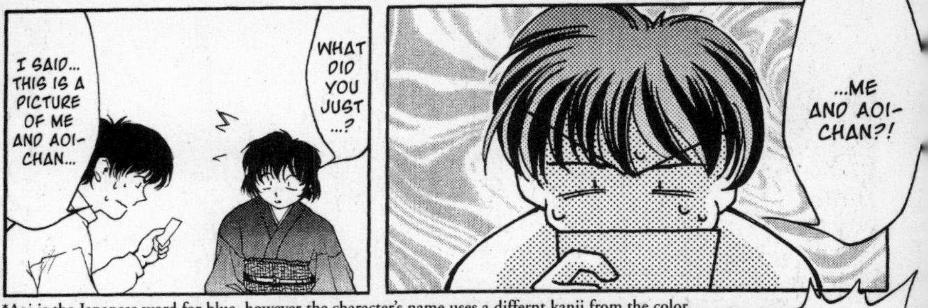
...ME AND AOI-CHAN?!
WHAT DID YOU JUST ...?
I SAID... THIS IS A PICTURE OF ME AND AOI-CHAN...

*Aoi is the Japanese word for blue, however the character's name uses a diffrent kanji from the color.

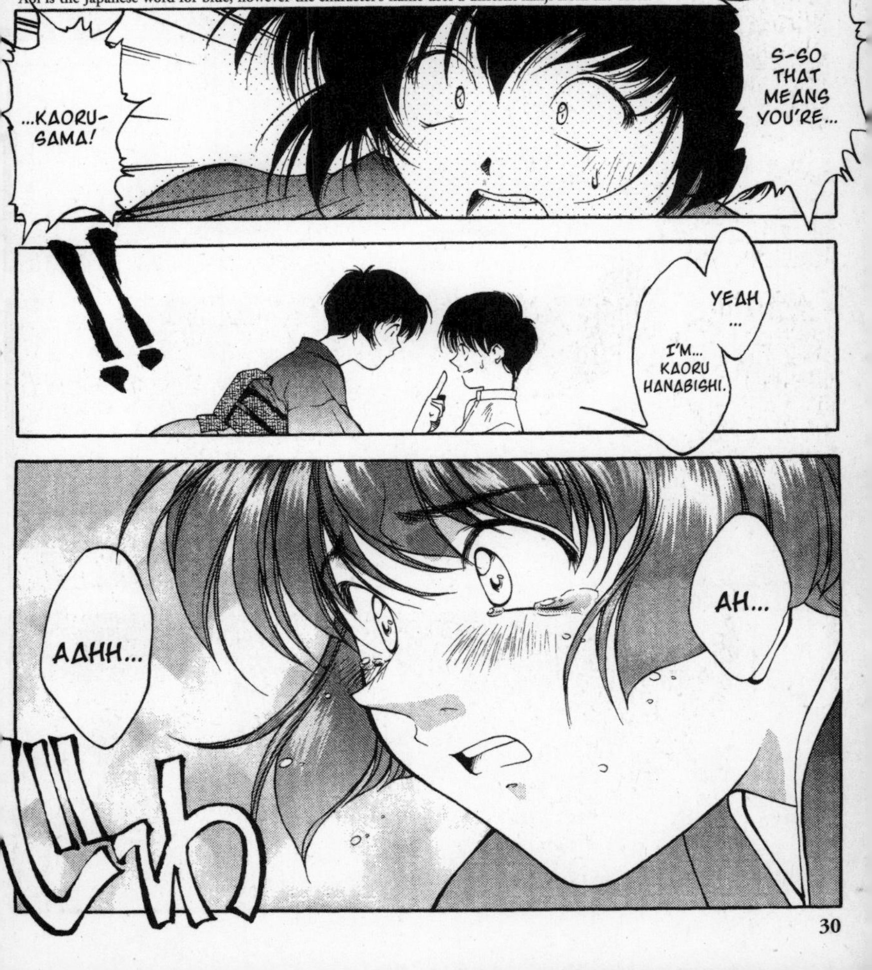
S-SO THAT MEANS YOU'RE...
...KAORU-SAMA!
YEAH ...
I'M... KAORU HANABISHI.
!!
AH...
AAHH...

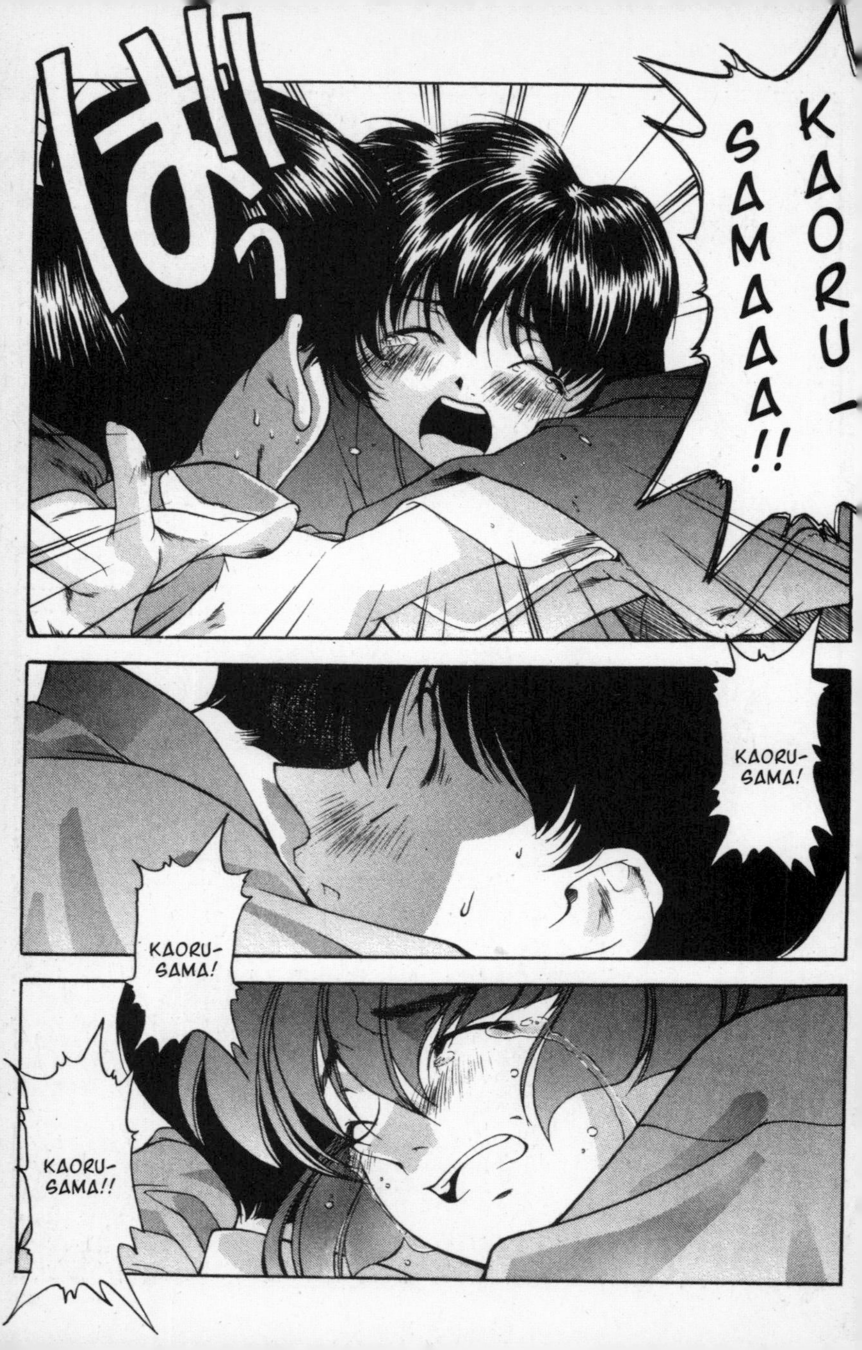

KAORU-SAMAAAA!!
ぱっ
KAORU-SAMA!
KAORU-SAMA!
KAORU-SAMA!!

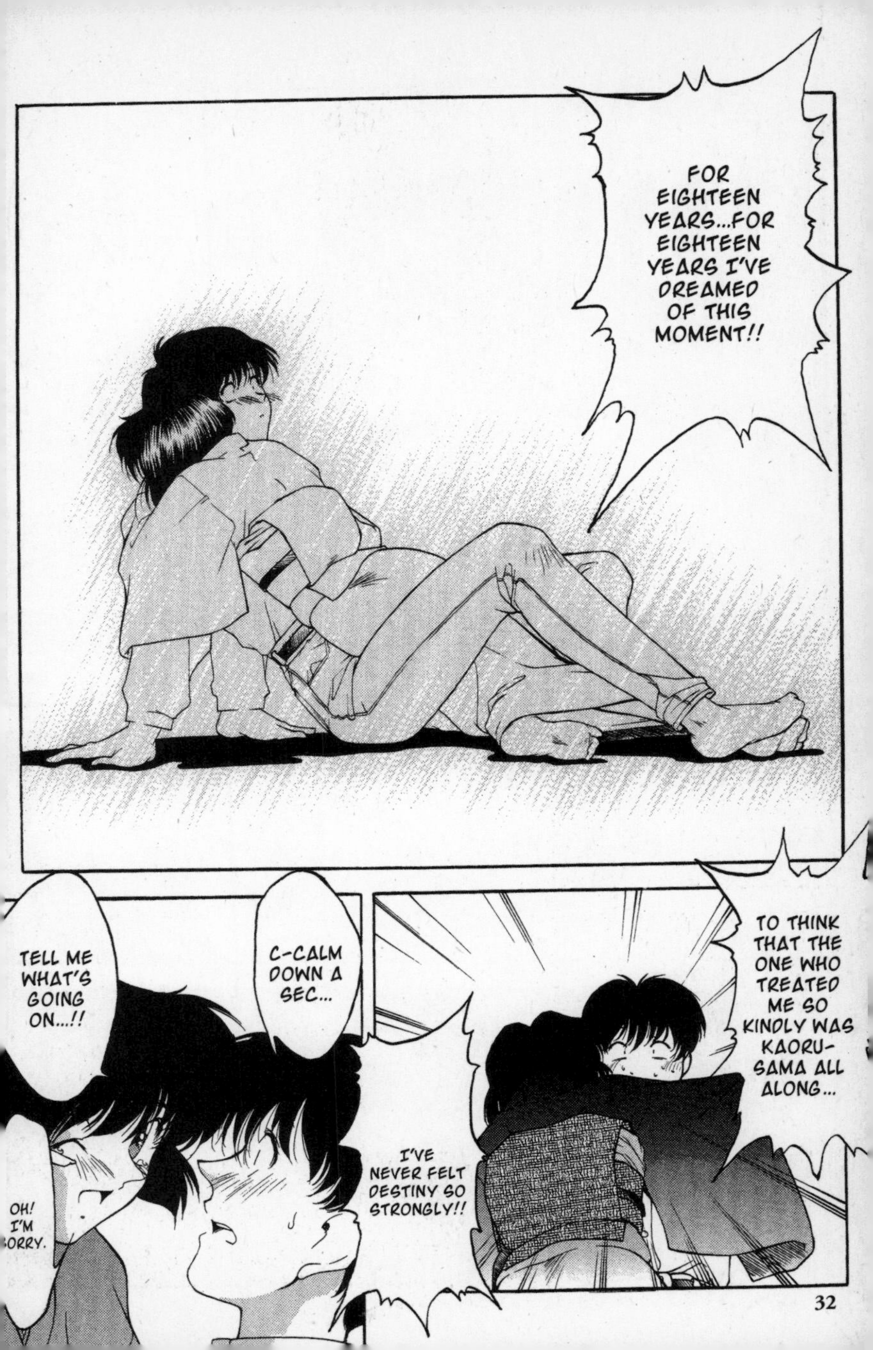
FOR EIGHTEEN YEARS...FOR EIGHTEEN YEARS I'VE DREAMED OF THIS MOMENT!!
TO THINK THAT THE ONE WHO TREATED ME SO KINDLY WAS KAORU-SAMA ALL ALONG...
I'VE NEVER FELT DESTINY SO STRONGLY!!
C-CALM DOWN A SEC...
TELL ME WHAT'S GOING ON...!!
OH! I'M SORRY.

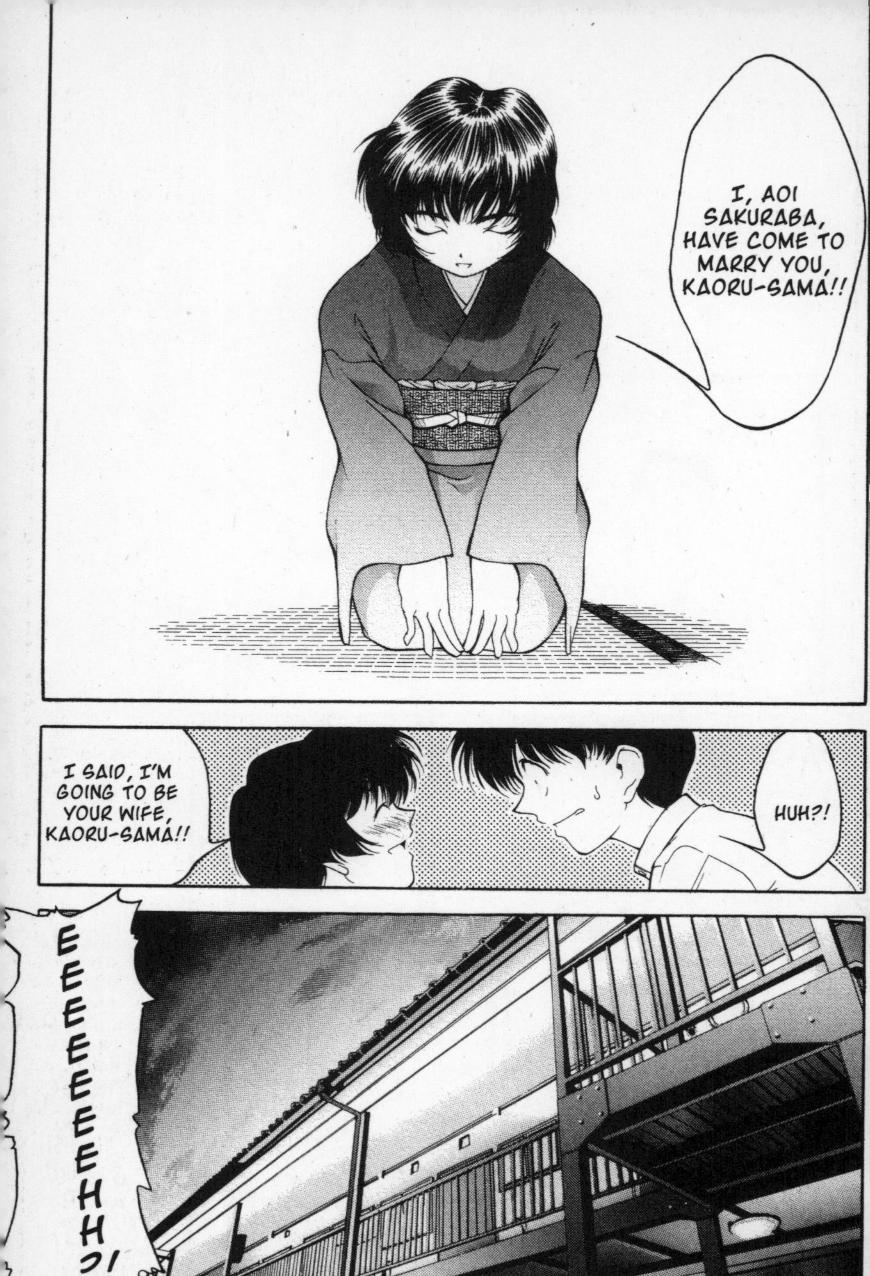
I, AOI SAKURABA, HAVE COME TO MARRY YOU, KAORU-SAMA!!
HUH?!
I SAID, I'M GOING TO BE YOUR WIFE, KAORU-SAMA!!
EEEEEEEEEEHH?!

End of Chapter 1: Enishi - Connection

Ai-Ao Theatre

part 1:
Go, go, our
Miyabi-san!!

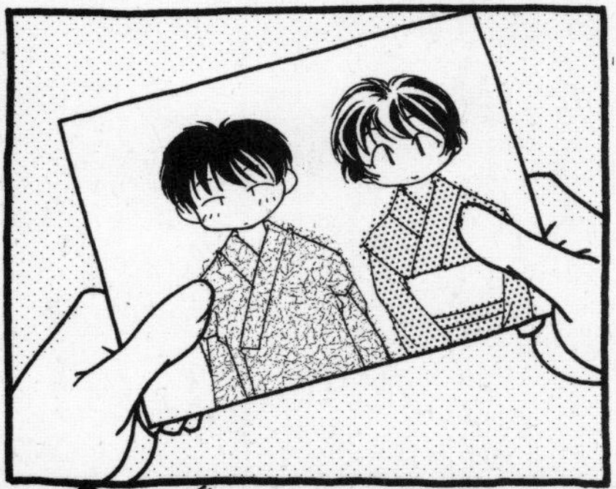

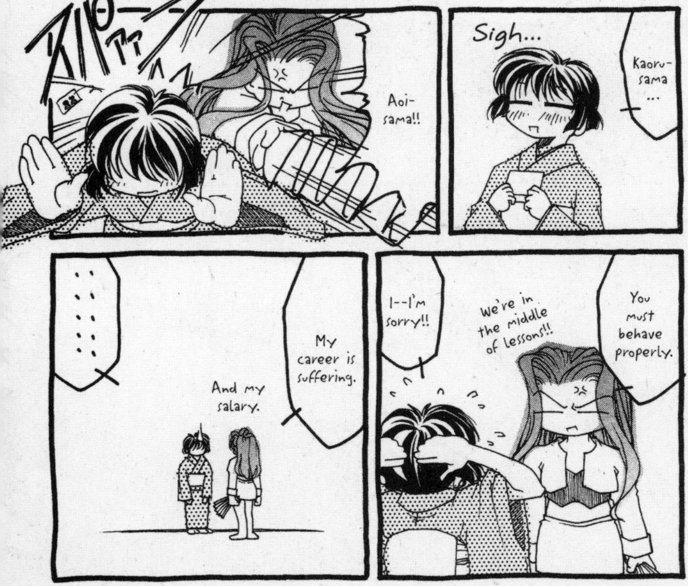
Sigh...
Kaoru-sama...
Aoi-sama!!
You must behave properly.
We're in the middle of lessons!!
I--I'm sorry!!
My career is suffering.
And my salary.
......

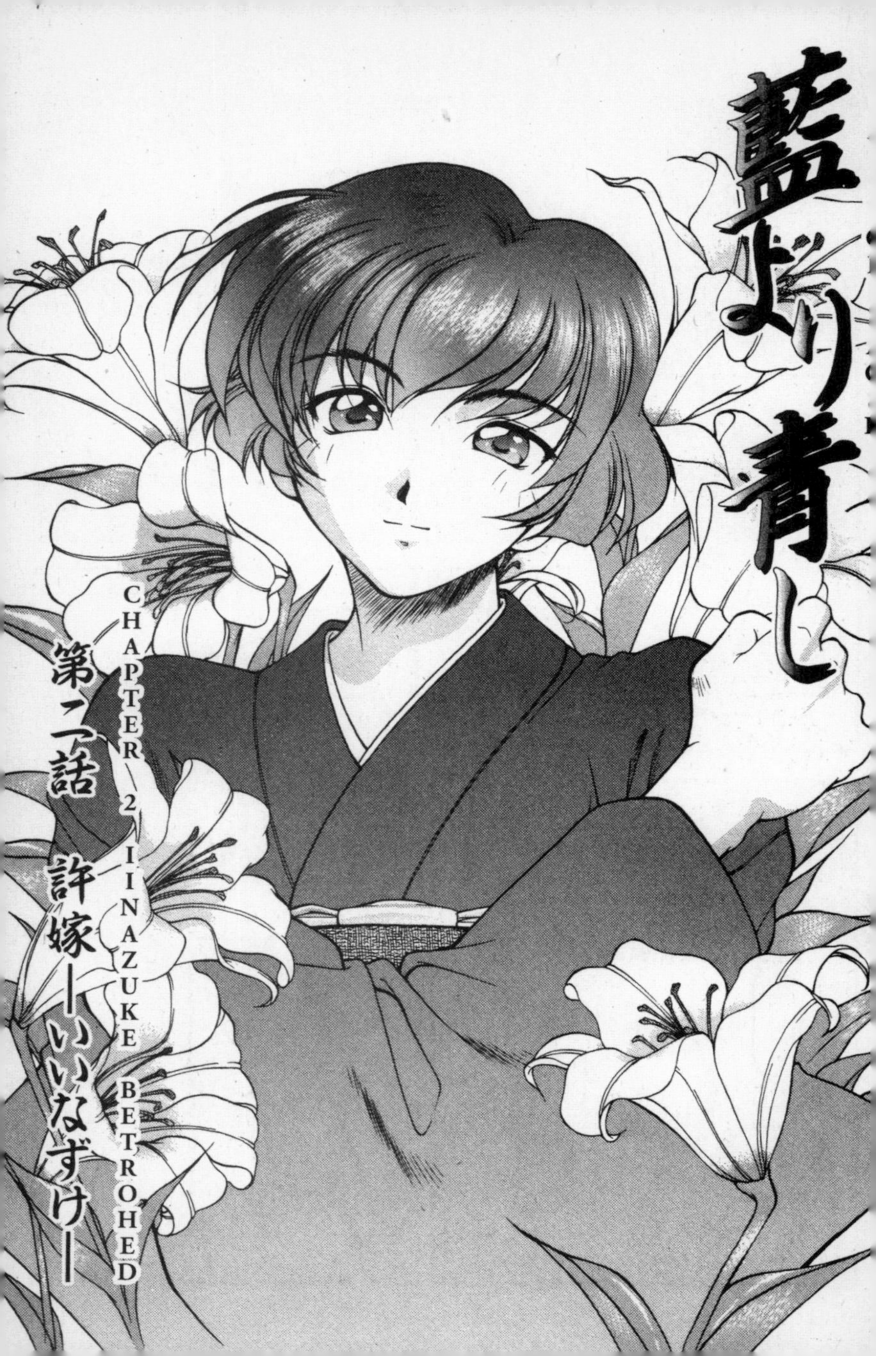
藍より青し
CHAPTER 2 IINAZUKE BETROHED
第二話 許嫁―いいなずけ―

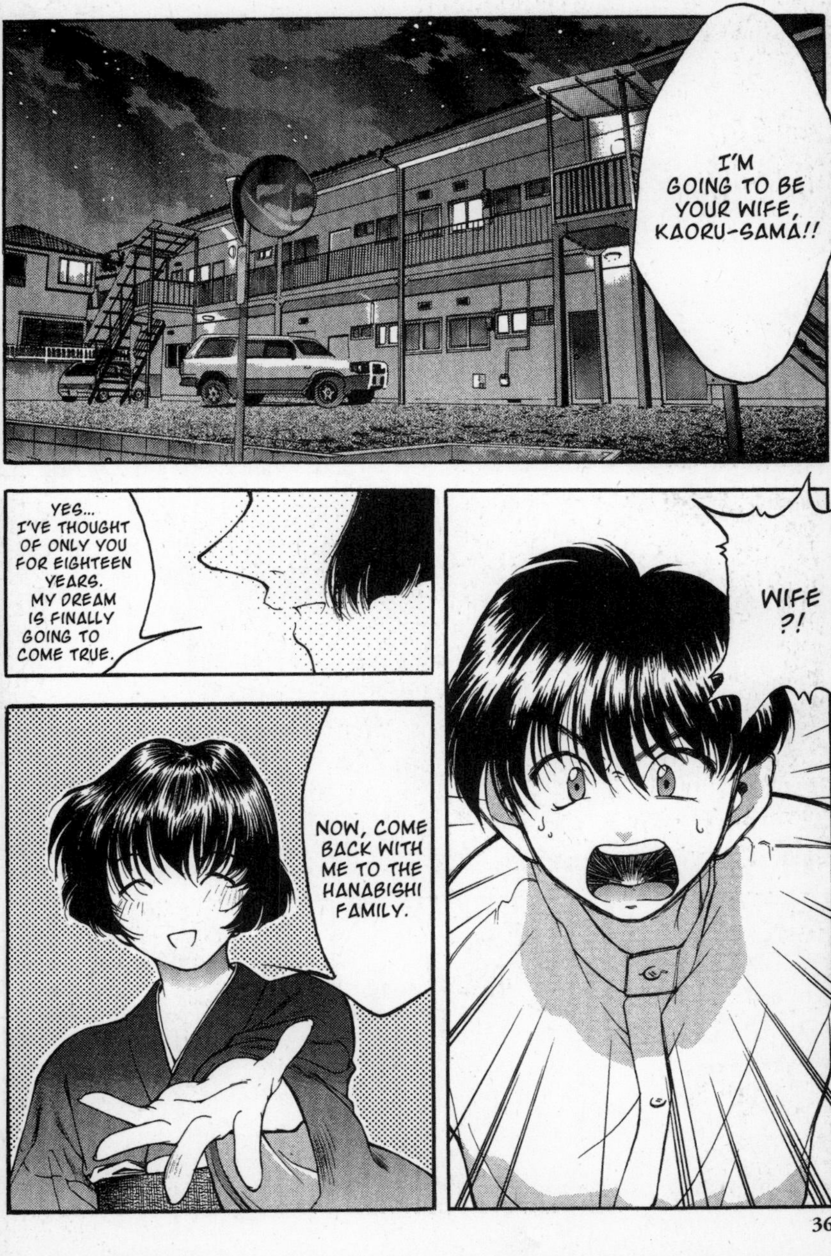
I'M GOING TO BE YOUR WIFE, KAORU-SAMA!!
WIFE ?!
YES... I'VE THOUGHT OF ONLY YOU FOR EIGHTEEN YEARS. MY DREAM IS FINALLY GOING TO COME TRUE.
NOW, COME BACK WITH ME TO THE HANABISHI FAMILY.

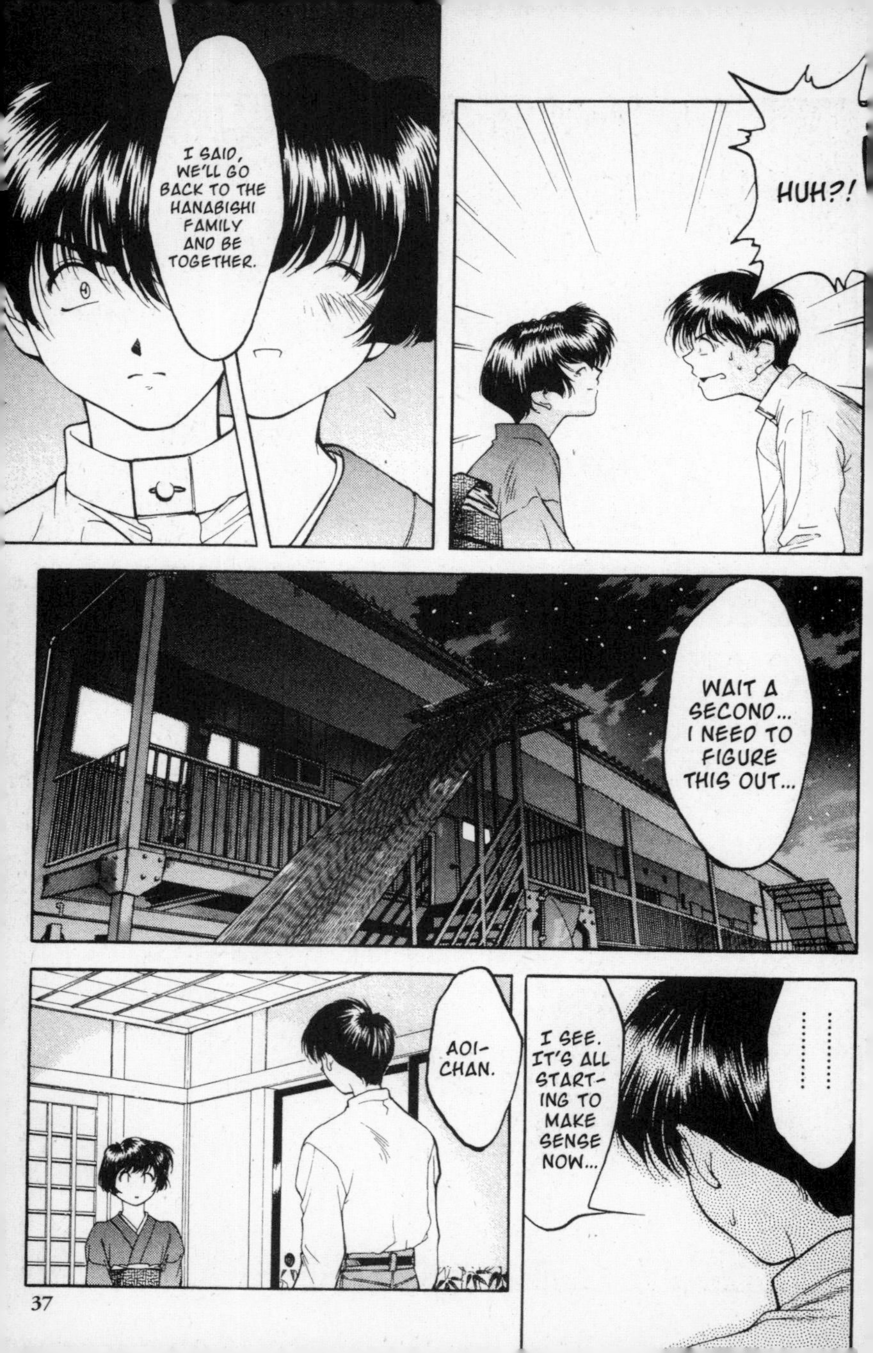
I SAID, WE'LL GO BACK TO THE HANABISHI FAMILY AND BE TOGETHER.
HUH?!
WAIT A SECOND... I NEED TO FIGURE THIS OUT...
AOI-CHAN.
I SEE. IT'S ALL STARTING TO MAKE SENSE NOW...
......

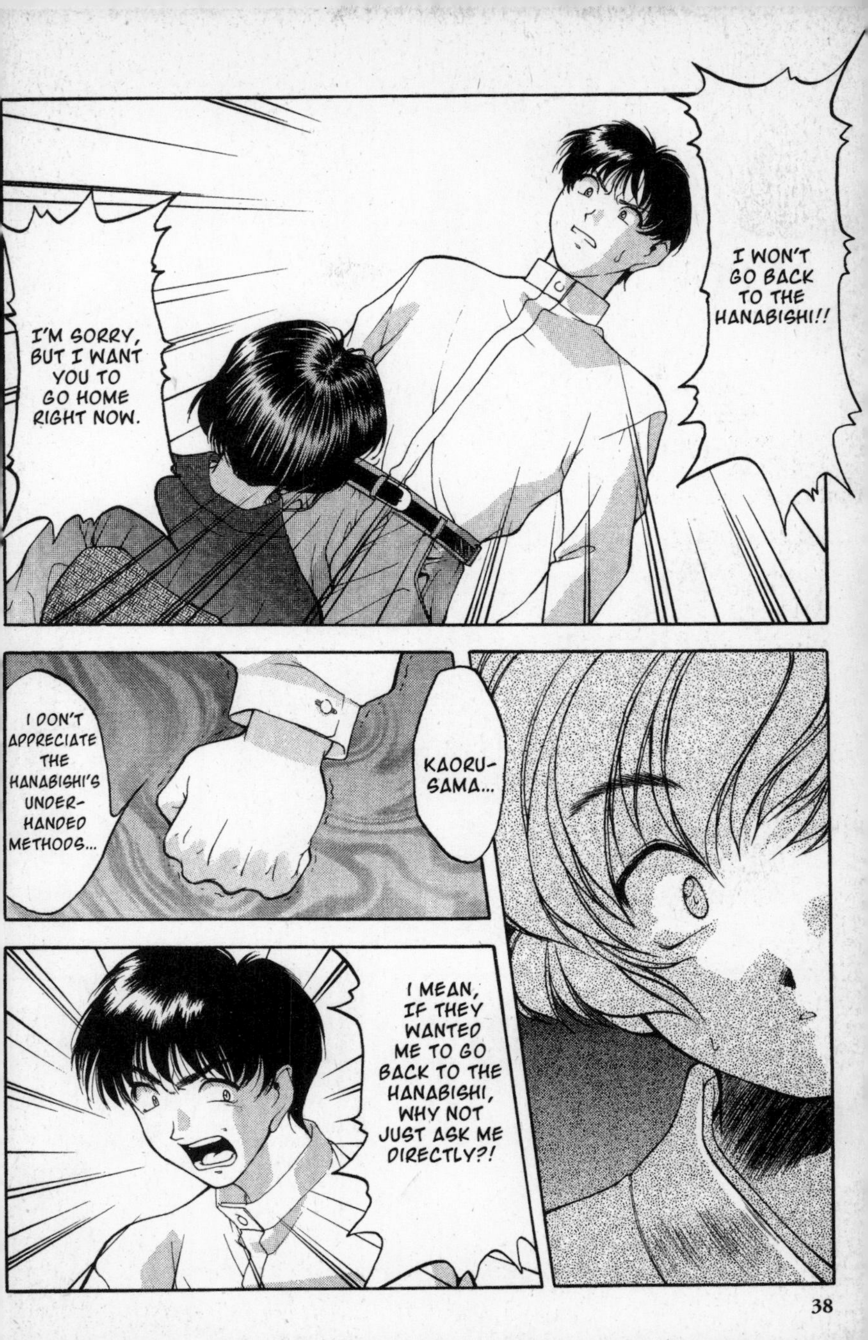
I WON'T GO BACK TO THE HANABISHI!!
I'M SORRY, BUT I WANT YOU TO GO HOME RIGHT NOW.
KAORU-SAMA...
I DON'T APPRECIATE THE HANABISHI'S UNDER-HANDED METHODS...
I MEAN, IF THEY WANTED ME TO GO BACK TO THE HANABISHI, WHY NOT JUST ASK ME DIRECTLY?!

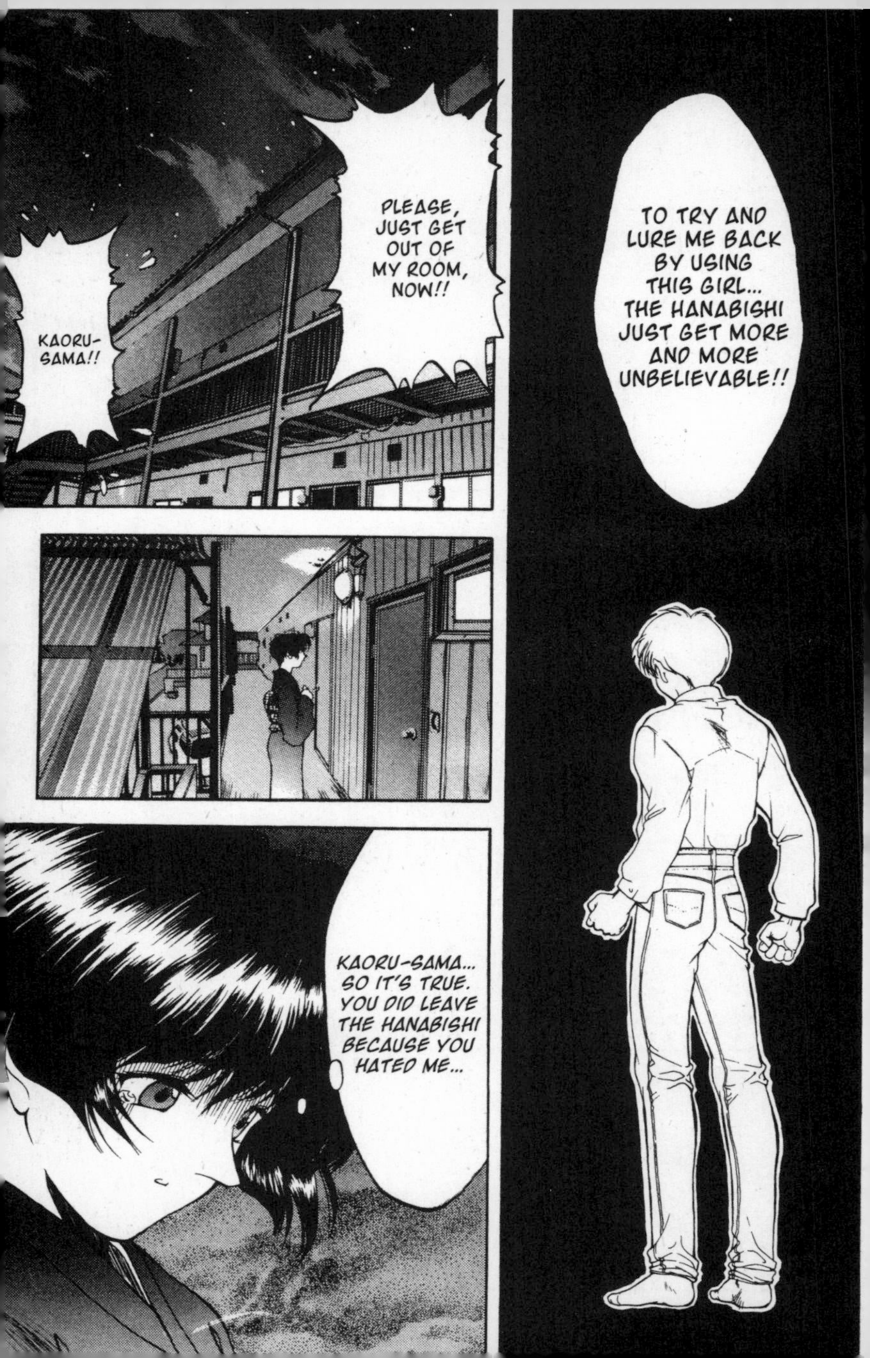
TO TRY AND LURE ME BACK BY USING THIS GIRL... THE HANABISHI JUST GET MORE AND MORE UNBELIEVABLE!!
PLEASE, JUST GET OUT OF MY ROOM, NOW!!
KAORU-SAMA!!
KAORU-SAMA... SO IT'S TRUE. YOU DID LEAVE THE HANABISHI BECAUSE YOU HATED ME...

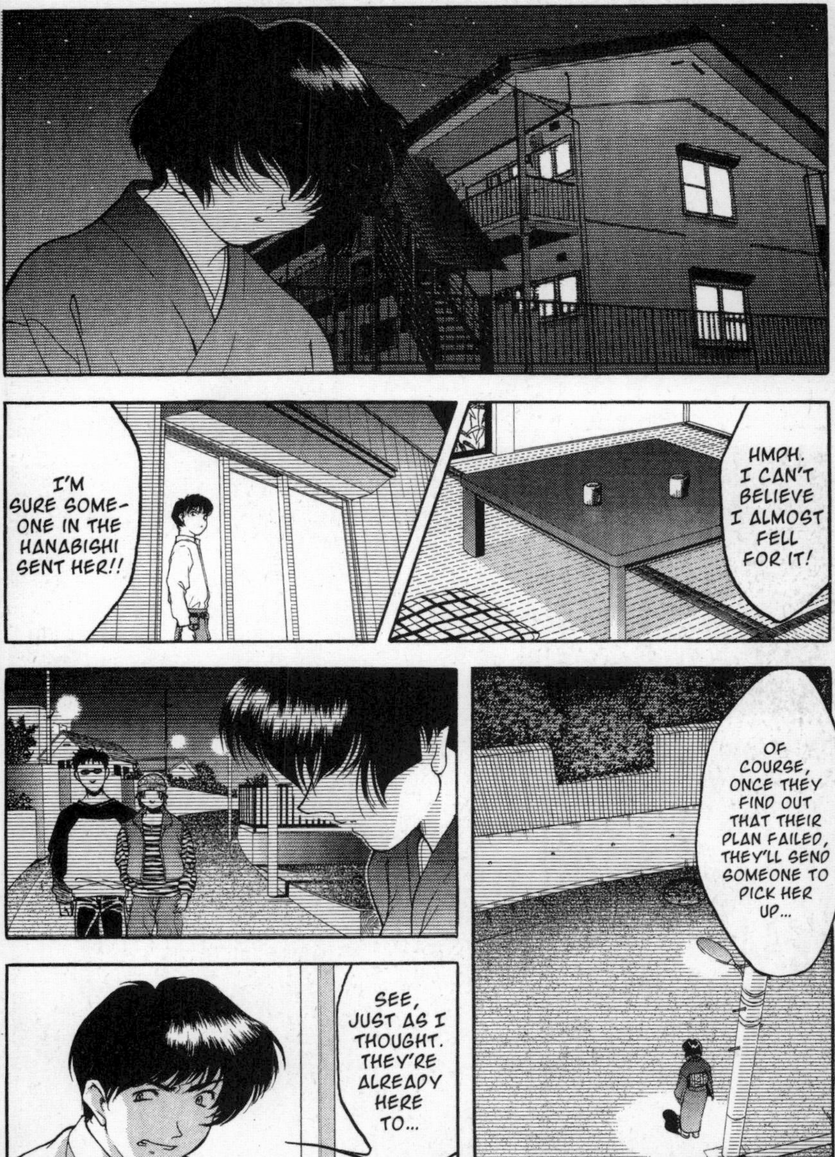
HMPH. I CAN'T BELIEVE I ALMOST FELL FOR IT!
I'M SURE SOME-ONE IN THE HANABISHI SENT HER!!
OF COURSE, ONCE THEY FIND OUT THAT THEIR PLAN FAILED, THEY'LL SEND SOMEONE TO PICK HER UP...
SEE, JUST AS I THOUGHT. THEY'RE ALREADY HERE TO...

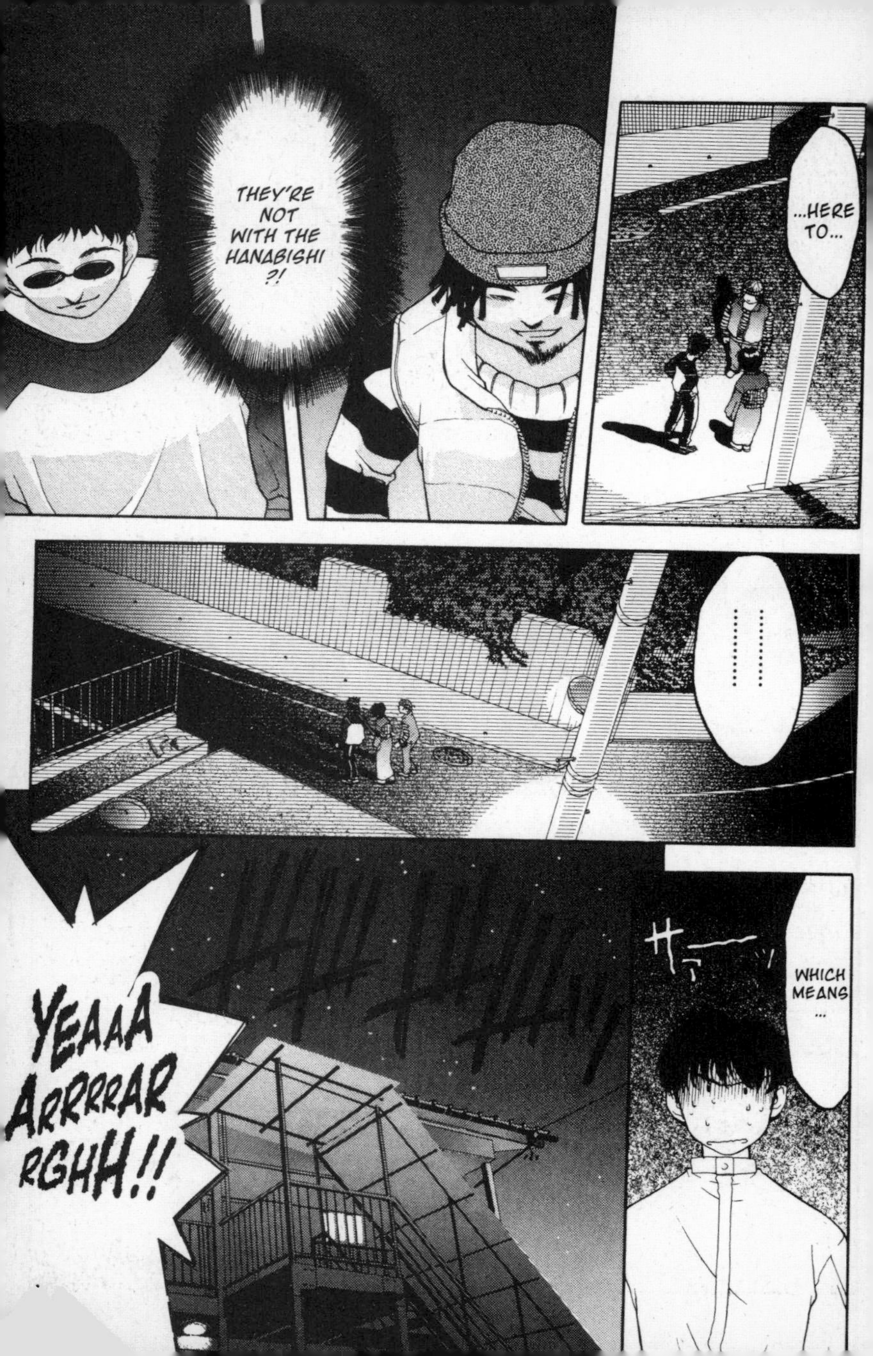
...HERE TO...
THEY'RE NOT WITH THE HANABISHI ?!
......
サーーッ
WHICH MEANS ...
YEAAA ARRRRAR RGHH!!

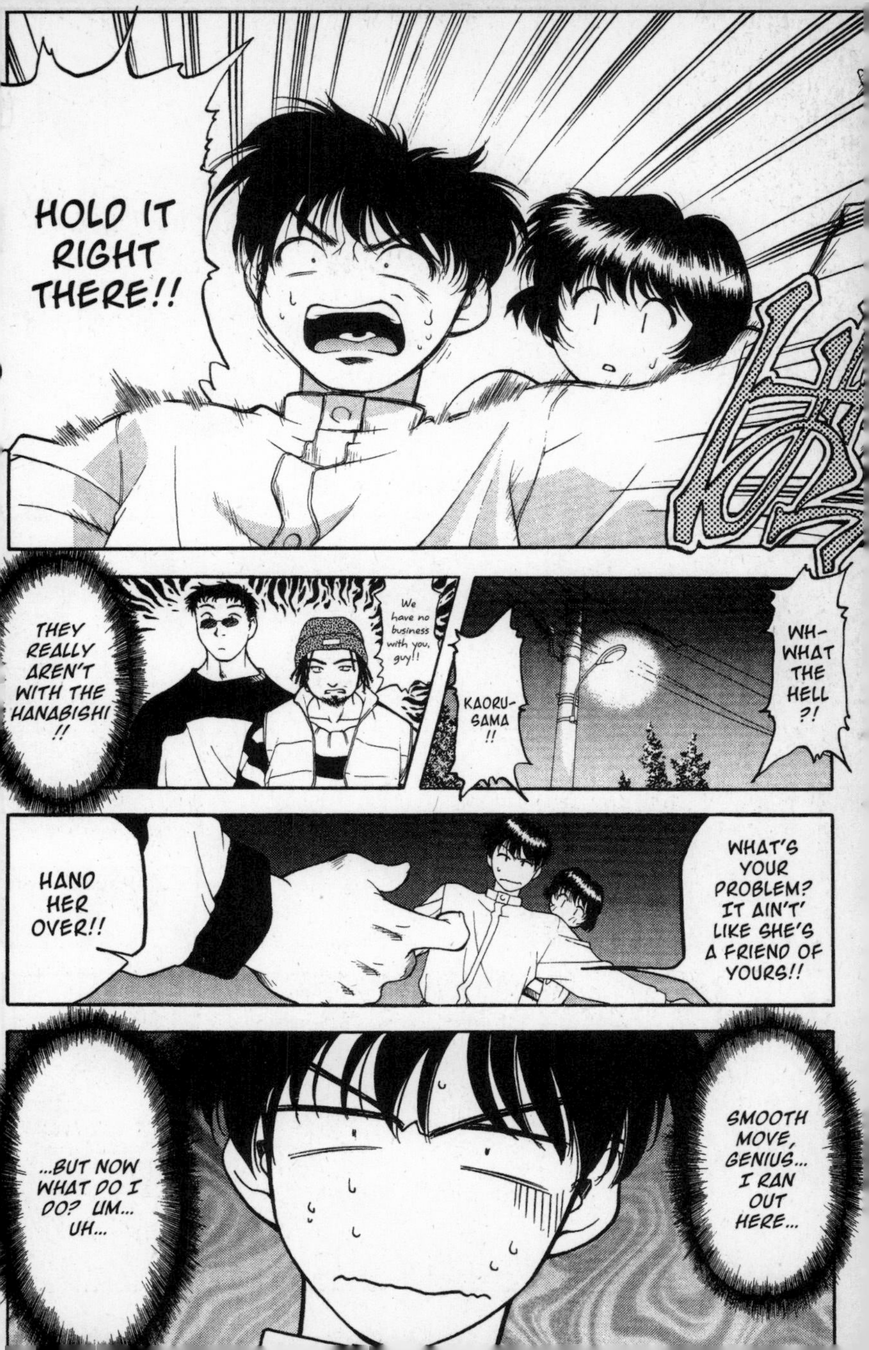
HOLD IT RIGHT THERE!!
WH-WHAT THE HELL?!
KAORU-SAMA!!
We have no business with you, guy!!
THEY REALLY AREN'T WITH THE HANABISHI!!
WHAT'S YOUR PROBLEM? IT AIN'T' LIKE SHE'S A FRIEND OF YOURS!!
HAND HER OVER!!
SMOOTH MOVE, GENIUS... I RAN OUT HERE...
...BUT NOW WHAT DO I DO? UM... UH...

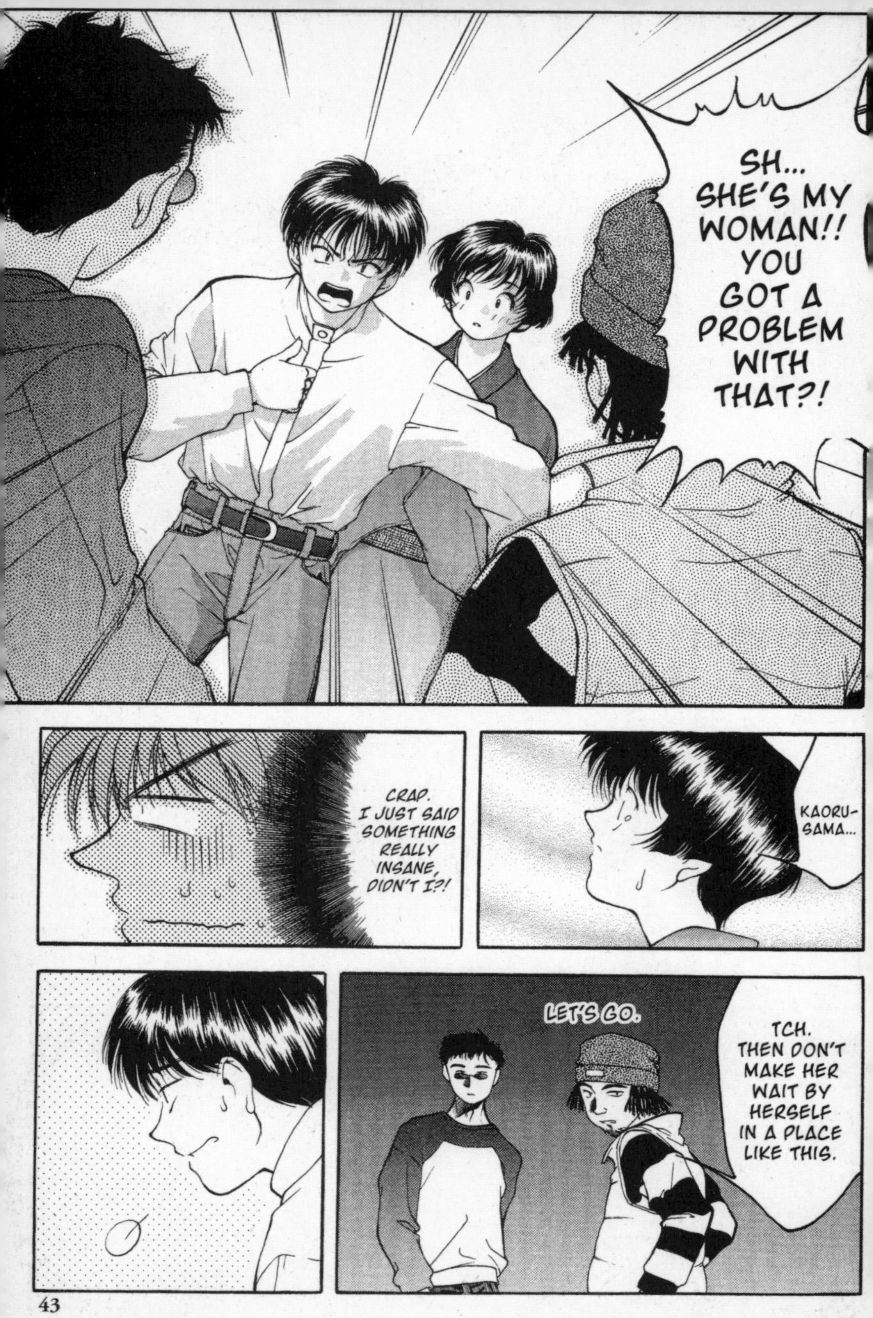
SH... SHE'S MY WOMAN!! YOU GOT A PROBLEM WITH THAT?!
KAORU-SAMA...
CRAP. I JUST SAID SOMETHING REALLY INSANE, DIDN'T I?!
TCH. THEN DON'T MAKE HER WAIT BY HERSELF IN A PLACE LIKE THIS.
LET'S GO.

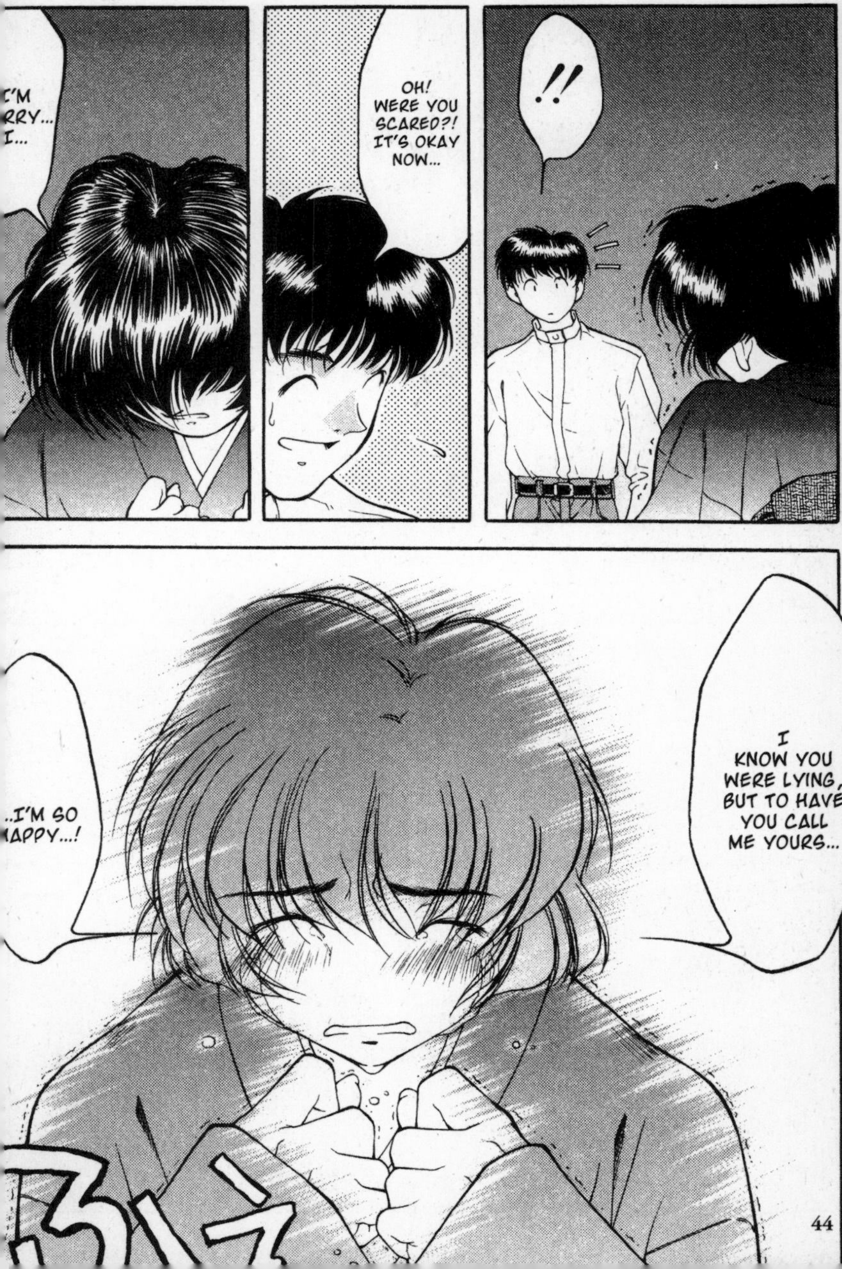
!!
OH! WERE YOU SCARED?! IT'S OKAY NOW...
I'M RRY... I...
I KNOW YOU WERE LYING, BUT TO HAVE YOU CALL ME YOURS...
..I'M SO APPY...!

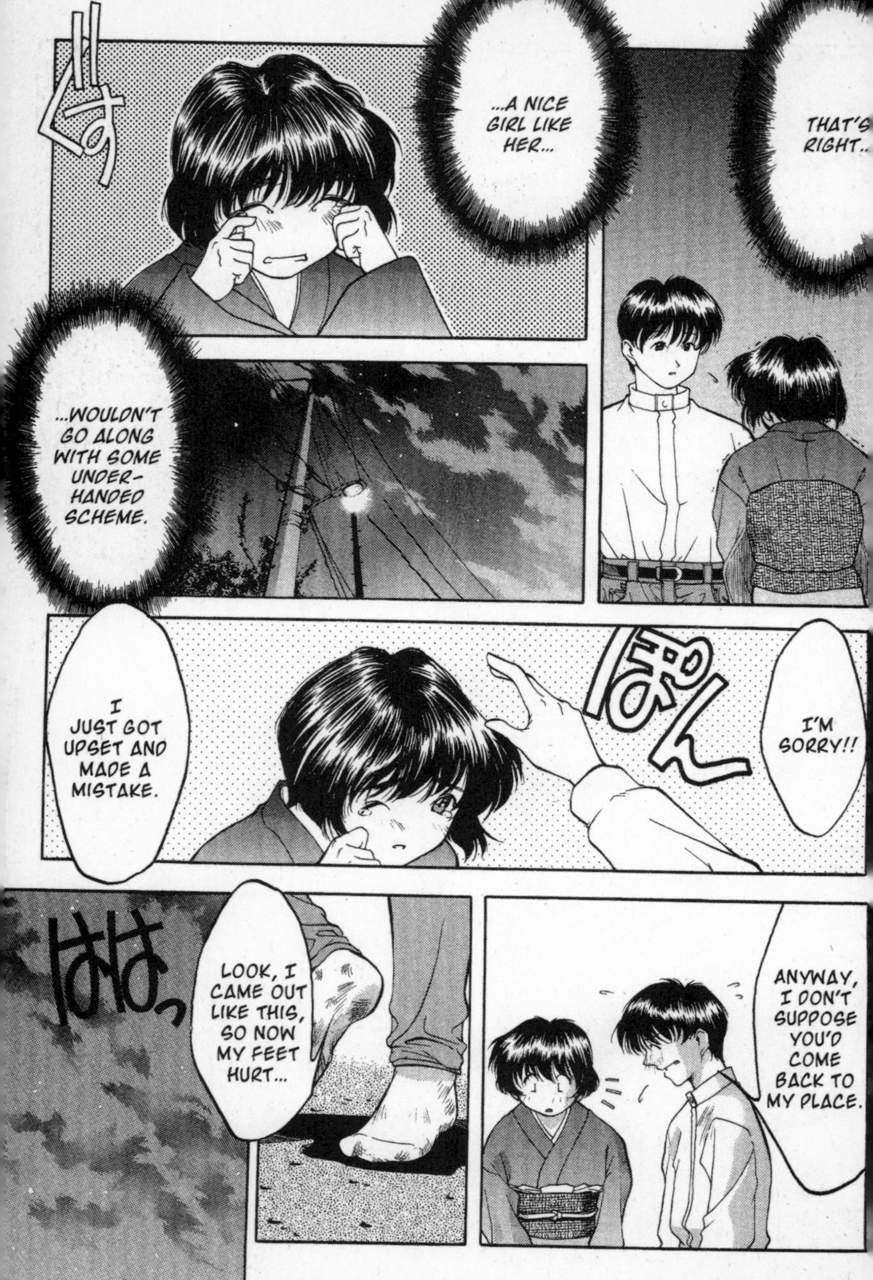
THAT'S RIGHT...
...A NICE GIRL LIKE HER...
ぐす
...WOULDN'T GO ALONG WITH SOME UNDER-HANDED SCHEME.
I'M SORRY!!
ぽん
I JUST GOT UPSET AND MADE A MISTAKE.
ANYWAY, I DON'T SUPPOSE YOU'D COME BACK TO MY PLACE.
LOOK, I CAME OUT LIKE THIS, SO NOW MY FEET HURT...
ははっ

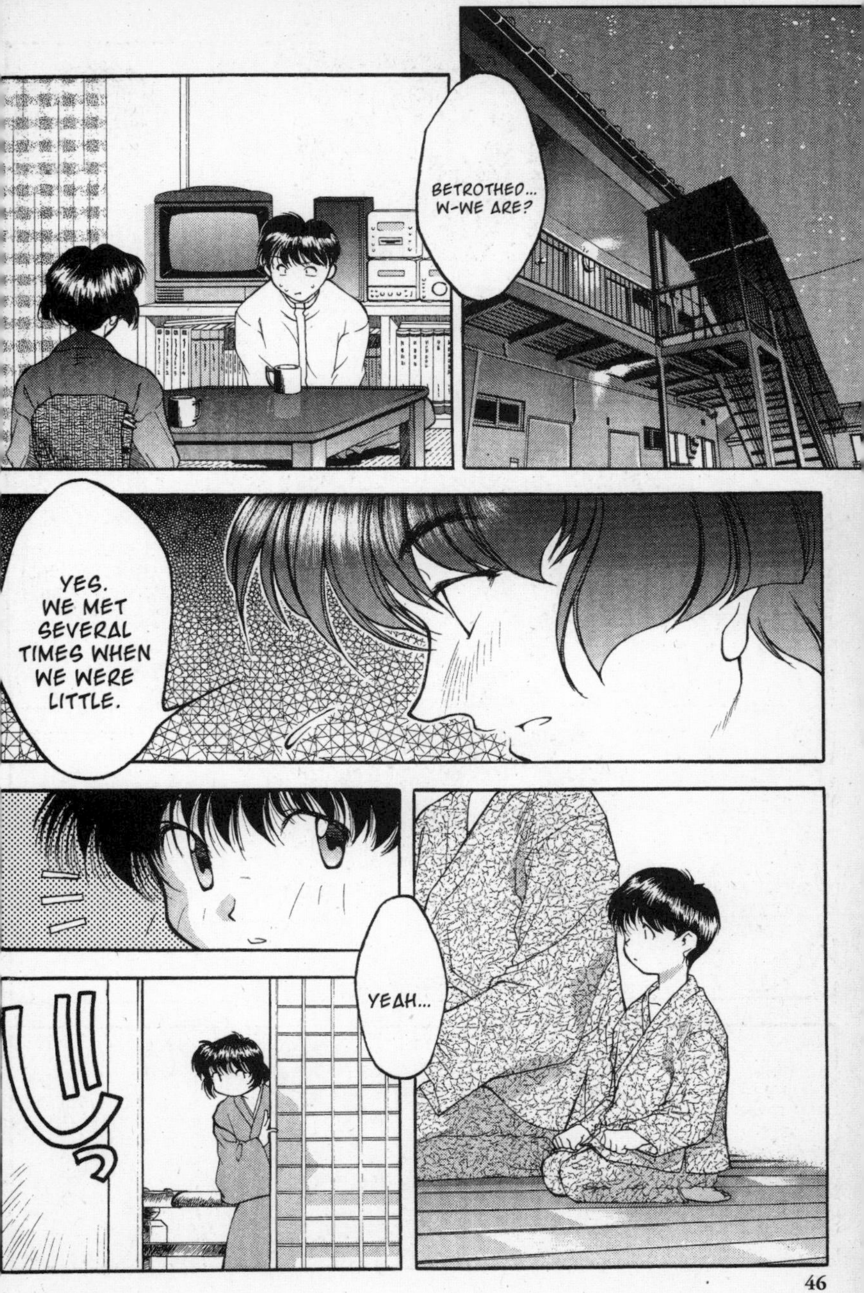

BETROTHED...
W-WE ARE?
YES.
WE MET
SEVERAL
TIMES WHEN
WE WERE
LITTLE.
YEAH...

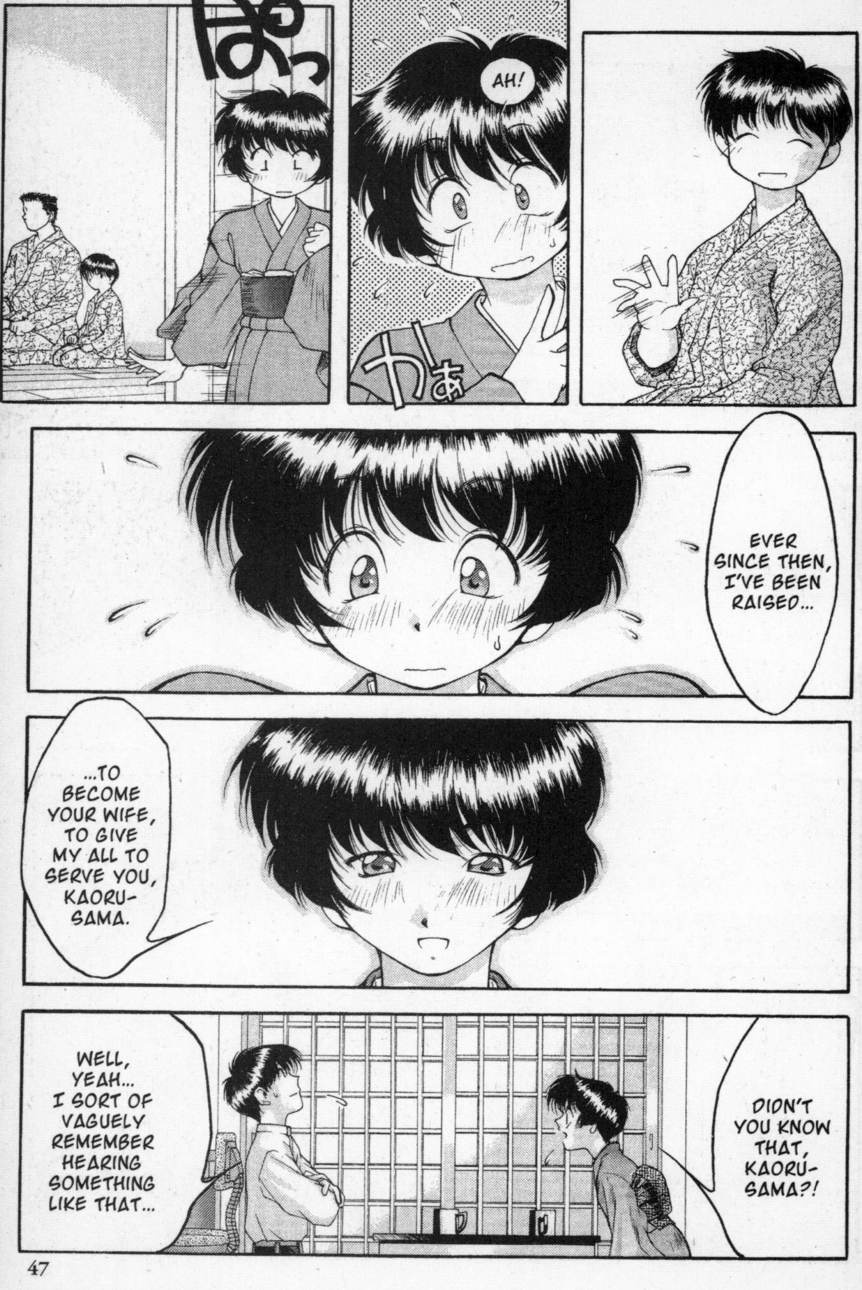
AH!
やぁ
ぱっ
EVER SINCE THEN, I'VE BEEN RAISED...
...TO BECOME YOUR WIFE, TO GIVE MY ALL TO SERVE YOU, KAORU-SAMA.
DIDN'T YOU KNOW THAT, KAORU-SAMA?!
WELL, YEAH... I SORT OF VAGUELY REMEMBER HEARING SOMETHING LIKE THAT...

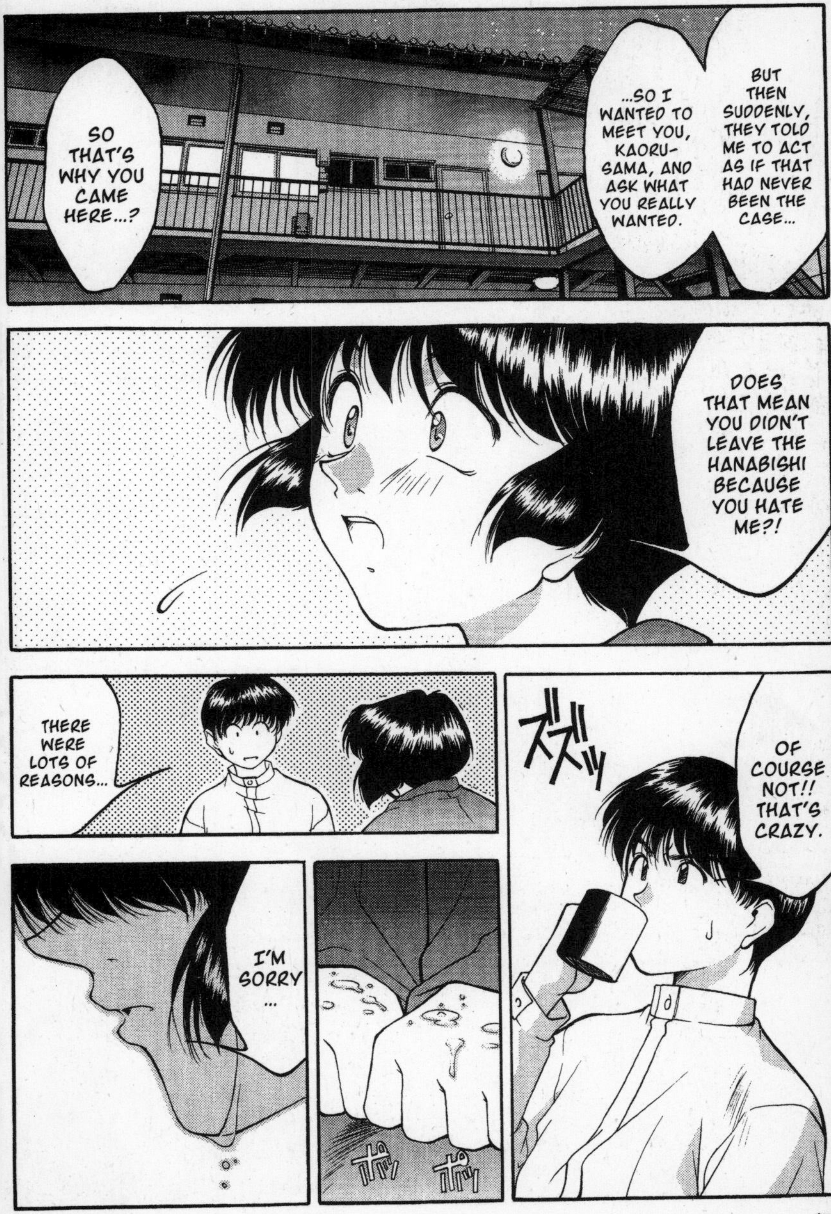
BUT THEN SUDDENLY, THEY TOLD ME TO ACT AS IF THAT HAD NEVER BEEN THE CASE...
...SO I WANTED TO MEET YOU, KAORU-SAMA, AND ASK WHAT YOU REALLY WANTED.
SO THAT'S WHY YOU CAME HERE...?
DOES THAT MEAN YOU DIDN'T LEAVE THE HANABISHI BECAUSE YOU HATE ME?!
ズズッ
OF COURSE NOT!! THAT'S CRAZY.
THERE WERE LOTS OF REASONS...
I'M SORRY ...

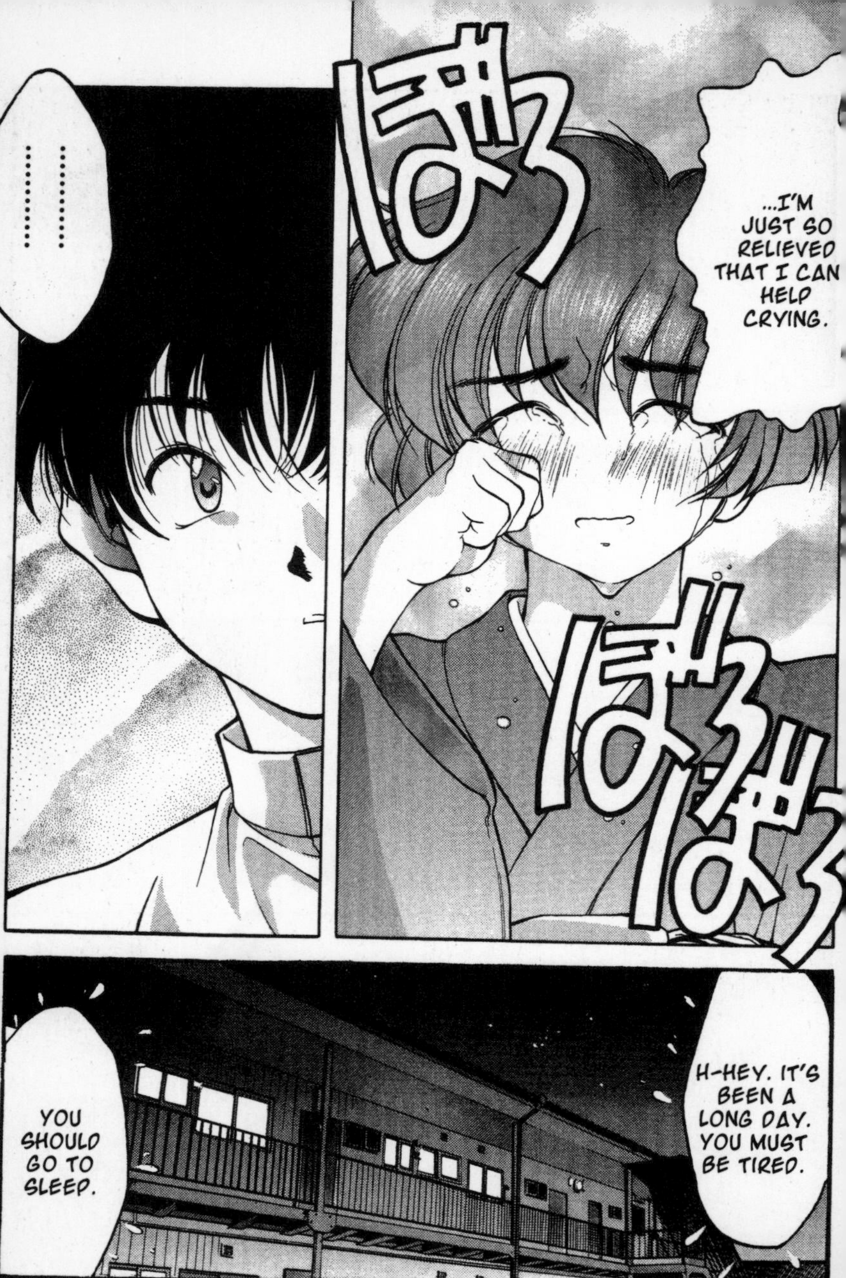
ぼろ
...I'M JUST SO RELIEVED THAT I CAN HELP CRYING.
ぼろぼろ
......
H-HEY. IT'S BEEN A LONG DAY. YOU MUST BE TIRED.
YOU SHOULD GO TO SLEEP.

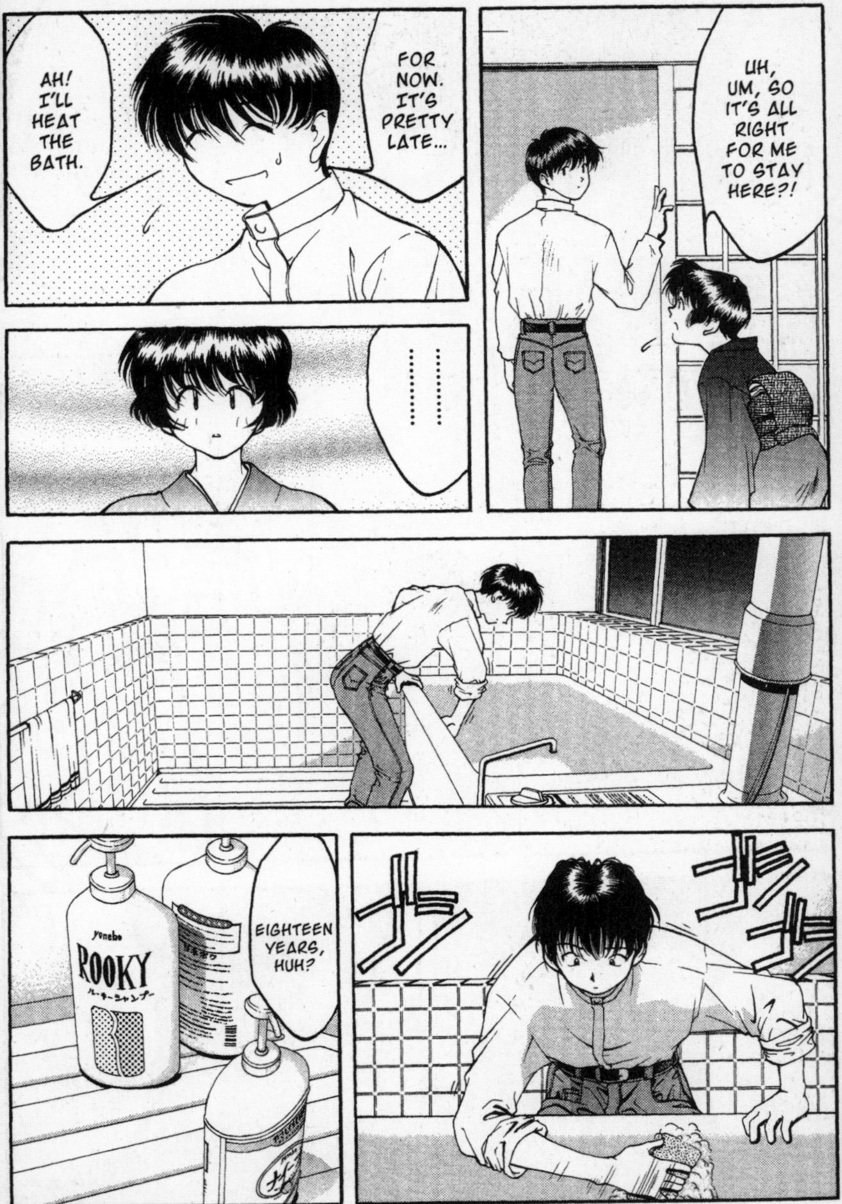
UH, UM, SO IT'S ALL RIGHT FOR ME TO STAY HERE?!
FOR NOW. IT'S PRETTY LATE...
AH! I'LL HEAT THE BATH.
......
EIGHTEEN YEARS, HUH?
yonebo
ROOKY

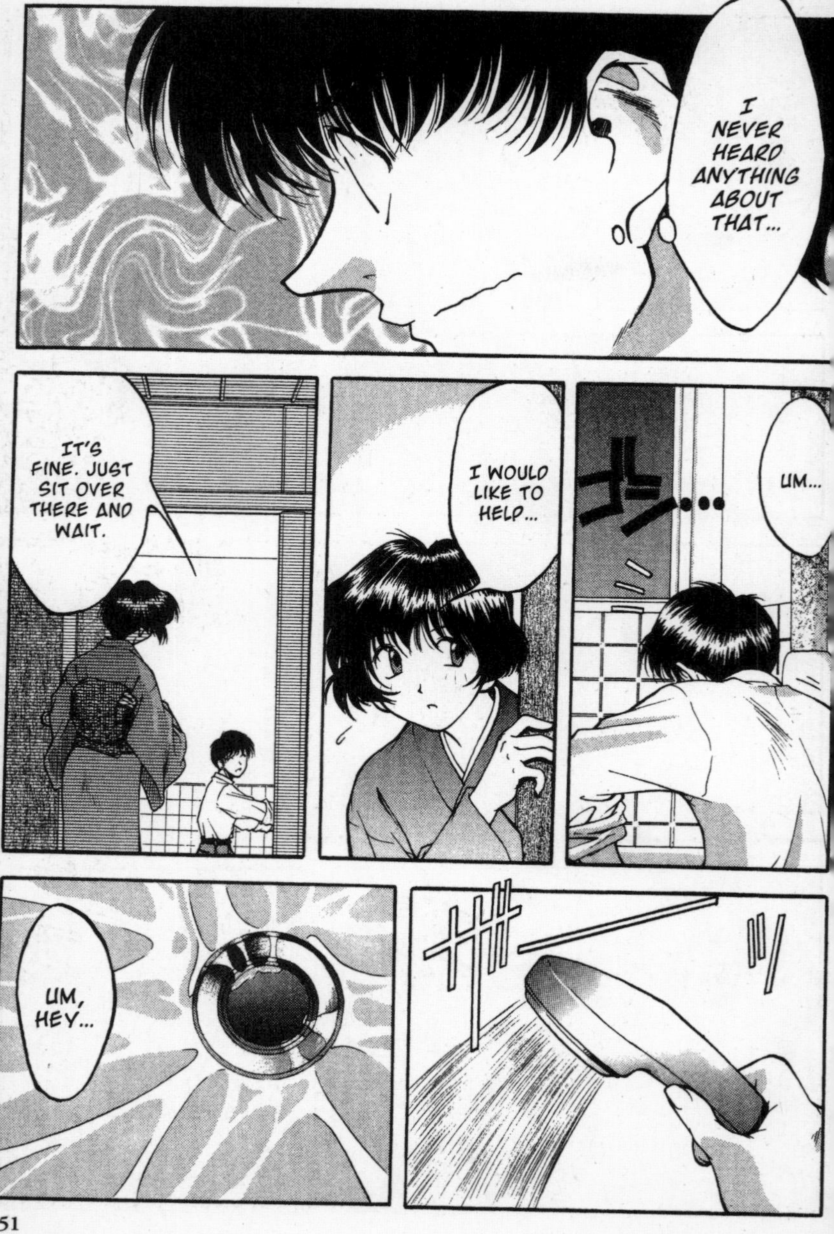
I NEVER HEARD ANYTHING ABOUT THAT...
UM...
I WOULD LIKE TO HELP...
IT'S FINE. JUST SIT OVER THERE AND WAIT.
UM, HEY...

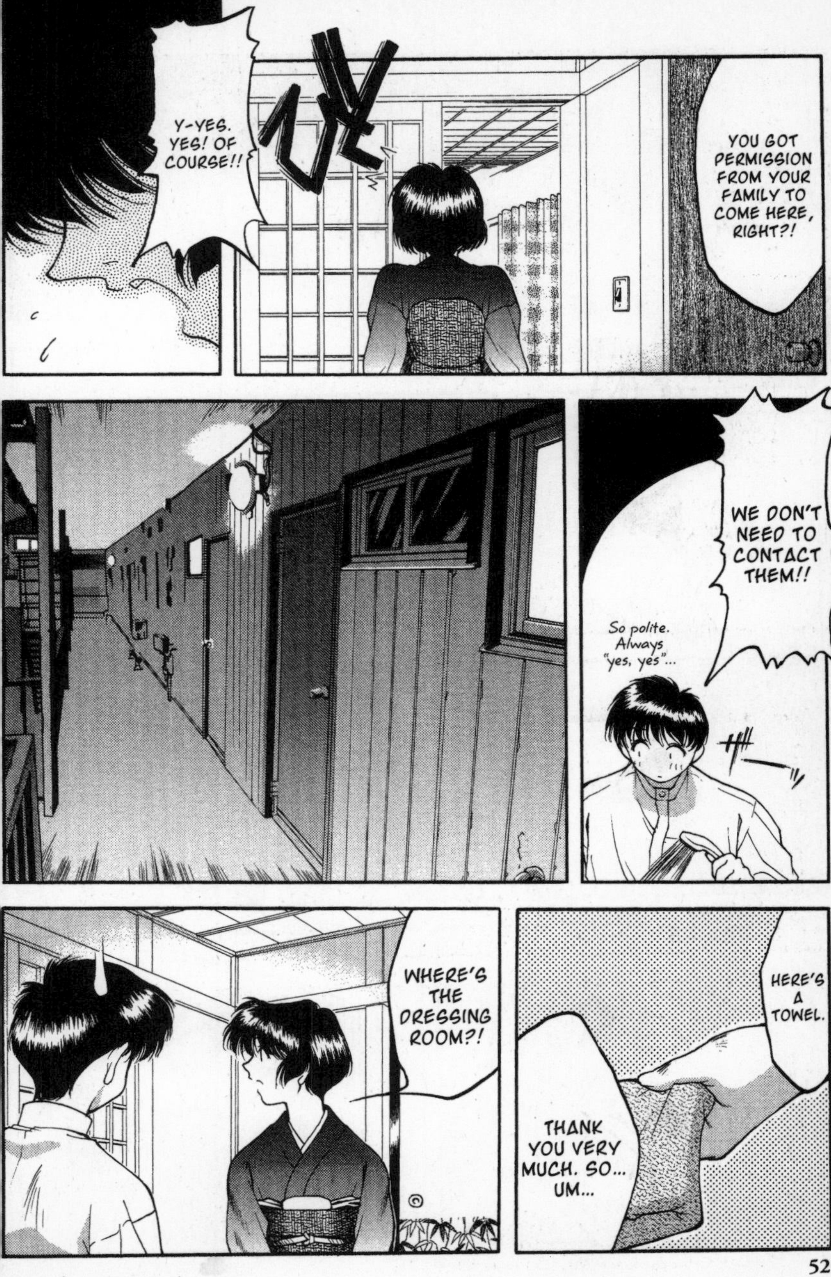
YOU GOT PERMISSION FROM YOUR FAMILY TO COME HERE, RIGHT?!
Y-YES. YES! OF COURSE!!
WE DON'T NEED TO CONTACT THEM!!
So polite. Always "yes, yes"...
HERE'S A TOWEL.
THANK YOU VERY MUCH. SO... UM...
WHERE'S THE DRESSING ROOM?!

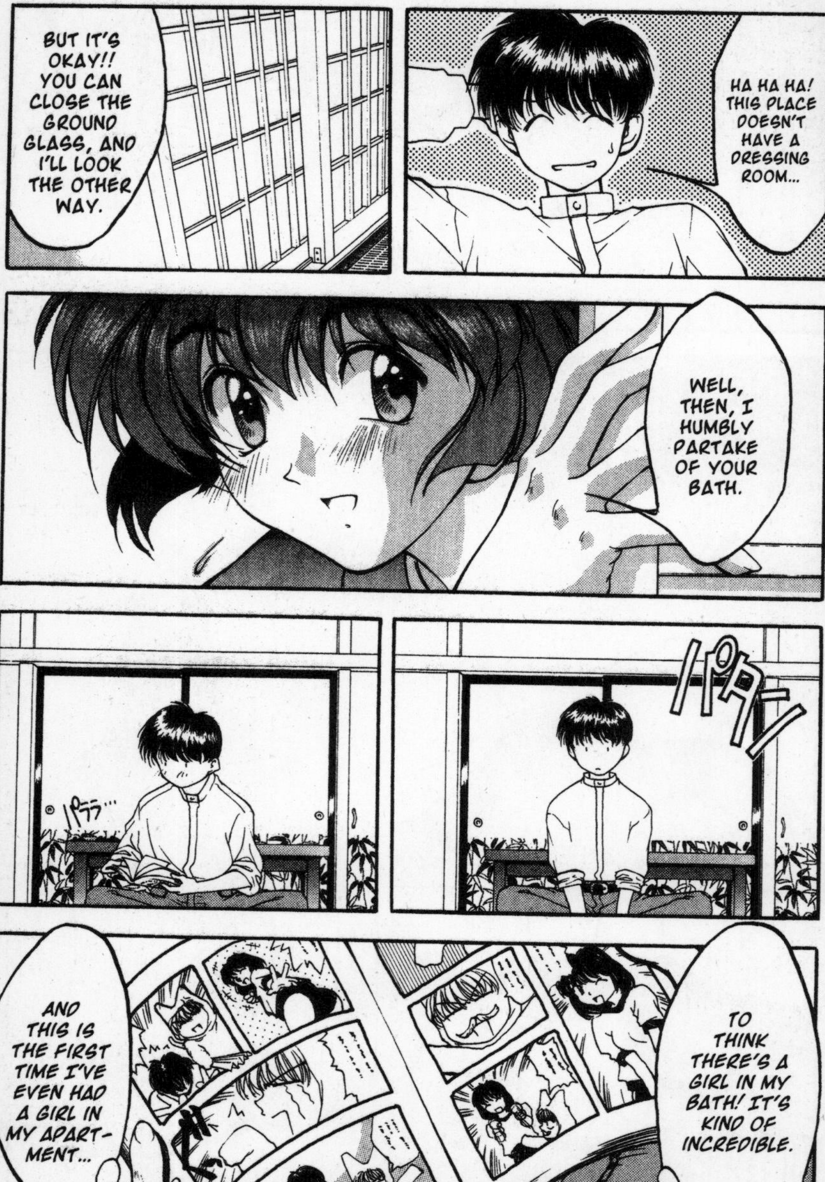
HA HA HA! THIS PLACE DOESN'T HAVE A DRESSING ROOM...
BUT IT'S OKAY!! YOU CAN CLOSE THE GROUND GLASS, AND I'LL LOOK THE OTHER WAY.
WELL, THEN, I HUMBLY PARTAKE OF YOUR BATH.
TO THINK THERE'S A GIRL IN MY BATH! IT'S KIND OF INCREDIBLE.
AND THIS IS THE FIRST TIME I'VE EVEN HAD A GIRL IN MY APARTMENT...

 Copyright: the Great Mari Koizumi-sensei

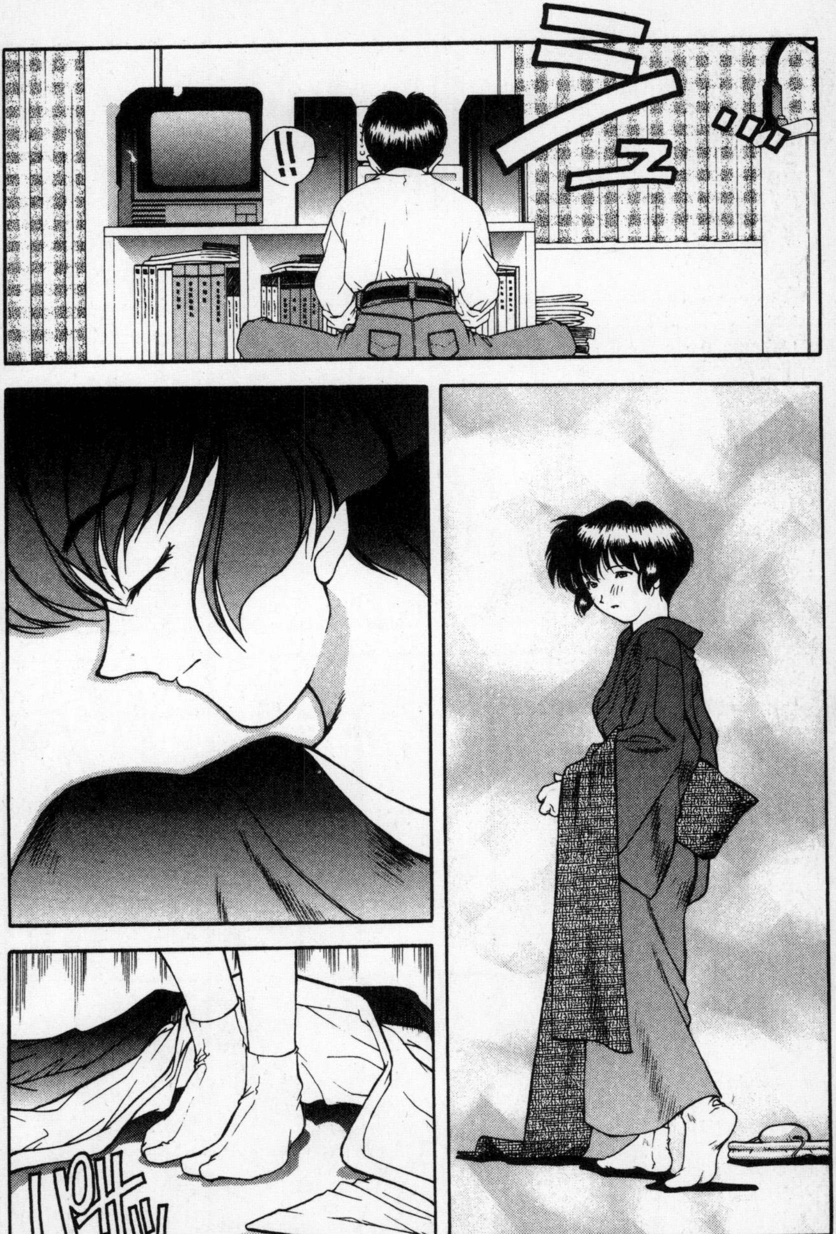
!!
ミシーン…
パサッ

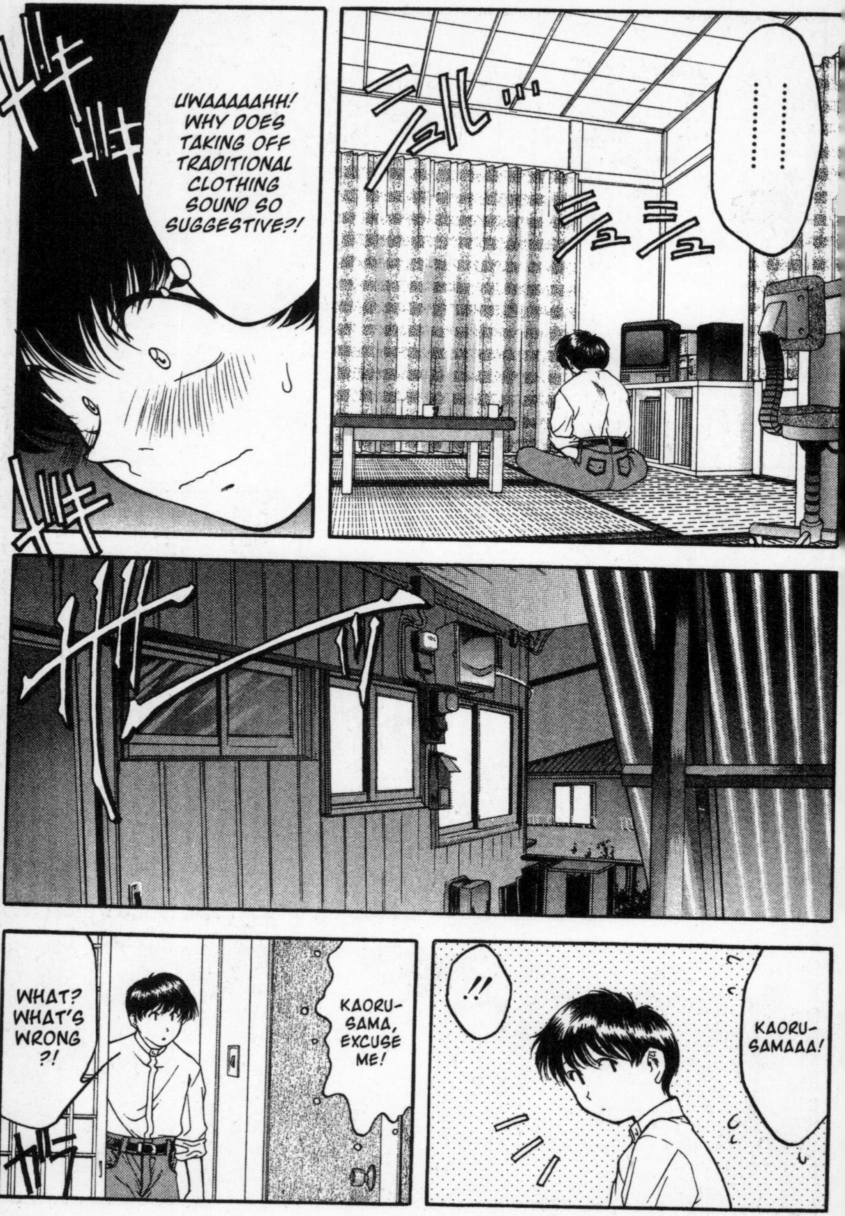
……
UWAAAAAHH! WHY DOES TAKING OFF TRADITIONAL CLOTHING SOUND SO SUGGESTIVE?!
!!
KAORU-SAMAAA!
KAORU-SAMA, EXCUSE ME!
WHAT? WHAT'S WRONG ?!

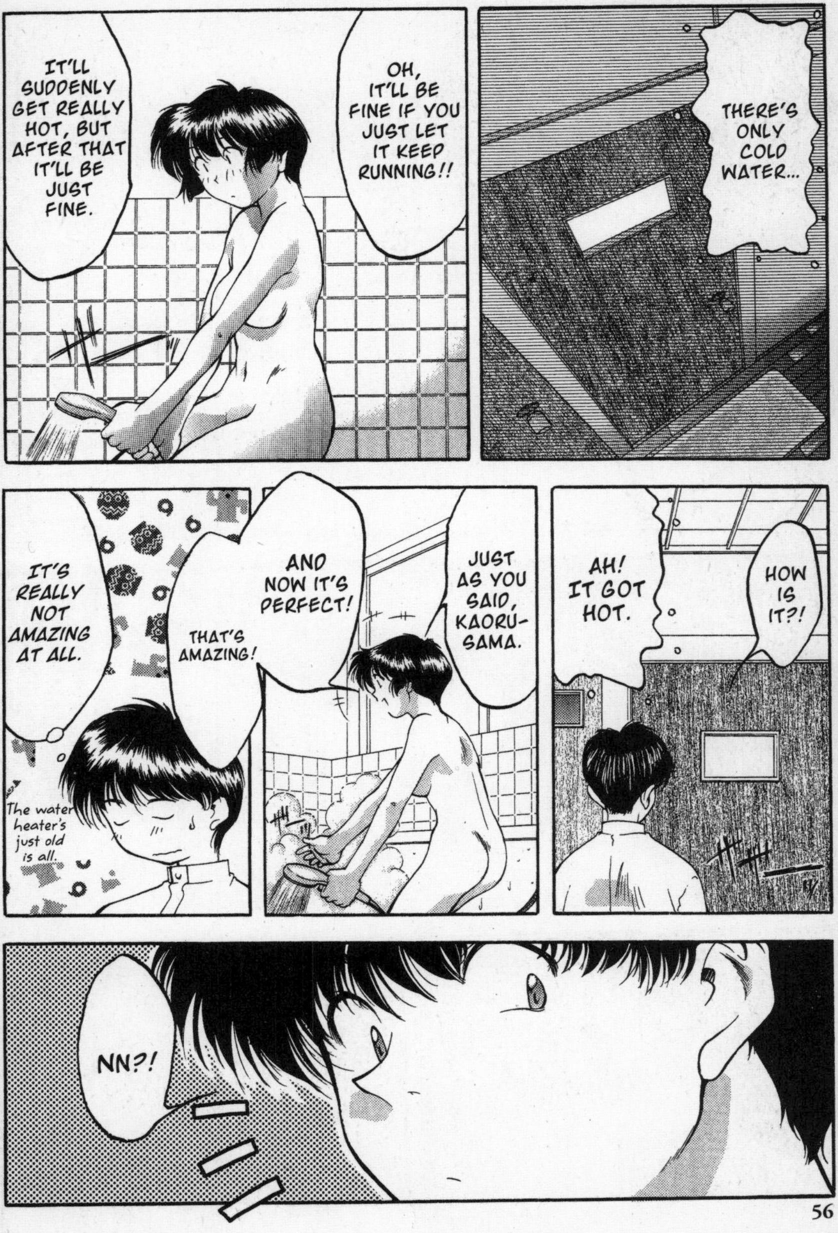
THERE'S ONLY COLD WATER...
OH, IT'LL BE FINE IF YOU JUST LET IT KEEP RUNNING!!
IT'LL SUDDENLY GET REALLY HOT, BUT AFTER THAT IT'LL BE JUST FINE.
HOW IS IT?!
AH! IT GOT HOT.
JUST AS YOU SAID, KAORU-SAMA.
AND NOW IT'S PERFECT!
THAT'S AMAZING!
IT'S REALLY NOT AMAZING AT ALL.
The water heater's just old is all.
NN?!

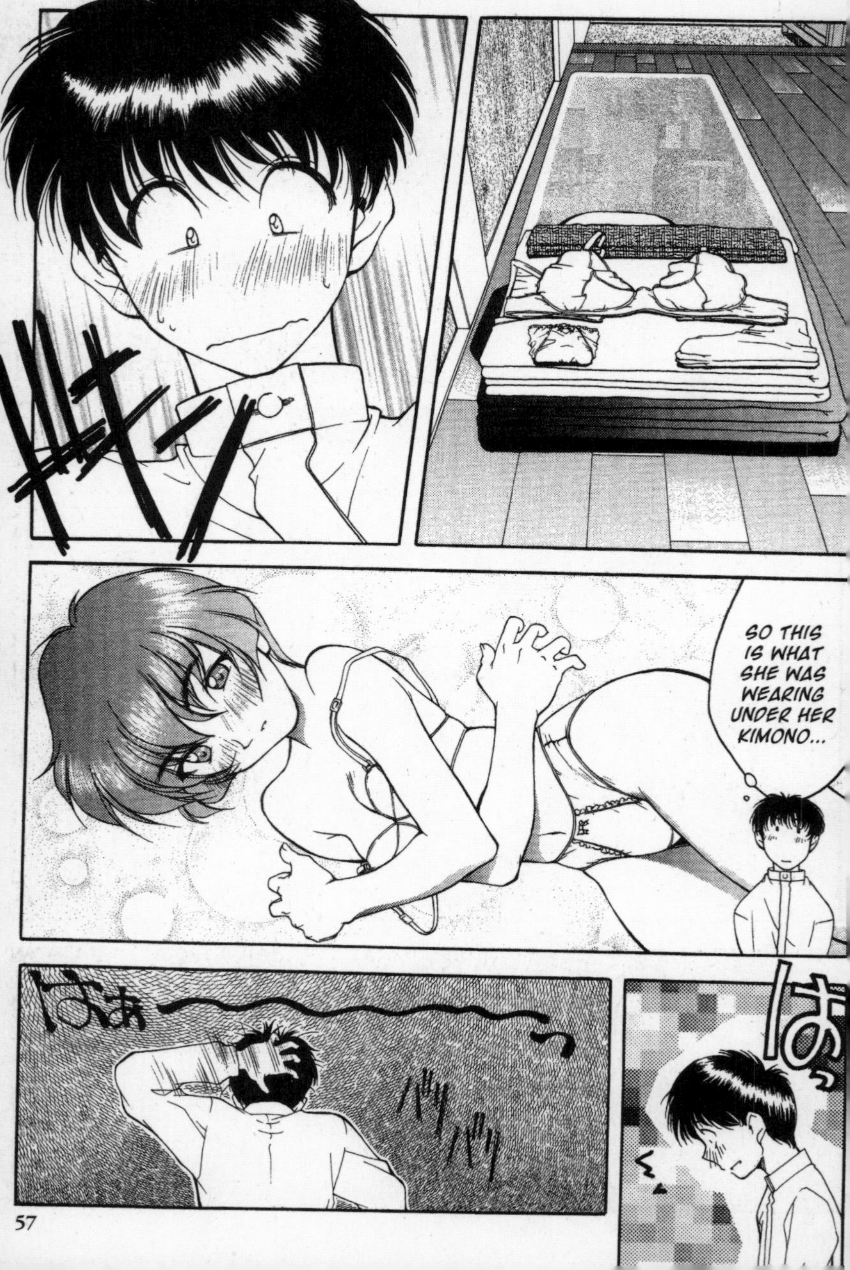
SO THIS IS WHAT SHE WAS WEARING UNDER HER KIMONO...
はっ
はぁ〜〜〜っ
バリバリ

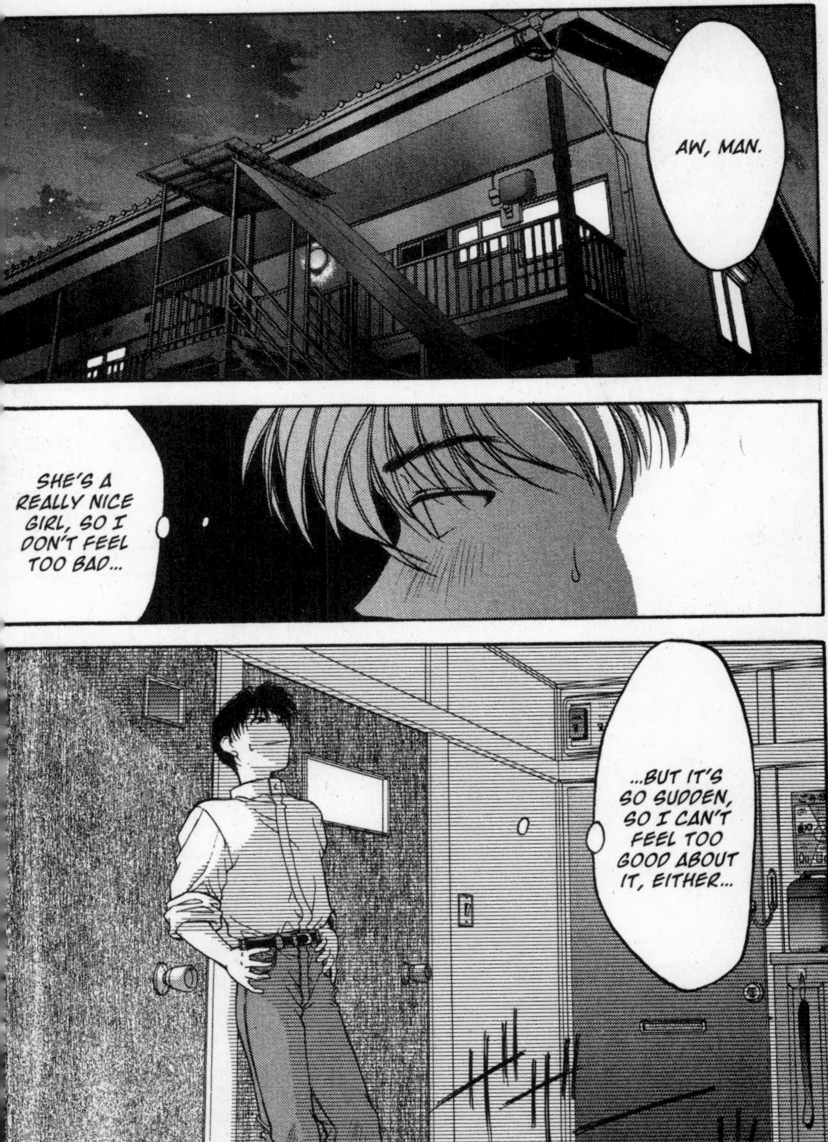
AW, MAN.
SHE'S A REALLY NICE GIRL, SO I DON'T FEEL TOO BAD...
...BUT IT'S SO SUDDEN, SO I CAN'T FEEL TOO GOOD ABOUT IT, EITHER...

End of Chapter 2: Iinazuke - Betrothed

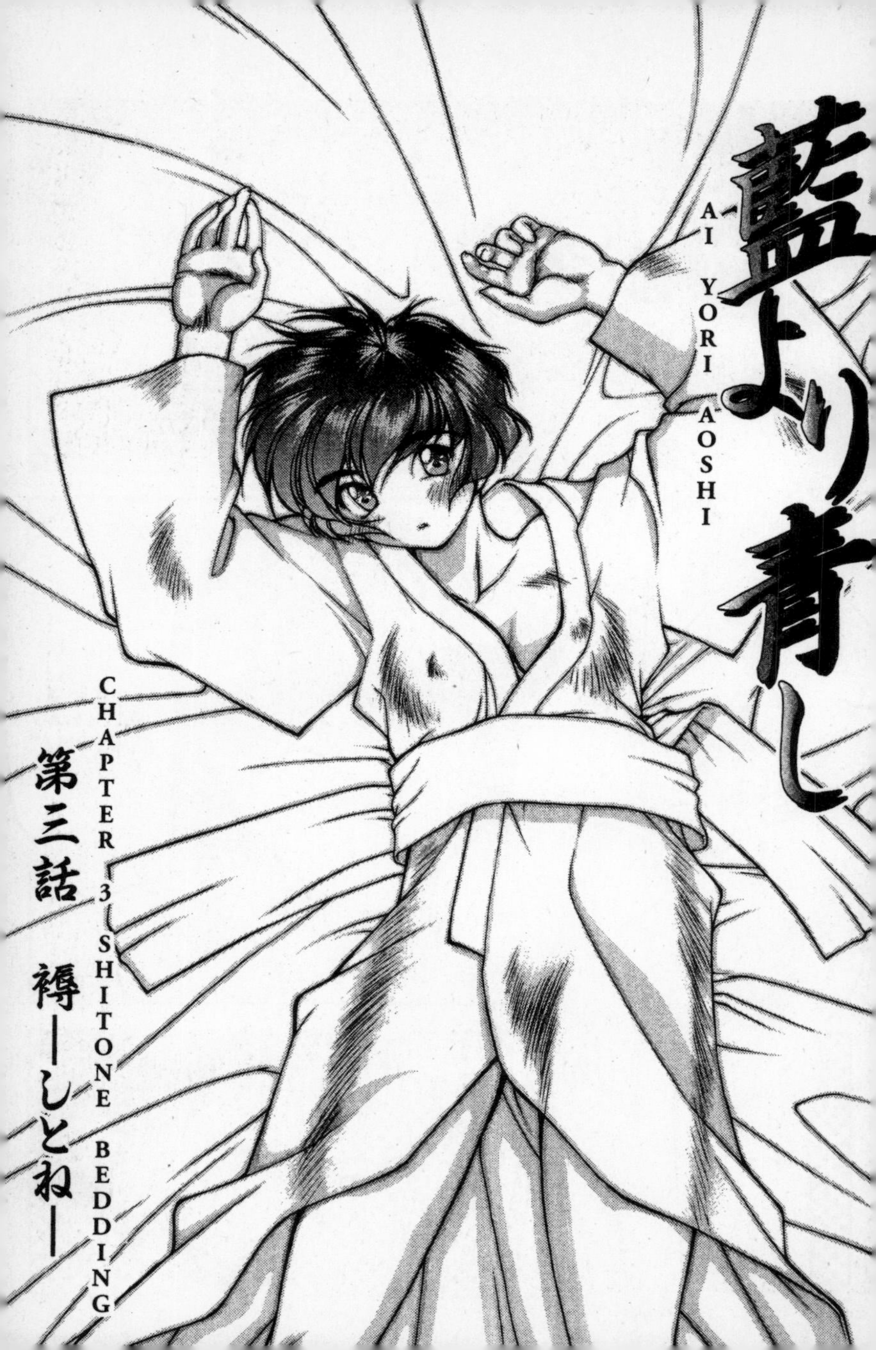
藍より青し
AI YORI AOSHI
第三話 褥―しとね―
CHAPTER 3 SHITONE BEDDING

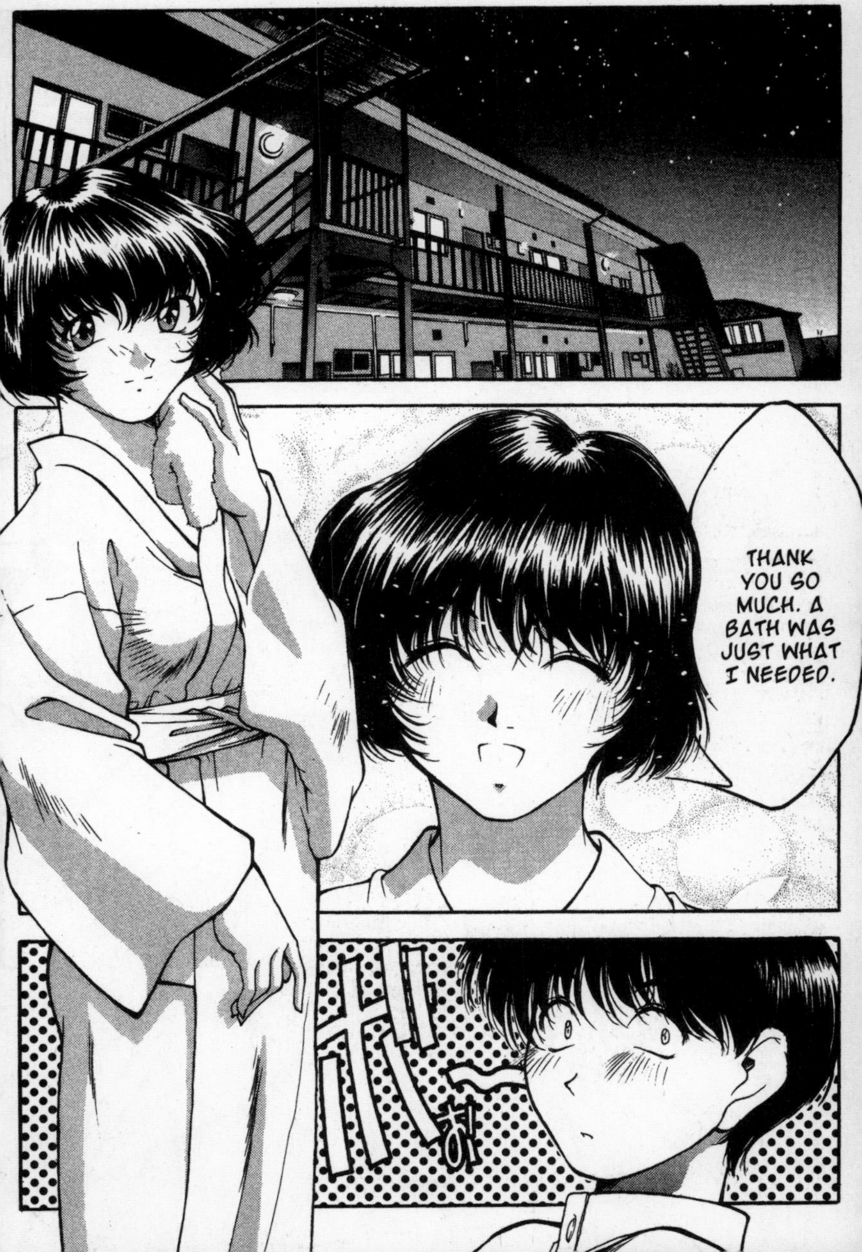
THANK YOU SO MUCH. A BATH WAS JUST WHAT I NEEDED.

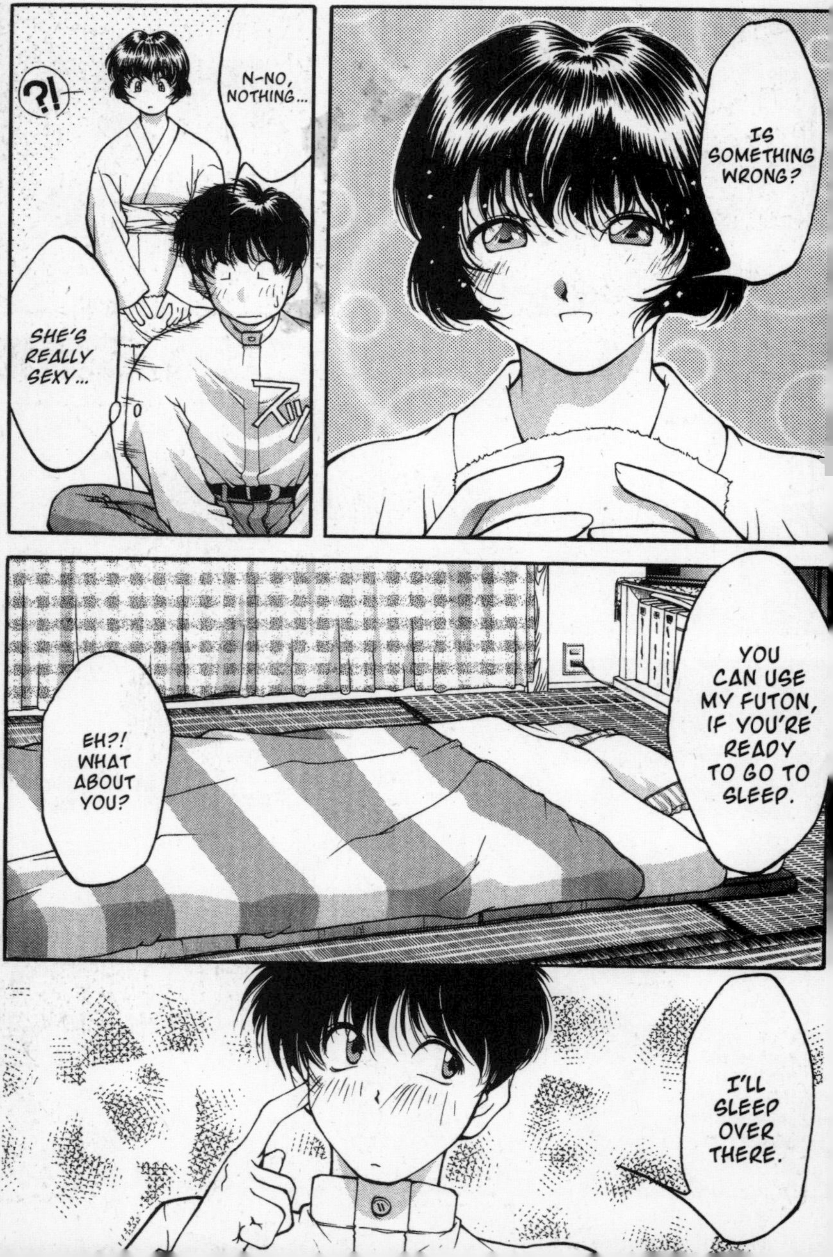
IS SOMETHING WRONG?
?!
N-NO, NOTHING...
SHE'S REALLY SEXY...
YOU CAN USE MY FUTON, IF YOU'RE READY TO GO TO SLEEP.
EH?! WHAT ABOUT YOU?
I'LL SLEEP OVER THERE.

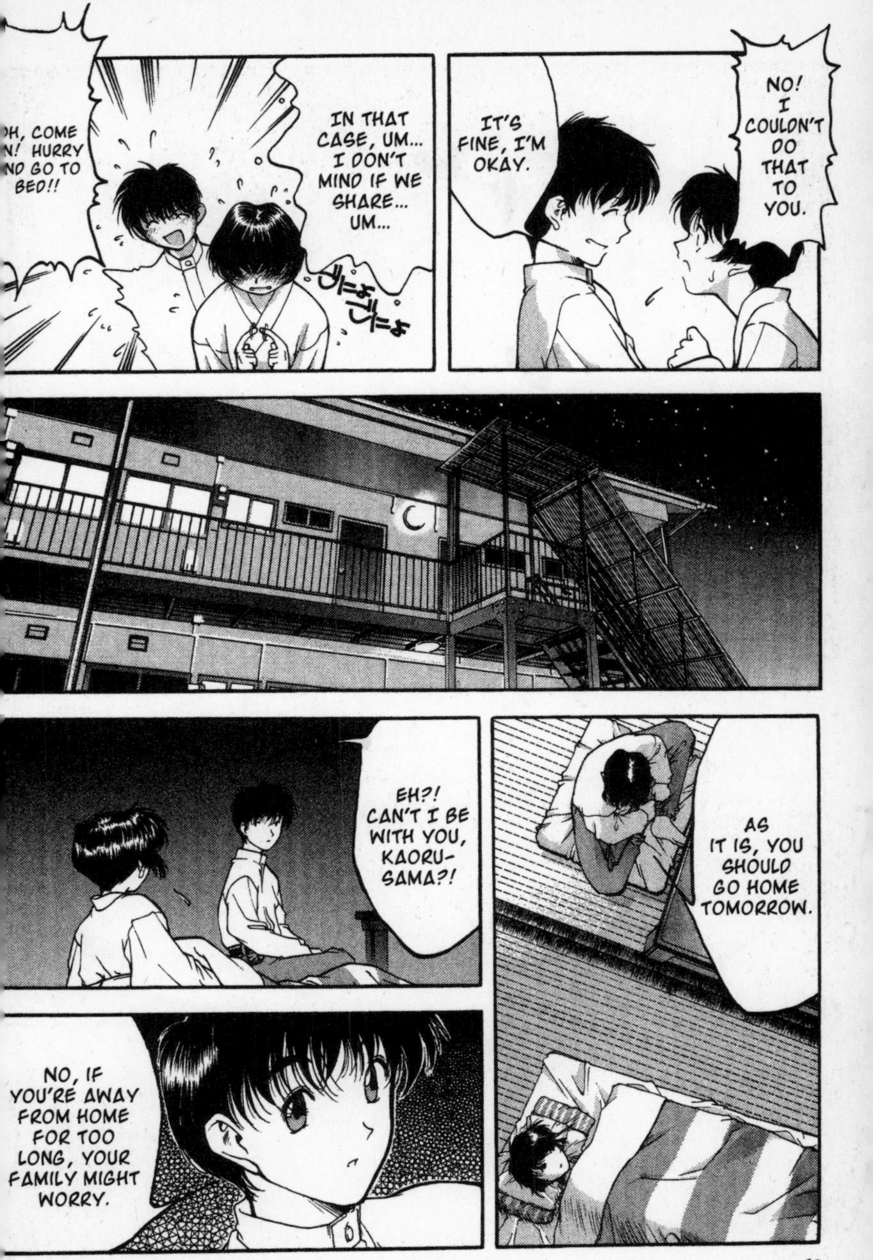
NO! I COULDN'T DO THAT TO YOU.
IT'S FINE, I'M OKAY.
IN THAT CASE, UM... I DON'T MIND IF WE SHARE... UM...
ごにょ ごにょ
H, COME N! HURRY ND GO TO BED!!
AS IT IS, YOU SHOULD GO HOME TOMORROW.
EH?! CAN'T I BE WITH YOU, KAORU-SAMA?!
NO, IF YOU'RE AWAY FROM HOME FOR TOO LONG, YOUR FAMILY MIGHT WORRY.

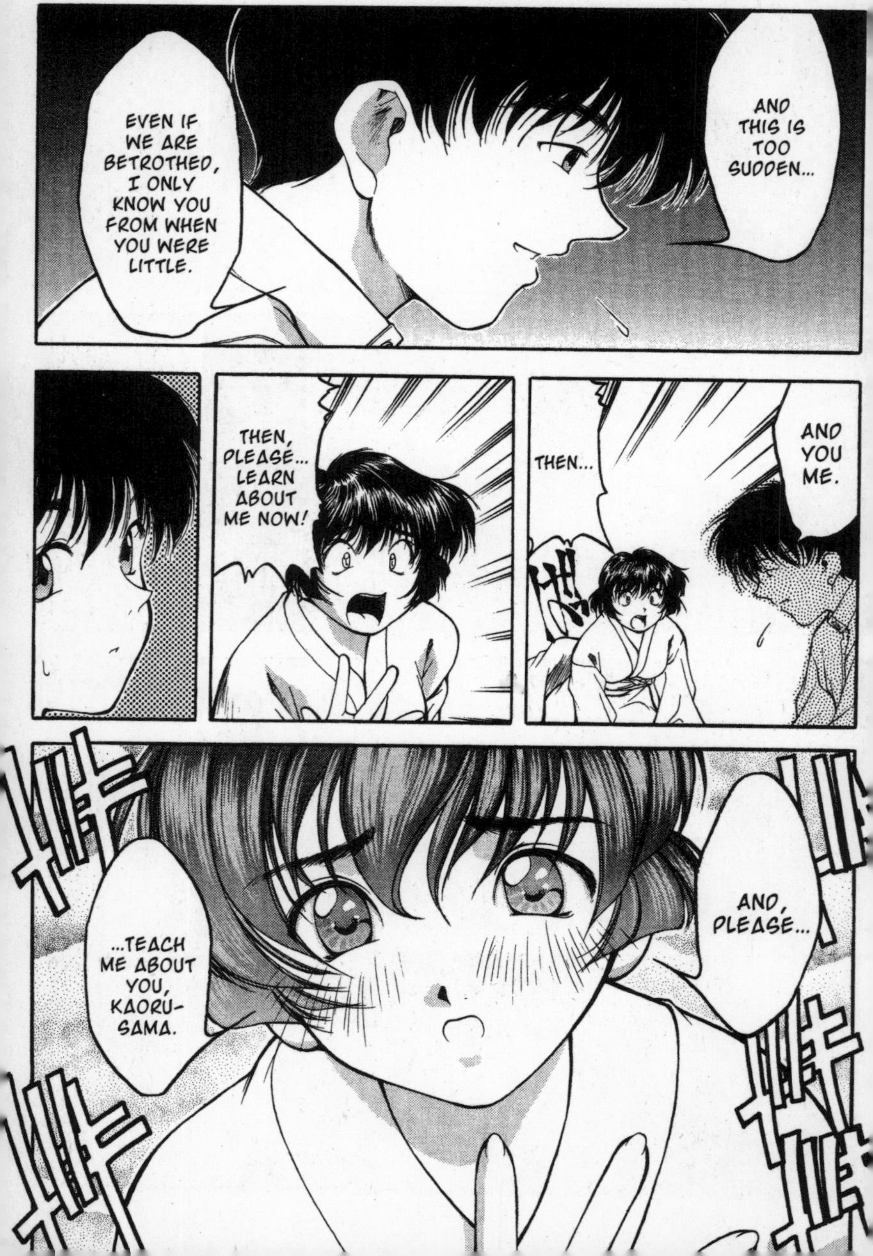
AND THIS IS TOO SUDDEN...
EVEN IF WE ARE BETROTHED, I ONLY KNOW YOU FROM WHEN YOU WERE LITTLE.
AND YOU ME.
THEN...
THEN, PLEASE... LEARN ABOUT ME NOW!
AND, PLEASE...
...TEACH ME ABOUT YOU, KAORU-SAMA.

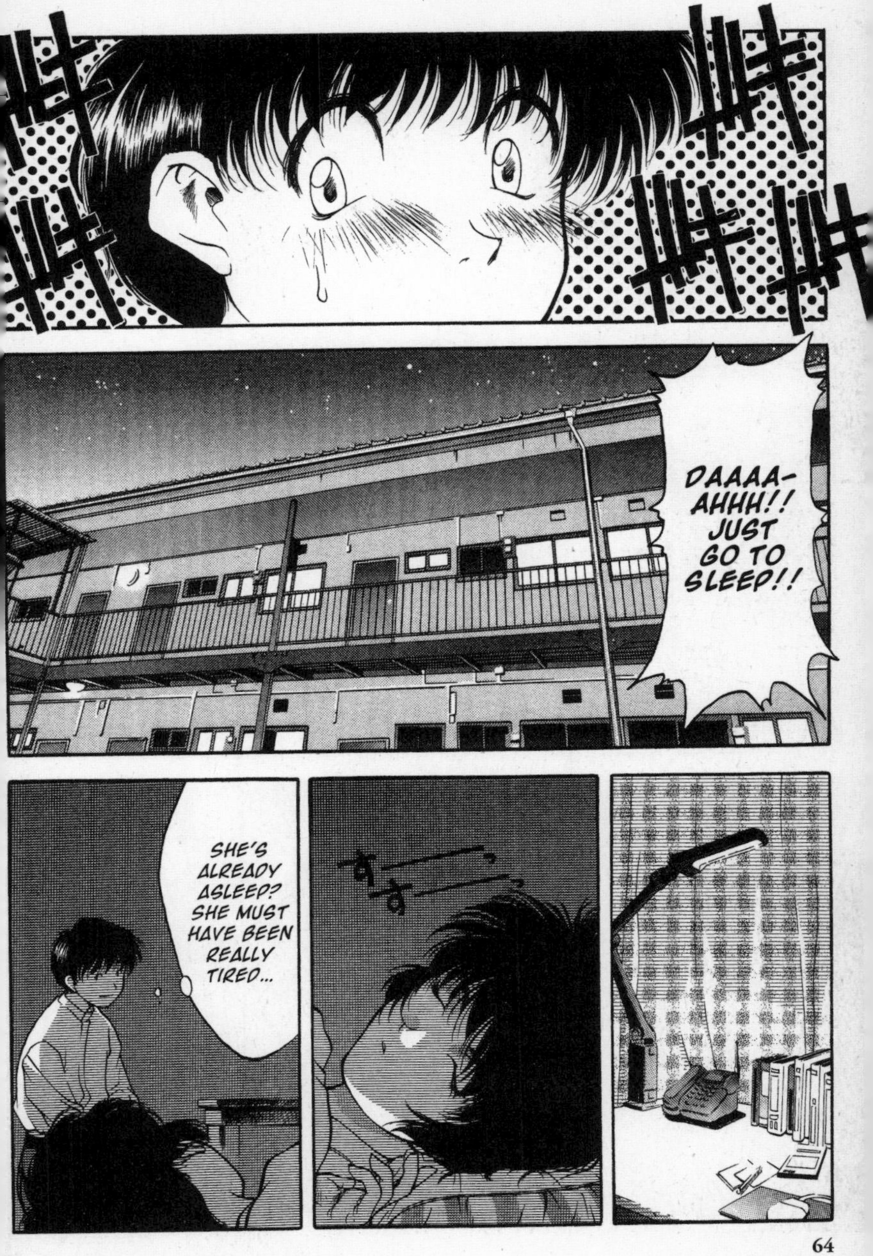
DAAAA-AHHH!! JUST GO TO SLEEP!!
す――
す――
SHE'S ALREADY ASLEEP? SHE MUST HAVE BEEN REALLY TIRED...

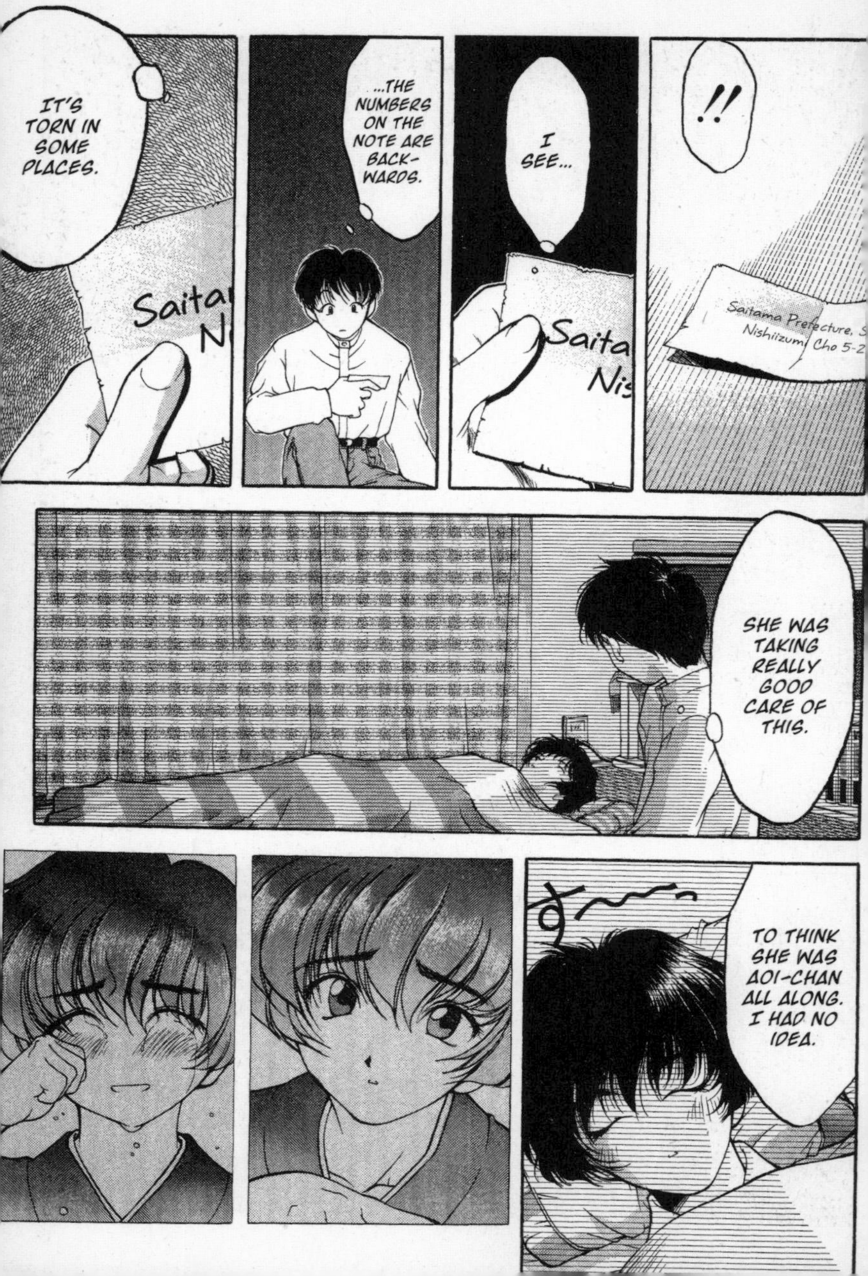
IT'S TORN IN SOME PLACES.
...THE NUMBERS ON THE NOTE ARE BACKWARDS.
I SEE...
!!
Saitama Prefecture, S
Nishiizumi Cho 5-2
SHE WAS TAKING REALLY GOOD CARE OF THIS.
す~~
TO THINK SHE WAS AOI-CHAN ALL ALONG. I HAD NO IDEA.

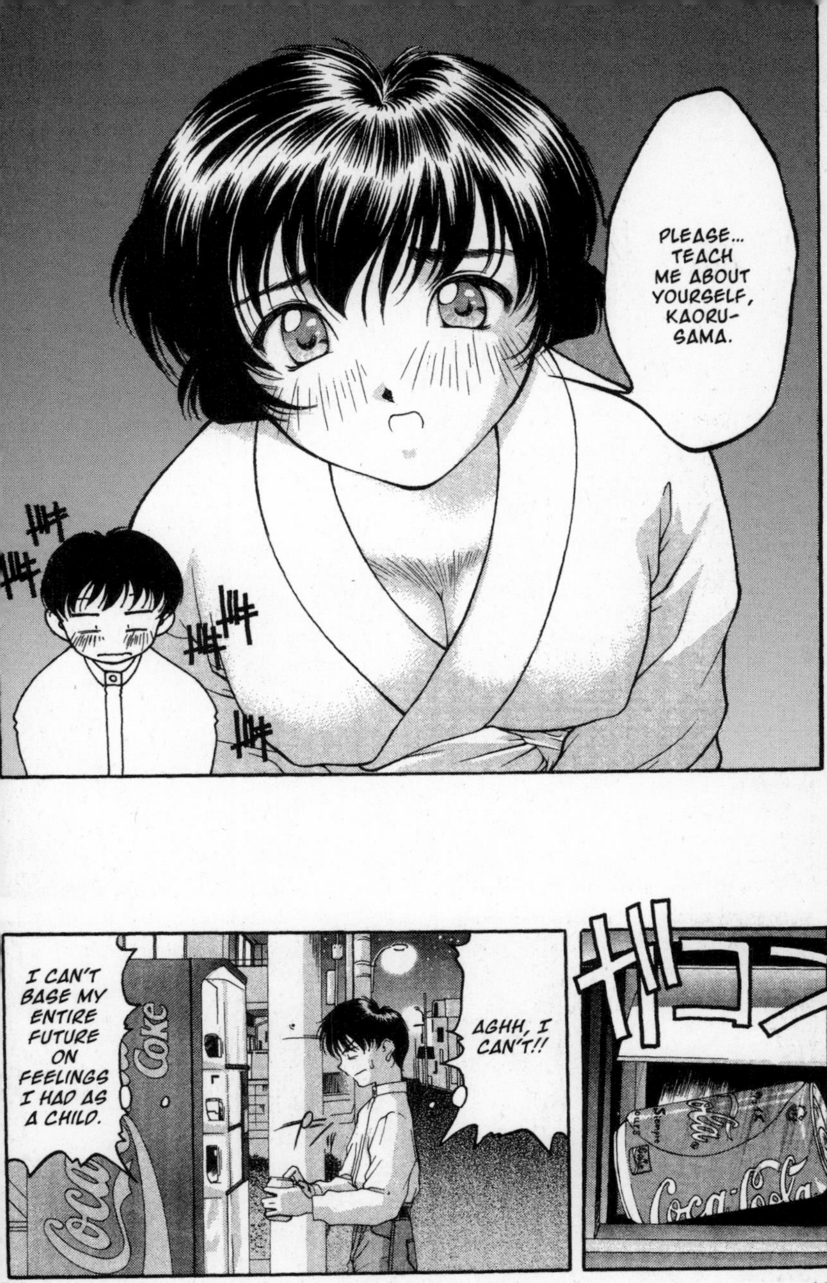
PLEASE... TEACH ME ABOUT YOURSELF, KAORU-SAMA.
Coca-Cola
AGHH, I CAN'T!!
I CAN'T BASE MY ENTIRE FUTURE ON FEELINGS I HAD AS A CHILD.
Coke
Coca

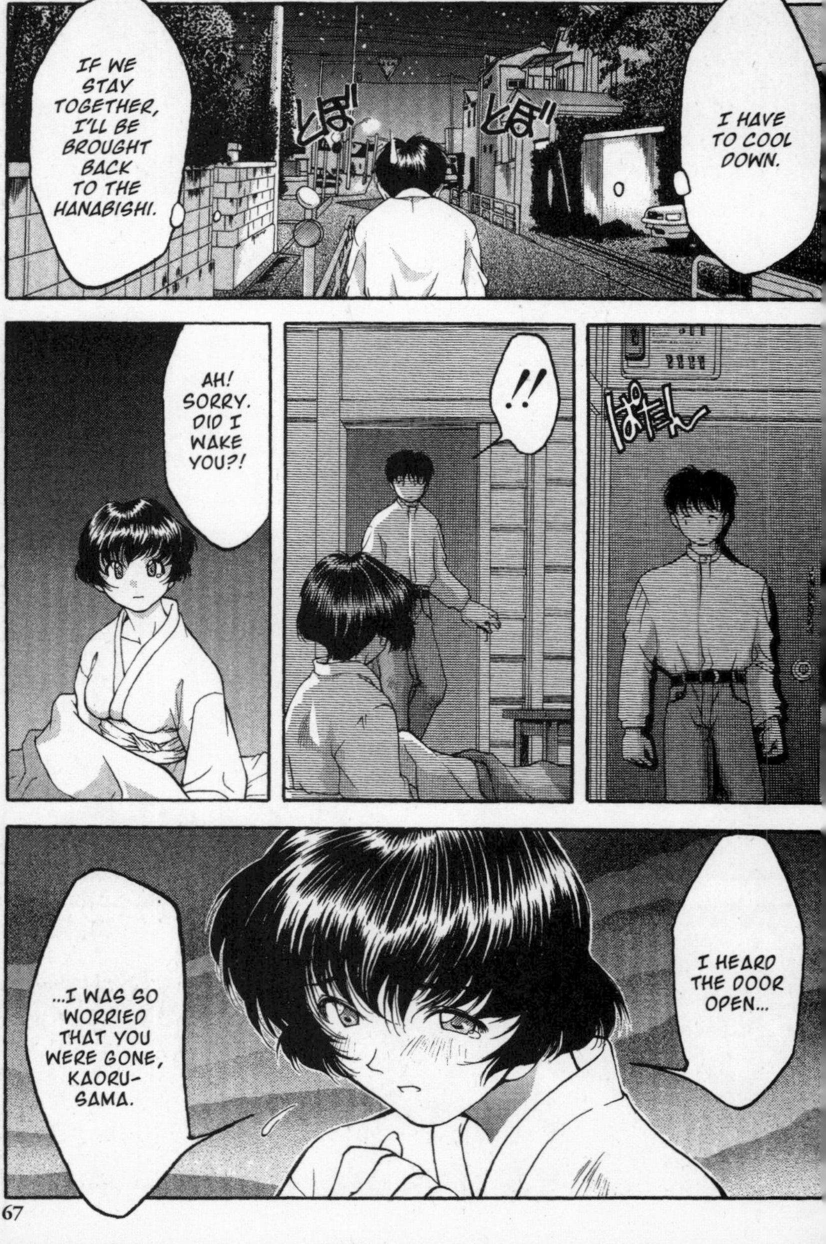

I HAVE TO COOL DOWN.
とぼ
とぼ
IF WE STAY TOGETHER, I'LL BE BROUGHT BACK TO THE HANABISHI.
ぱたん
!!
AH! SORRY. DID I WAKE YOU?!
I HEARD THE DOOR OPEN...
...I WAS SO WORRIED THAT YOU WERE GONE, KAORU-SAMA.

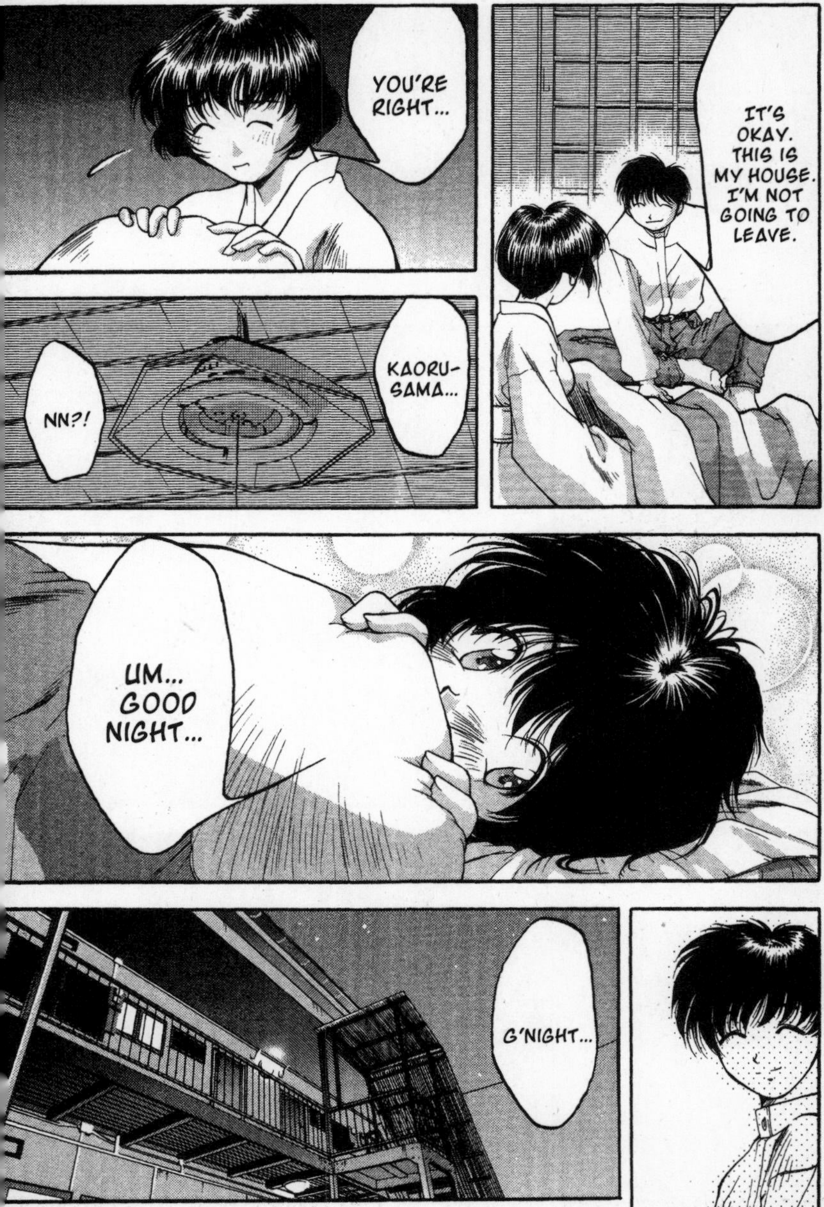
IT'S OKAY. THIS IS MY HOUSE. I'M NOT GOING TO LEAVE.
YOU'RE RIGHT...
KAORU-SAMA...
NN?!
UM... GOOD NIGHT...
G'NIGHT...

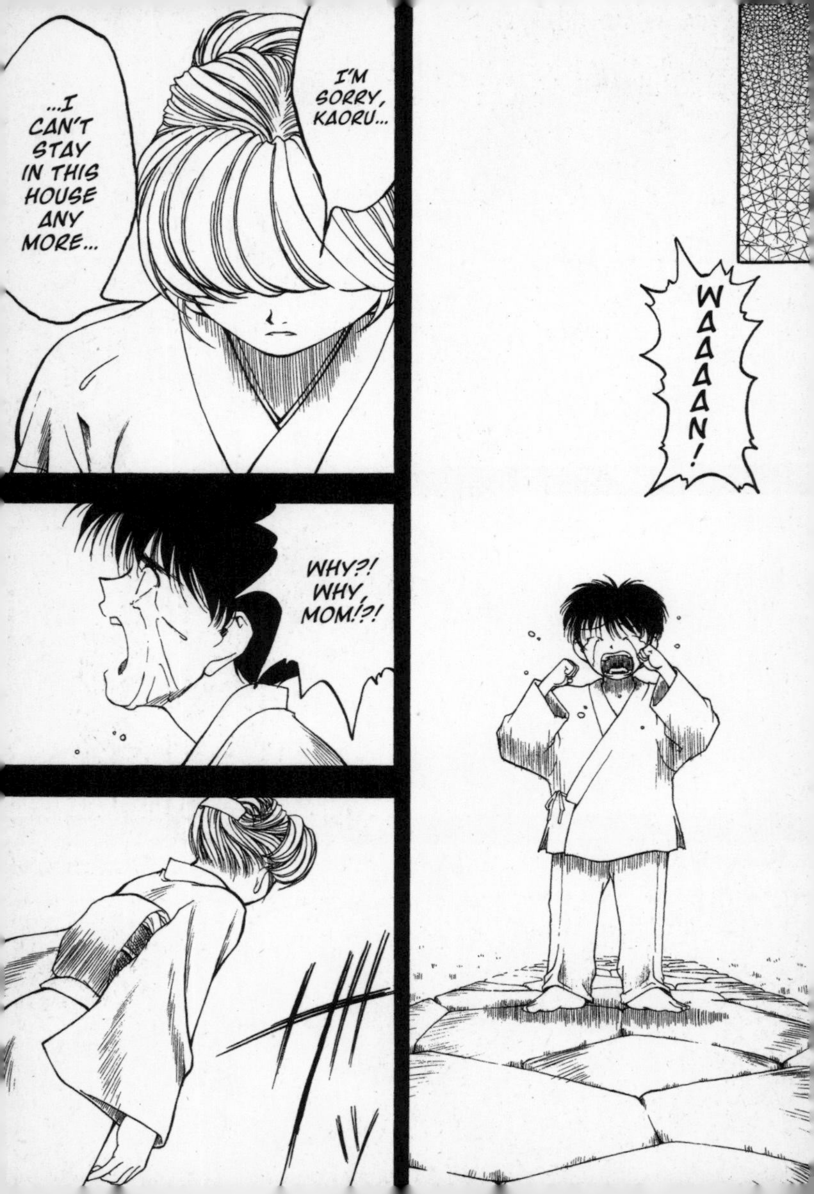
I'M SORRY, KAORU...
...I CAN'T STAY IN THIS HOUSE ANY MORE...
WHY?! WHY, MOM!?!
WAAAAAN!

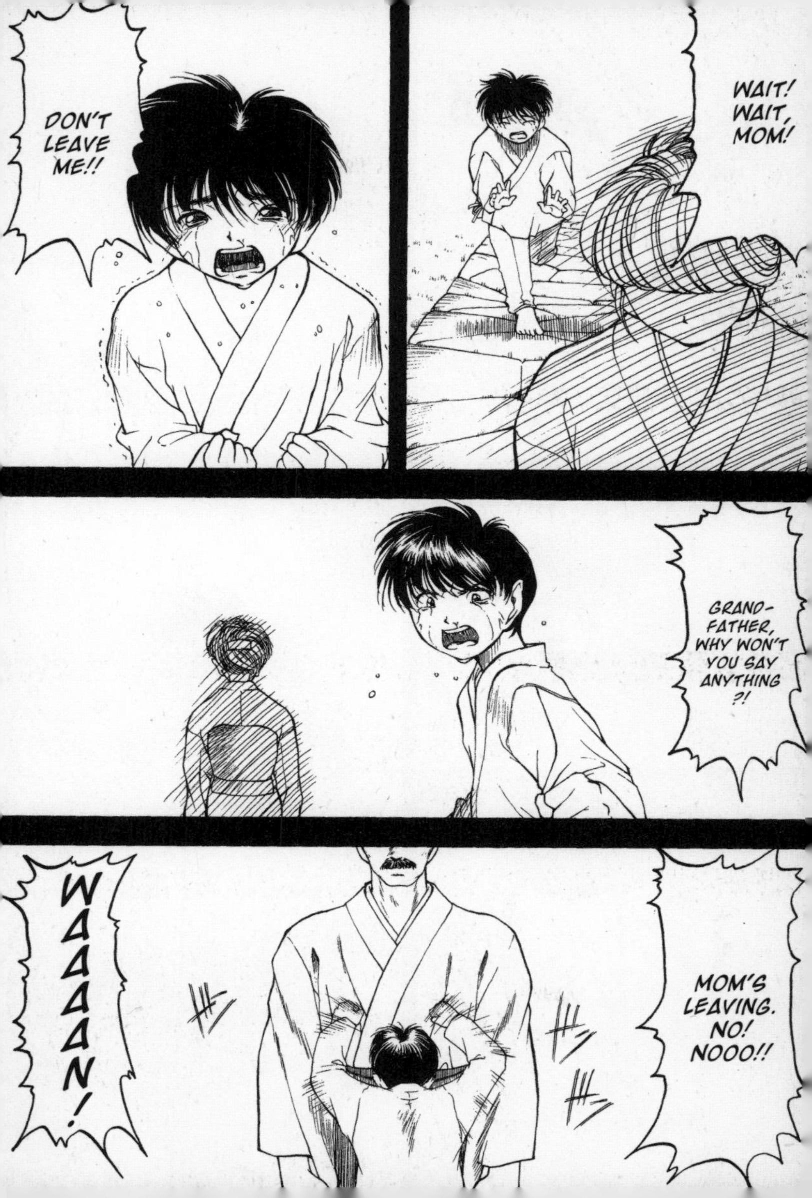
WAIT! WAIT, MOM!
DON'T LEAVE ME!!
GRAND-FATHER, WHY WON'T YOU SAY ANYTHING ?!
MOM'S LEAVING. NO! NOOO!!
WAAAAAN!

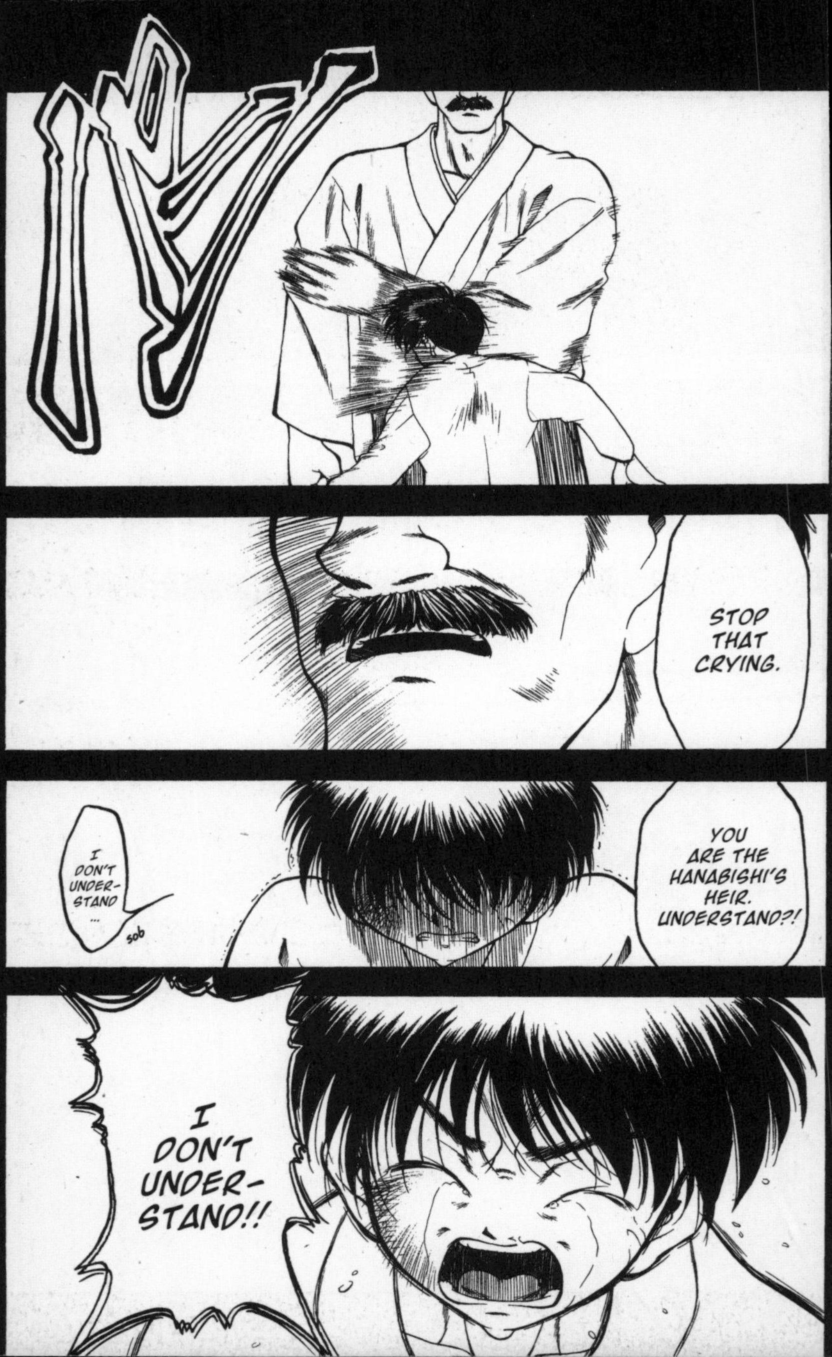
STOP THAT CRYING.
YOU ARE THE HANABISHI'S HEIR. UNDERSTAND?!
I DON'T UNDER-STAND...
sob
I DON'T UNDER-STAND!!

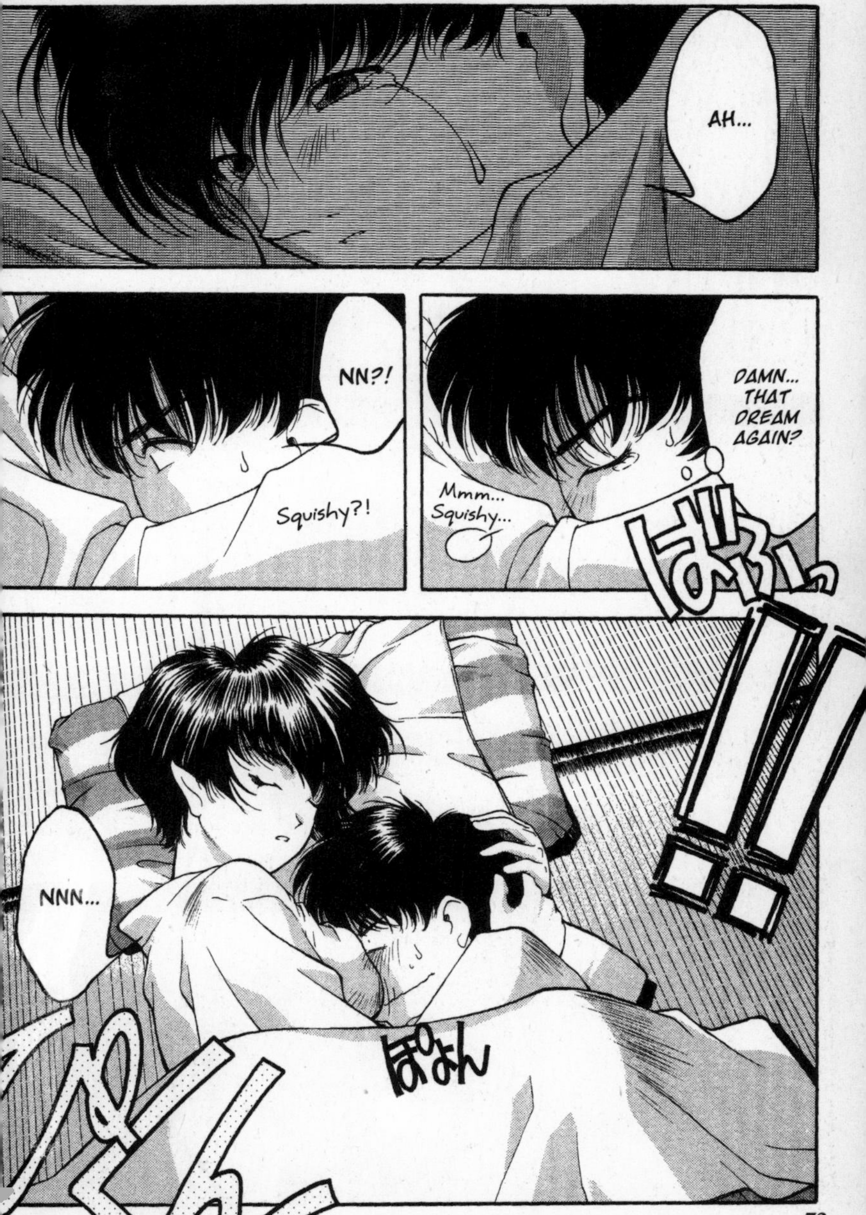
AH...
DAMN... THAT DREAM AGAIN?
Mmm... Squishy...
NN?!
Squishy?!
ばふっ!!
NNN...
ぽよん

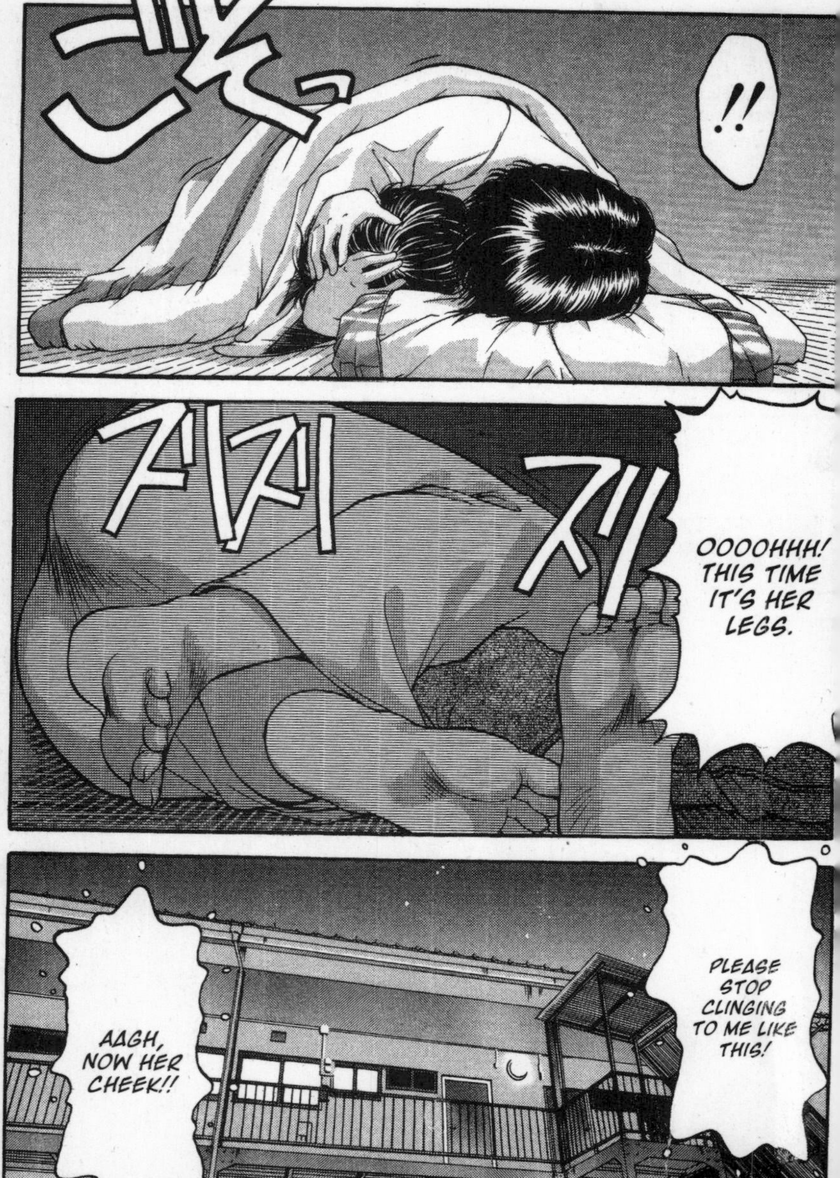
!!
OOOOHHH! THIS TIME IT'S HER LEGS.
PLEASE STOP CLINGING TO ME LIKE THIS!
AAGH, NOW HER CHEEK!!

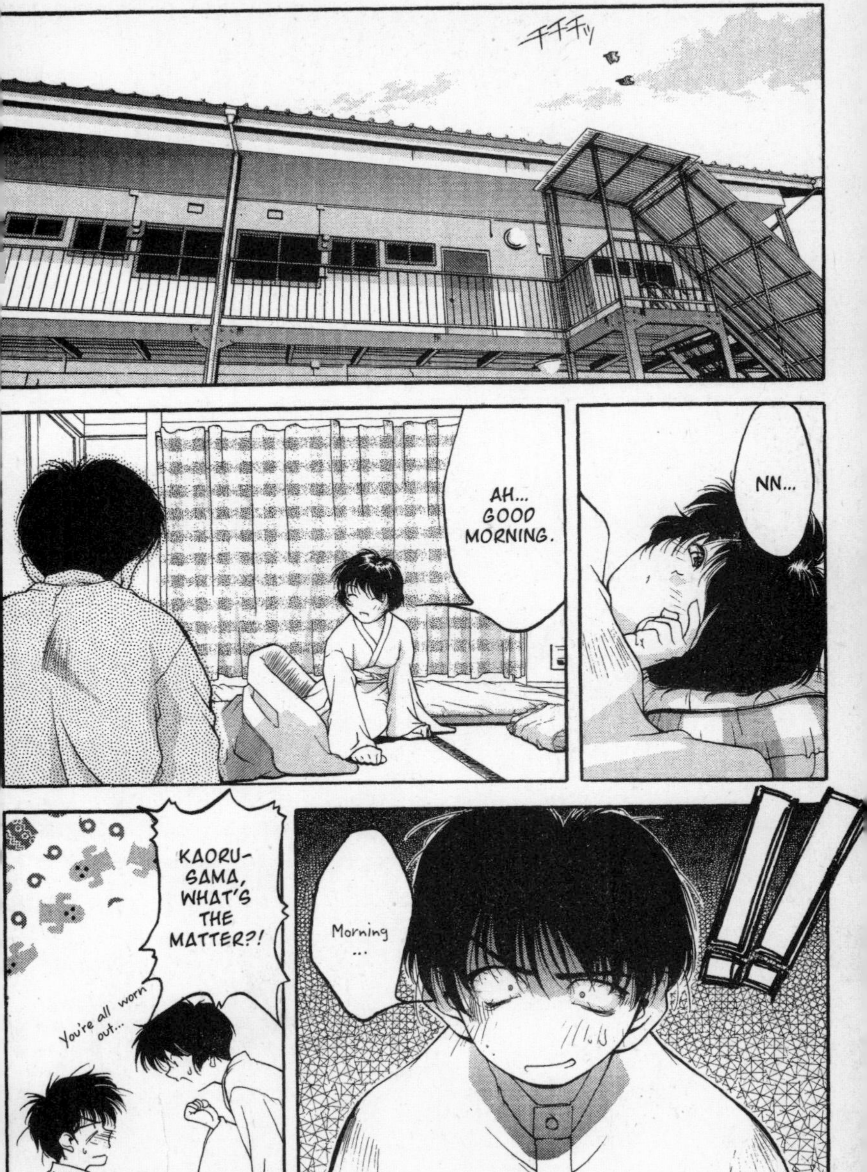
チチチッ
NN...
AH... GOOD MORNING.
Morning ...
KAORU-SAMA, WHAT'S THE MATTER?!
You're all worn out...

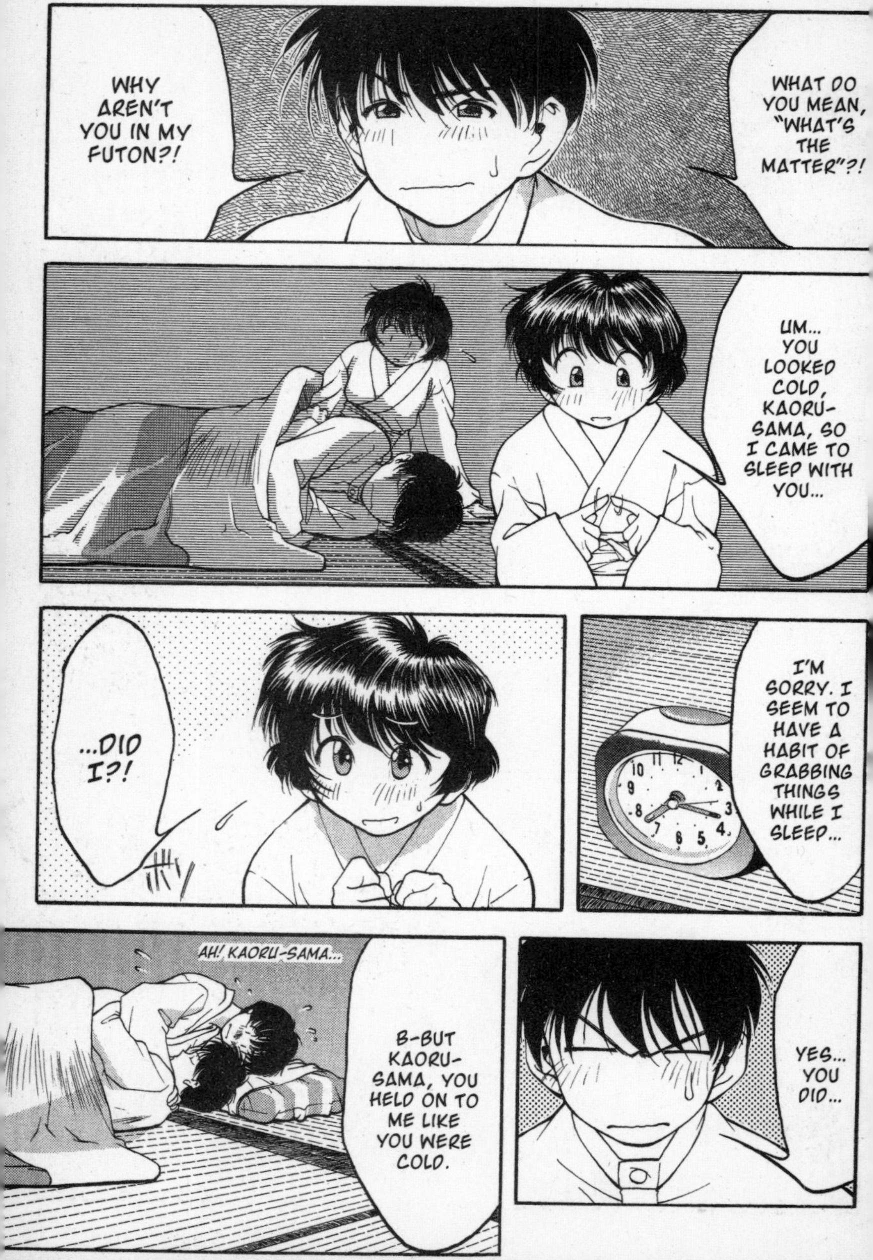
WHAT DO YOU MEAN, "WHAT'S THE MATTER"?!
WHY AREN'T YOU IN MY FUTON?!
UM... YOU LOOKED COLD, KAORU-SAMA, SO I CAME TO SLEEP WITH YOU...
I'M SORRY. I SEEM TO HAVE A HABIT OF GRABBING THINGS WHILE I SLEEP...
...DID I?!
YES... YOU DID...
AH! KAORU-SAMA...
B-BUT KAORU-SAMA, YOU HELD ON TO ME LIKE YOU WERE COLD.

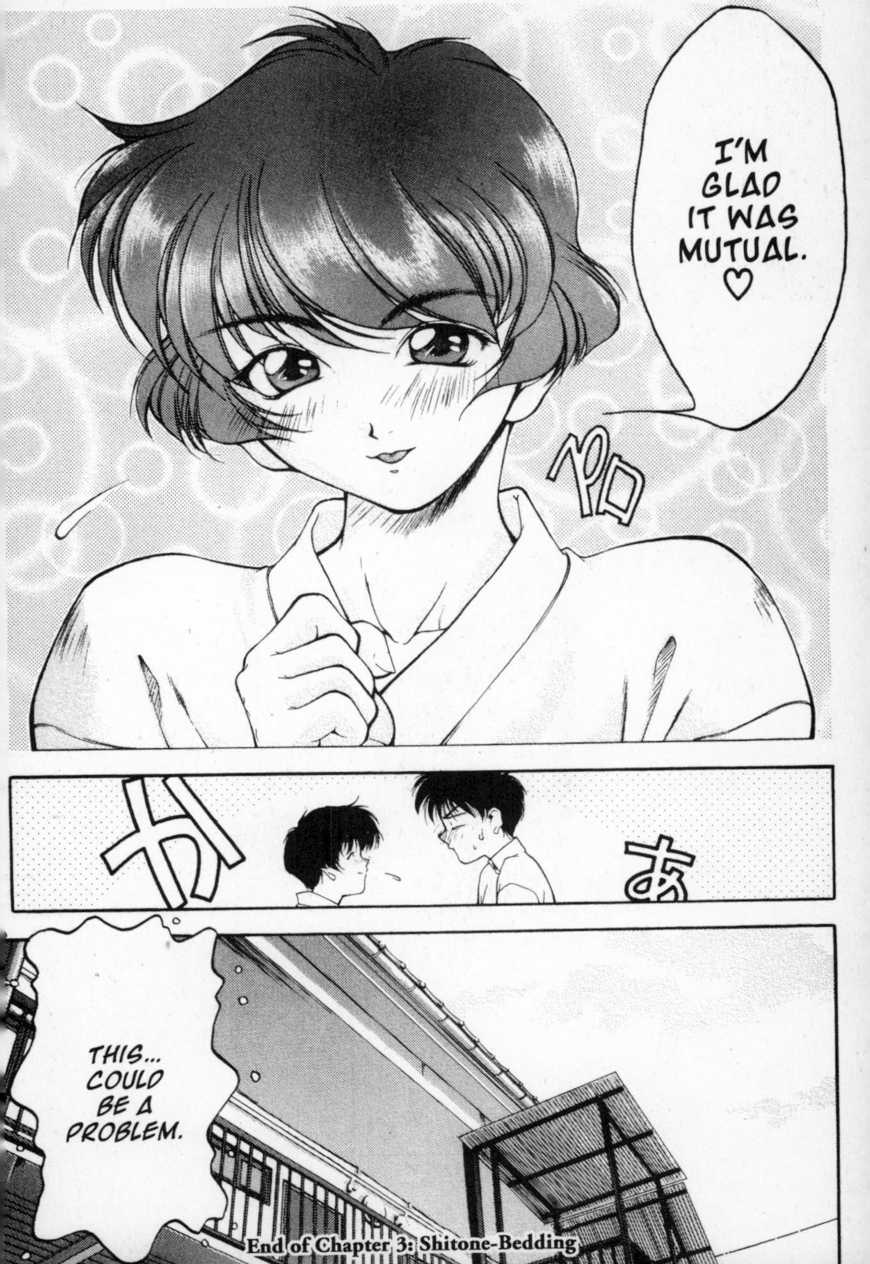
I'M GLAD IT WAS MUTUAL. ♡
ペロ
かあ
THIS... COULD BE A PROBLEM.
End of Chapter 3: Shitone-Bedding

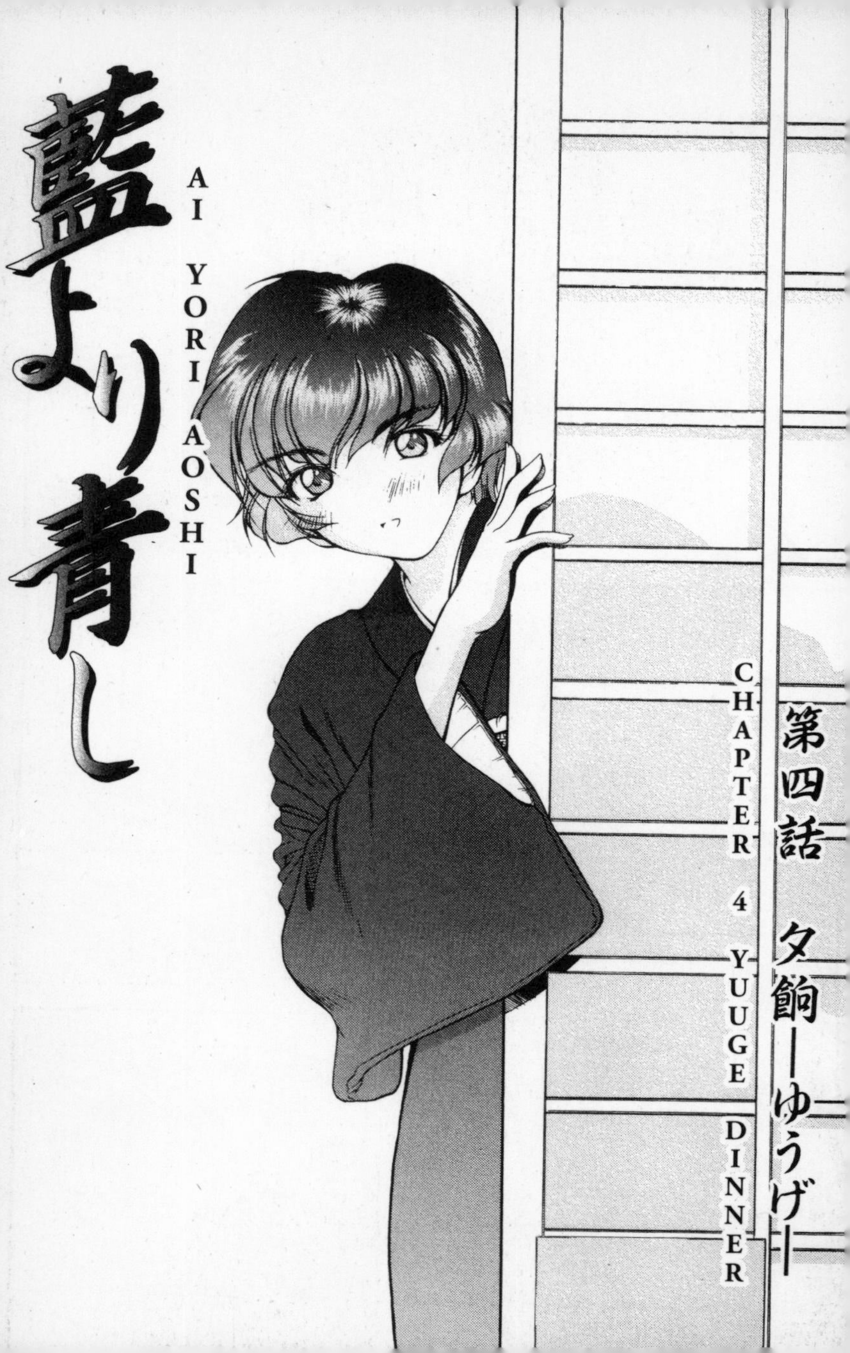
藍より青し
AI YORI AOSHI
第四話 夕餉―ゆうげ―
CHAPTER 4 YUUGE DINNER

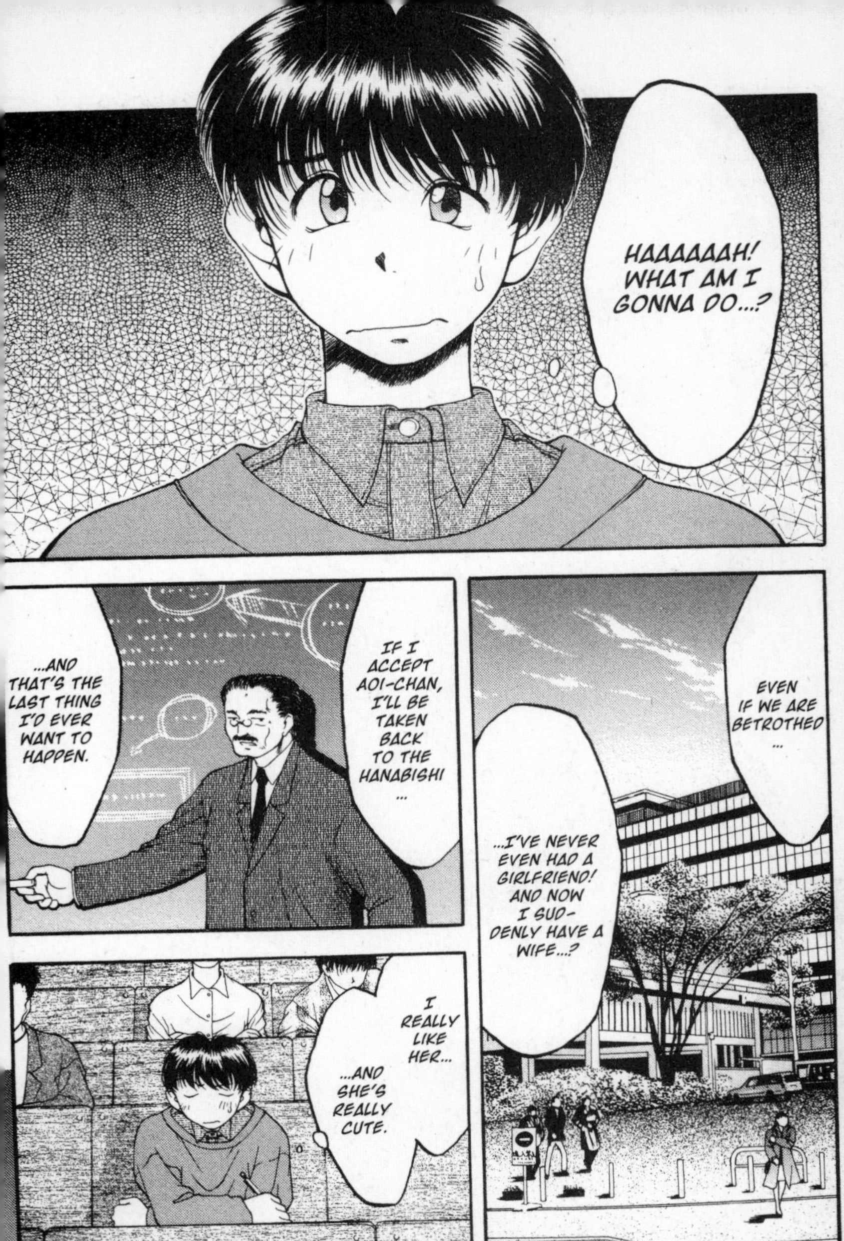
HAAAAAAH! WHAT AM I GONNA DO...?
EVEN IF WE ARE BETROTHED ...
...I'VE NEVER EVEN HAD A GIRLFRIEND! AND NOW I SUD-DENLY HAVE A WIFE...?
IF I ACCEPT AOI-CHAN, I'LL BE TAKEN BACK TO THE HANABISHI ...
...AND THAT'S THE LAST THING I'D EVER WANT TO HAPPEN.
I REALLY LIKE HER...
...AND SHE'S REALLY CUTE.

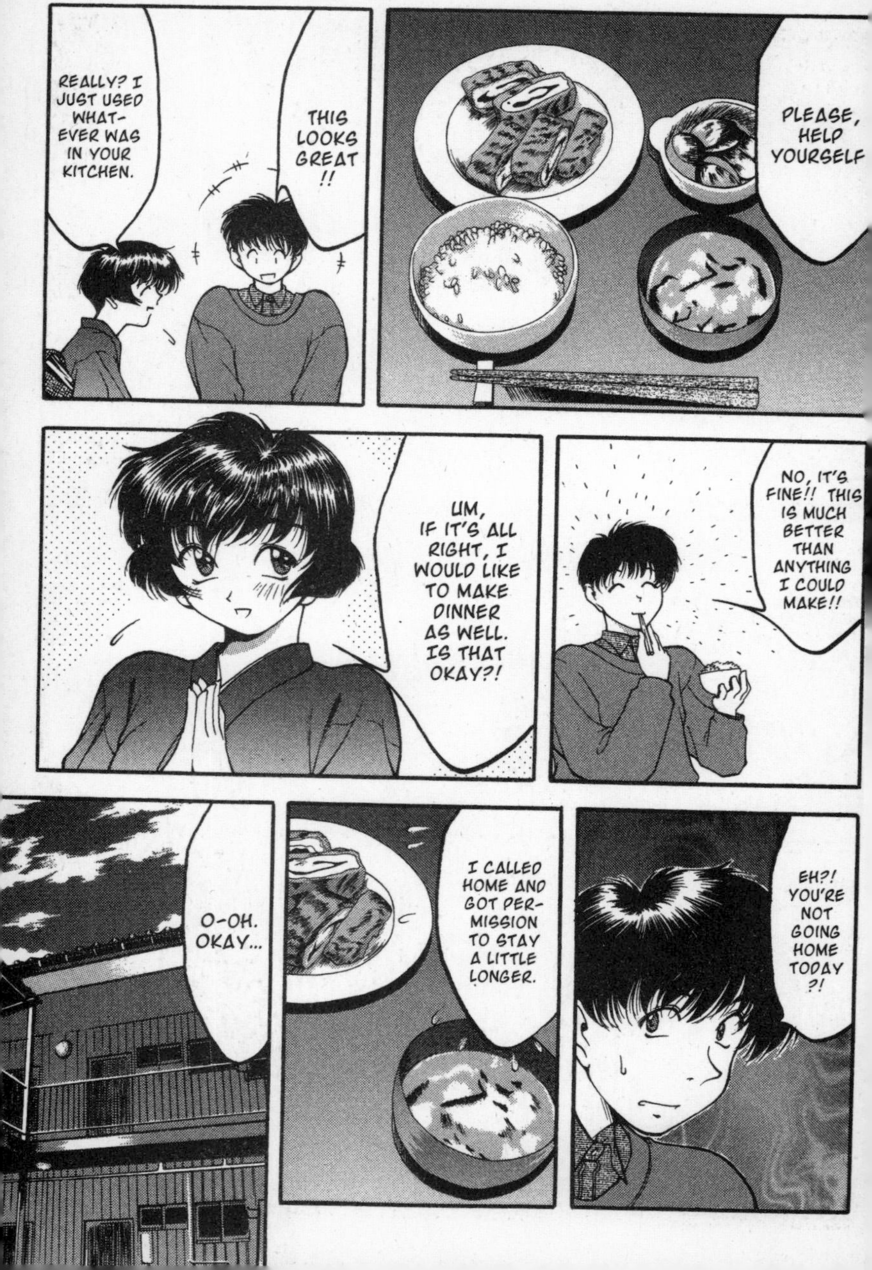
PLEASE, HELP YOURSELF
THIS LOOKS GREAT!!
REALLY? I JUST USED WHAT-EVER WAS IN YOUR KITCHEN.
NO, IT'S FINE!! THIS IS MUCH BETTER THAN ANYTHING I COULD MAKE!!
UM, IF IT'S ALL RIGHT, I WOULD LIKE TO MAKE DINNER AS WELL. IS THAT OKAY?!
EH?! YOU'RE NOT GOING HOME TODAY?!
I CALLED HOME AND GOT PER-MISSION TO STAY A LITTLE LONGER.
O-OH. OKAY...

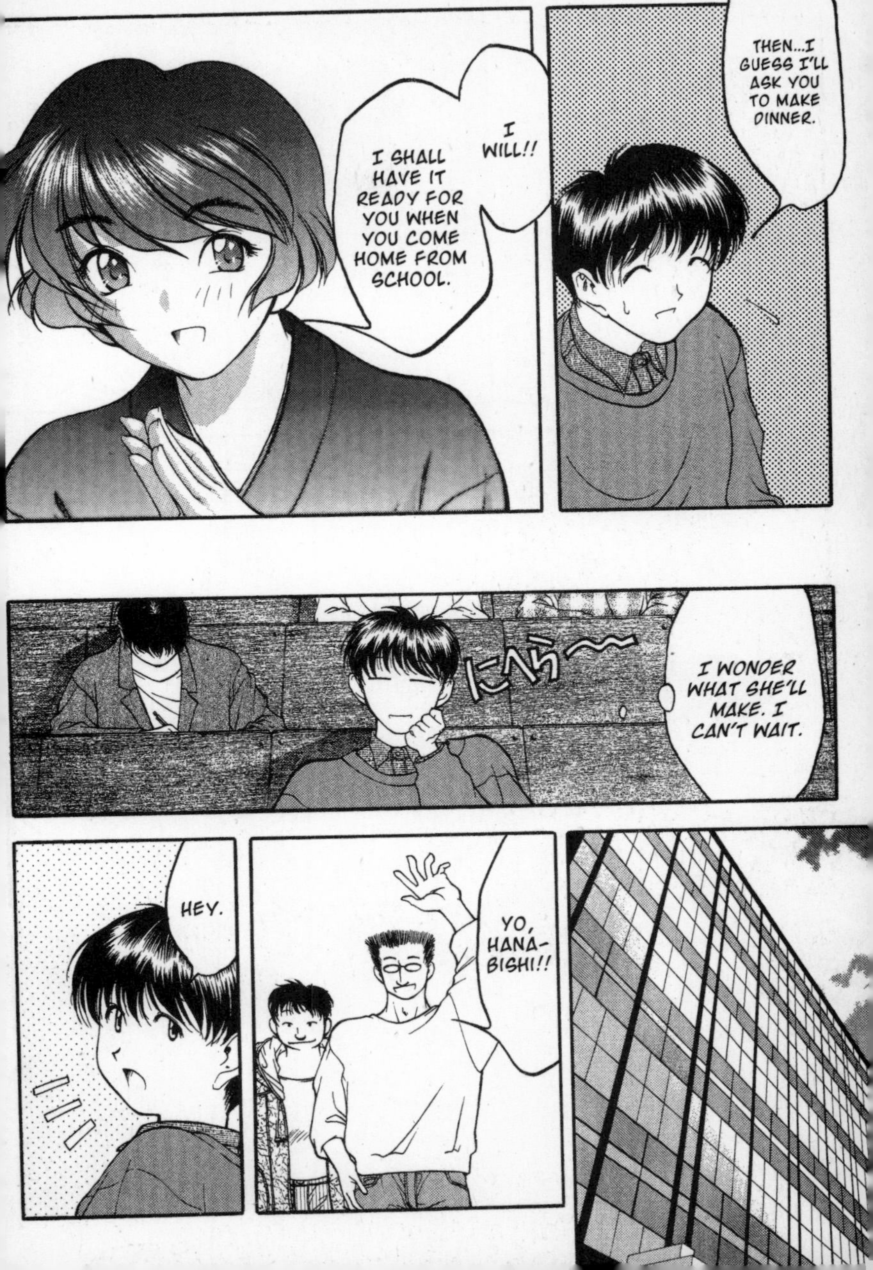
THEN...I GUESS I'LL ASK YOU TO MAKE DINNER.
I WILL!!
I SHALL HAVE IT READY FOR YOU WHEN YOU COME HOME FROM SCHOOL.
I WONDER WHAT SHE'LL MAKE. I CAN'T WAIT.
にへら〜〜
YO, HANA-BISHI!!
HEY.

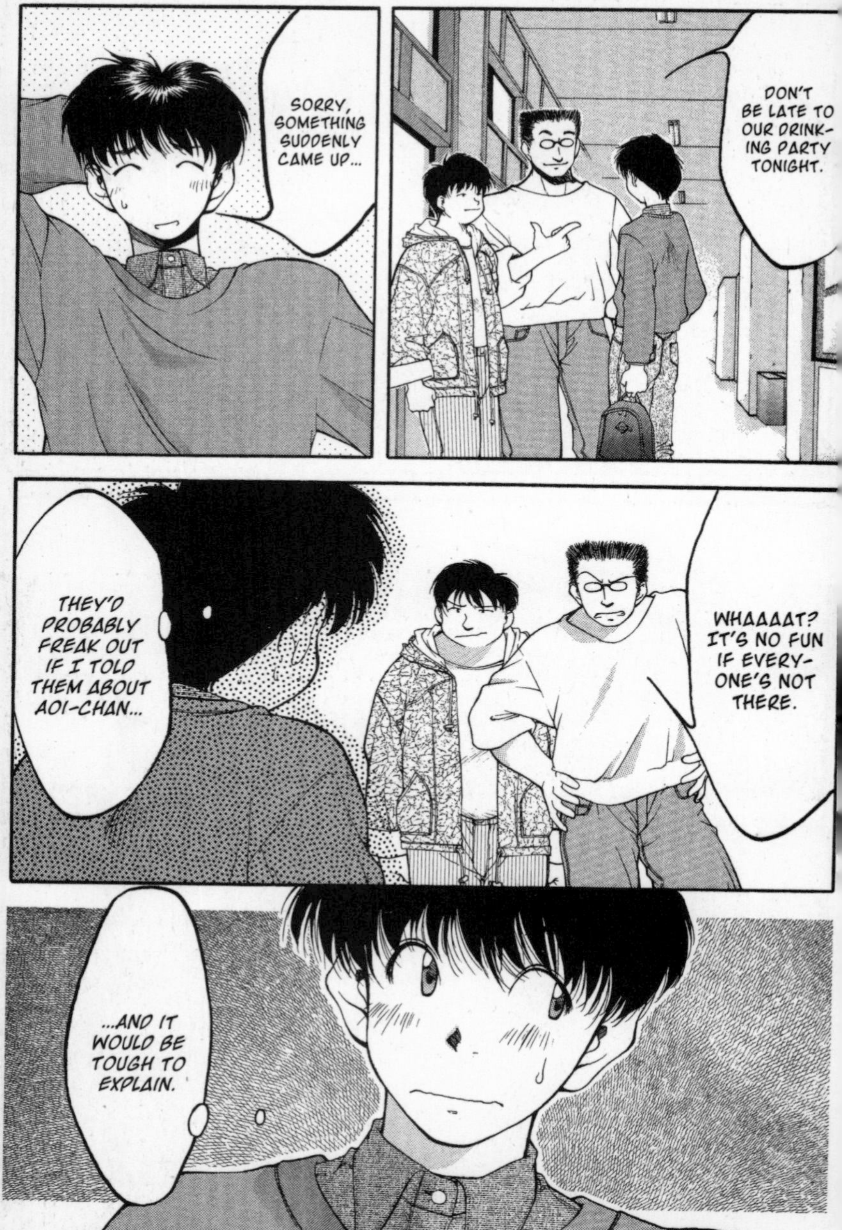
DON'T BE LATE TO OUR DRINK-ING PARTY TONIGHT.
SORRY, SOMETHING SUDDENLY CAME UP...
WHAAAAT? IT'S NO FUN IF EVERY-ONE'S NOT THERE.
THEY'D PROBABLY FREAK OUT IF I TOLD THEM ABOUT AOI-CHAN...
...AND IT WOULD BE TOUGH TO EXPLAIN.

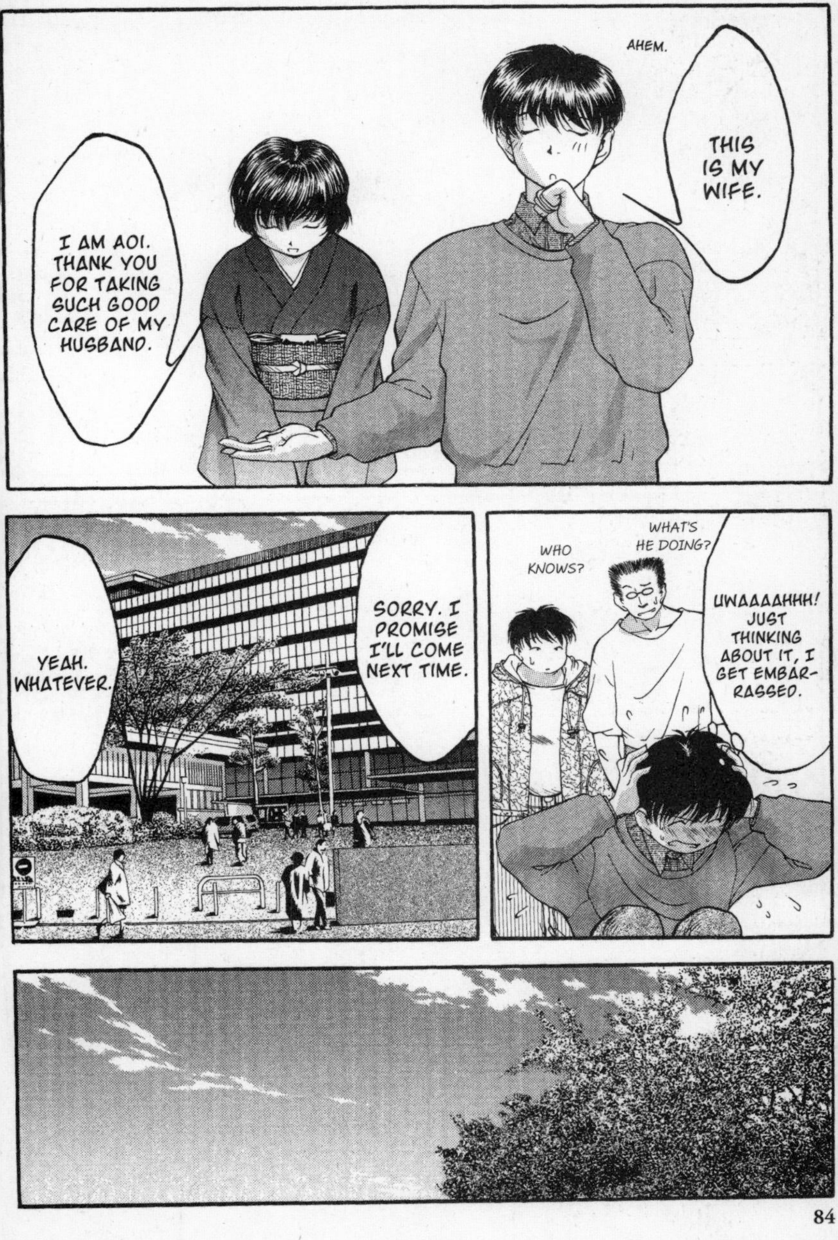
AHEM.
THIS IS MY WIFE.
I AM AOI. THANK YOU FOR TAKING SUCH GOOD CARE OF MY HUSBAND.
UWAAAAHHH! JUST THINKING ABOUT IT, I GET EMBARRASSED.
WHAT'S HE DOING?
WHO KNOWS?
SORRY. I PROMISE I'LL COME NEXT TIME.
YEAH. WHATEVER.

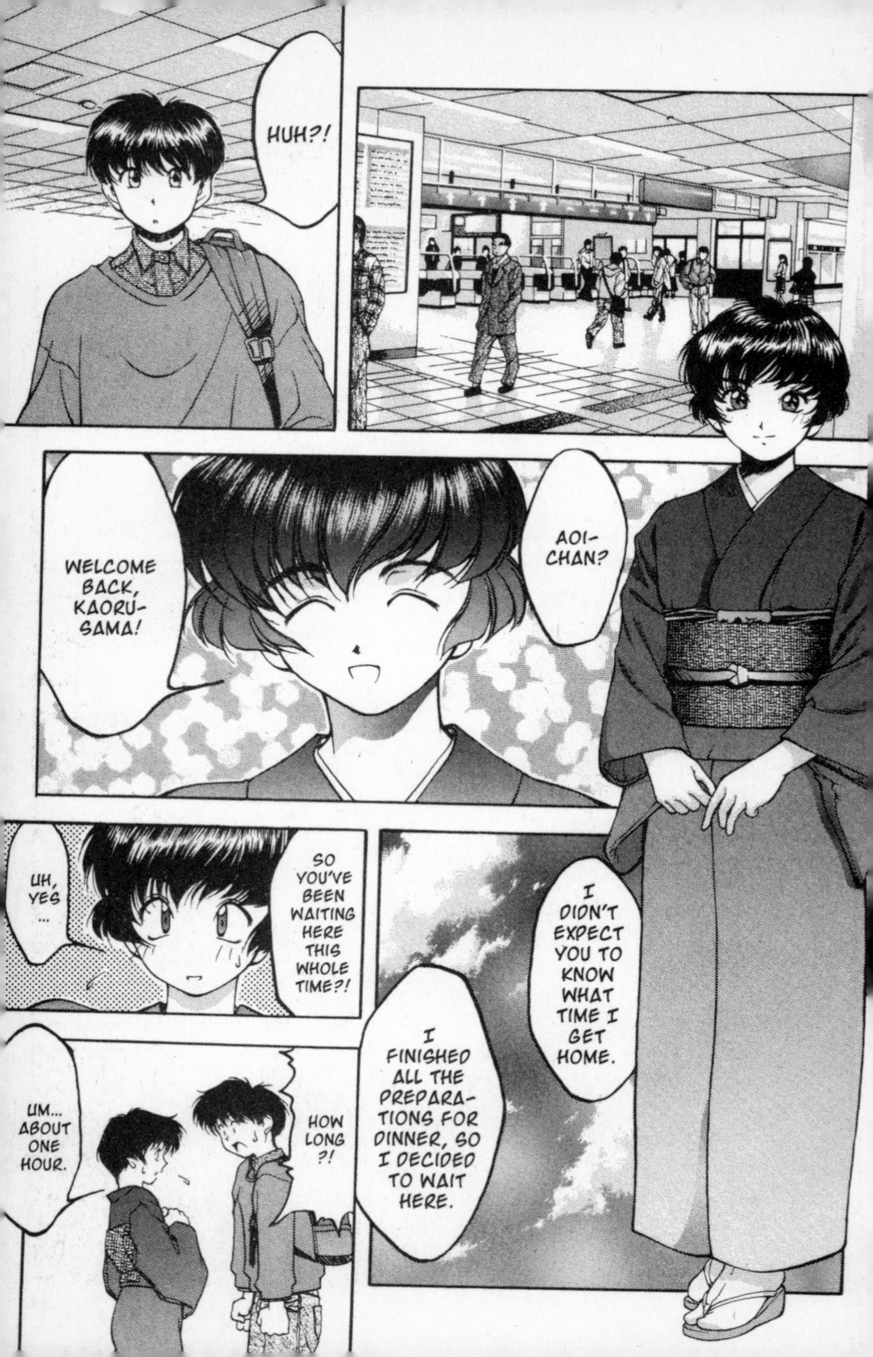
HUH?!
AOI-CHAN?
WELCOME BACK, KAORU-SAMA!
I DIDN'T EXPECT YOU TO KNOW WHAT TIME I GET HOME.
I FINISHED ALL THE PREPARATIONS FOR DINNER, SO I DECIDED TO WAIT HERE.
SO YOU'VE BEEN WAITING HERE THIS WHOLE TIME?!
UH, YES ...
HOW LONG ?!
UM... ABOUT ONE HOUR.

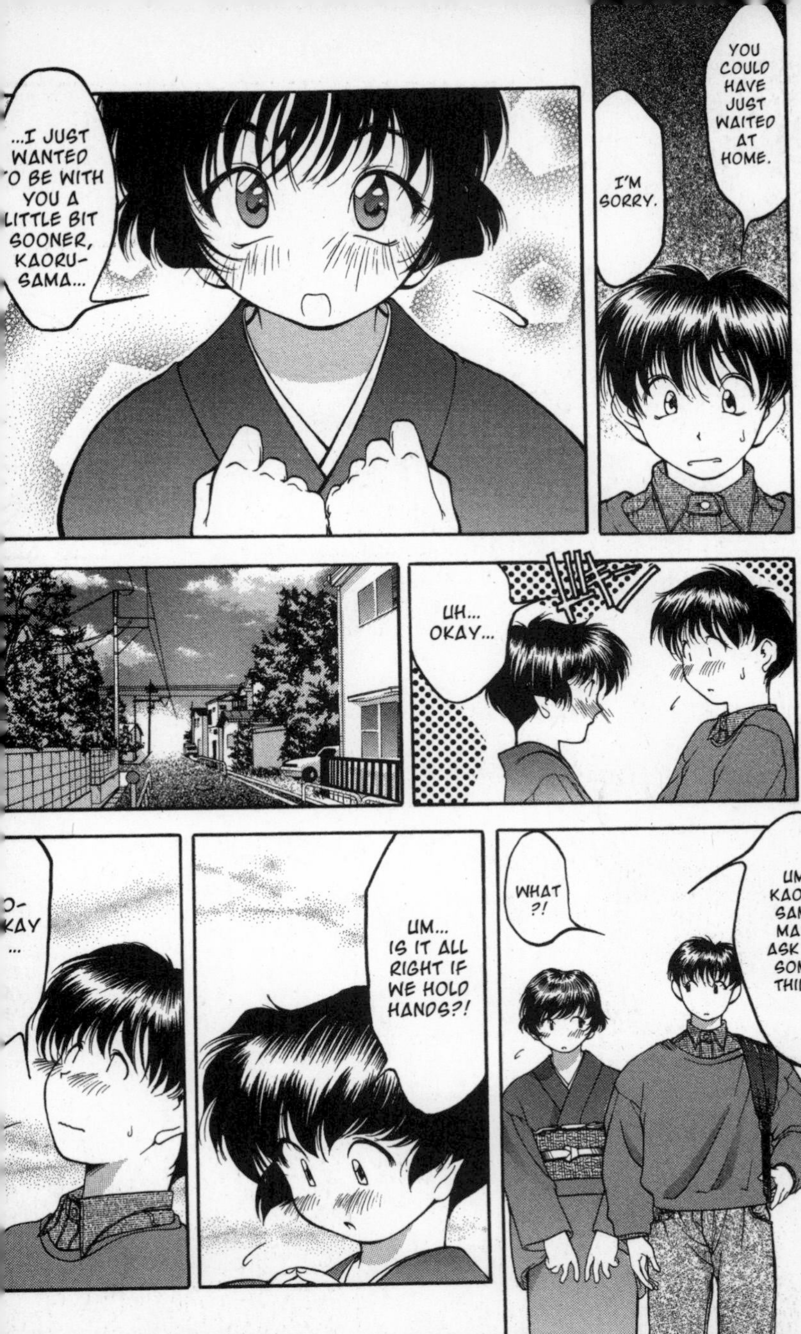
YOU COULD HAVE JUST WAITED AT HOME.
I'M SORRY.
...I JUST WANTED O BE WITH YOU A LITTLE BIT SOONER, KAORU-SAMA...
UH... OKAY...
UM... KAORU-SAMA, MAY I ASK YOU SOMETHING?
WHAT?!
UM... IS IT ALL RIGHT IF WE HOLD HANDS?!
O-KAY ...

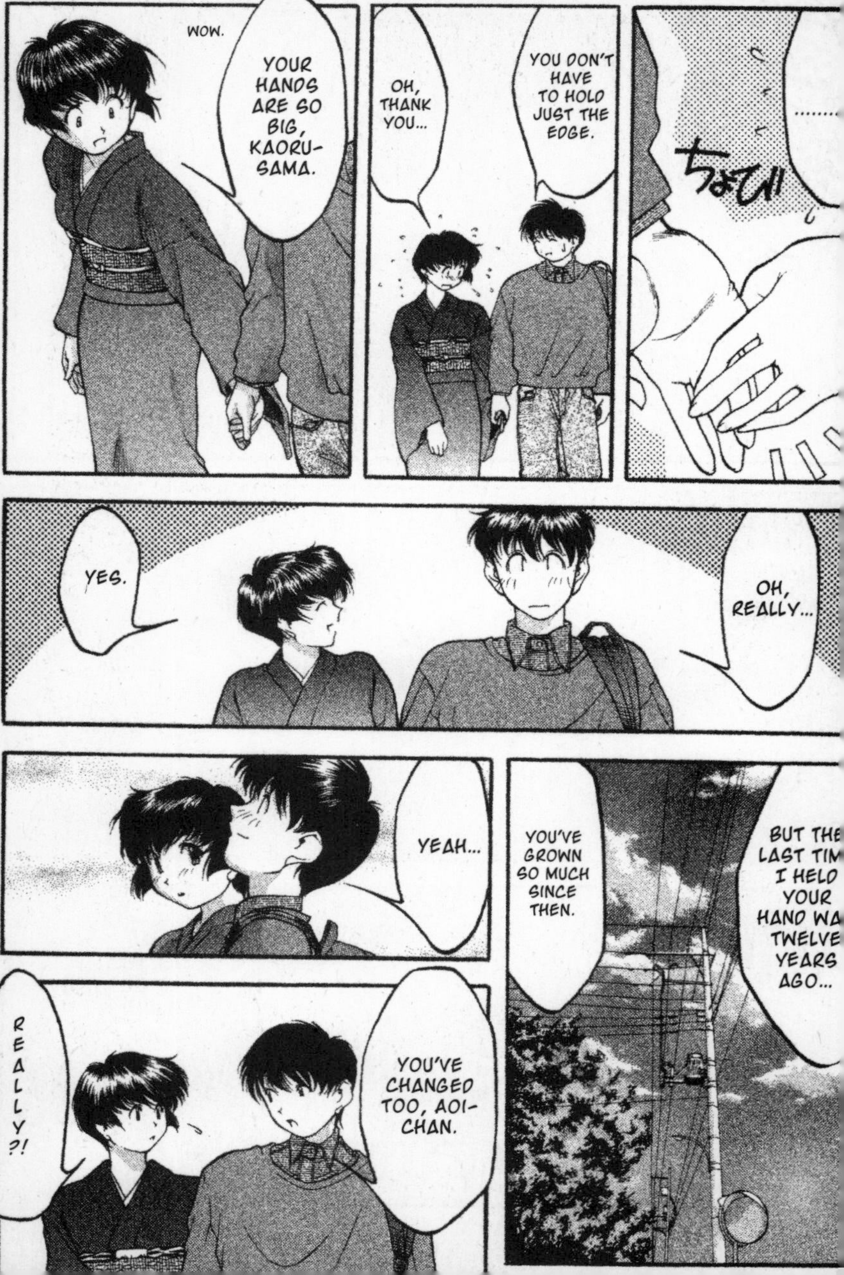
........
ちょひ!!
YOU DON'T HAVE TO HOLD JUST THE EDGE.
OH, THANK YOU...
YOUR HANDS ARE SO BIG, KAORU-SAMA.
WOW.
OH, REALLY...
YES.
BUT THE LAST TIM I HELD YOUR HAND WA TWELVE YEARS AGO...
YOU'VE GROWN SO MUCH SINCE THEN.
YEAH...
YOU'VE CHANGED TOO, AOI-CHAN.
REALLY?!

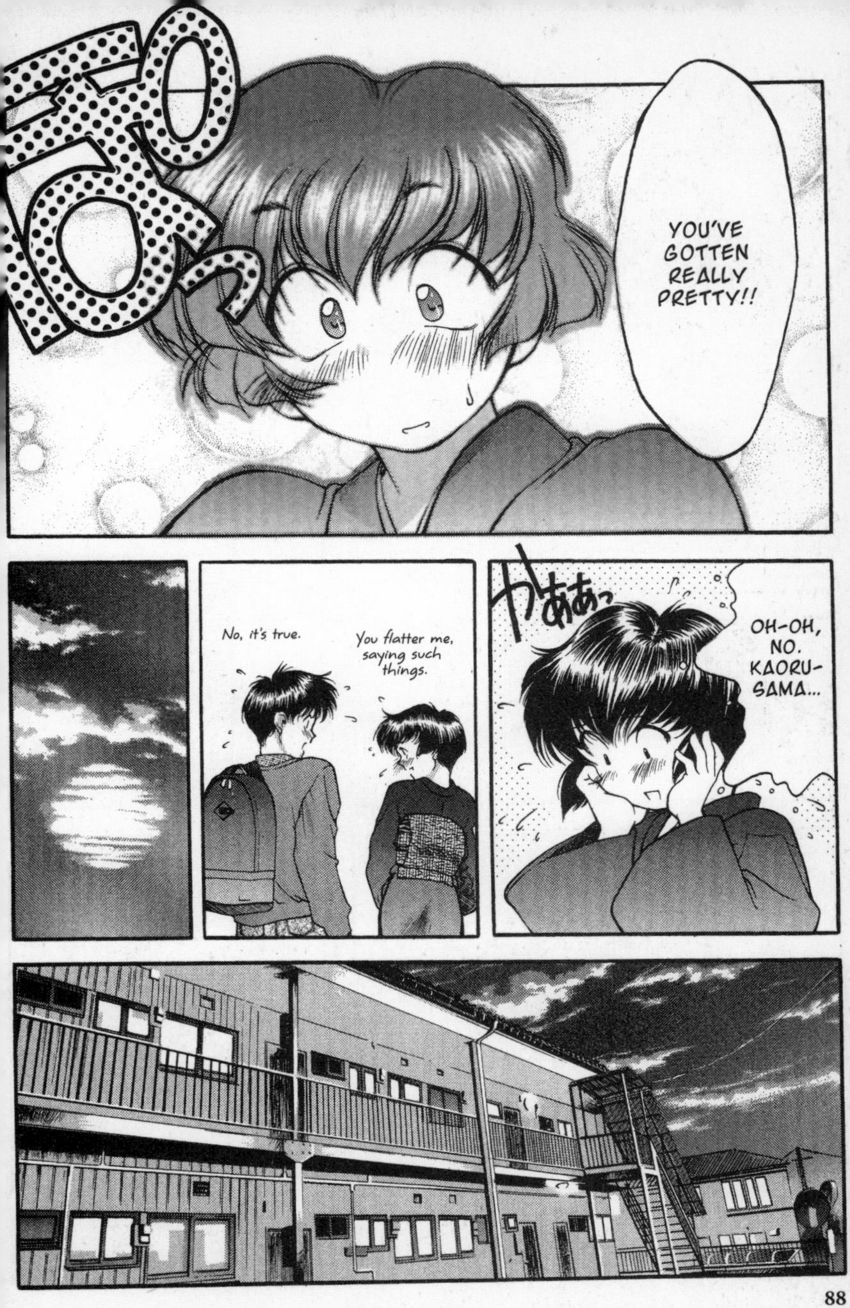
YOU'VE GOTTEN REALLY PRETTY!!
OH-OH, NO. KAORU-SAMA...
やーあぁっ
You flatter me, saying such things.
No, it's true.

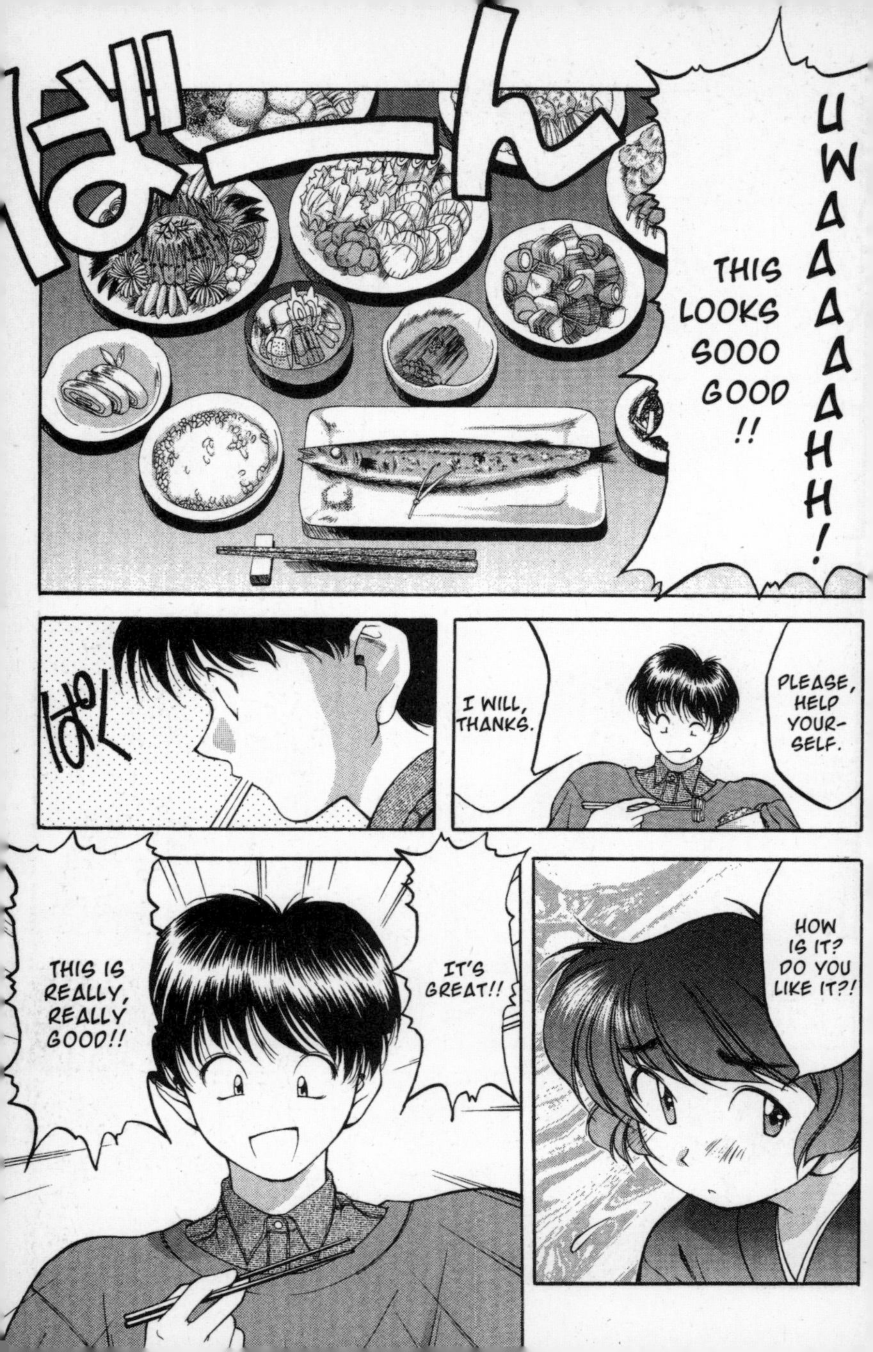
UWAAAAAHH!
THIS LOOKS SOOO GOOD!!
ばーん
PLEASE, HELP YOURSELF.
I WILL, THANKS.
ぱく
HOW IS IT? DO YOU LIKE IT?!
IT'S GREAT!!
THIS IS REALLY, REALLY GOOD!!

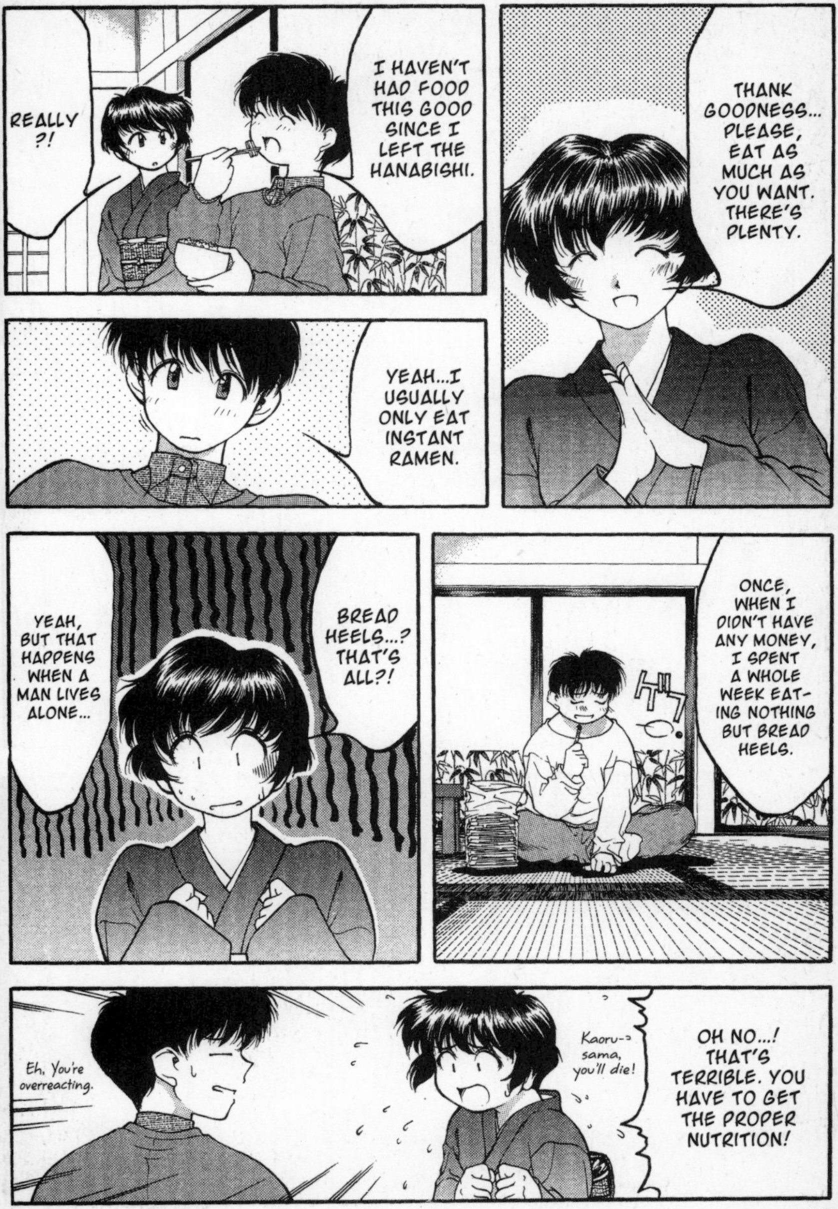
I HAVEN'T HAD FOOD THIS GOOD SINCE I LEFT THE HANABISHI.
REALLY ?!
THANK GOODNESS... PLEASE, EAT AS MUCH AS YOU WANT. THERE'S PLENTY.
YEAH...I USUALLY ONLY EAT INSTANT RAMEN.
ONCE, WHEN I DIDN'T HAVE ANY MONEY, I SPENT A WHOLE WEEK EATING NOTHING BUT BREAD HEELS.
BREAD HEELS...? THAT'S ALL?!
YEAH, BUT THAT HAPPENS WHEN A MAN LIVES ALONE...
OH NO...! THAT'S TERRIBLE. YOU HAVE TO GET THE PROPER NUTRITION!
Kaoru-sama, you'll die!
Eh, You're overreacting.

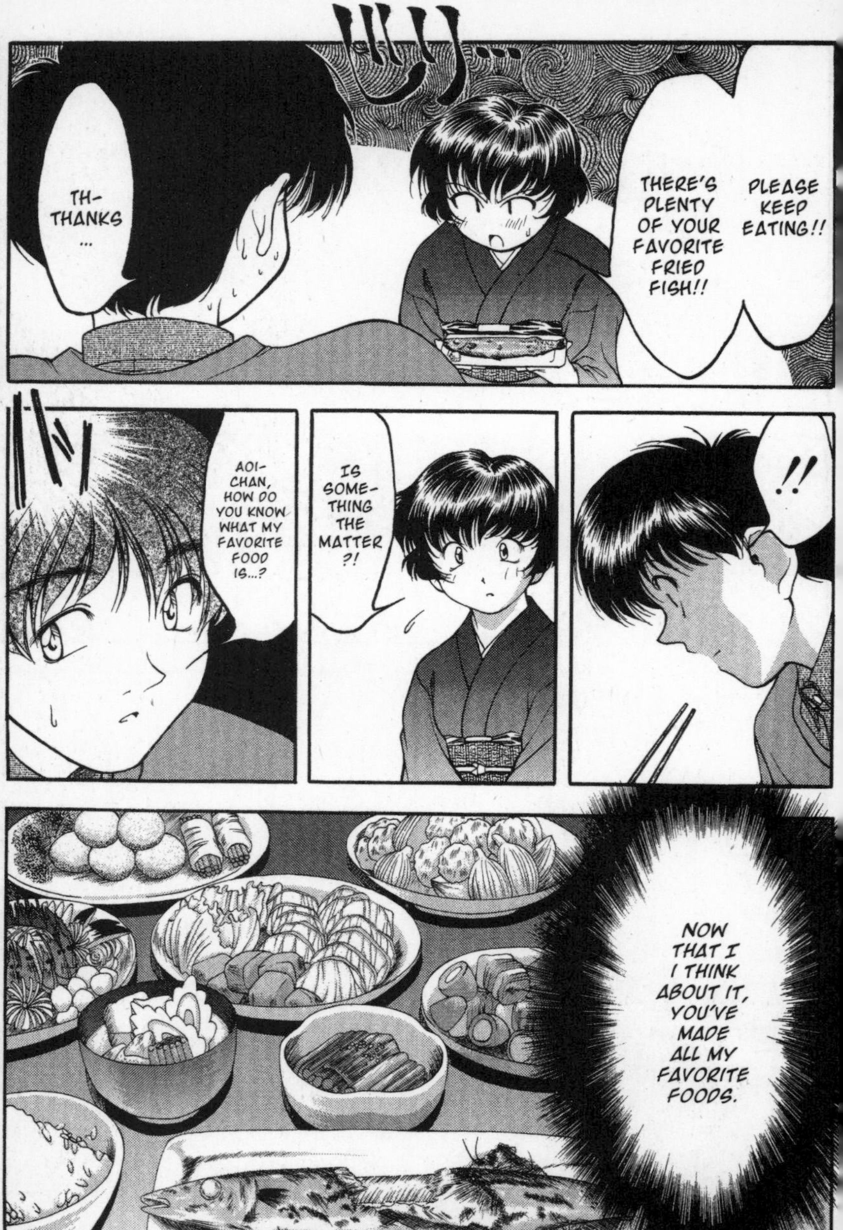
PLEASE KEEP EATING!!
THERE'S PLENTY OF YOUR FAVORITE FRIED FISH!!
TH-THANKS...
!!
IS SOMETHING THE MATTER?!
AOI-CHAN, HOW DO YOU KNOW WHAT MY FAVORITE FOOD IS...?
NOW THAT I I THINK ABOUT IT, YOU'VE MADE ALL MY FAVORITE FOODS.

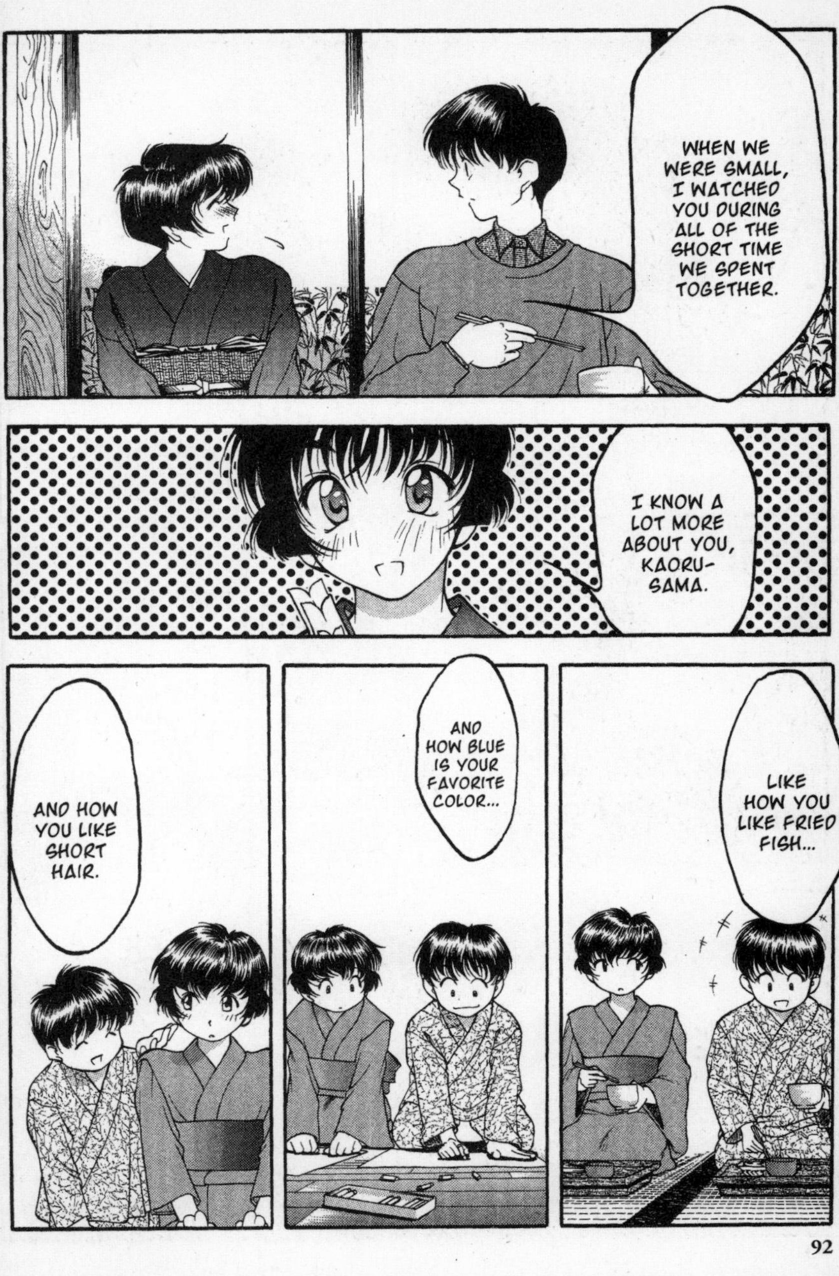
WHEN WE WERE SMALL, I WATCHED YOU DURING ALL OF THE SHORT TIME WE SPENT TOGETHER.
I KNOW A LOT MORE ABOUT YOU, KAORU-SAMA.
LIKE HOW YOU LIKE FRIED FISH...
AND HOW BLUE IS YOUR FAVORITE COLOR...
AND HOW YOU LIKE SHORT HAIR.

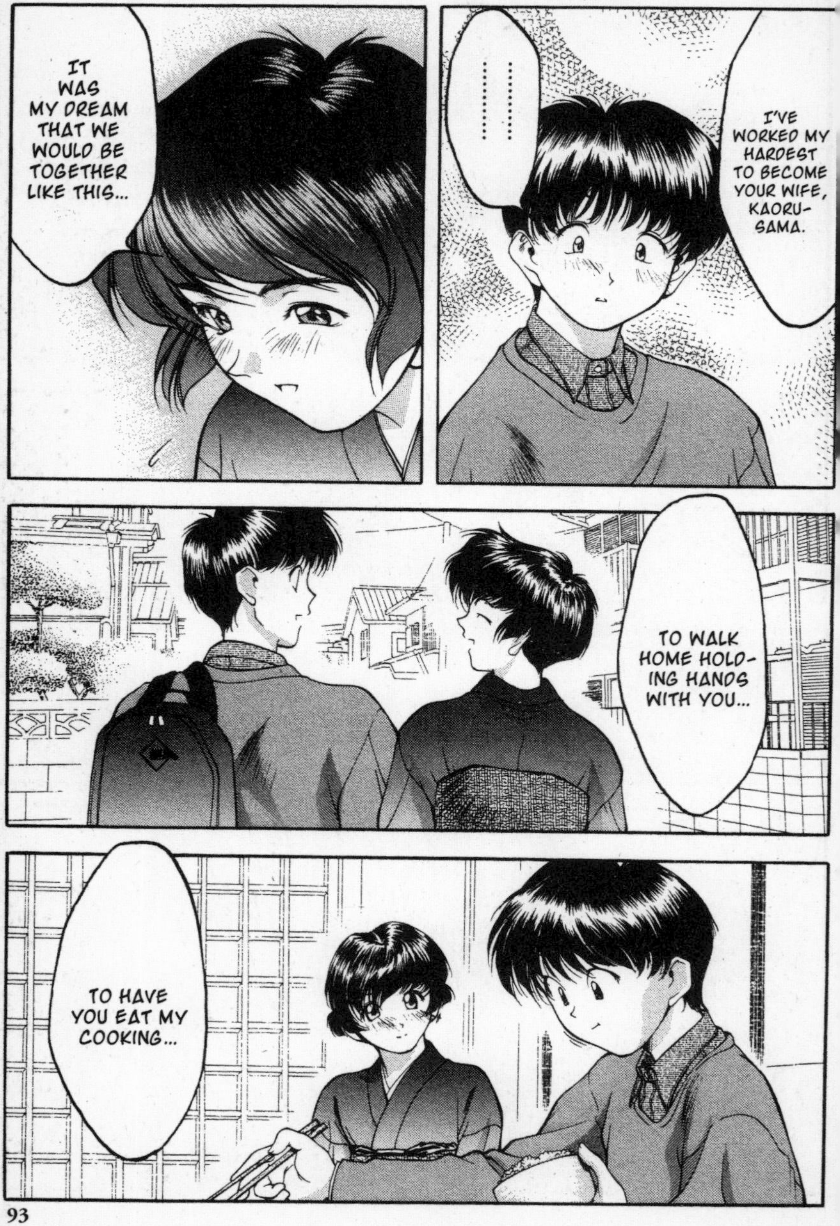
......
I'VE WORKED MY HARDEST TO BECOME YOUR WIFE, KAORU-SAMA.
IT WAS MY DREAM THAT WE WOULD BE TOGETHER LIKE THIS...
TO WALK HOME HOLDING HANDS WITH YOU...
TO HAVE YOU EAT MY COOKING...

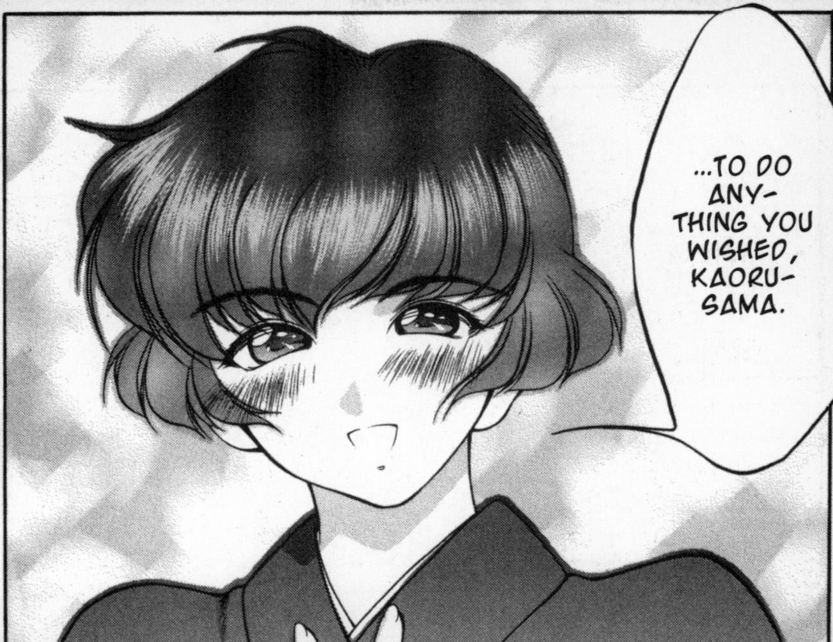
...TO DO ANY-THING YOU WISHED, KAORU-SAMA.
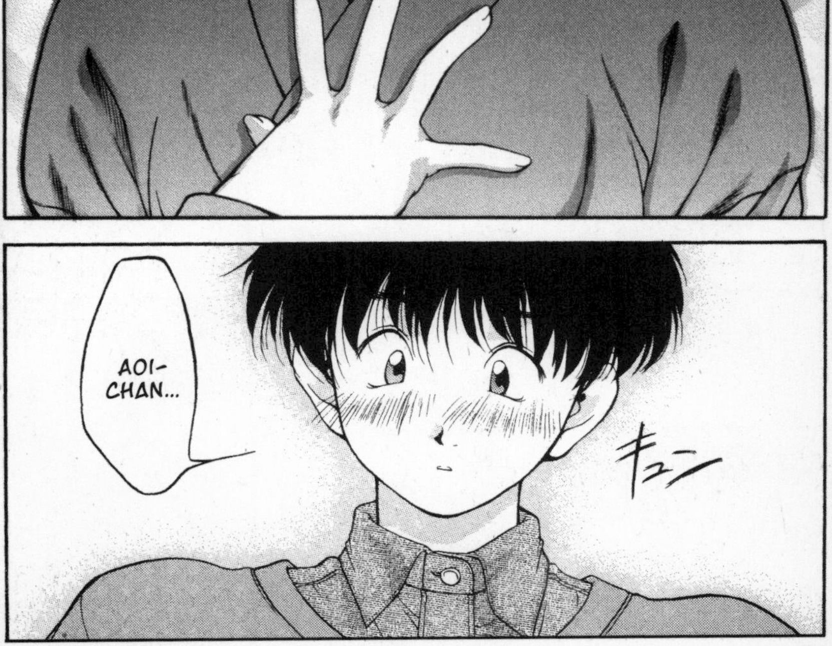
AOI-CHAN...
キュン

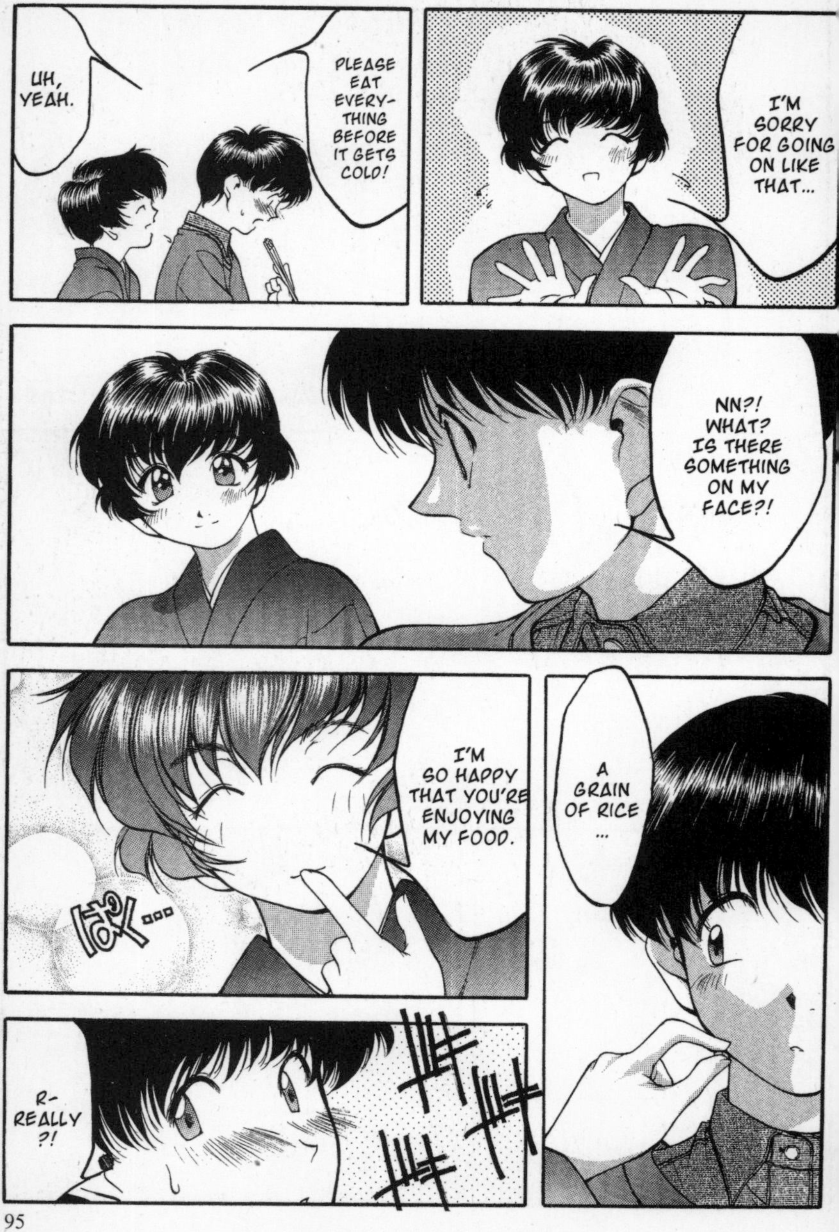
I'M SORRY FOR GOING ON LIKE THAT...
PLEASE EAT EVERY-THING BEFORE IT GETS COLD!
UH, YEAH.
NN?! WHAT? IS THERE SOMETHING ON MY FACE?!
A GRAIN OF RICE ...
I'M SO HAPPY THAT YOU'RE ENJOYING MY FOOD.
R-REALLY ?!

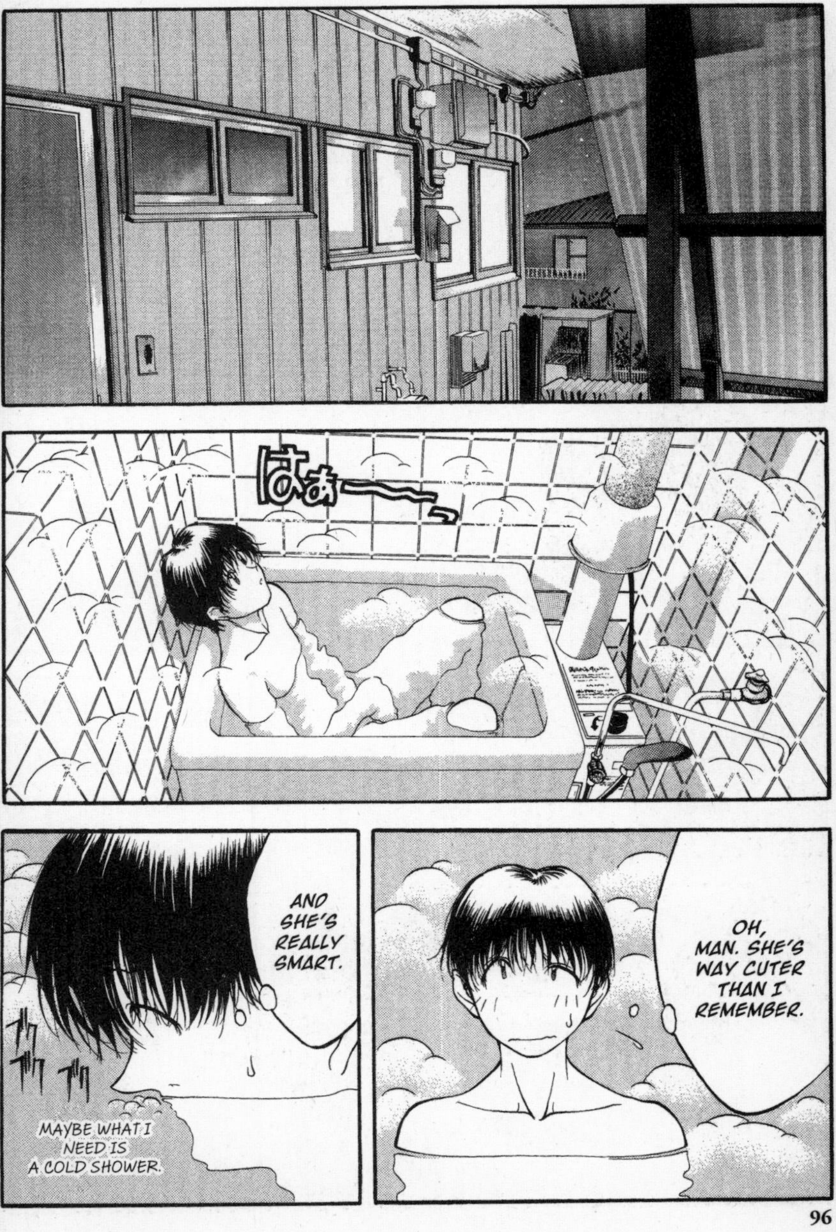
はぁ〜〜っ
OH, MAN. SHE'S WAY CUTER THAN I REMEMBER.
AND SHE'S REALLY SMART.
ブクブク ブク
MAYBE WHAT I NEED IS A COLD SHOWER.

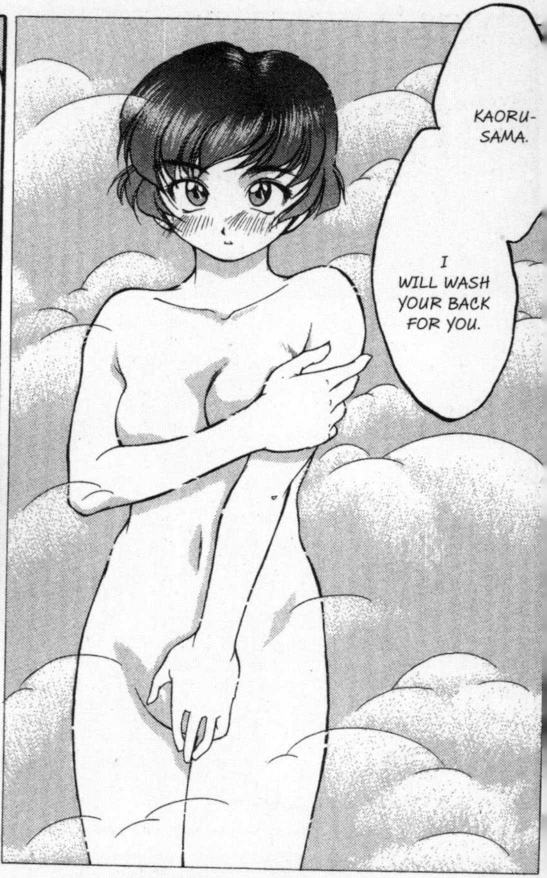
KAORU-SAMA.
I WILL WASH YOUR BACK FOR YOU.
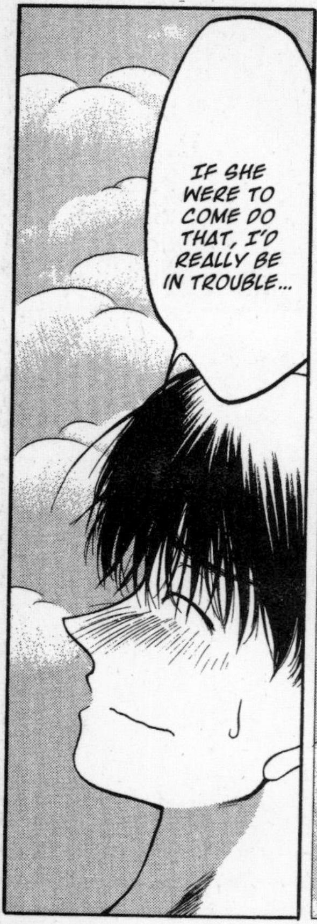
IF SHE WERE TO COME DO THAT, I'D REALLY BE IN TROUBLE...
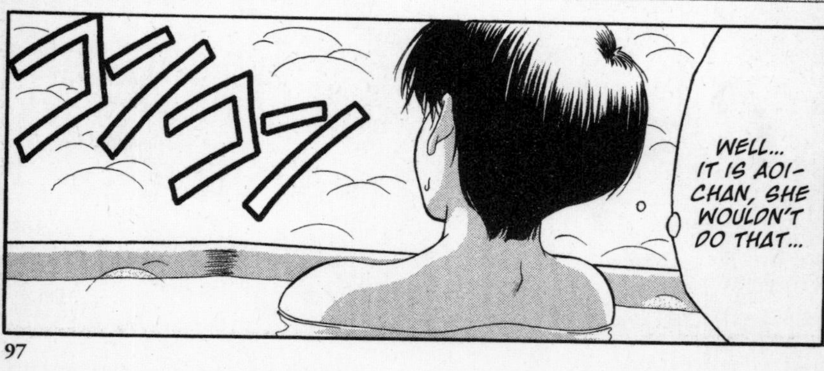
WELL... IT IS AOI-CHAN, SHE WOULDN'T DO THAT...

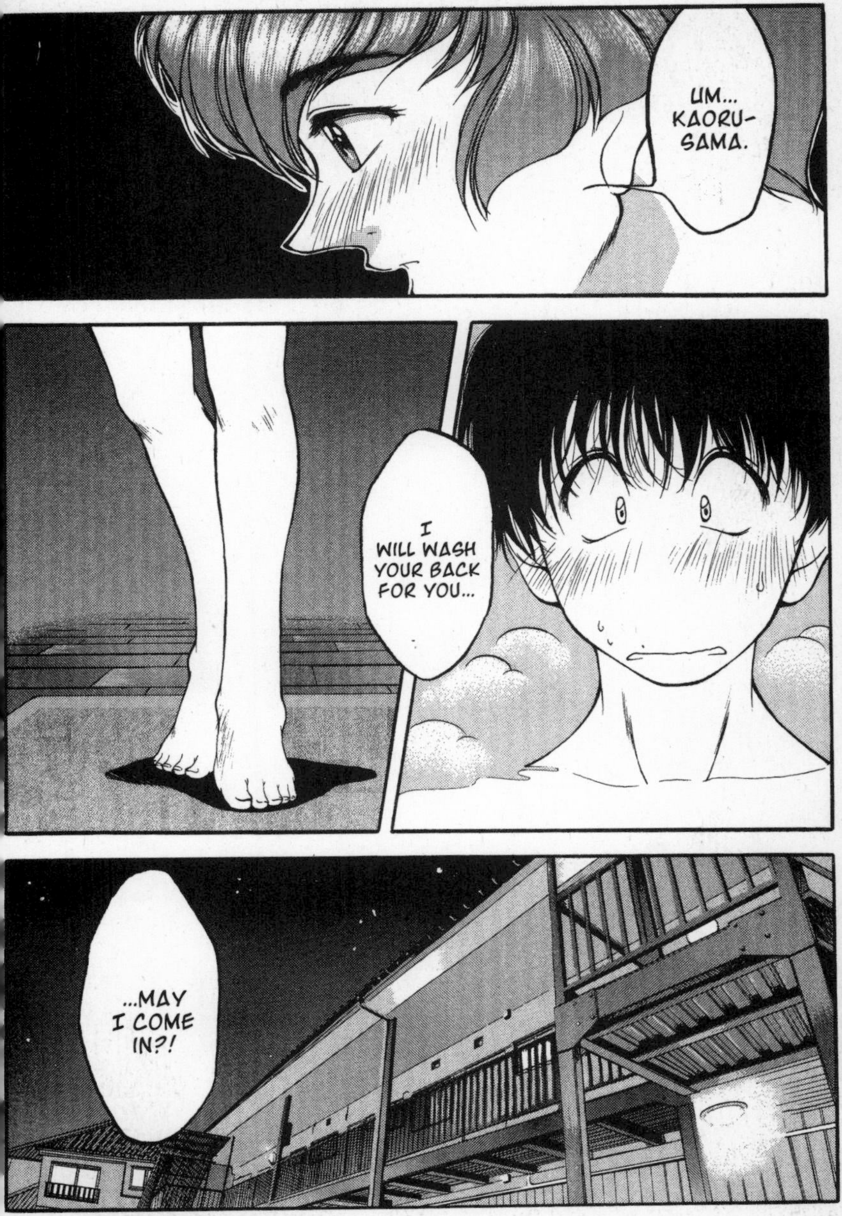
UM... KAORU-SAMA.
I WILL WASH YOUR BACK FOR YOU...
...MAY I COME IN?!

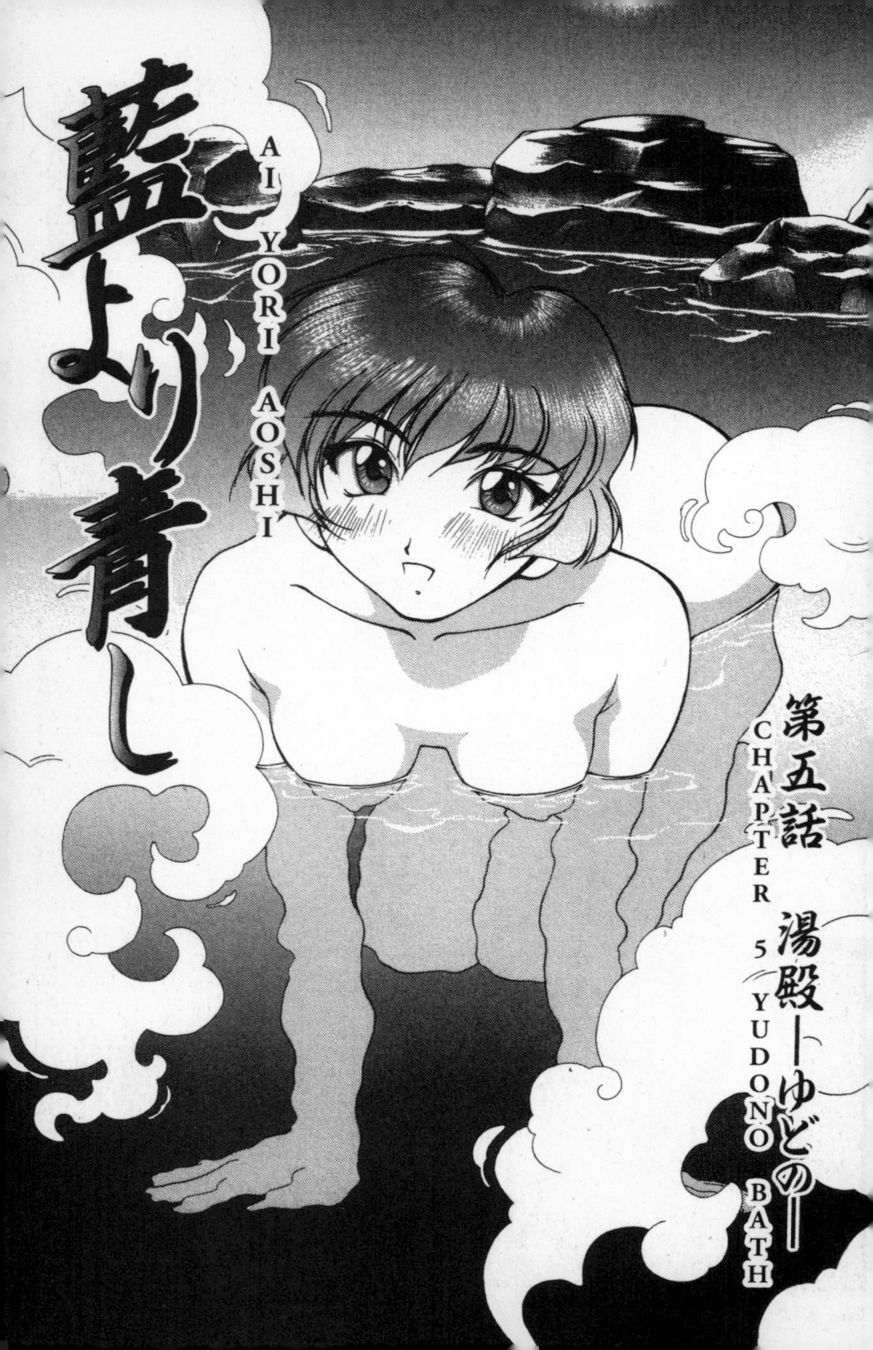
藍より青し
AI YORI AOSHI
第五話 湯殿―ゆどの―
CHAPTER 5 YUDONO BATH

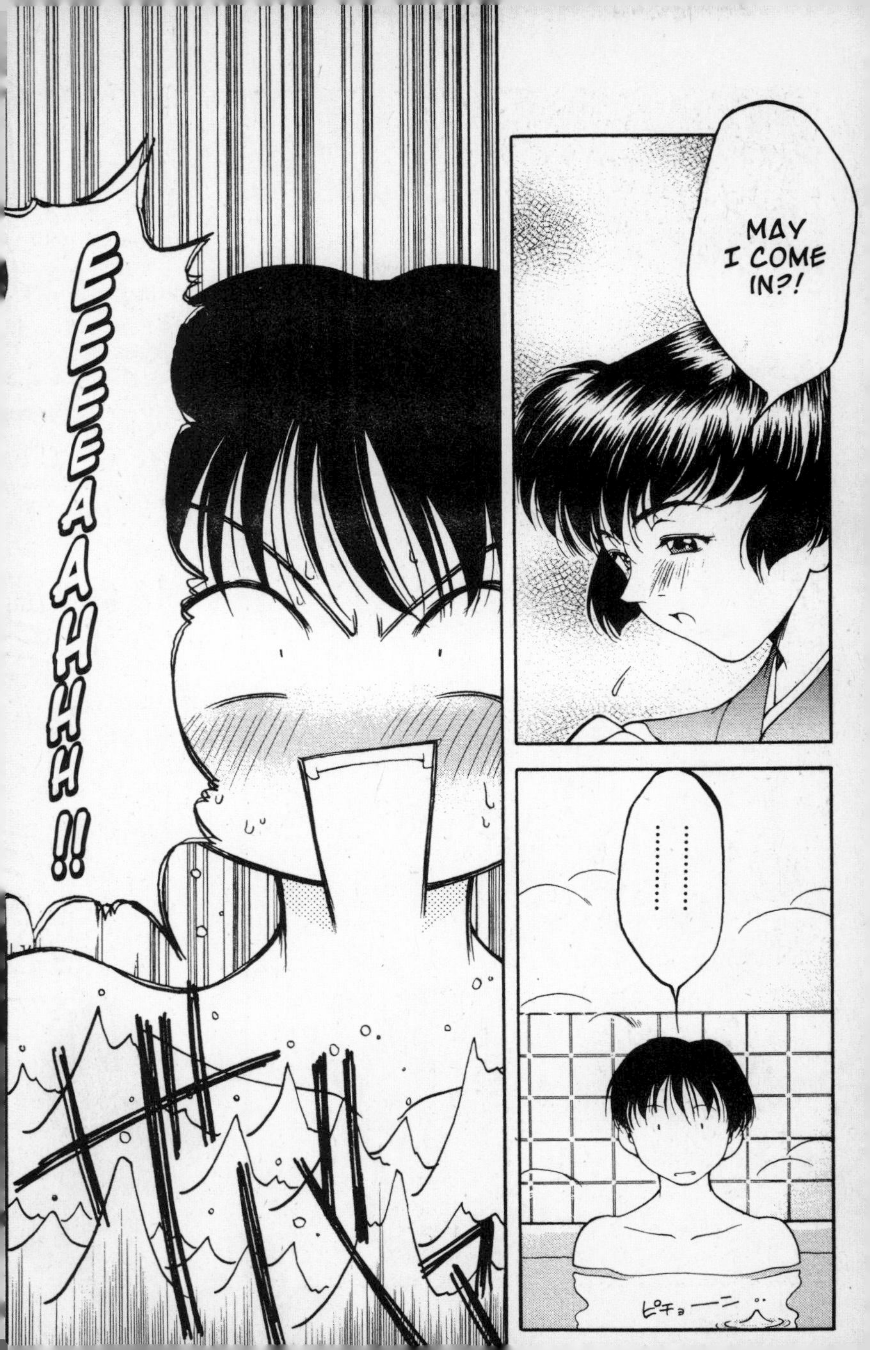
MAY I COME IN?!
......
ピチョーン
EEEEAAAHHHH!!

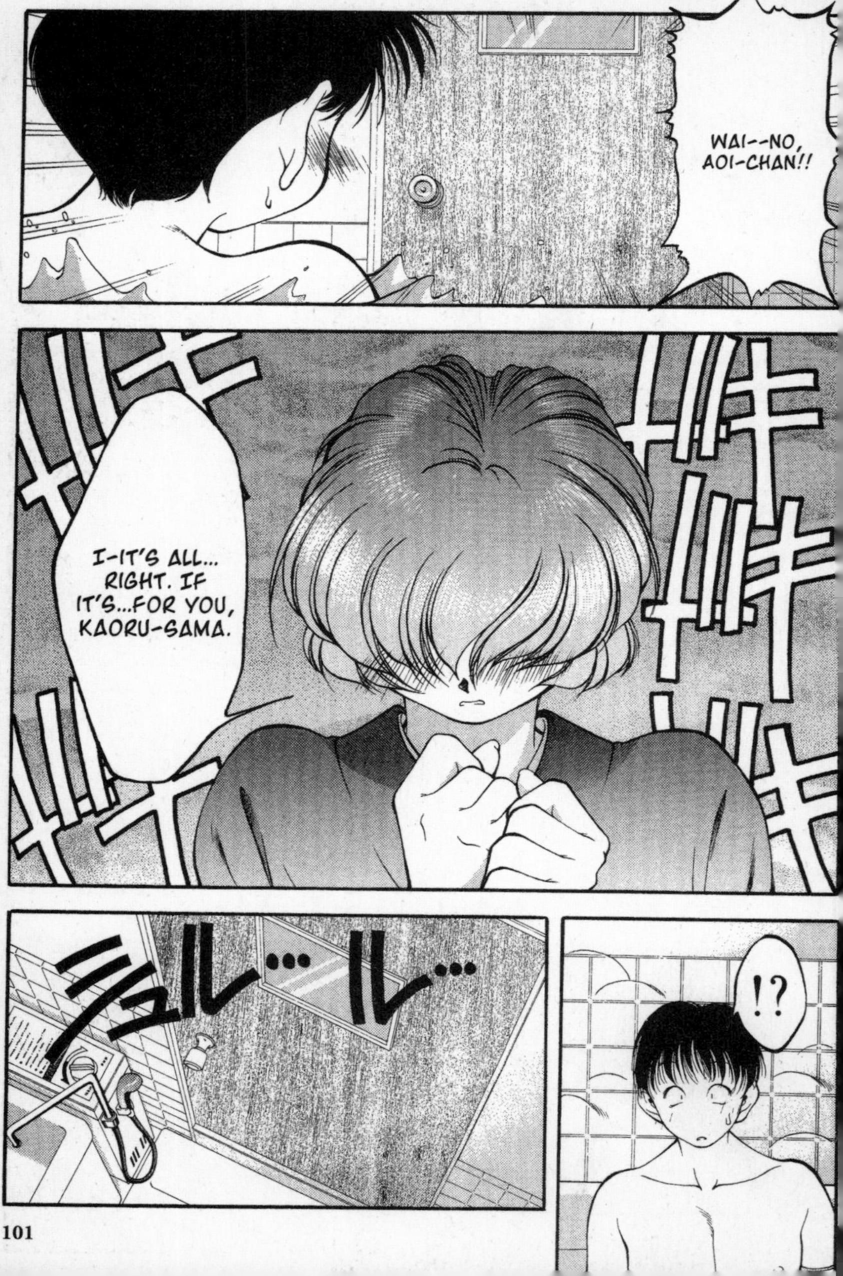
WAI--NO, AOI-CHAN!!
I-IT'S ALL... RIGHT. IF IT'S...FOR YOU, KAORU-SAMA.
!?
シュル… ル…

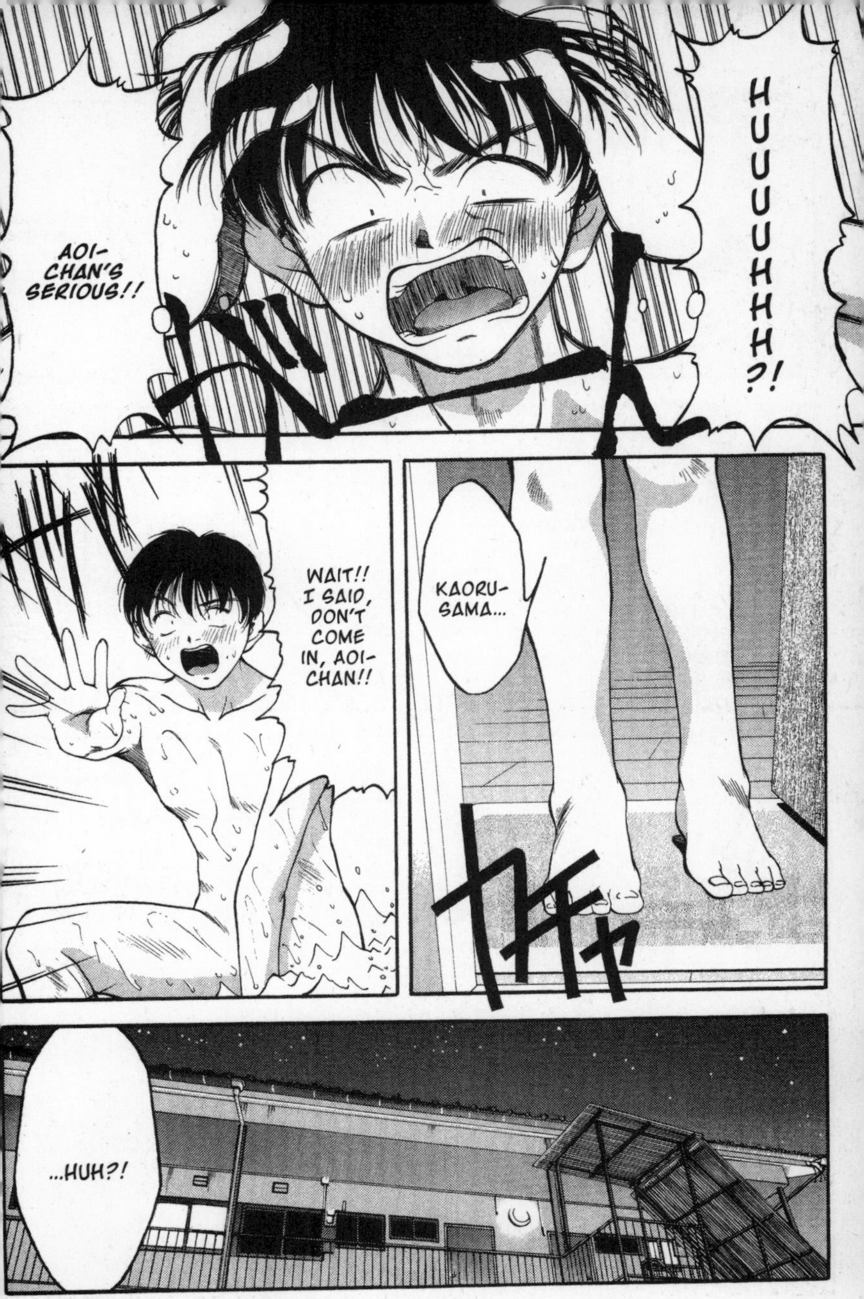
HUUUUHHHH?!
AOI-CHAN'S SERIOUS!!
KAORU-SAMA...
カチャ
WAIT!! I SAID, DON'T COME IN, AOI-CHAN!!
...HUH?!

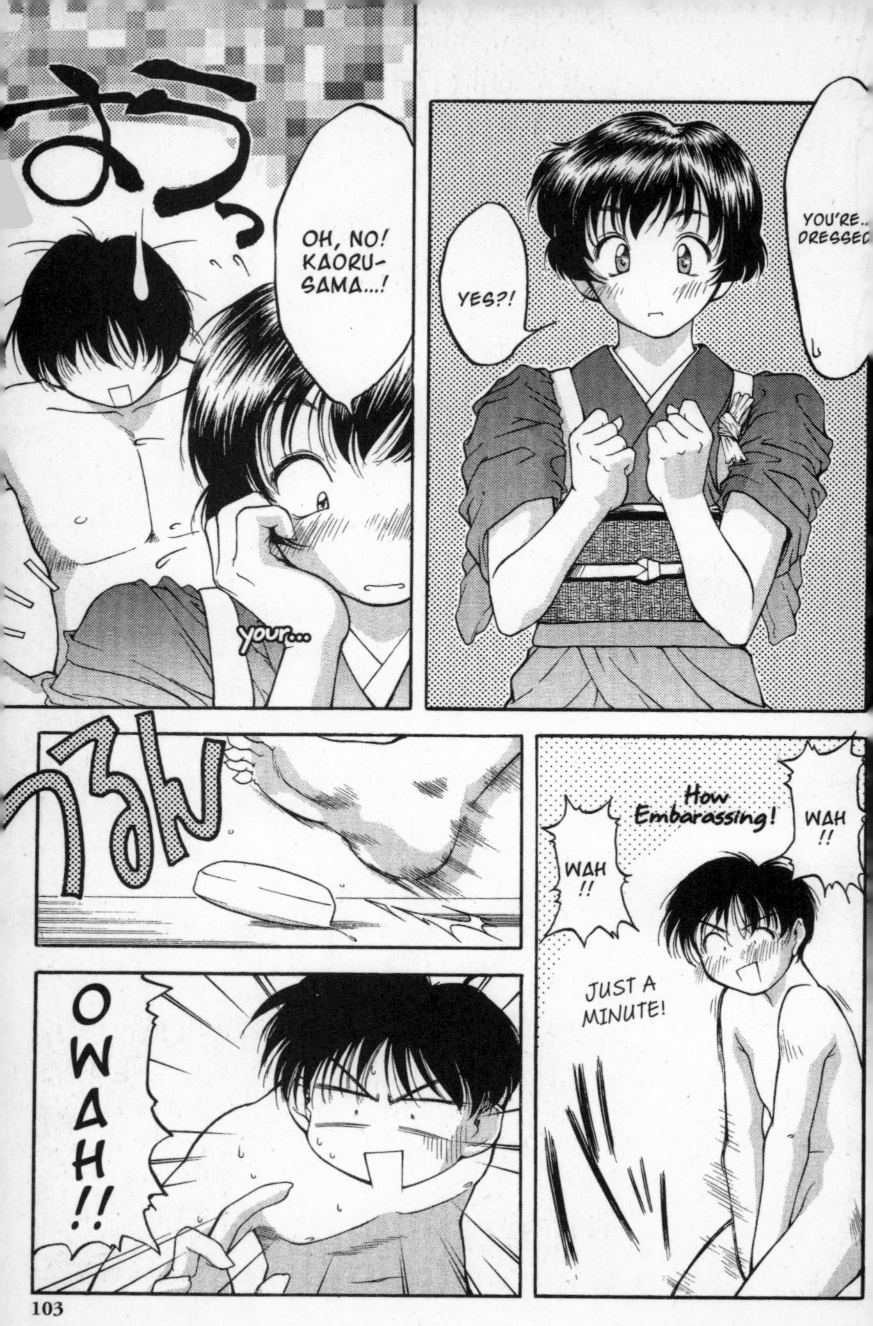
YOU'RE... DRESSED
YES?!
OH, NO! KAORU-SAMA...!
your...
How Embarassing!
WAH !!
WAH !!
JUST A MINUTE!
OWAH!!

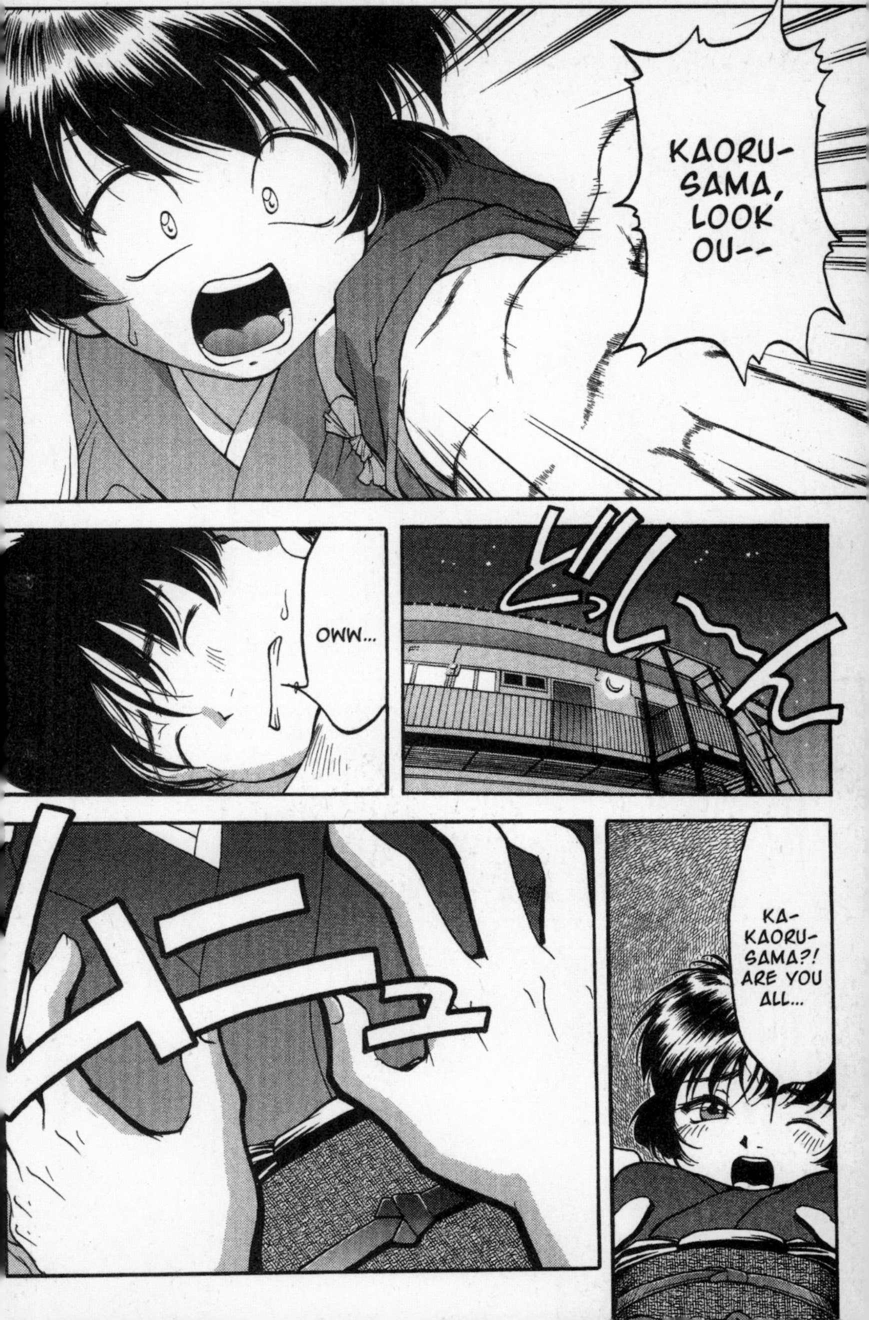
KAORU-SAMA, LOOK OU--
どっし～ん
OWW...
KA-KAORU-SAMA?! ARE YOU ALL...

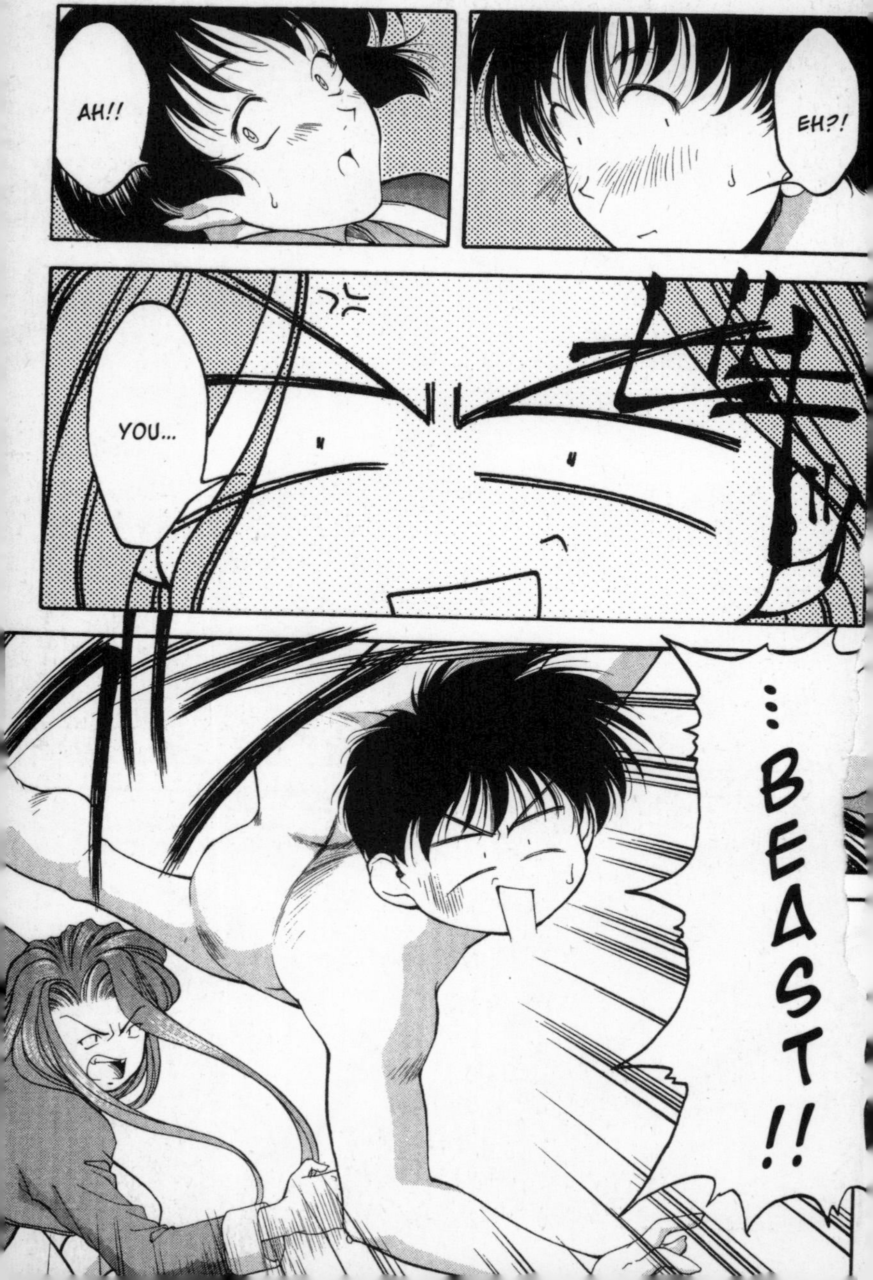
EH?!
AH!!
YOU...
...BEAST!!

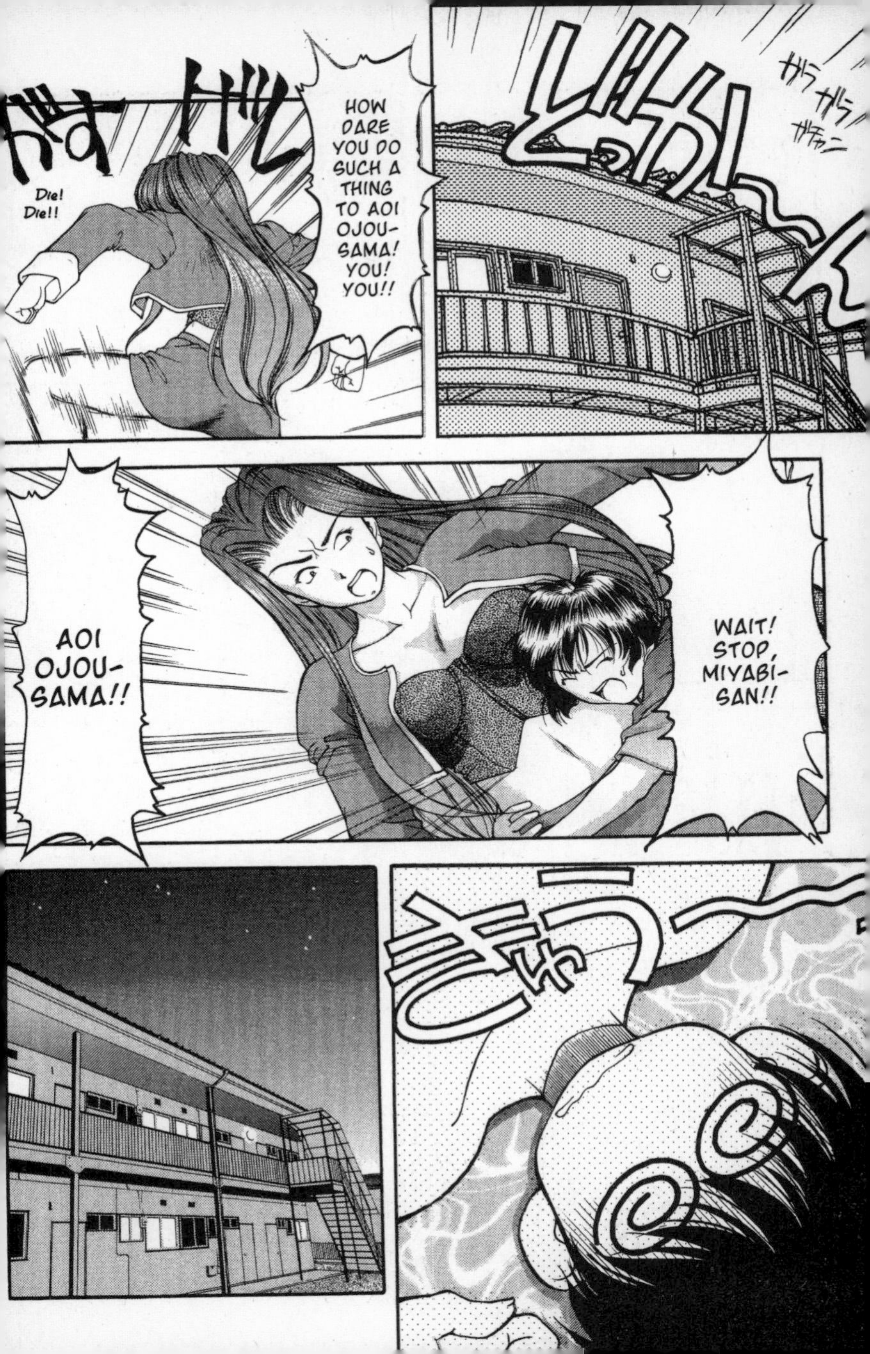

どっし～～ん
ガラ ガラ ガチャン
がす げし
HOW DARE YOU DO SUCH A THING TO AOI OJOU-SAMA! YOU! YOU!!
Die! Die!!
WAIT! STOP, MIYABI-SAN!!
AOI OJOU-SAMA!!
きゅう～

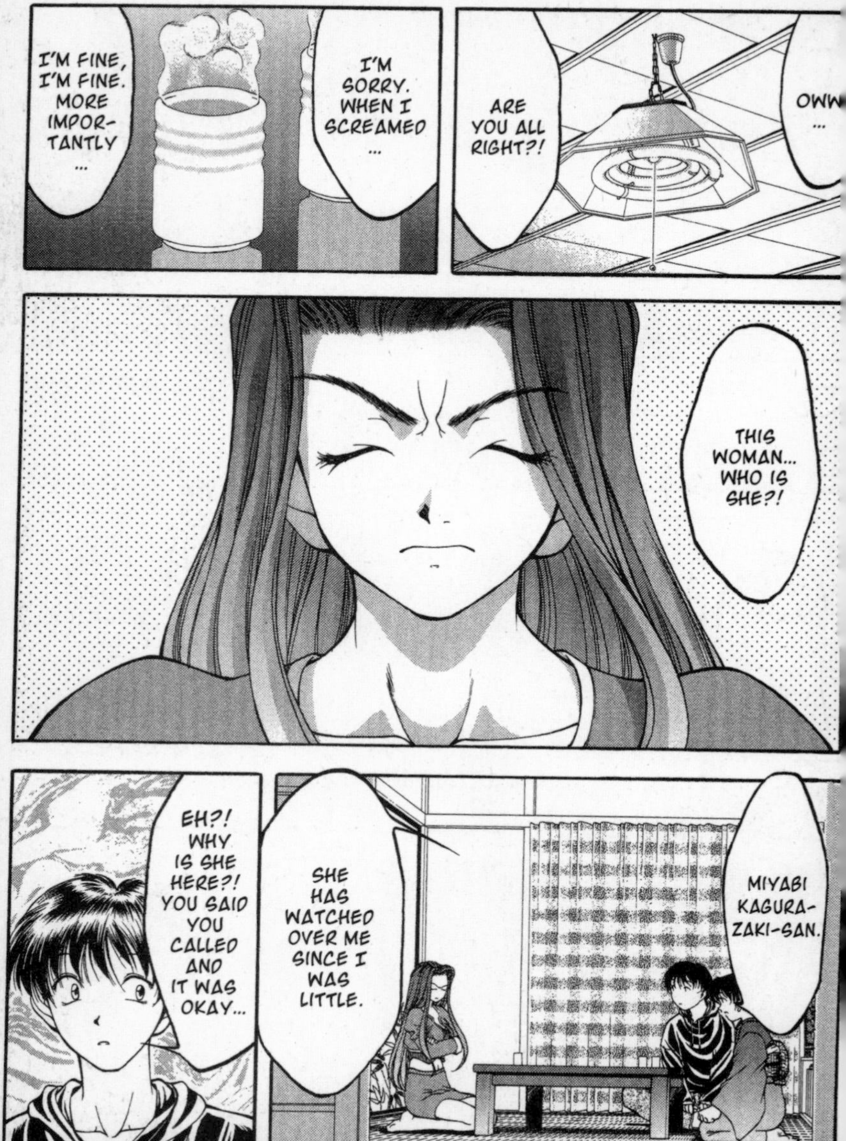
OWW ...
ARE YOU ALL RIGHT?!
I'M SORRY. WHEN I SCREAMED ...
I'M FINE, I'M FINE. MORE IMPORTANTLY ...
THIS WOMAN... WHO IS SHE?!
MIYABI KAGURAZAKI-SAN.
SHE HAS WATCHED OVER ME SINCE I WAS LITTLE.
EH?! WHY IS SHE HERE?! YOU SAID YOU CALLED AND IT WAS OKAY...

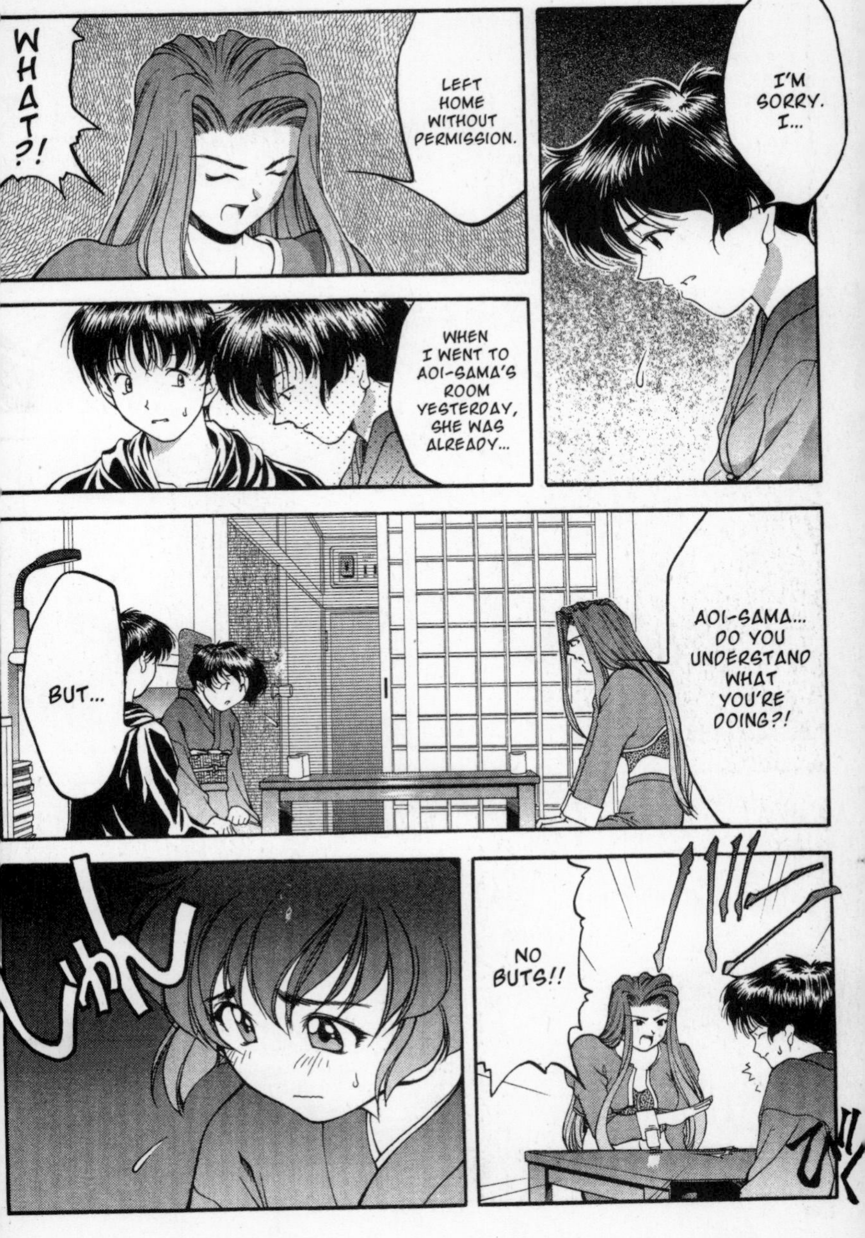
I'M SORRY. I...
LEFT HOME WITHOUT PERMISSION.
WHAT?!
WHEN I WENT TO AOI-SAMA'S ROOM YESTERDAY, SHE WAS ALREADY...
AOI-SAMA... DO YOU UNDERSTAND WHAT YOU'RE DOING?!
BUT...
NO BUTS!!
しゅん

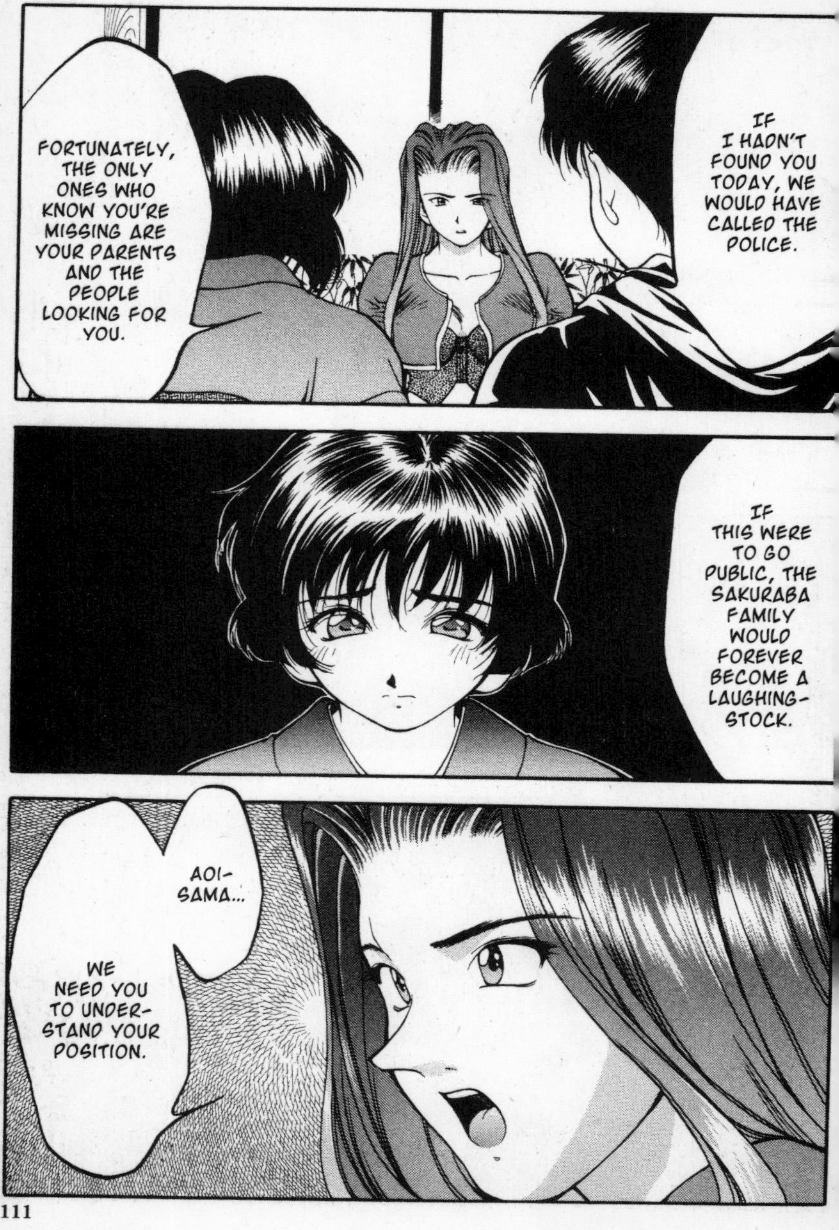
IF I HADN'T FOUND YOU TODAY, WE WOULD HAVE CALLED THE POLICE.
FORTUNATELY, THE ONLY ONES WHO KNOW YOU'RE MISSING ARE YOUR PARENTS AND THE PEOPLE LOOKING FOR YOU.
IF THIS WERE TO GO PUBLIC, THE SAKURABA FAMILY WOULD FOREVER BECOME A LAUGHING-STOCK.
AOI-SAMA...
WE NEED YOU TO UNDER-STAND YOUR POSITION.

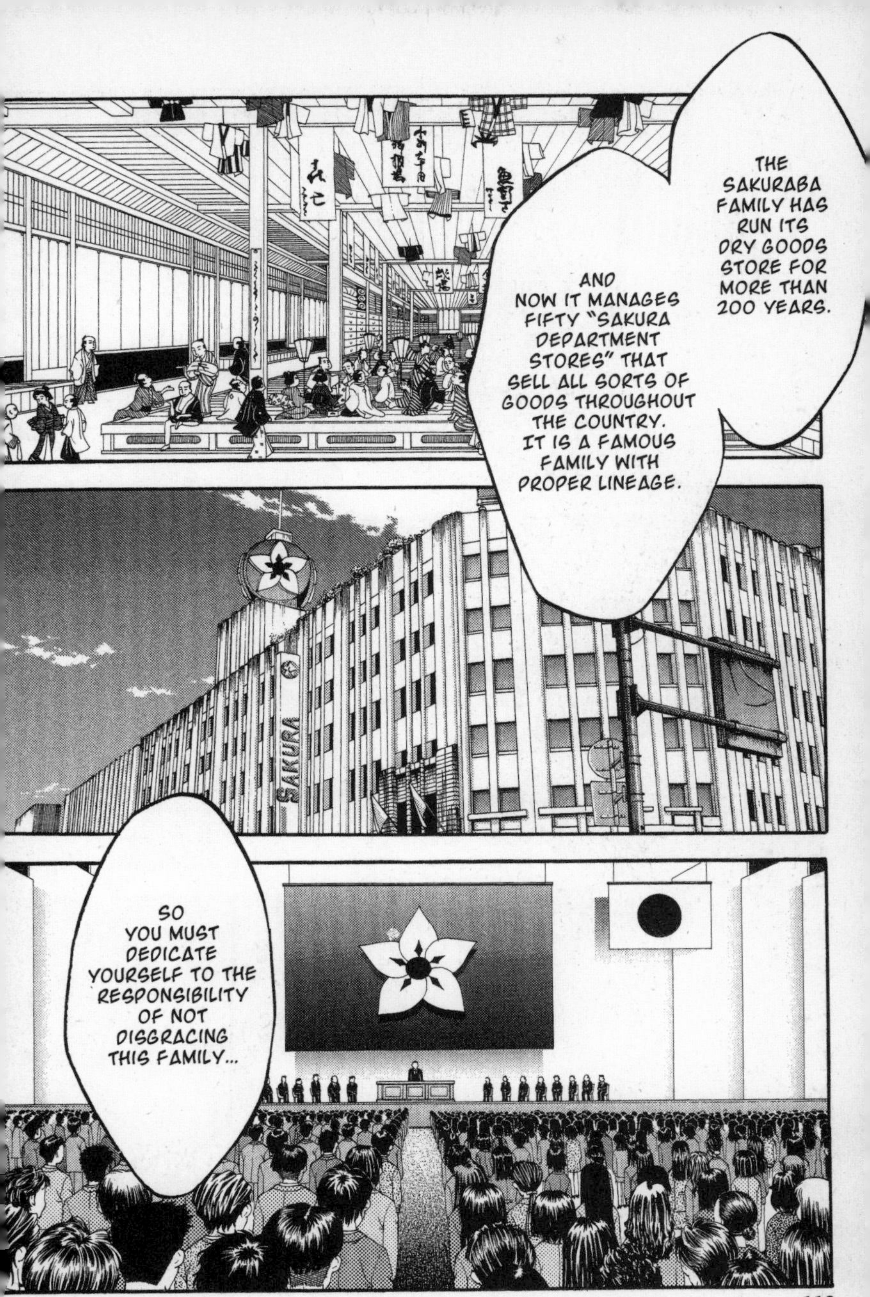
THE SAKURABA FAMILY HAS RUN ITS DRY GOODS STORE FOR MORE THAN 200 YEARS.
AND NOW IT MANAGES FIFTY "SAKURA DEPARTMENT STORES" THAT SELL ALL SORTS OF GOODS THROUGHOUT THE COUNTRY. IT IS A FAMOUS FAMILY WITH PROPER LINEAGE.
SAKURA
SO YOU MUST DEDICATE YOURSELF TO THE RESPONSIBILITY OF NOT DISGRACING THIS FAMILY...

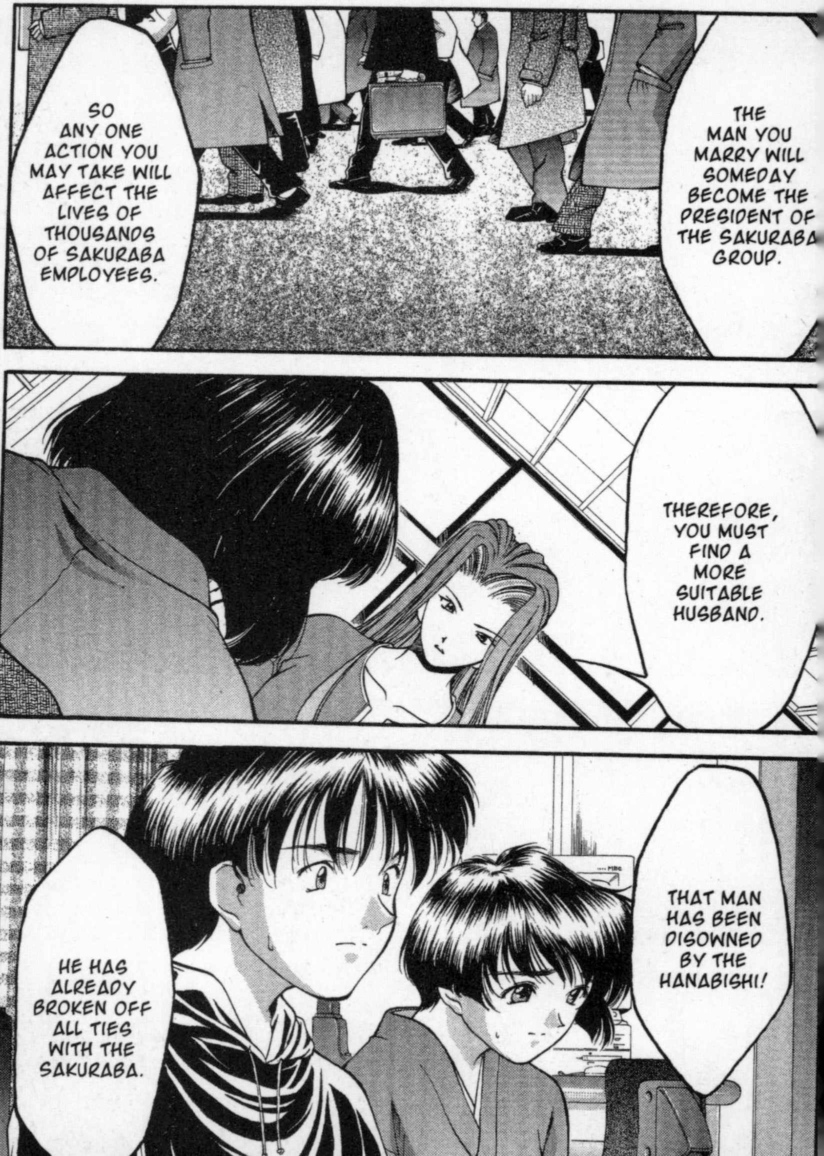
THE MAN YOU MARRY WILL SOMEDAY BECOME THE PRESIDENT OF THE SAKURABA GROUP.
SO ANY ONE ACTION YOU MAY TAKE WILL AFFECT THE LIVES OF THOUSANDS OF SAKURABA EMPLOYEES.
THEREFORE, YOU MUST FIND A MORE SUITABLE HUSBAND.
THAT MAN HAS BEEN DISOWNED BY THE HANABISHI!
HE HAS ALREADY BROKEN OFF ALL TIES WITH THE SAKURABA.

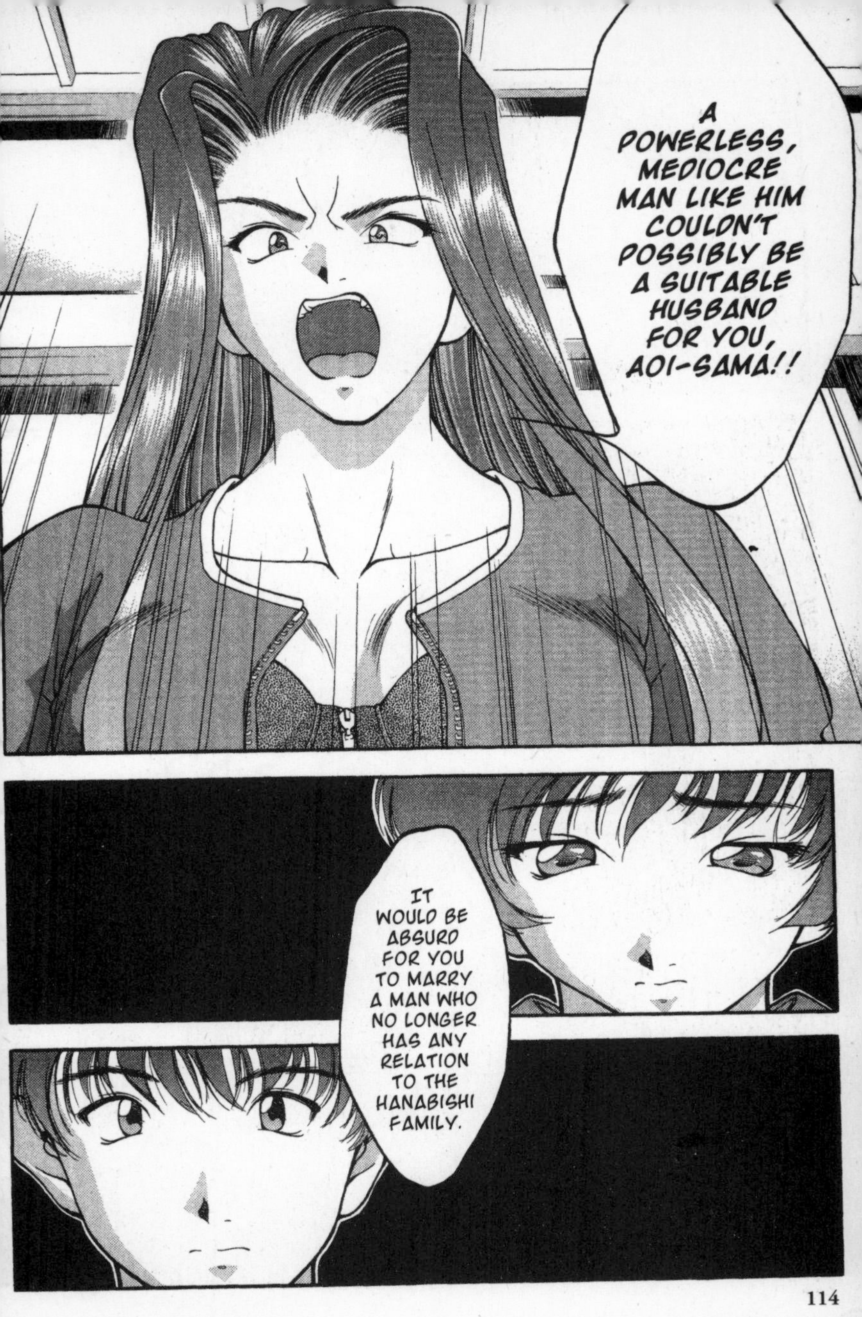
A POWERLESS, MEDIOCRE MAN LIKE HIM COULDN'T POSSIBLY BE A SUITABLE HUSBAND FOR YOU, AOI-SAMA!!
IT WOULD BE ABSURD FOR YOU TO MARRY A MAN WHO NO LONGER HAS ANY RELATION TO THE HANABISHI FAMILY.

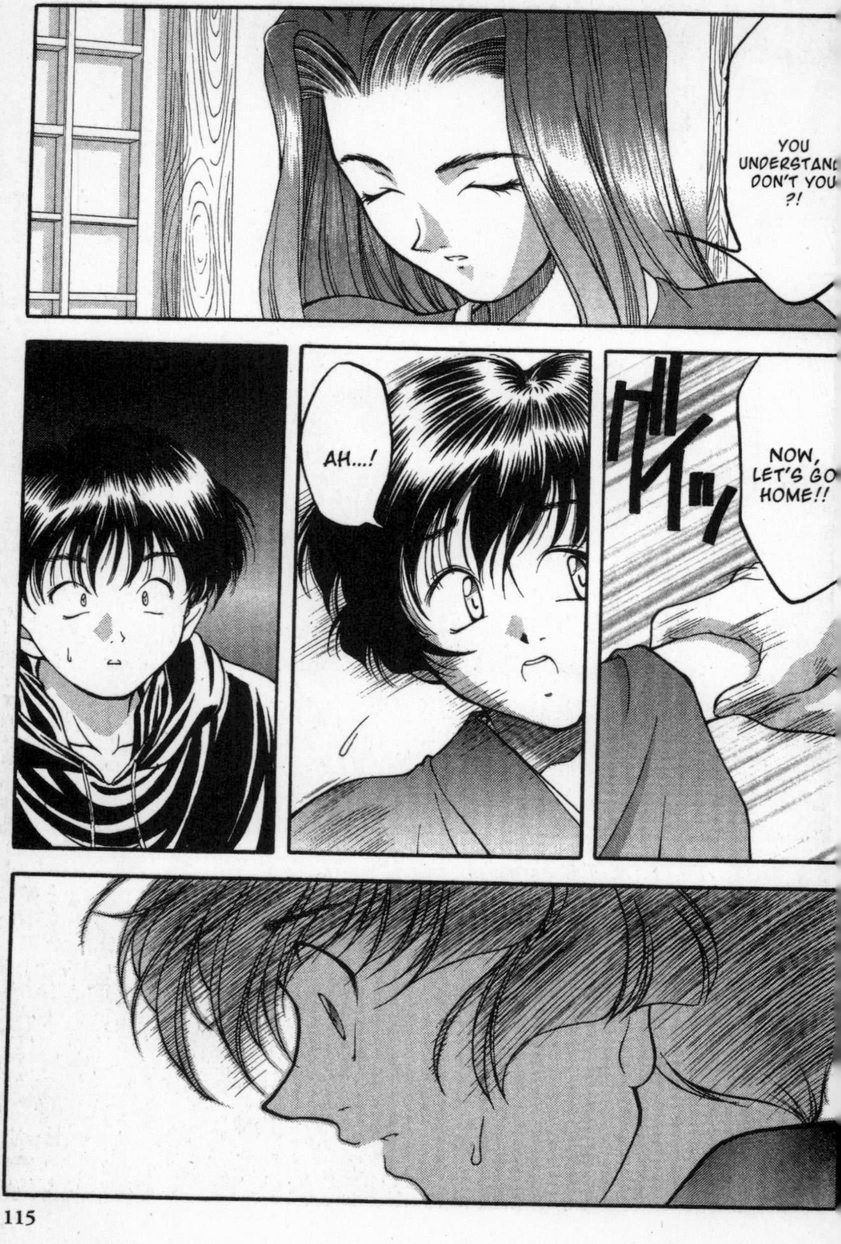
YOU UNDERSTAND DON'T YOU ?!
NOW, LET'S GO HOME!!
AH...!

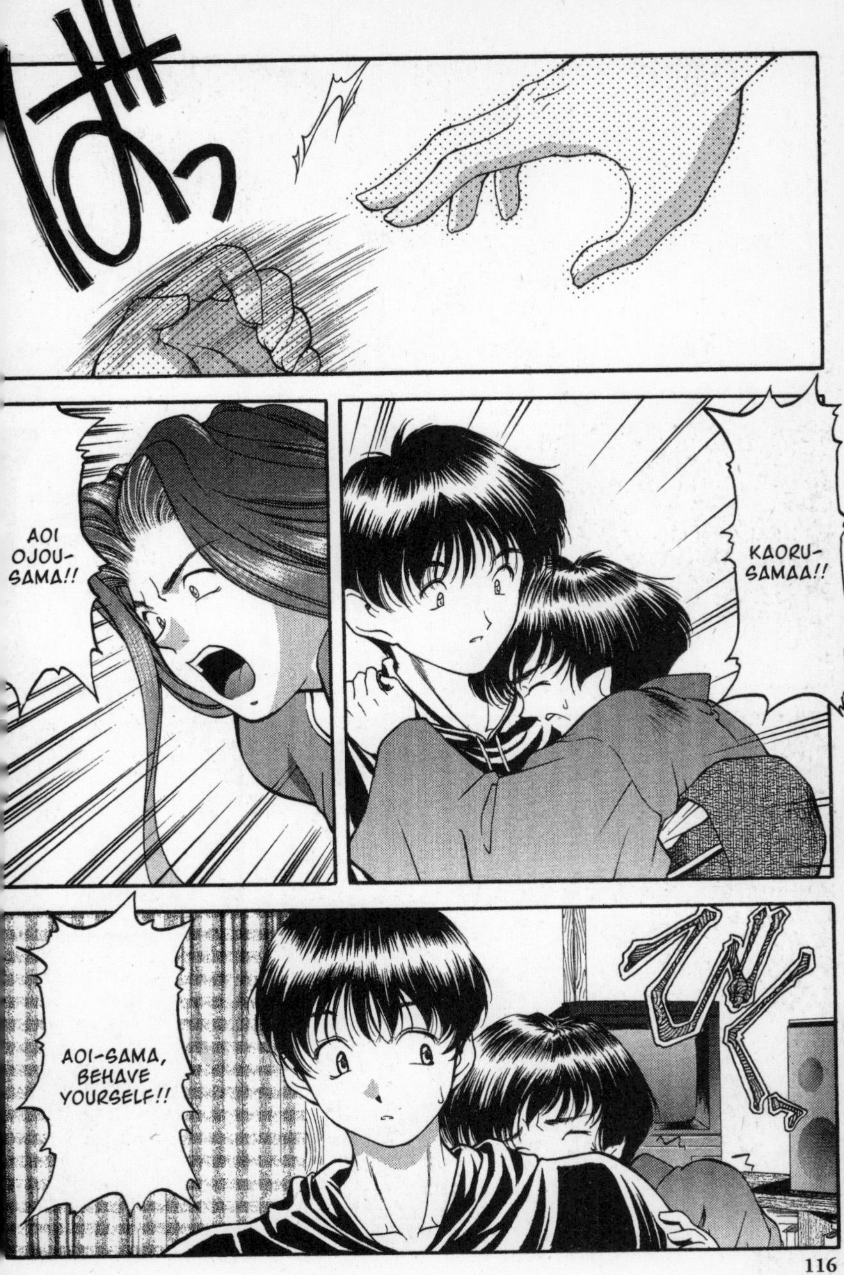
ぱっ
KAORU-SAMAA!!
AOI OJOU-SAMA!!
AOI-SAMA, BEHAVE YOURSELF!!

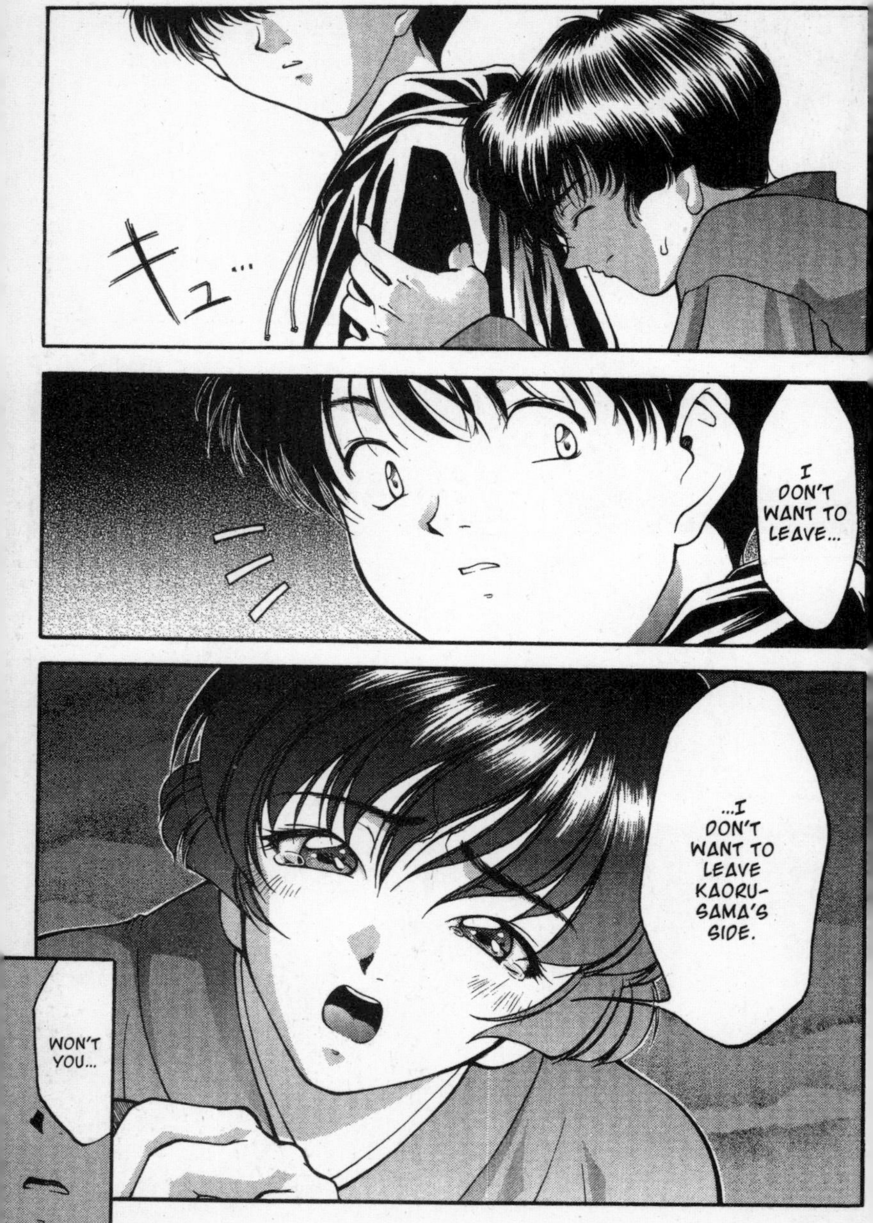
キュ…
I DON'T WANT TO LEAVE...
...I DON'T WANT TO LEAVE KAORU-SAMA'S SIDE.
WON'T YOU...

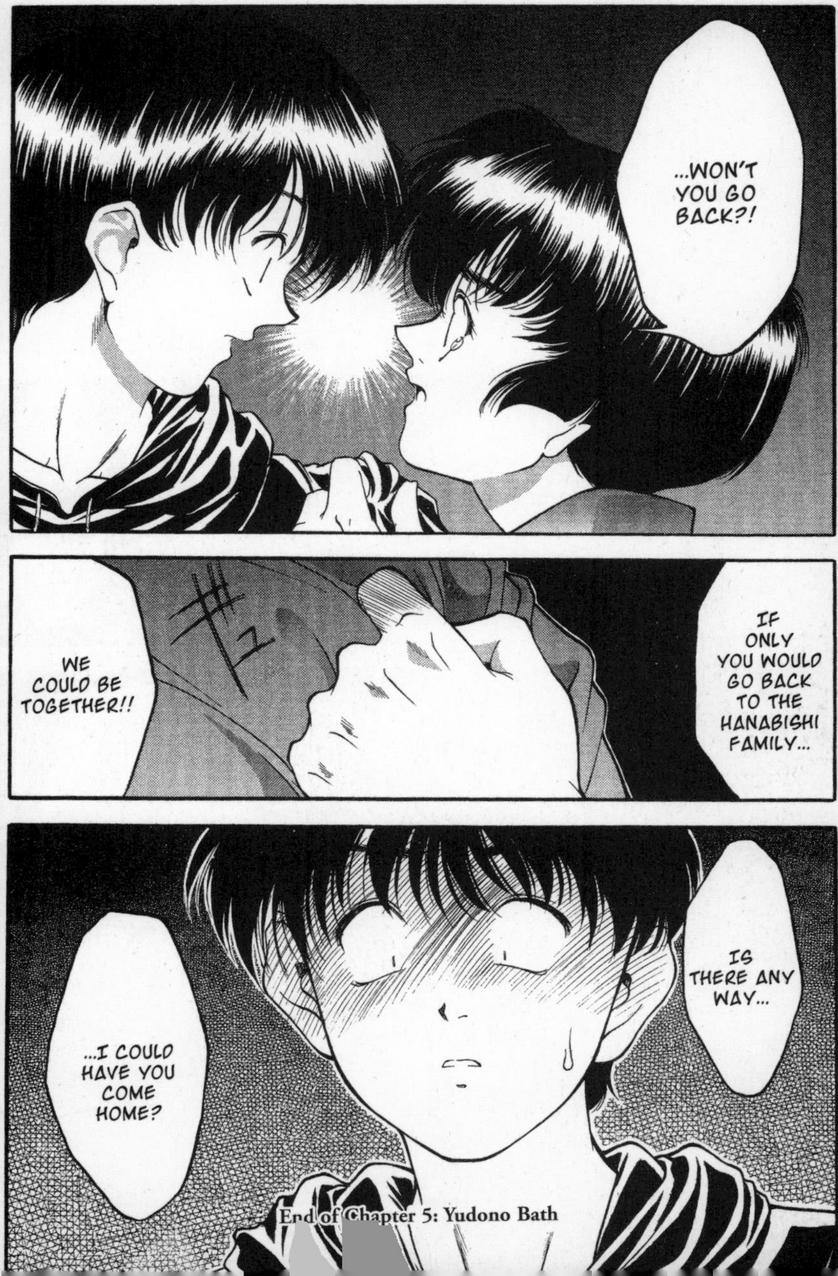
...WON'T YOU GO BACK?!
IF ONLY YOU WOULD GO BACK TO THE HANABISHI FAMILY...
ギュ
WE COULD BE TOGETHER!!
IS THERE ANY WAY...
...I COULD HAVE YOU COME HOME?
End of Chapter 5: Yudono Bath

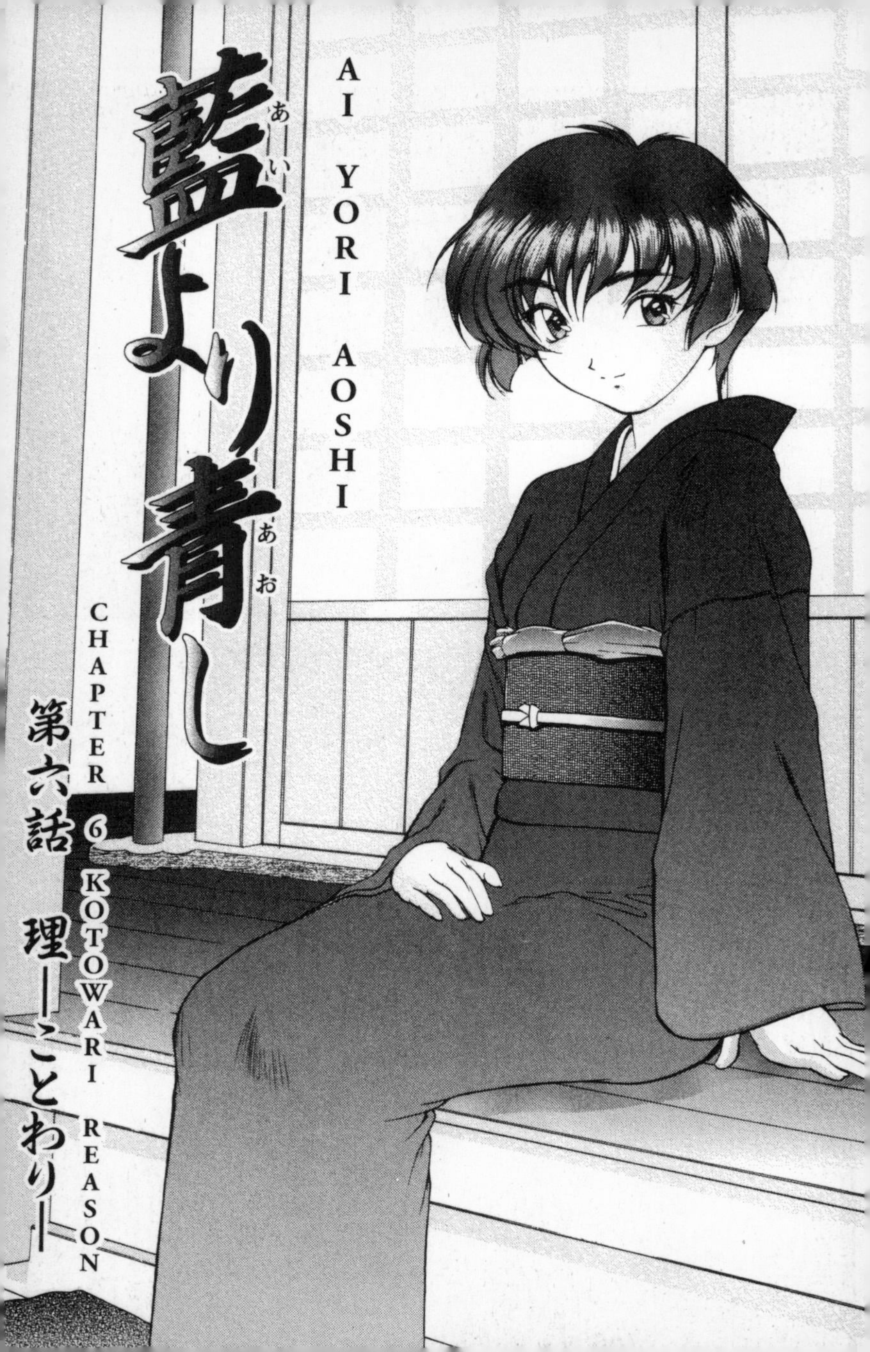
藍より青し
AI YORI AOSHI
第六話 理—ことわり—
CHAPTER 6 KOTOWARI REASON

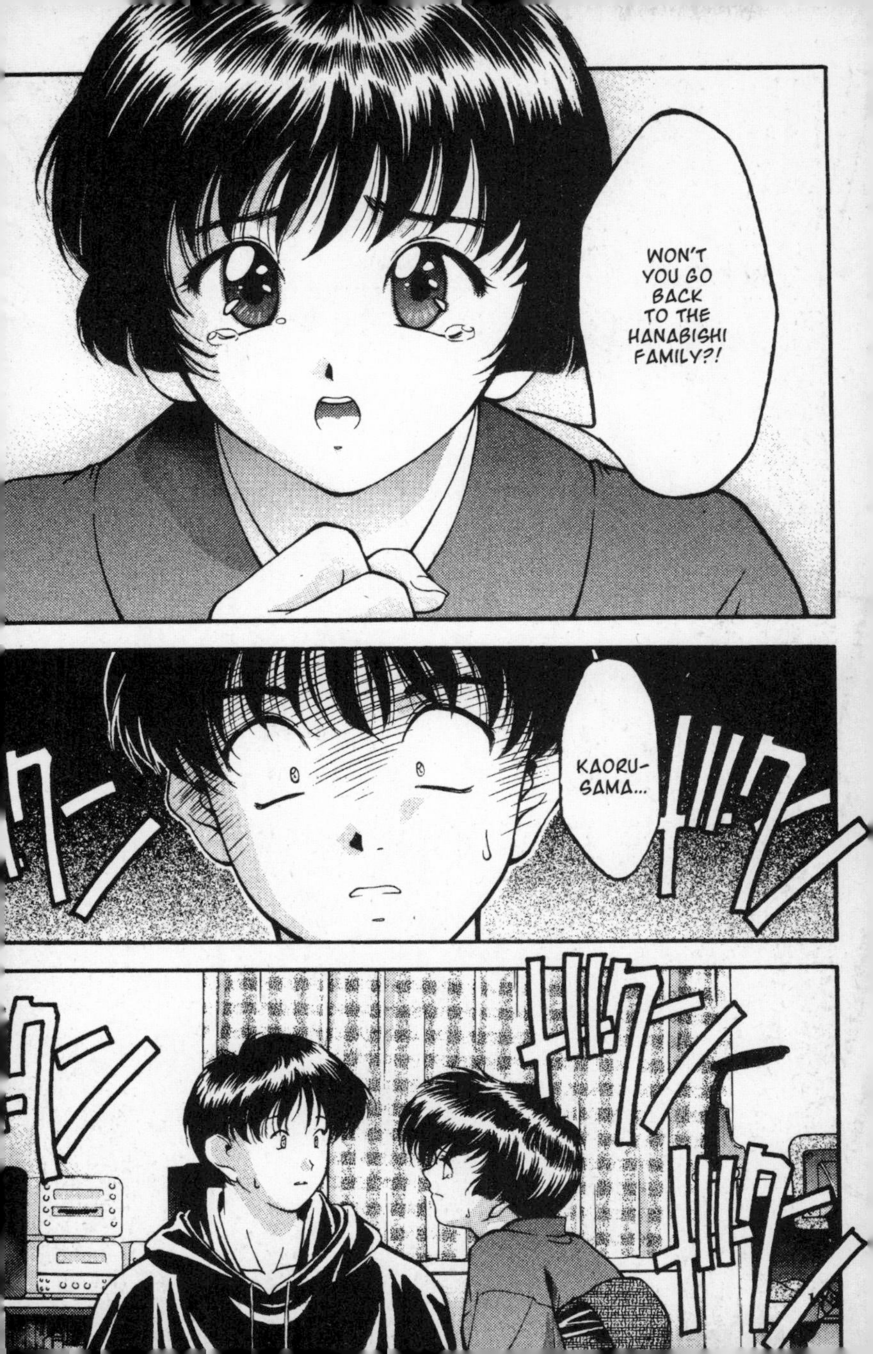
WON'T YOU GO BACK TO THE HANABISHI FAMILY?!
KAORU-SAMA...

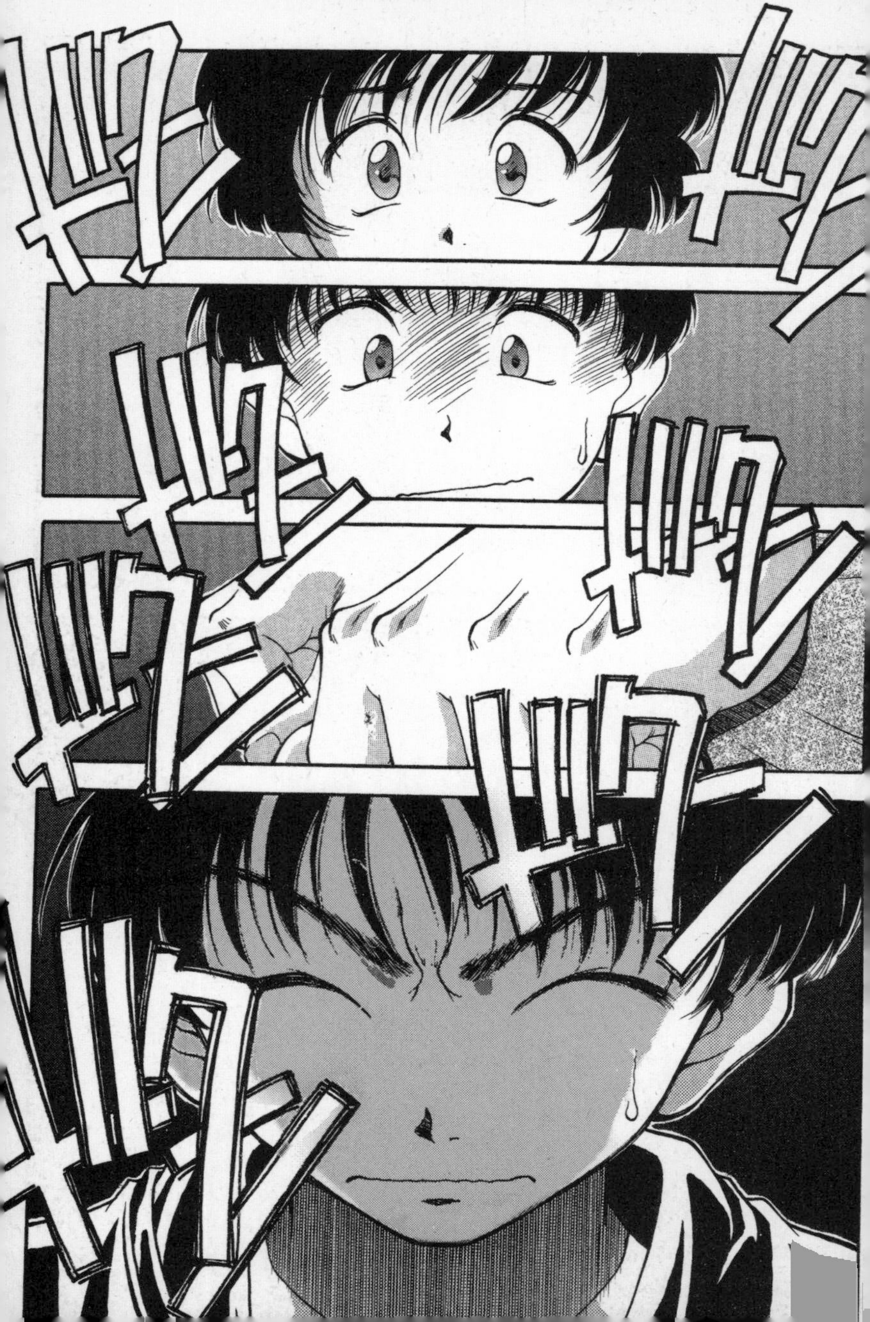
ドキン
ドキン
ドキン
ドキン
ドキン
ドキン
ドキン

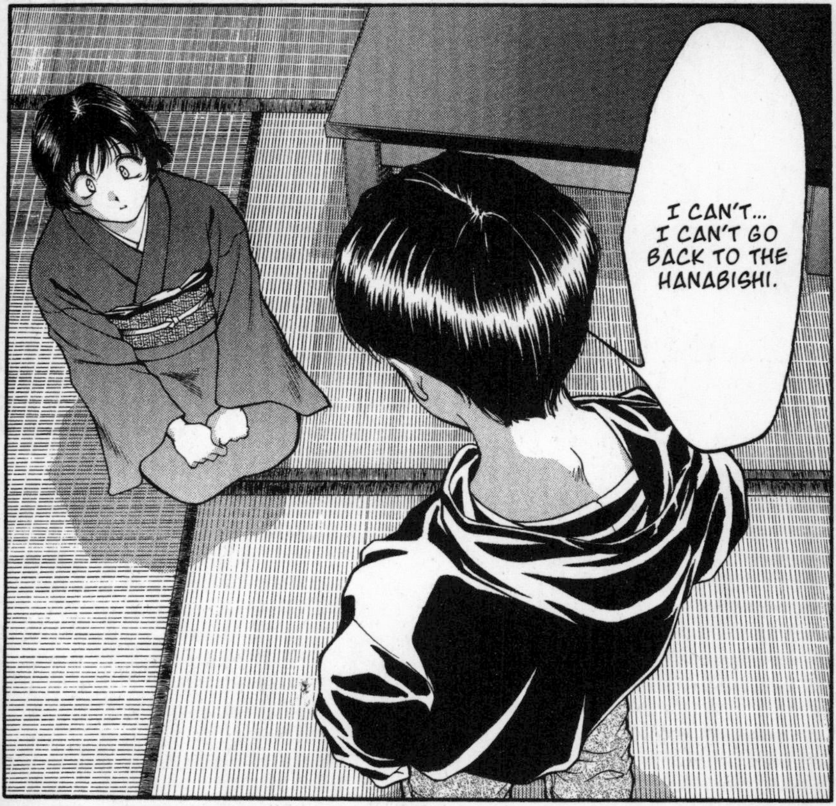
I CAN'T... I CAN'T GO BACK TO THE HANABISHI.
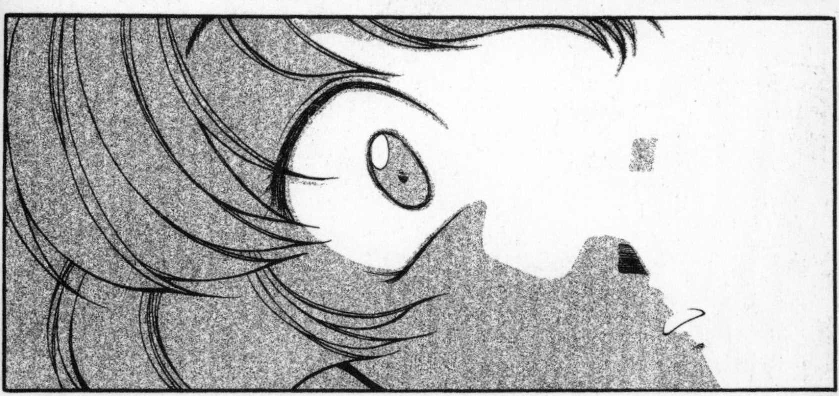

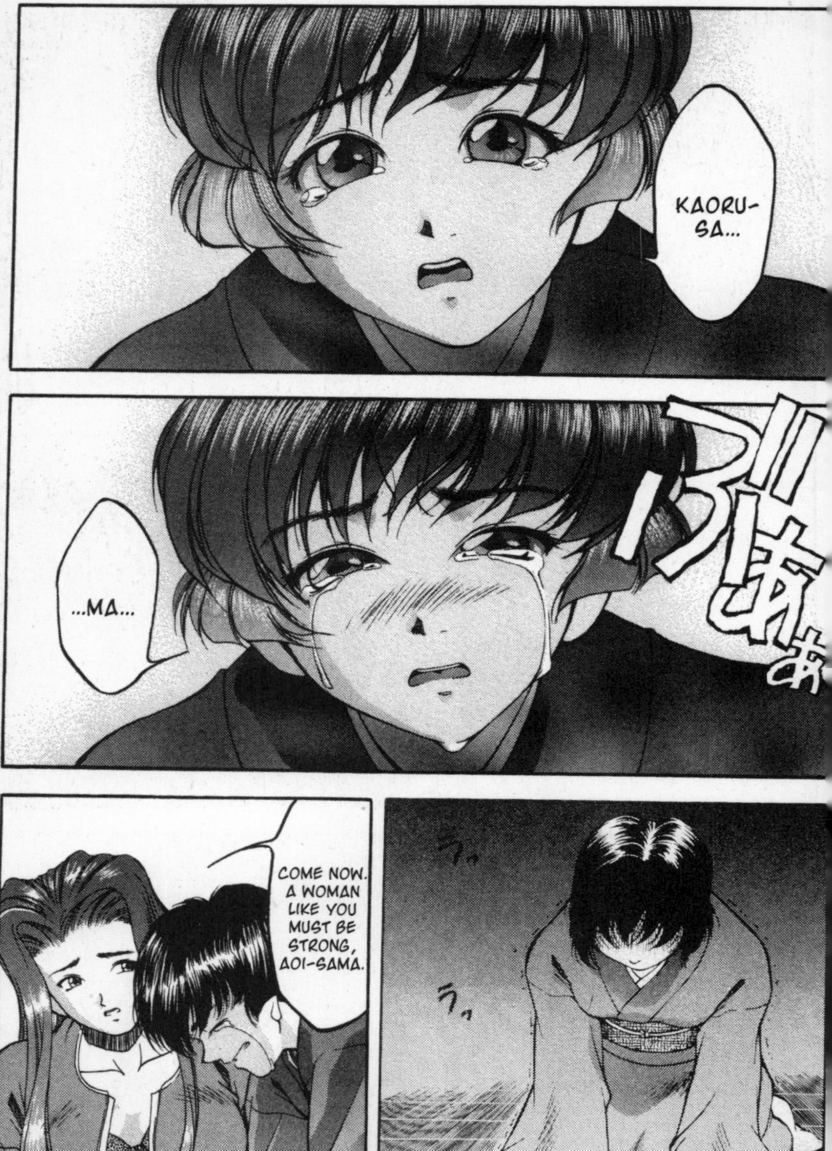
KAORU-SA...
...MA...
COME NOW. A WOMAN LIKE YOU MUST BE STRONG, AOI-SAMA.

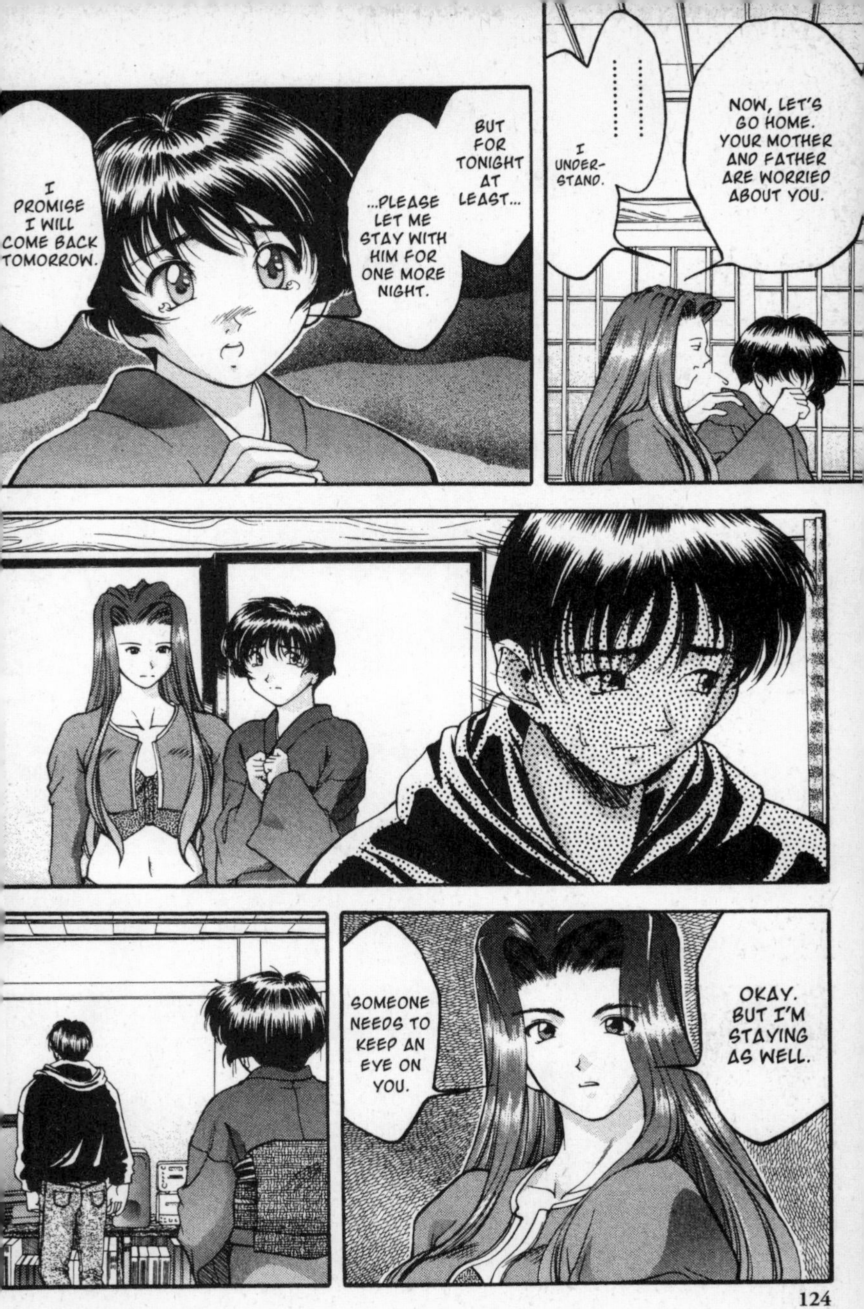
NOW, LET'S GO HOME. YOUR MOTHER AND FATHER ARE WORRIED ABOUT YOU.
......
I UNDER-STAND.
BUT FOR TONIGHT AT LEAST...
...PLEASE LET ME STAY WITH HIM FOR ONE MORE NIGHT.
I PROMISE I WILL COME BACK TOMORROW.
OKAY. BUT I'M STAYING AS WELL.
SOMEONE NEEDS TO KEEP AN EYE ON YOU.

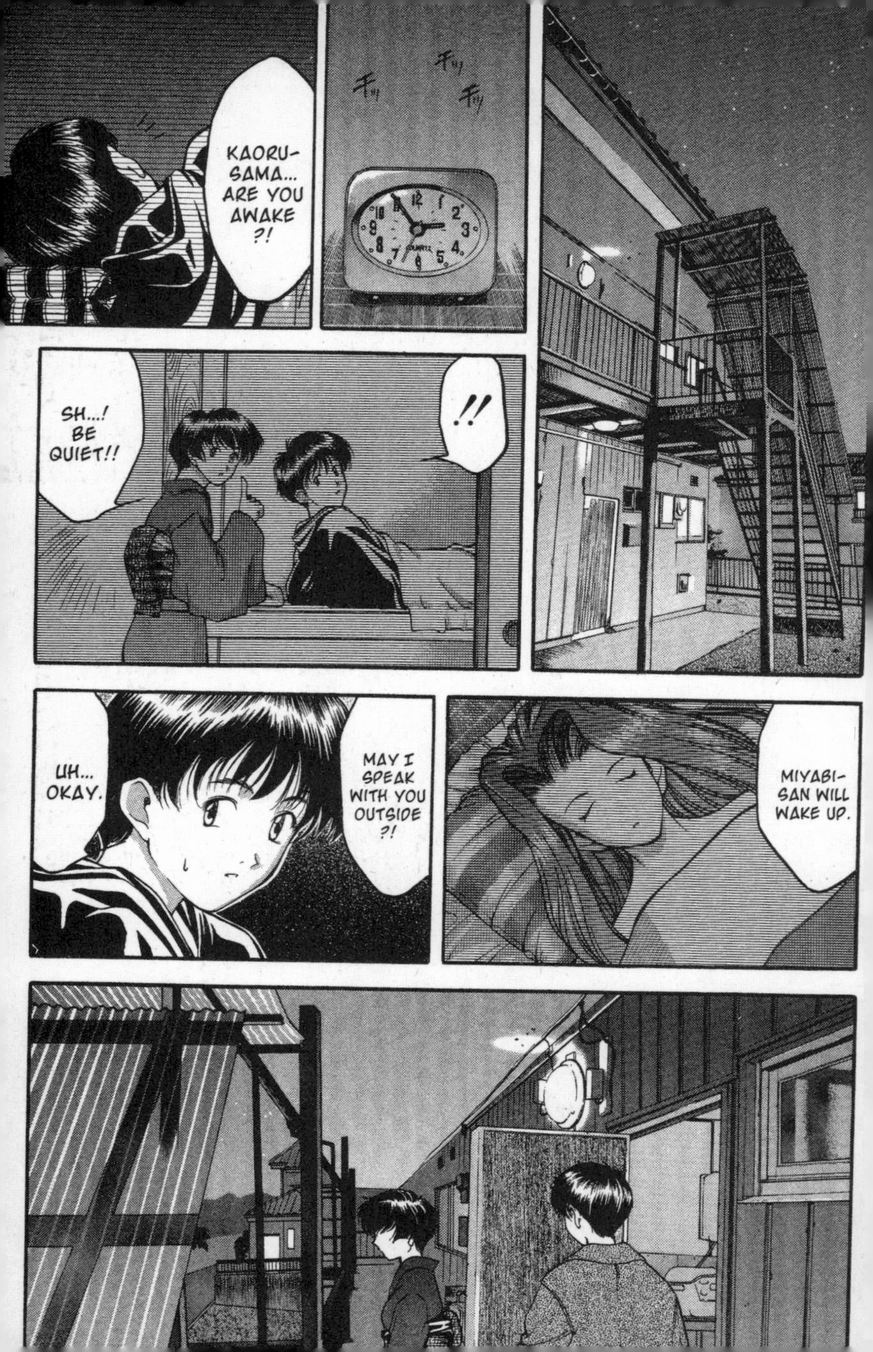

チッ
チッ
チッ
KAORU-SAMA... ARE YOU AWAKE ?!
!!
SH...! BE QUIET!!
MIYABI-SAN WILL WAKE UP.
MAY I SPEAK WITH YOU OUTSIDE ?!
UH... OKAY.

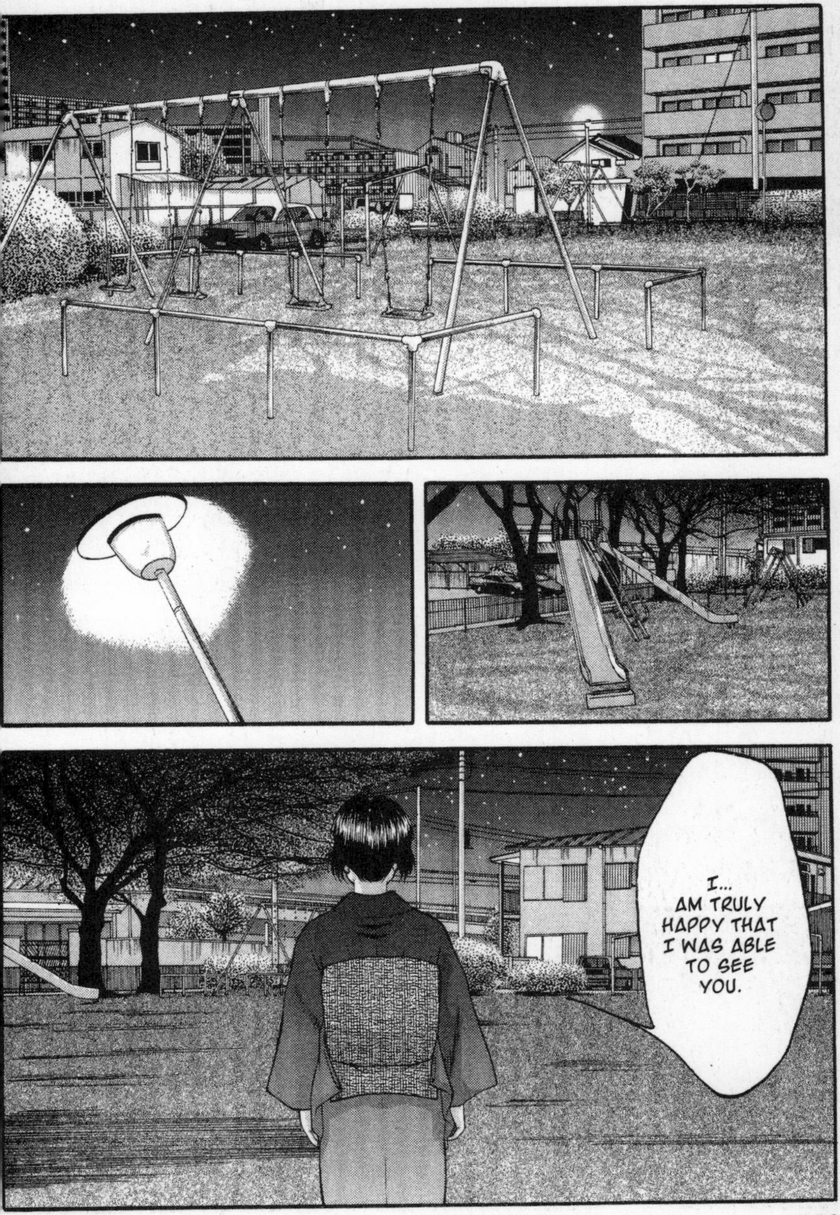
I... AM TRULY HAPPY THAT I WAS ABLE TO SEE YOU.

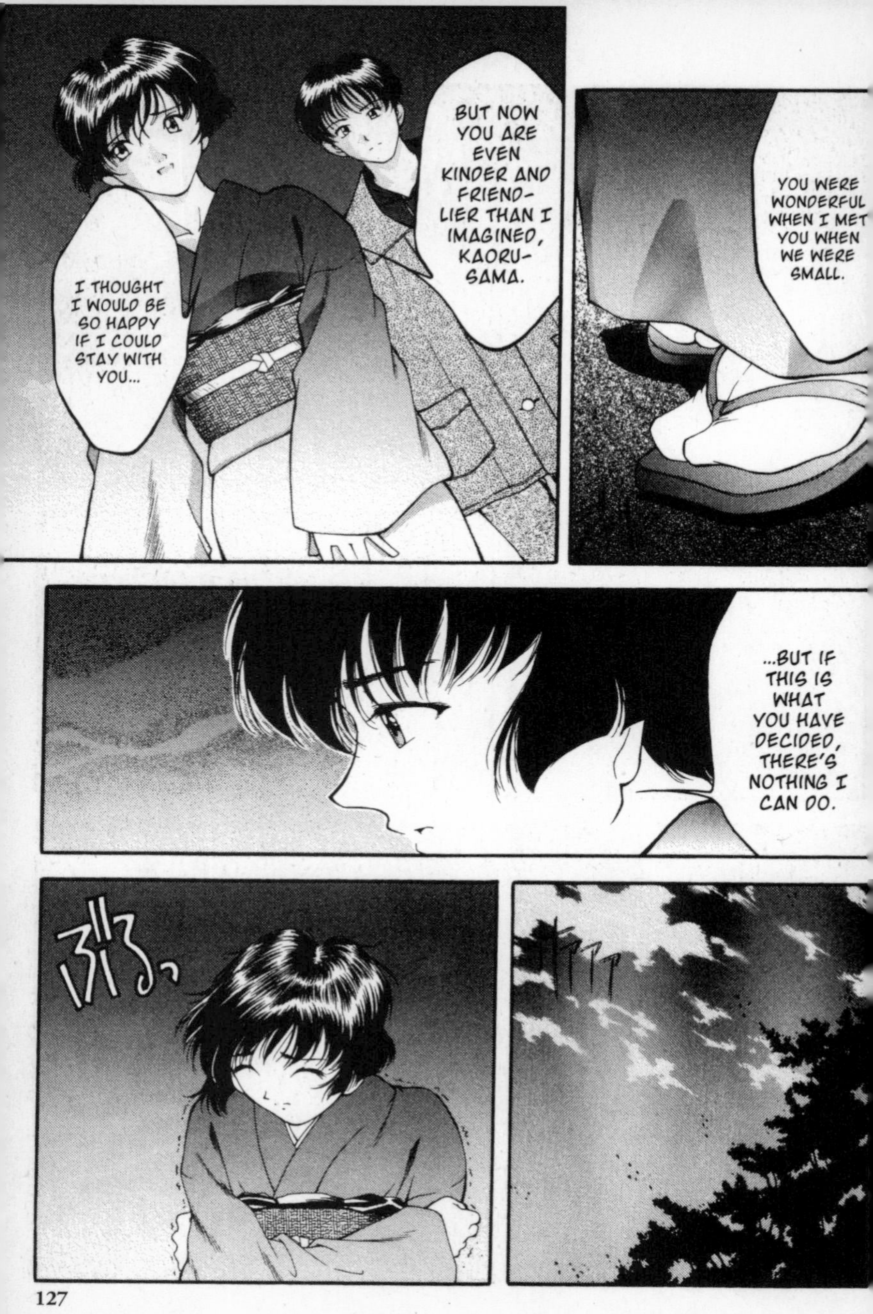
YOU WERE WONDERFUL WHEN I MET YOU WHEN WE WERE SMALL.
BUT NOW YOU ARE EVEN KINDER AND FRIEND-LIER THAN I IMAGINED, KAORU-SAMA.
I THOUGHT I WOULD BE SO HAPPY IF I COULD STAY WITH YOU...
...BUT IF THIS IS WHAT YOU HAVE DECIDED, THERE'S NOTHING I CAN DO.
ぶるっ

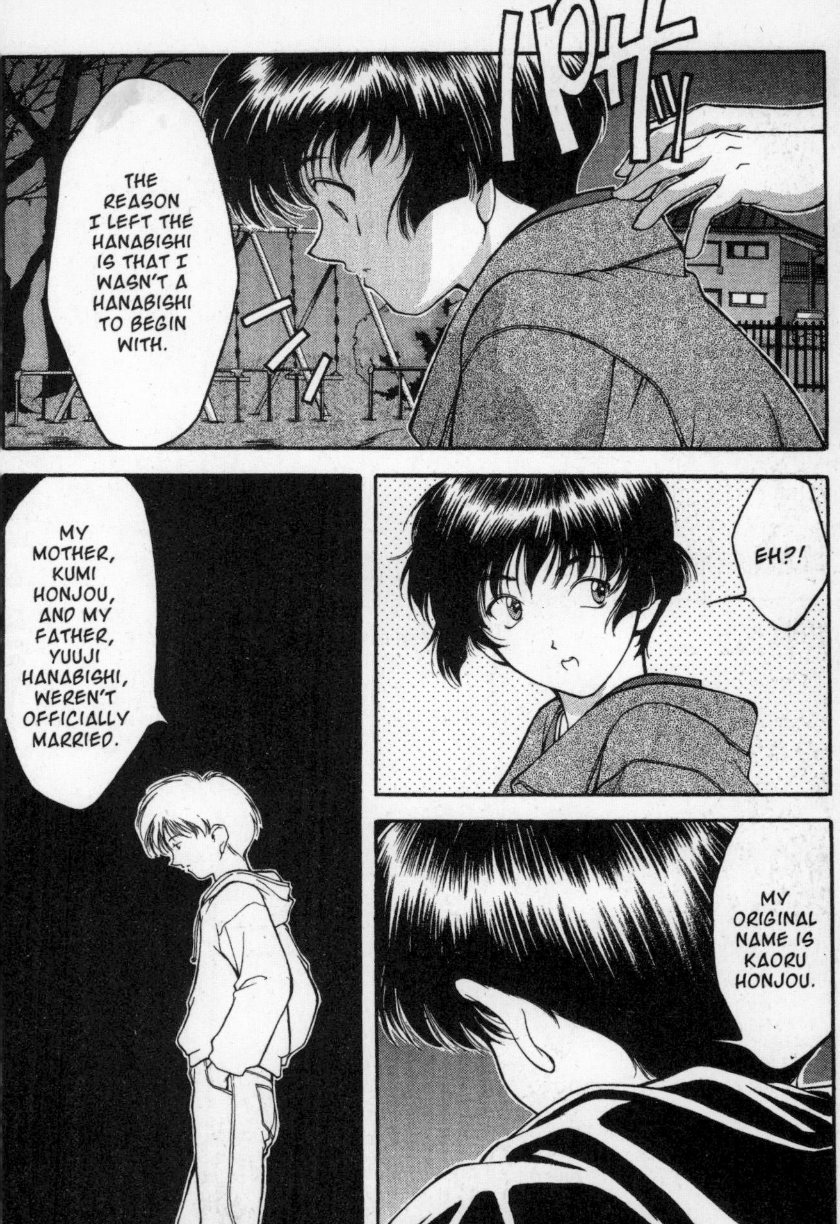

パサッ
THE REASON I LEFT THE HANABISHI IS THAT I WASN'T A HANABISHI TO BEGIN WITH.
EH?!
MY ORIGINAL NAME IS KAORU HONJOU.
MY MOTHER, KUMI HONJOU, AND MY FATHER, YUUJI HANABISHI, WEREN'T OFFICIALLY MARRIED.

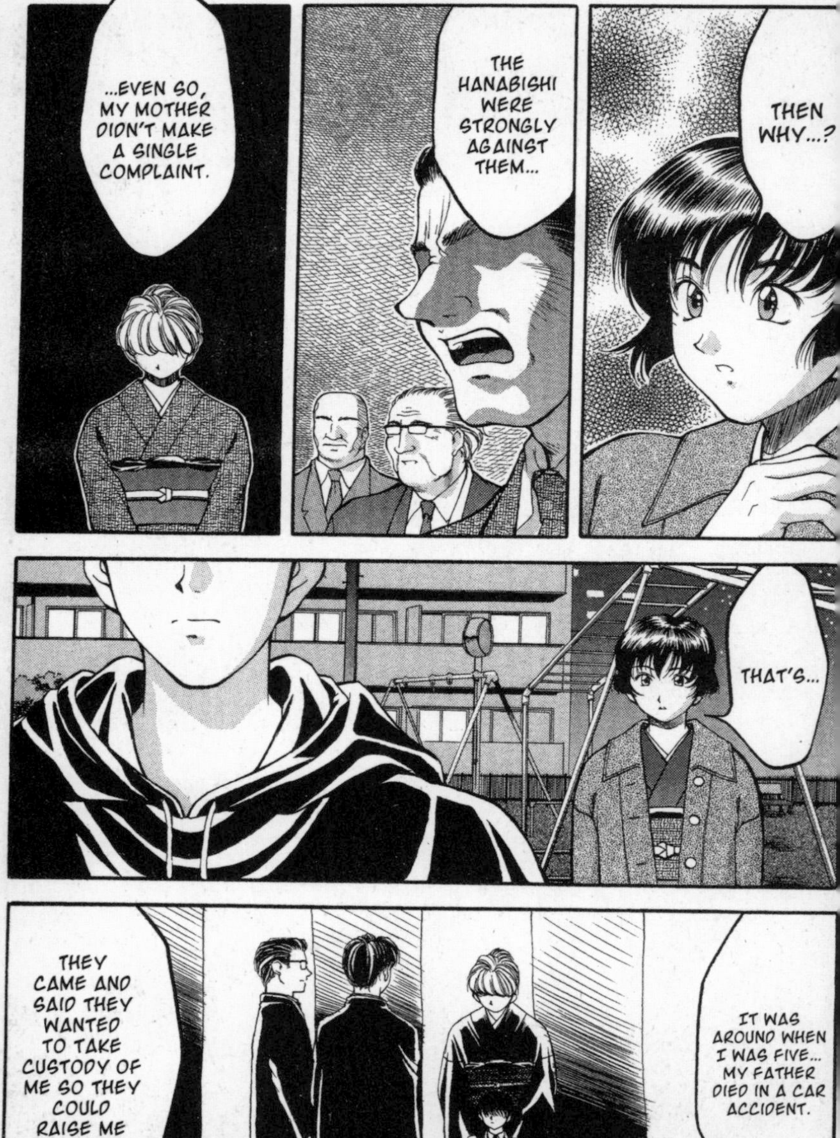
THEN WHY...?
THE HANABISHI WERE STRONGLY AGAINST THEM...
...EVEN SO, MY MOTHER DIDN'T MAKE A SINGLE COMPLAINT.
THAT'S...
IT WAS AROUND WHEN I WAS FIVE... MY FATHER DIED IN A CAR ACCIDENT.
THEY CAME AND SAID THEY WANTED TO TAKE CUSTODY OF ME SO THEY COULD RAISE ME PROPERLY.

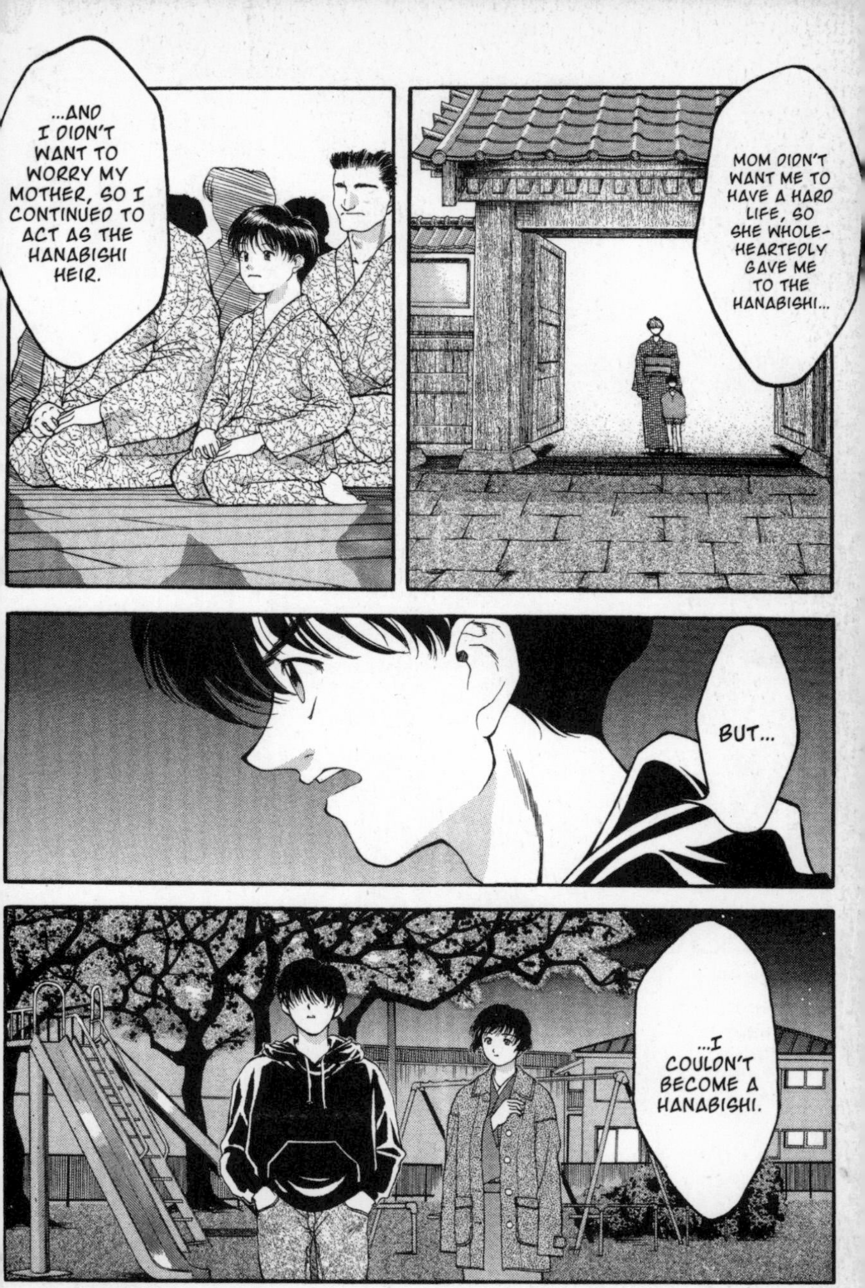
MOM DIDN'T WANT ME TO HAVE A HARD LIFE, SO SHE WHOLE-HEARTEDLY GAVE ME TO THE HANABISHI...
...AND I DIDN'T WANT TO WORRY MY MOTHER, SO I CONTINUED TO ACT AS THE HANABISHI HEIR.
BUT...
...I COULDN'T BECOME A HANABISHI.

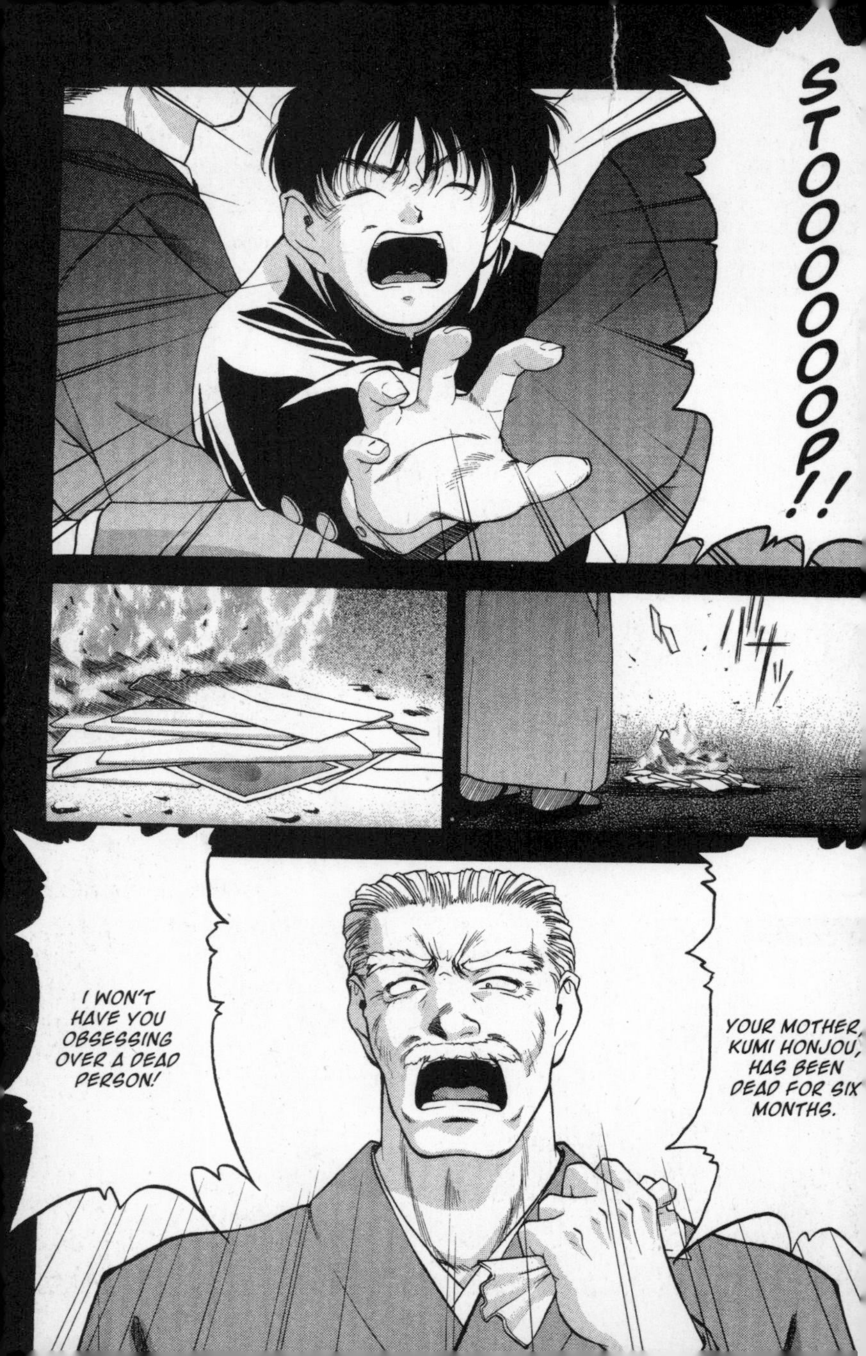
STOOOOOOOP!!
YOUR MOTHER, KUMI HONJOU, HAS BEEN DEAD FOR SIX MONTHS.
I WON'T HAVE YOU OBSESSING OVER A DEAD PERSON!

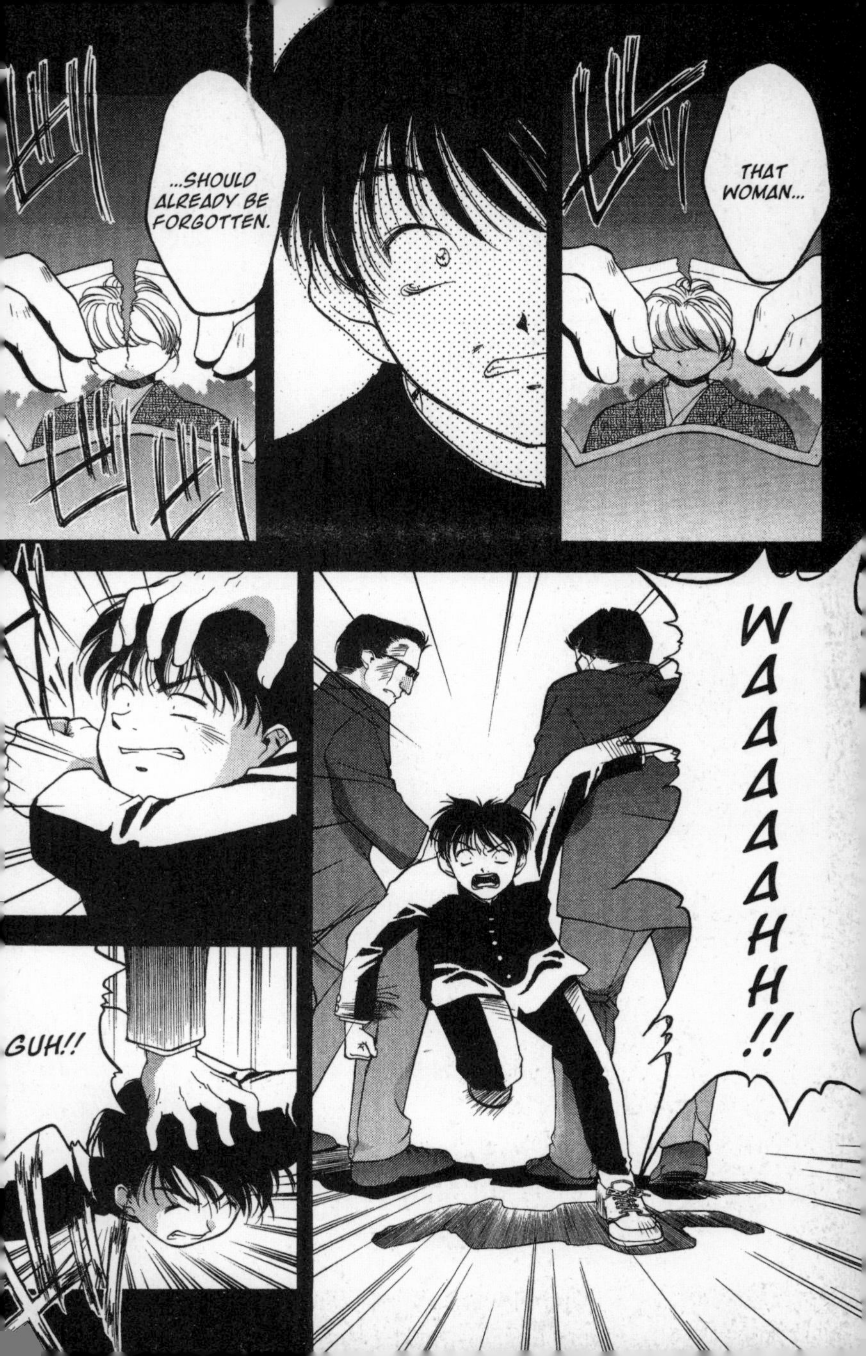
THAT WOMAN...
...SHOULD ALREADY BE FORGOTTEN.
WAAAAAAHH!!
GUH!!

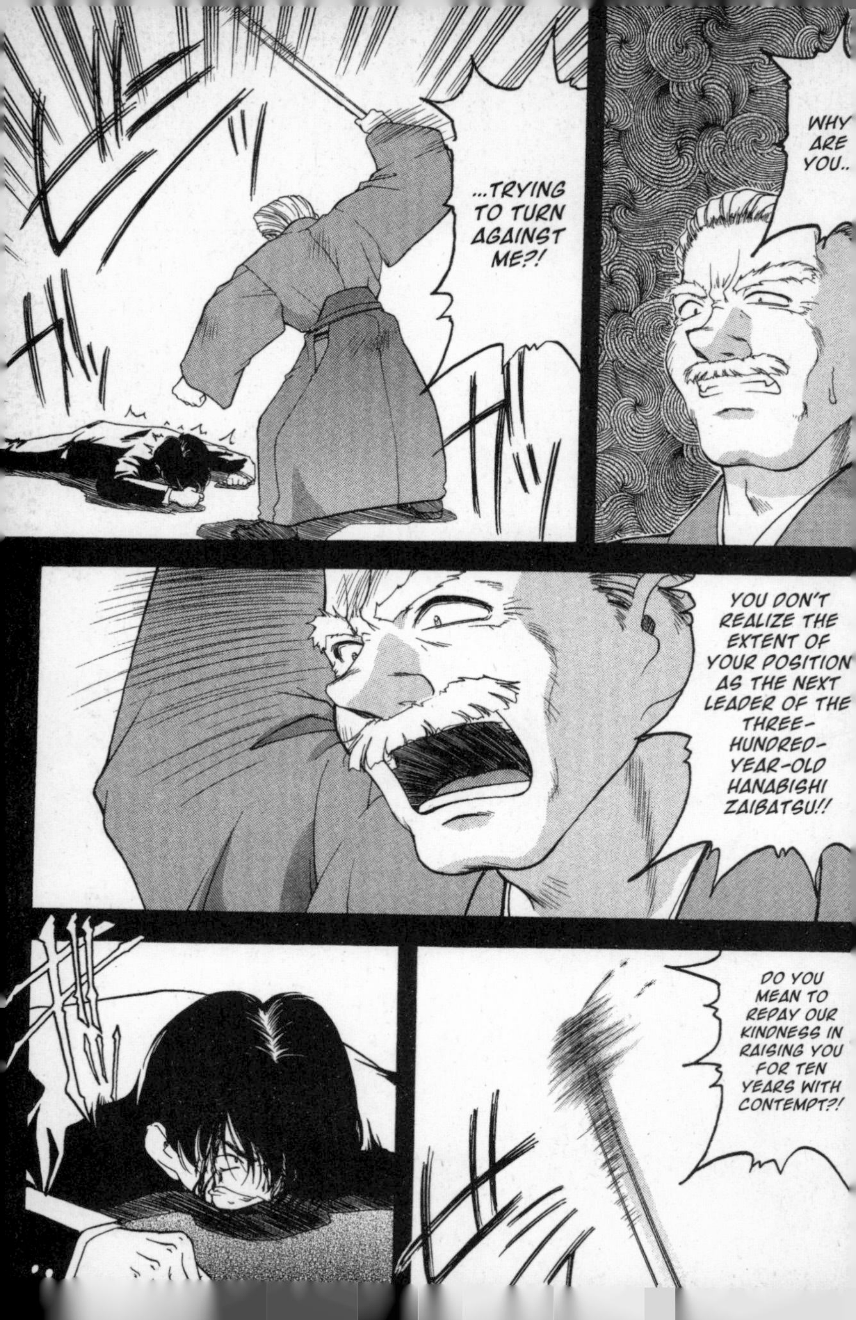
WHY ARE YOU..
...TRYING TO TURN AGAINST ME?!
YOU DON'T REALIZE THE EXTENT OF YOUR POSITION AS THE NEXT LEADER OF THE THREE-HUNDRED-YEAR-OLD HANABISHI ZAIBATSU!!
DO YOU MEAN TO REPAY OUR KINDNESS IN RAISING YOU FOR TEN YEARS WITH CONTEMPT?!
...

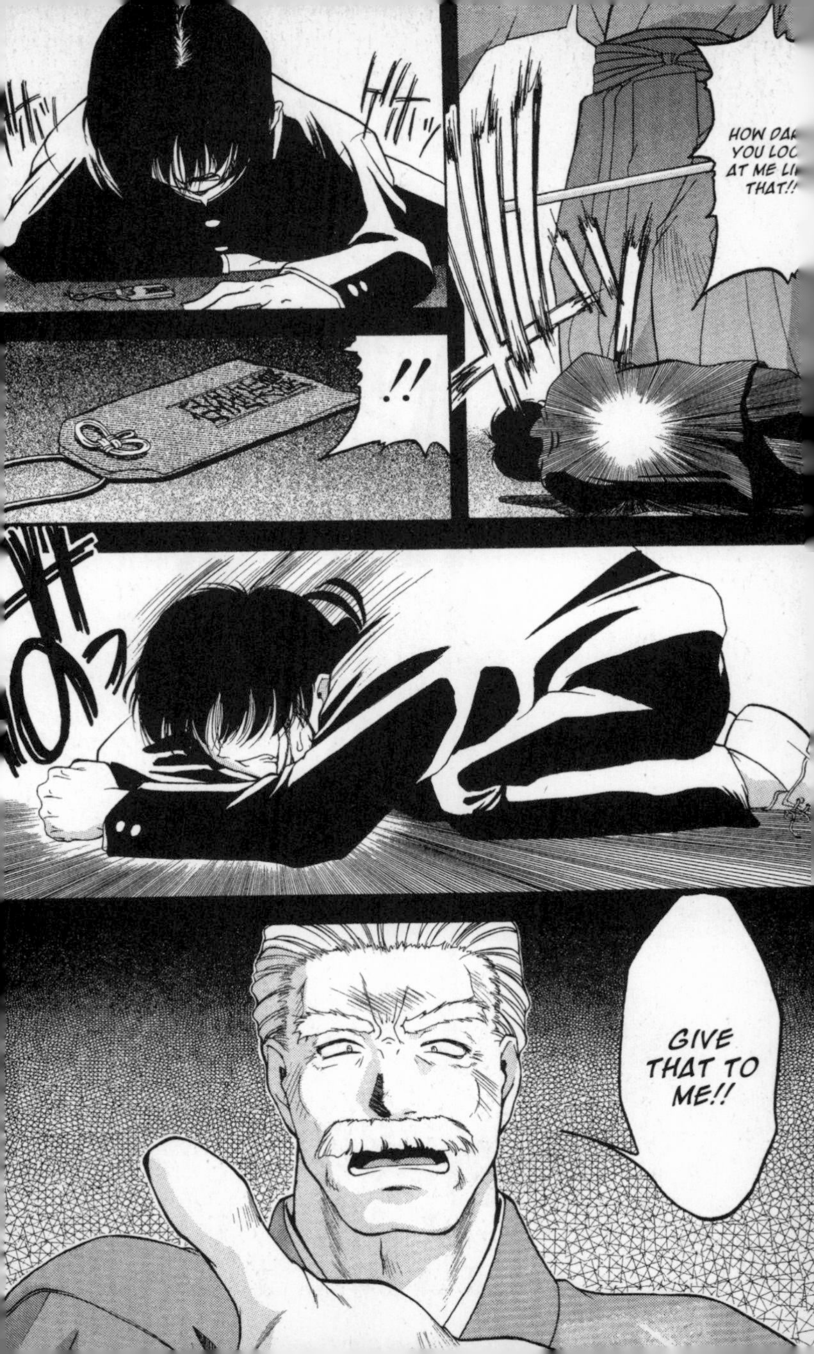
HOW DAR YOU LOO AT ME LI THAT!!
!!
GIVE THAT TO ME!!

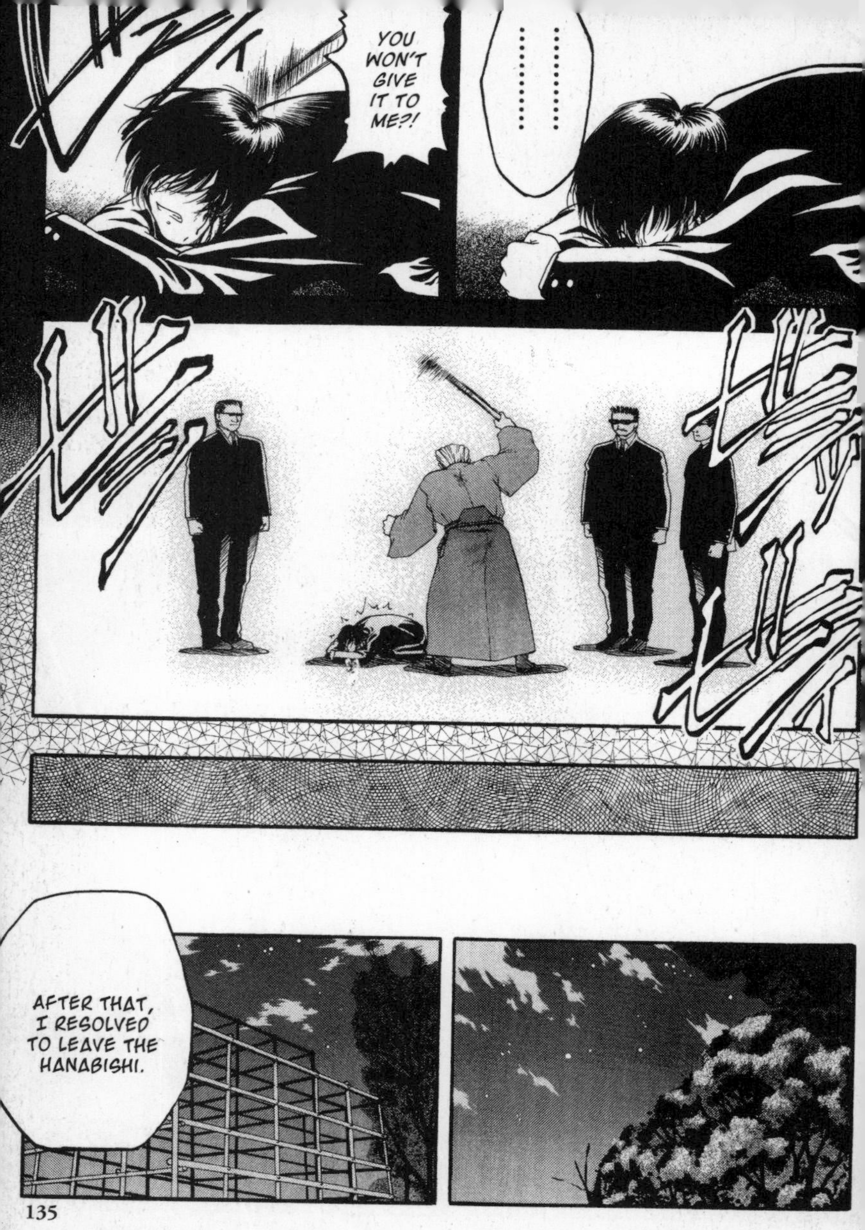
......
YOU WON'T GIVE IT TO ME?!
AFTER THAT, I RESOLVED TO LEAVE THE HANABISHI.

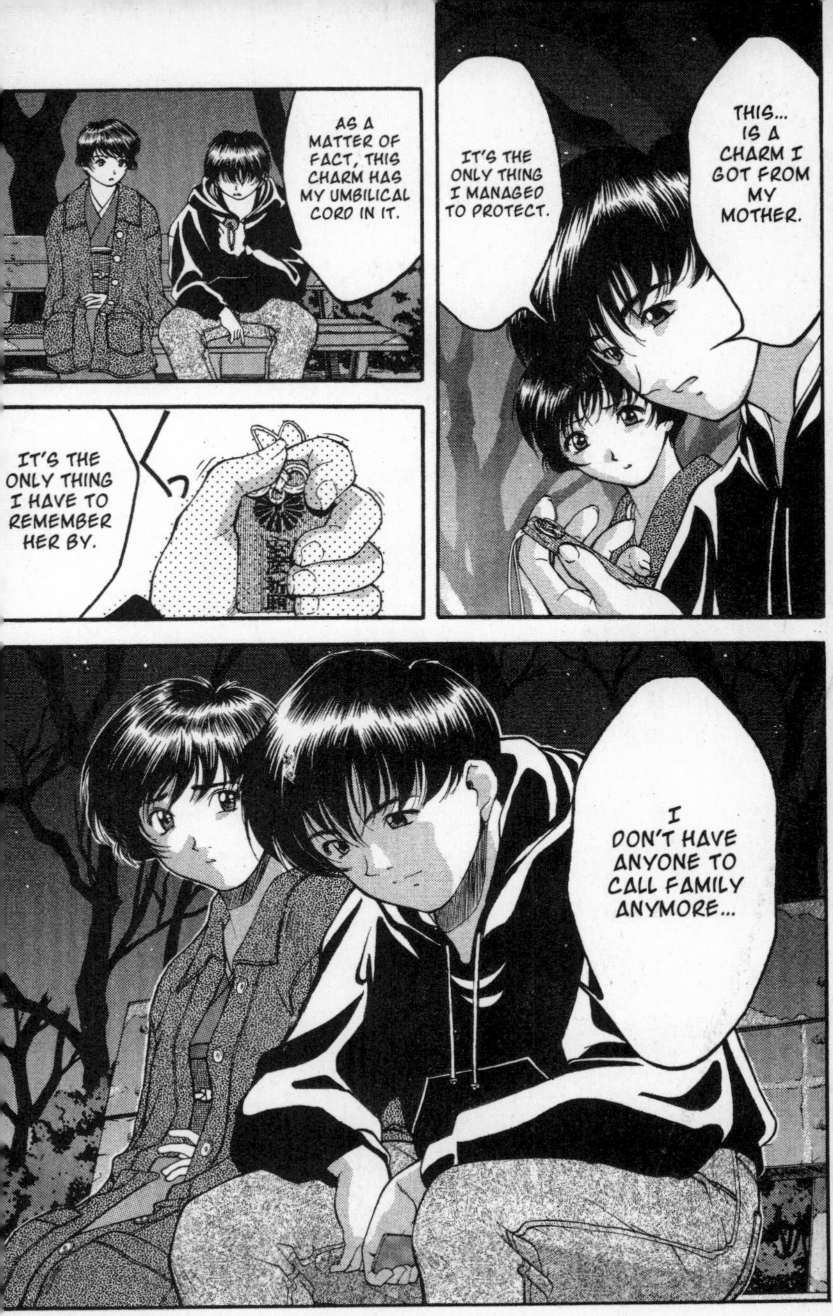
THIS... IS A CHARM I GOT FROM MY MOTHER.
IT'S THE ONLY THING I MANAGED TO PROTECT.
AS A MATTER OF FACT, THIS CHARM HAS MY UMBILICAL CORD IN IT.
IT'S THE ONLY THING I HAVE TO REMEMBER HER BY.
I DON'T HAVE ANYONE TO CALL FAMILY ANYMORE...

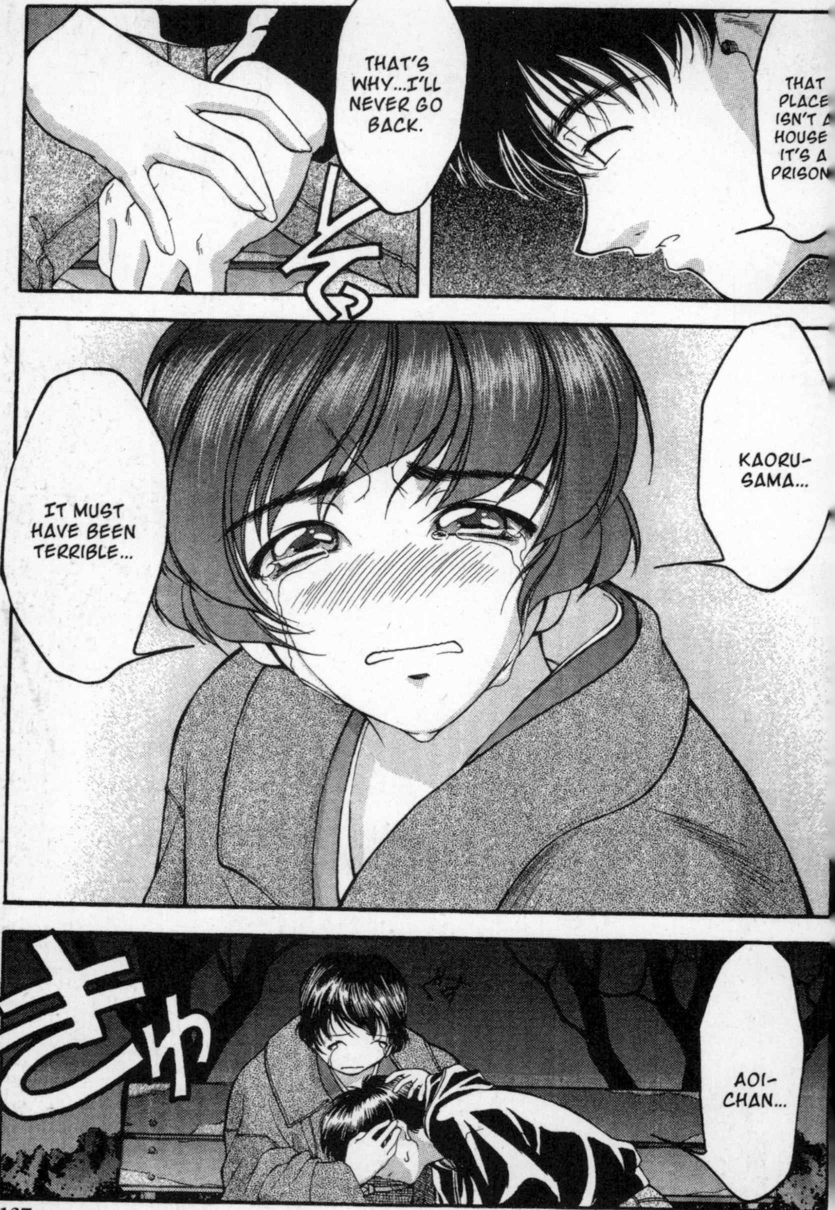
THAT PLACE ISN'T A HOUSE IT'S A PRISON
THAT'S WHY...I'LL NEVER GO BACK.
KAORU-SAMA...
IT MUST HAVE BEEN TERRIBLE...
AOI-CHAN...
きゅ

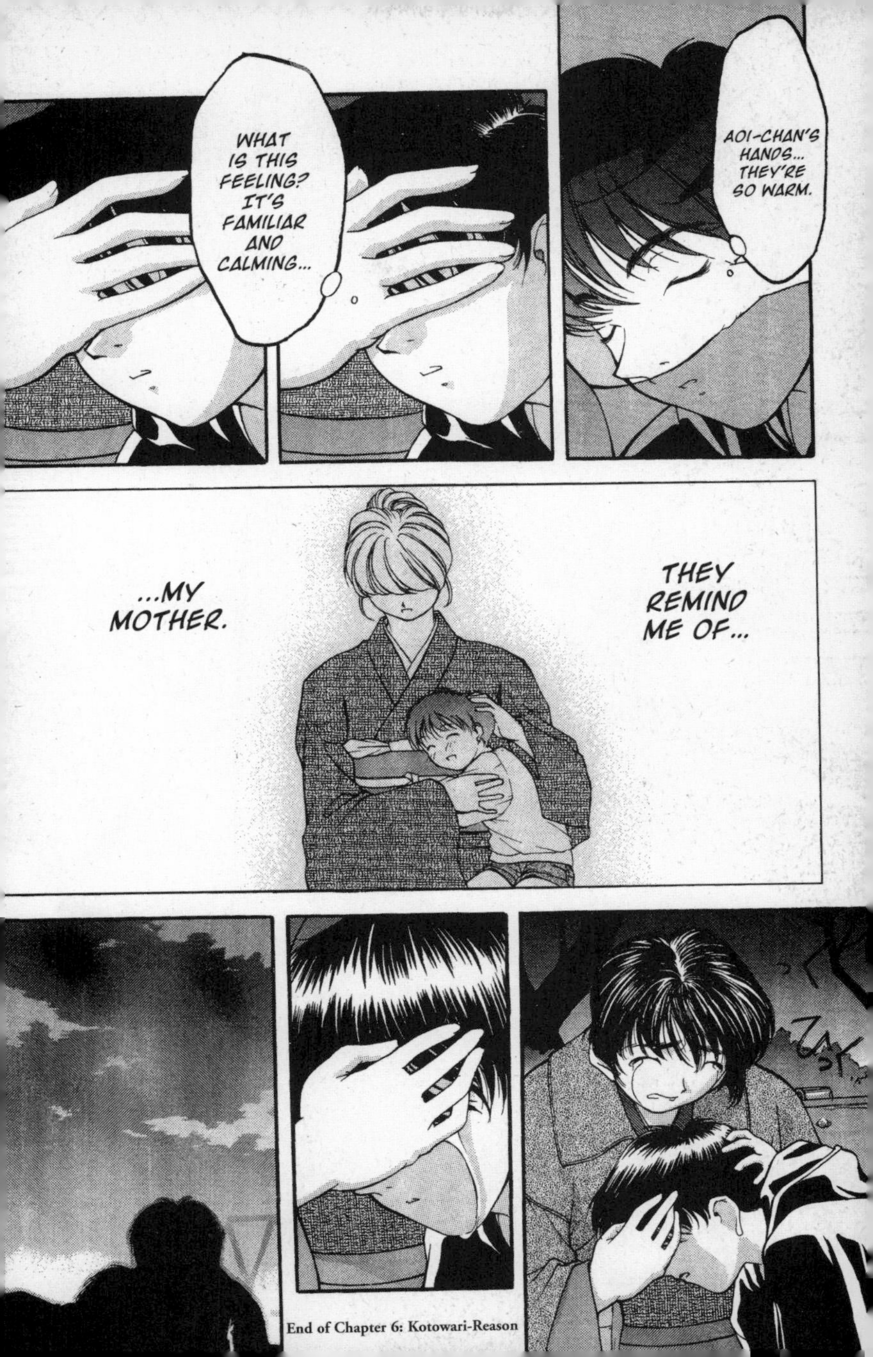
AOI-CHAN'S HANDS... THEY'RE SO WARM.
WHAT IS THIS FEELING? IT'S FAMILIAR AND CALMING...
THEY REMIND ME OF...
...MY MOTHER.
End of Chapter 6: Kotowari-Reason

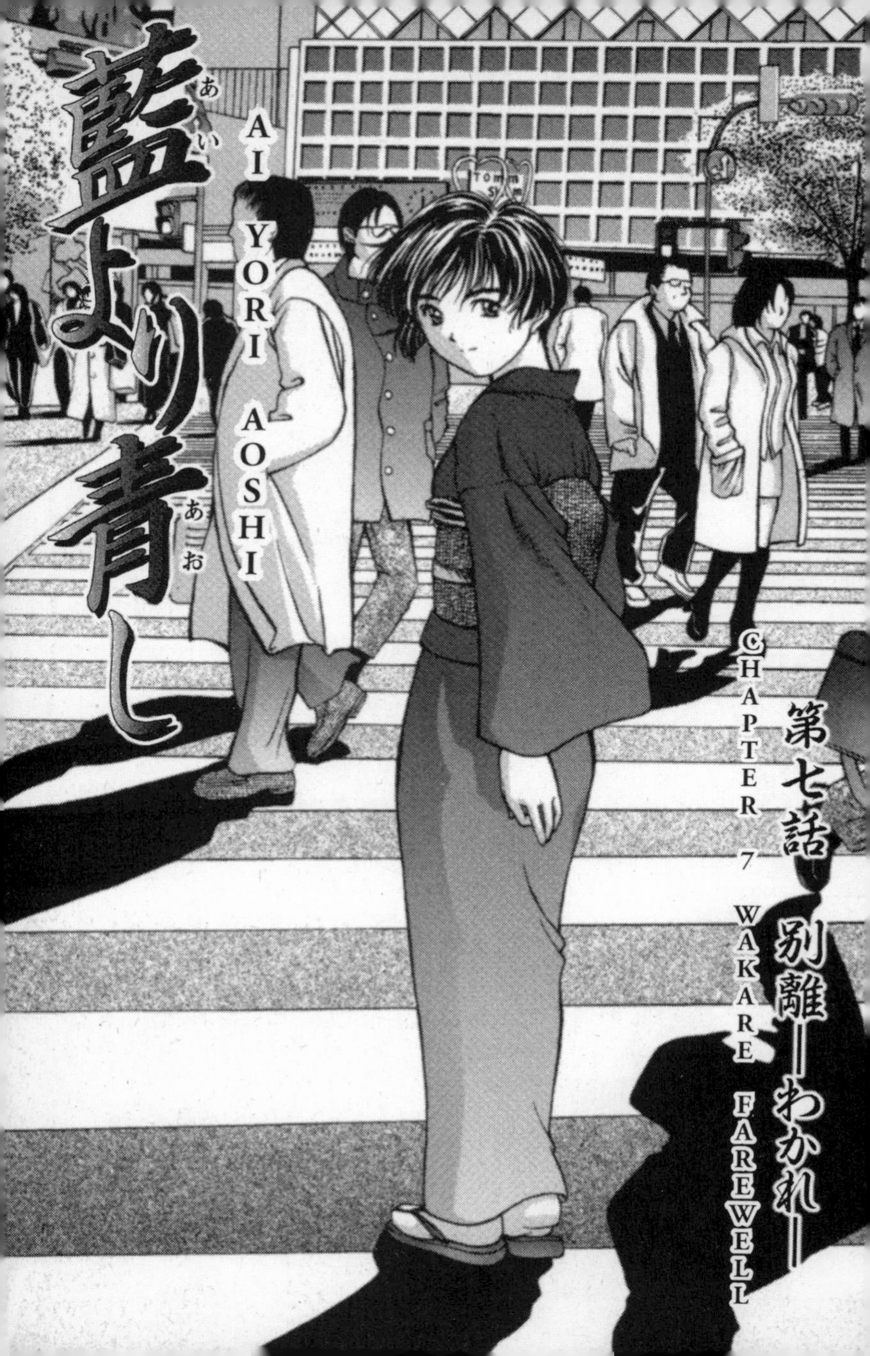
藍より青し
AI YORI AOSHI
第七話 別離—わかれ—
CHAPTER 7 WAKARE FAREWELL

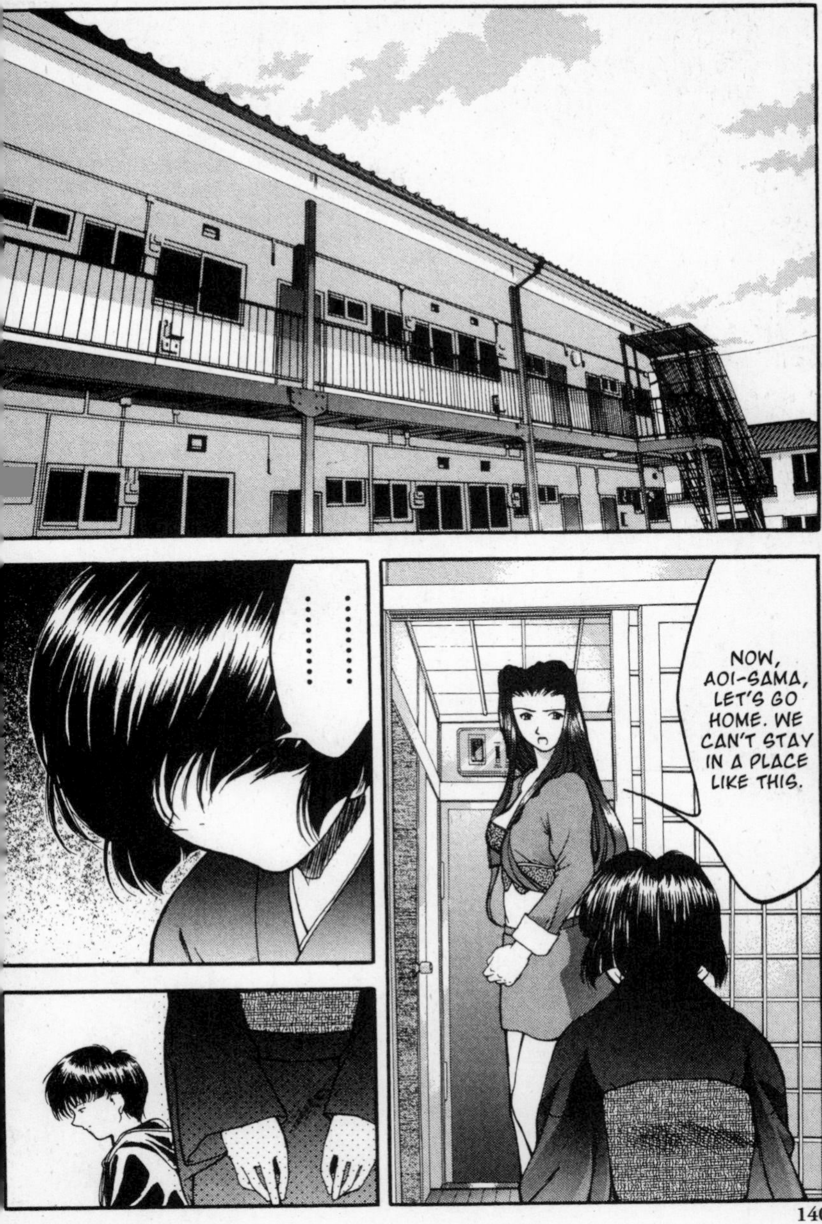
NOW, AOI-SAMA, LET'S GO HOME. WE CAN'T STAY IN A PLACE LIKE THIS.
......

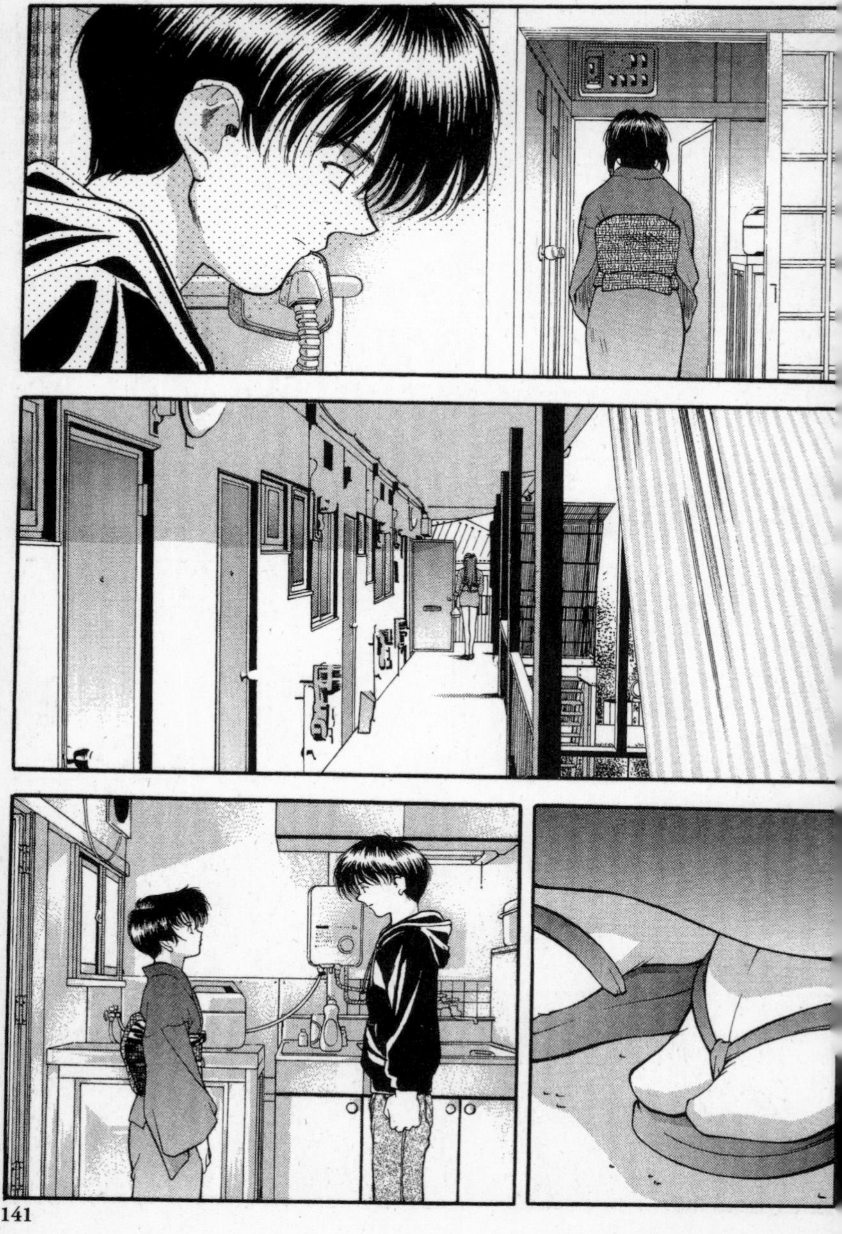

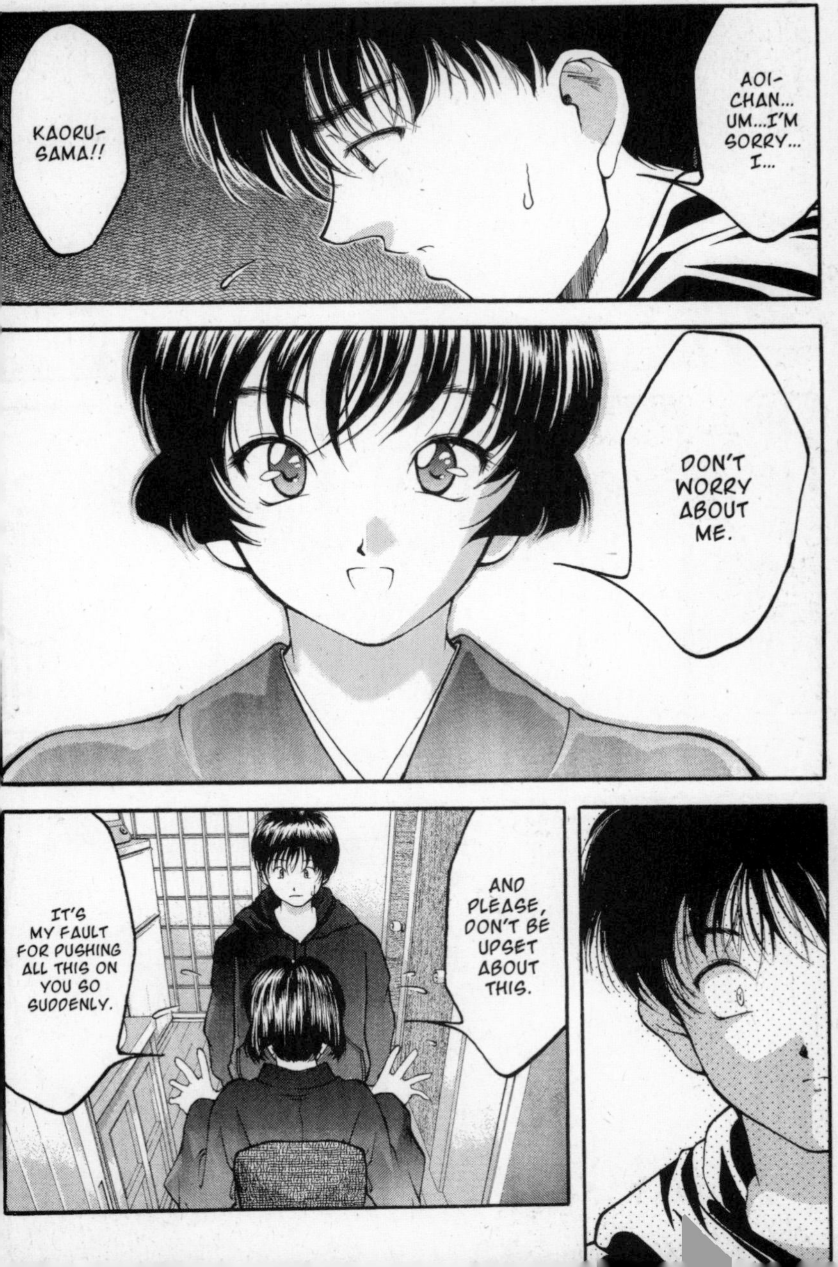
AOI-CHAN... UM...I'M SORRY... I...
KAORU-SAMA!!
DON'T WORRY ABOUT ME.
AND PLEASE, DON'T BE UPSET ABOUT THIS.
IT'S MY FAULT FOR PUSHING ALL THIS ON YOU SO SUDDENLY.

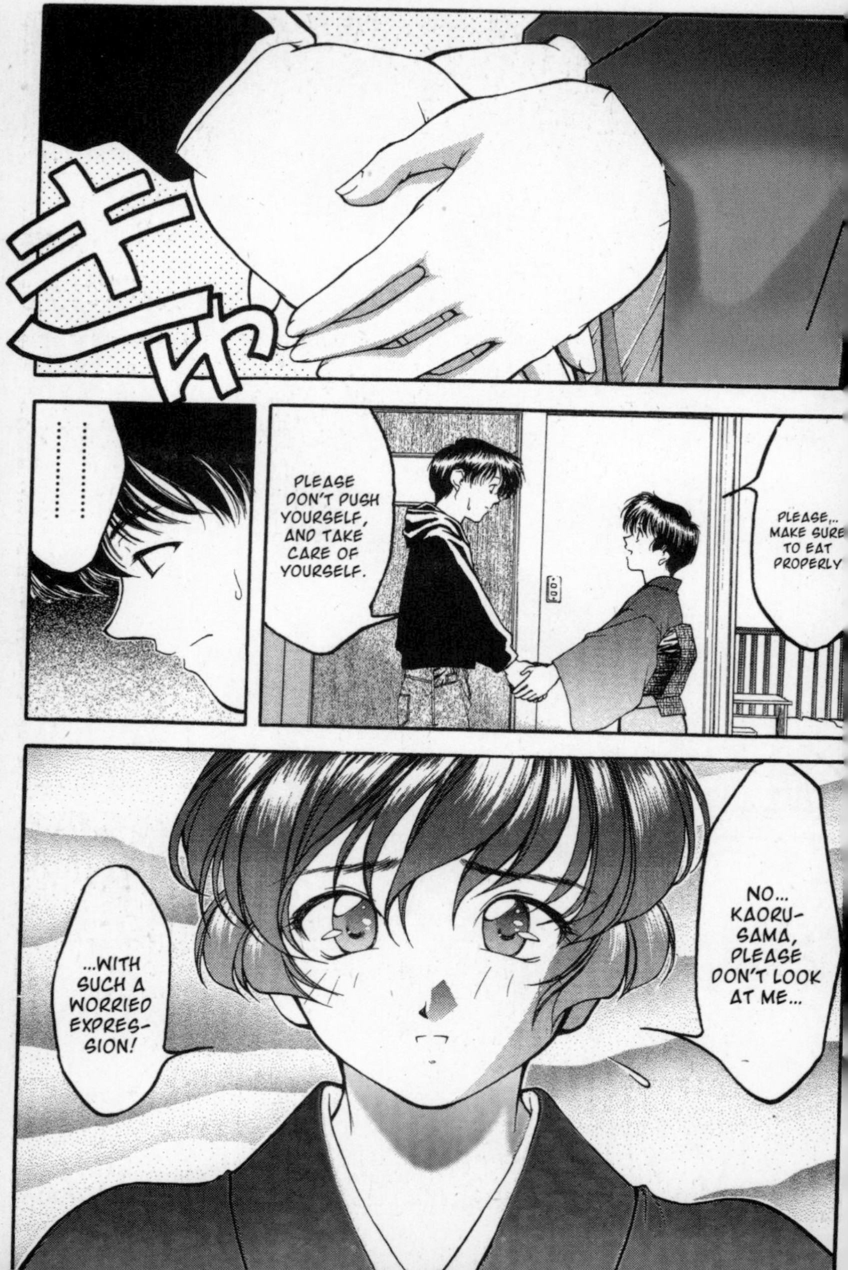
キュ
PLEASE,.. MAKE SURE TO EAT PROPERLY
PLEASE DON'T PUSH YOURSELF, AND TAKE CARE OF YOURSELF.
......
NO... KAORU-SAMA, PLEASE DON'T LOOK AT ME...
...WITH SUCH A WORRIED EXPRESSION!

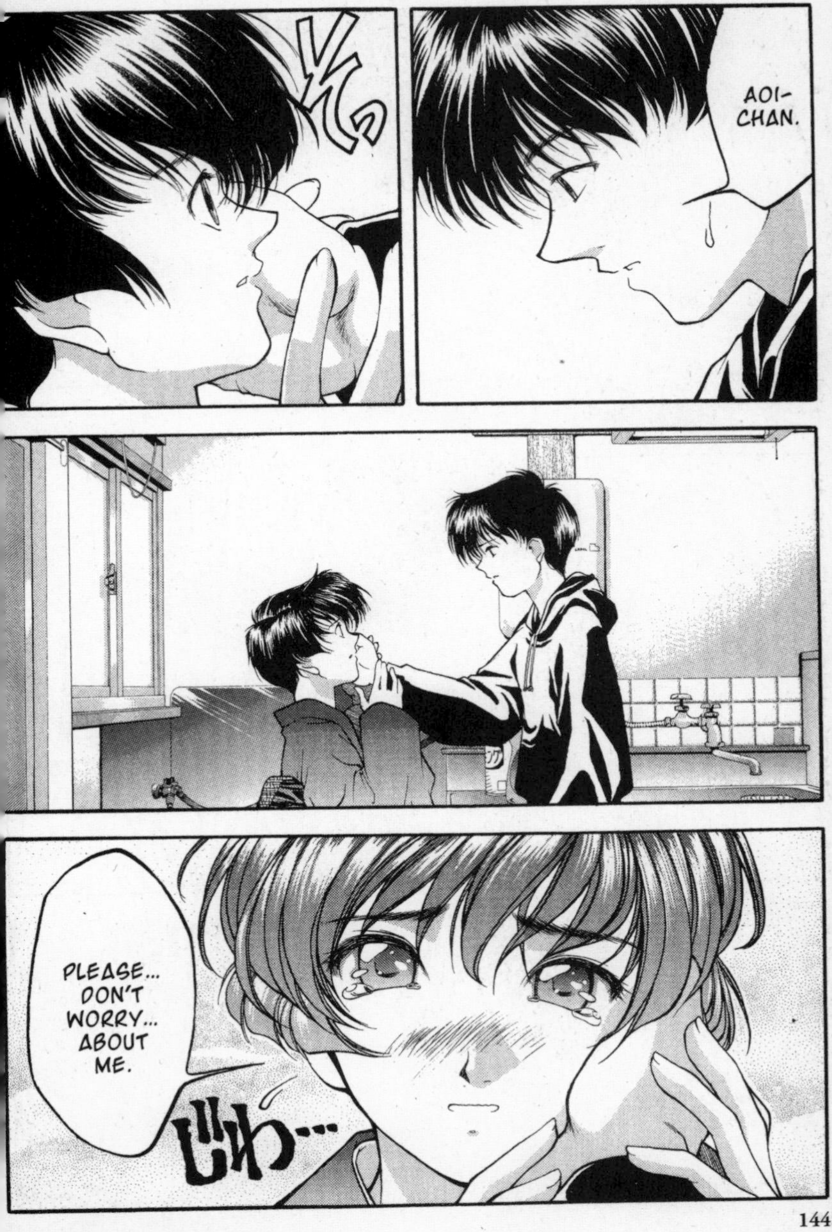
AOI-CHAN.
んっ
PLEASE... DON'T WORRY... ABOUT ME.
じわ…

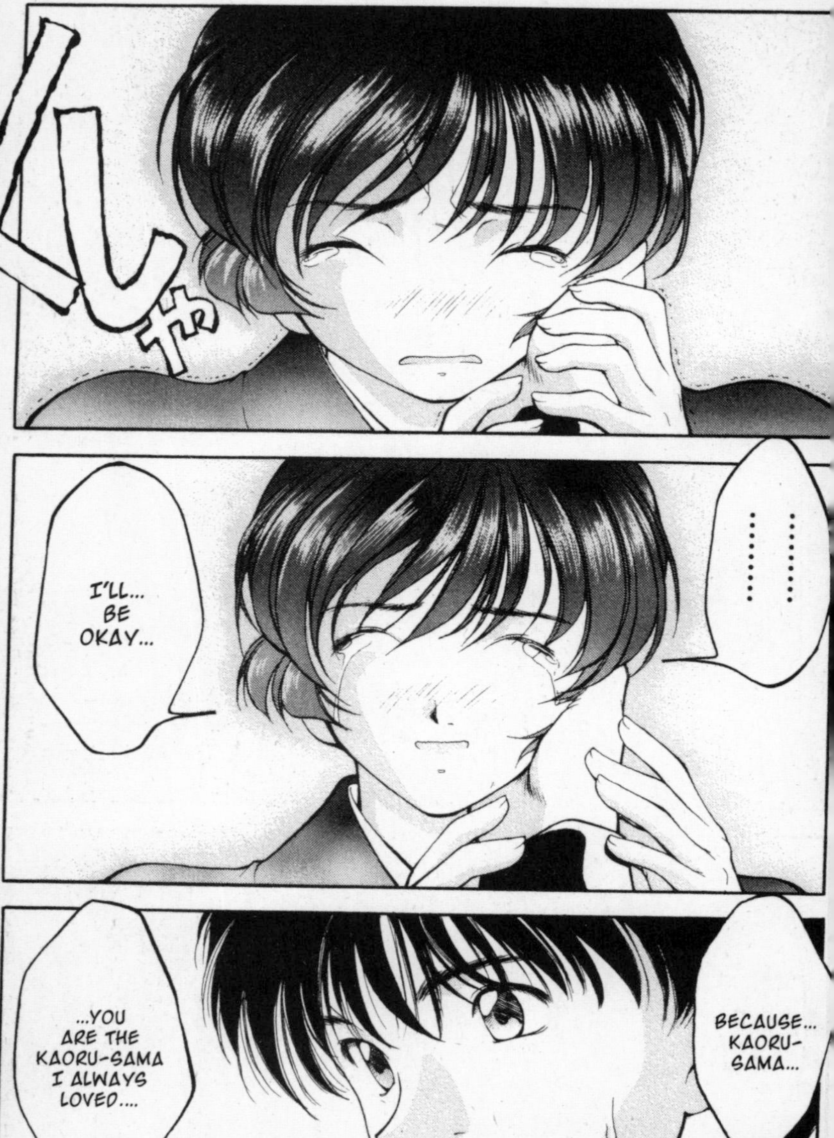
......
I'LL... BE OKAY...
BECAUSE... KAORU-SAMA...
...YOU ARE THE KAORU-SAMA I ALWAYS LOVED....

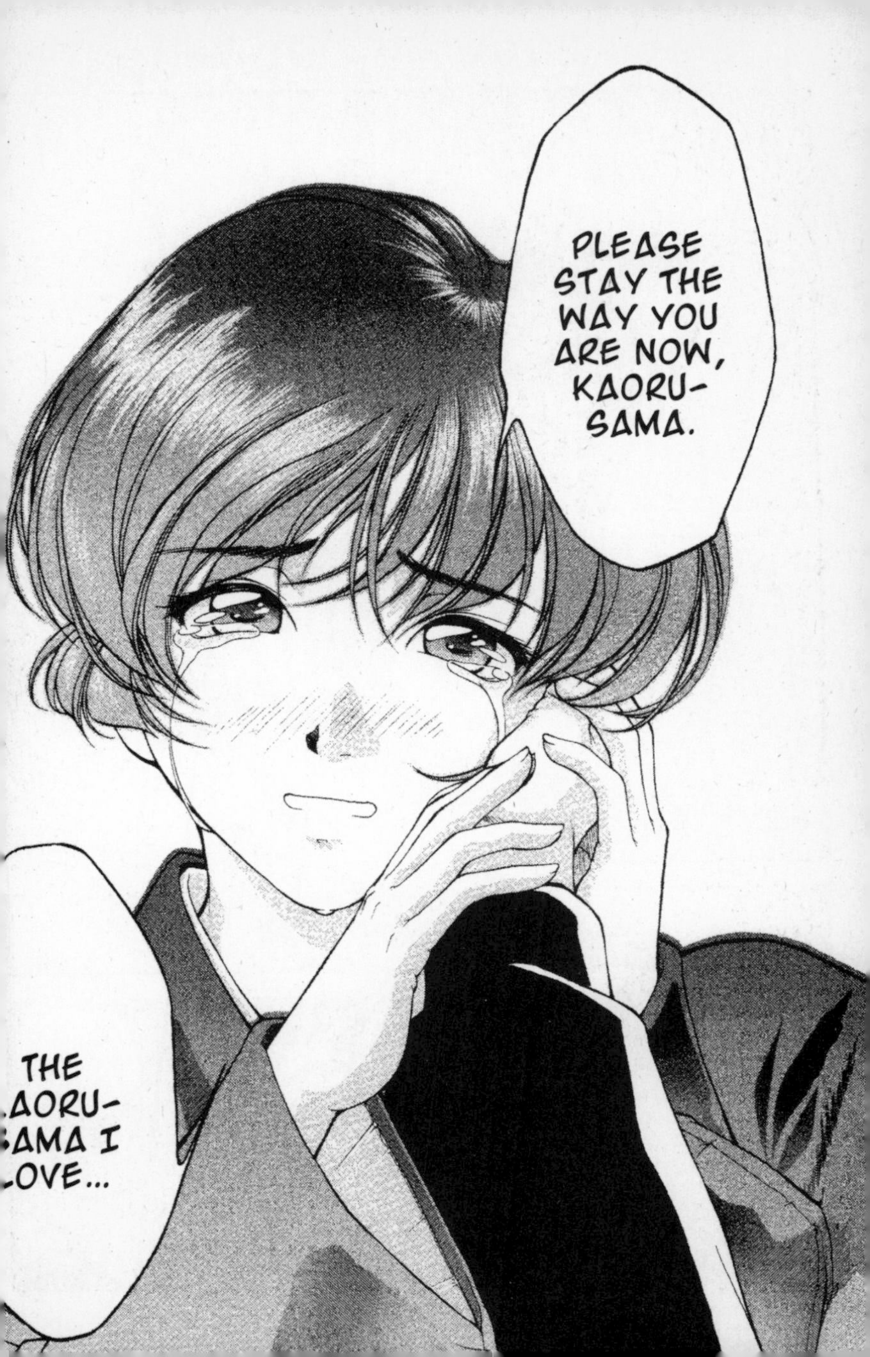
PLEASE STAY THE WAY YOU ARE NOW, KAORU-SAMA.
THE AORU-AMA I OVE...

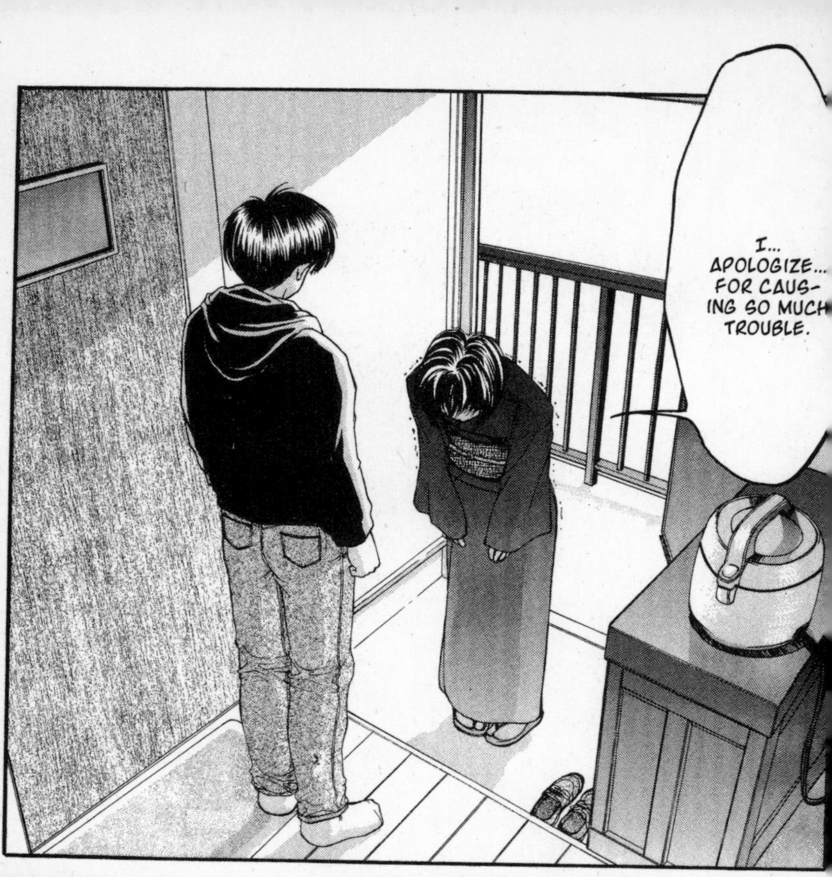
I... APOLOGIZE... FOR CAUSING SO MUCH TROUBLE.
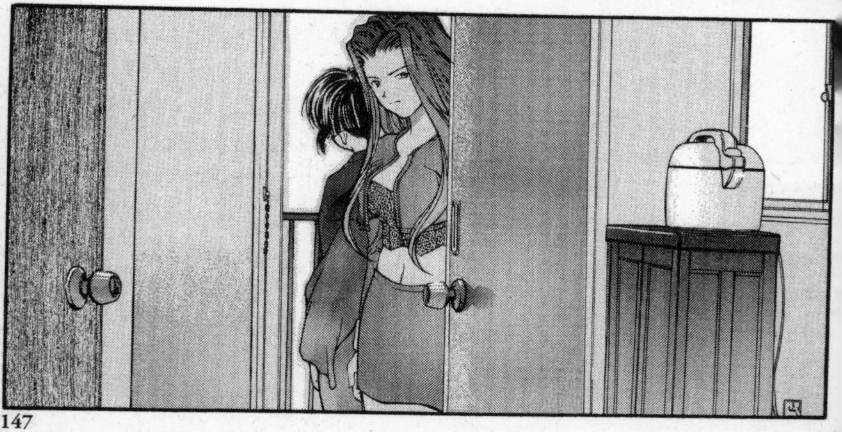

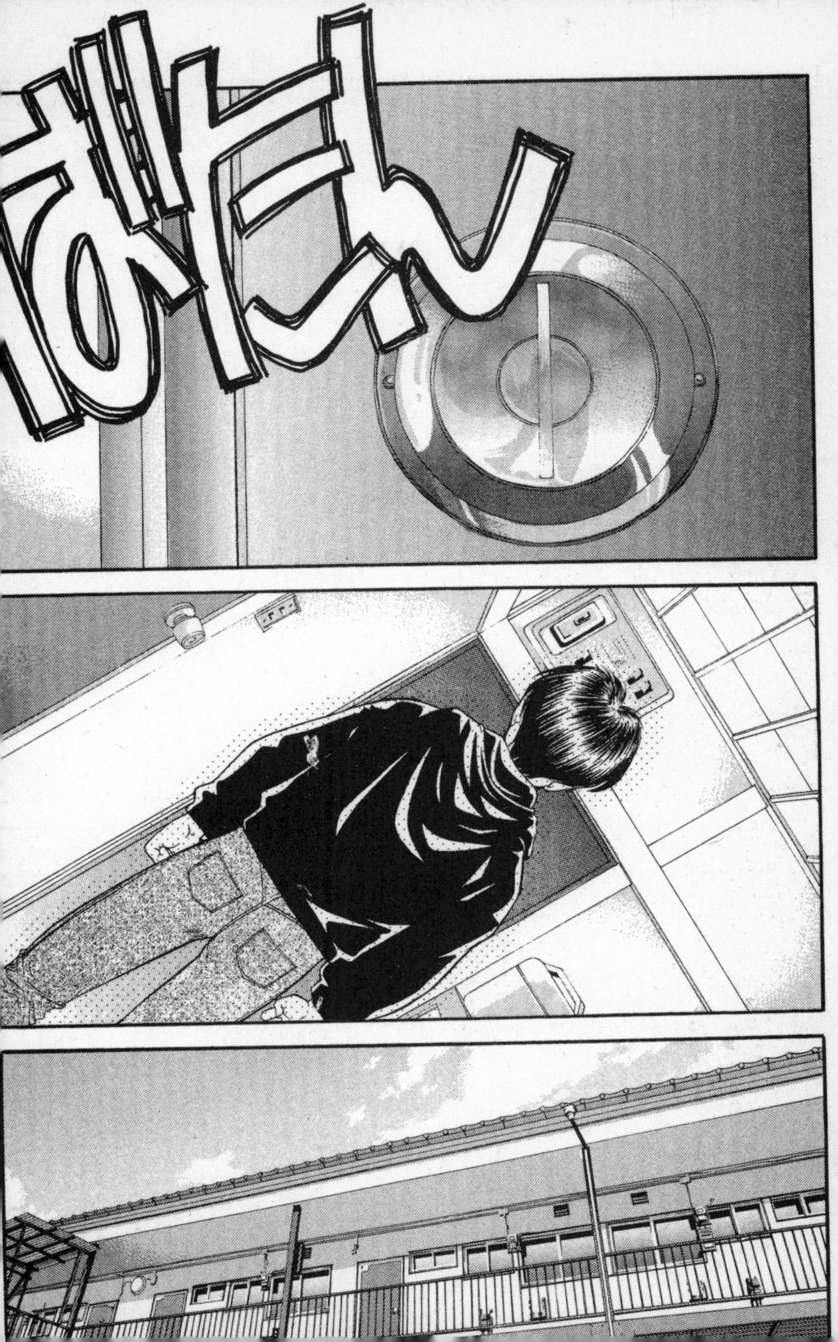
ばたん

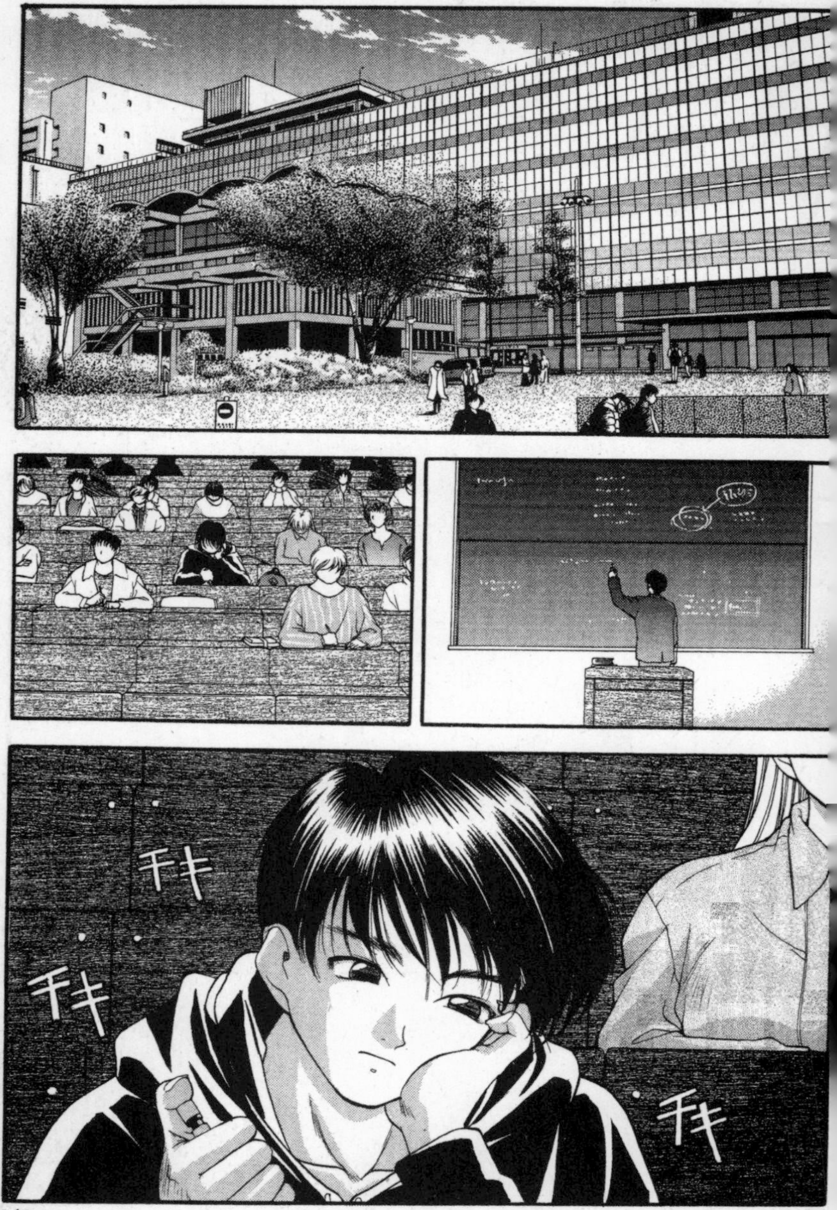
チキ
チキ
チキ

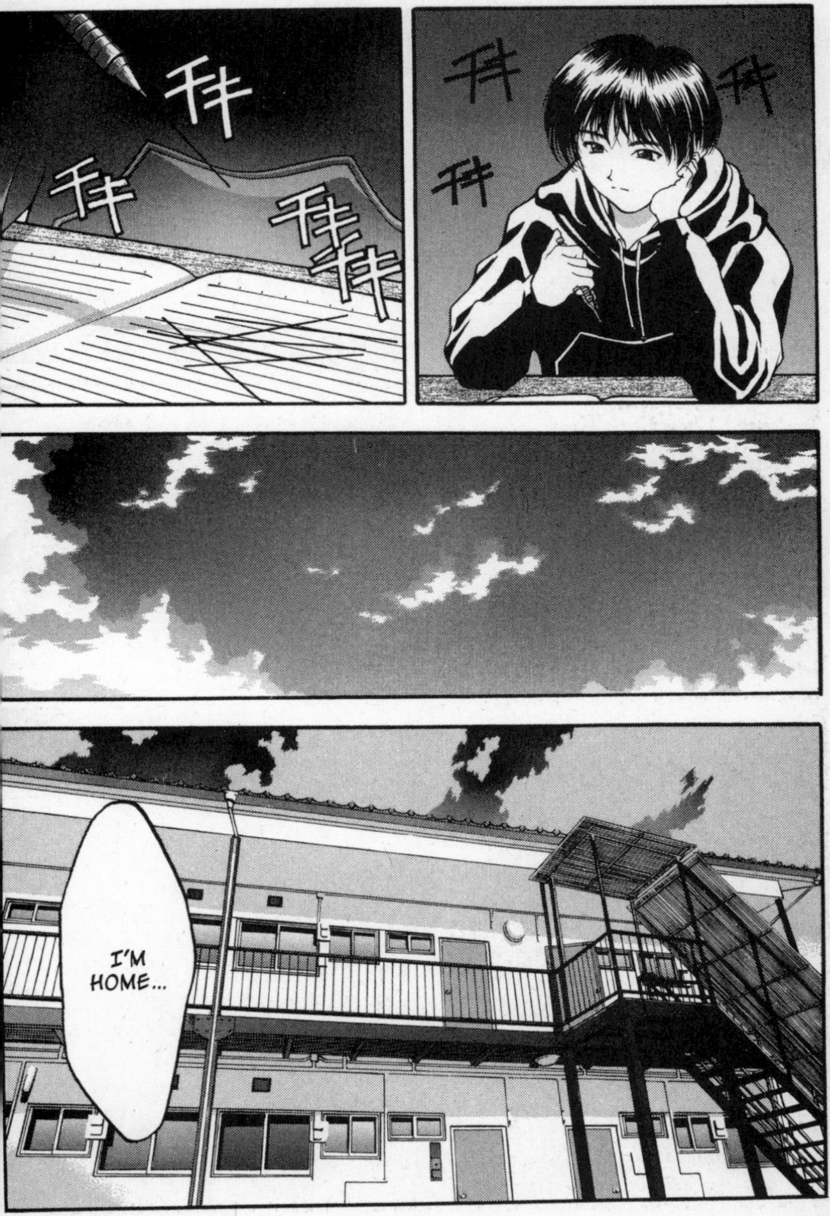
チキ
チキ
チキ
チキ
チキ
チキ
チキ
I'M HOME...

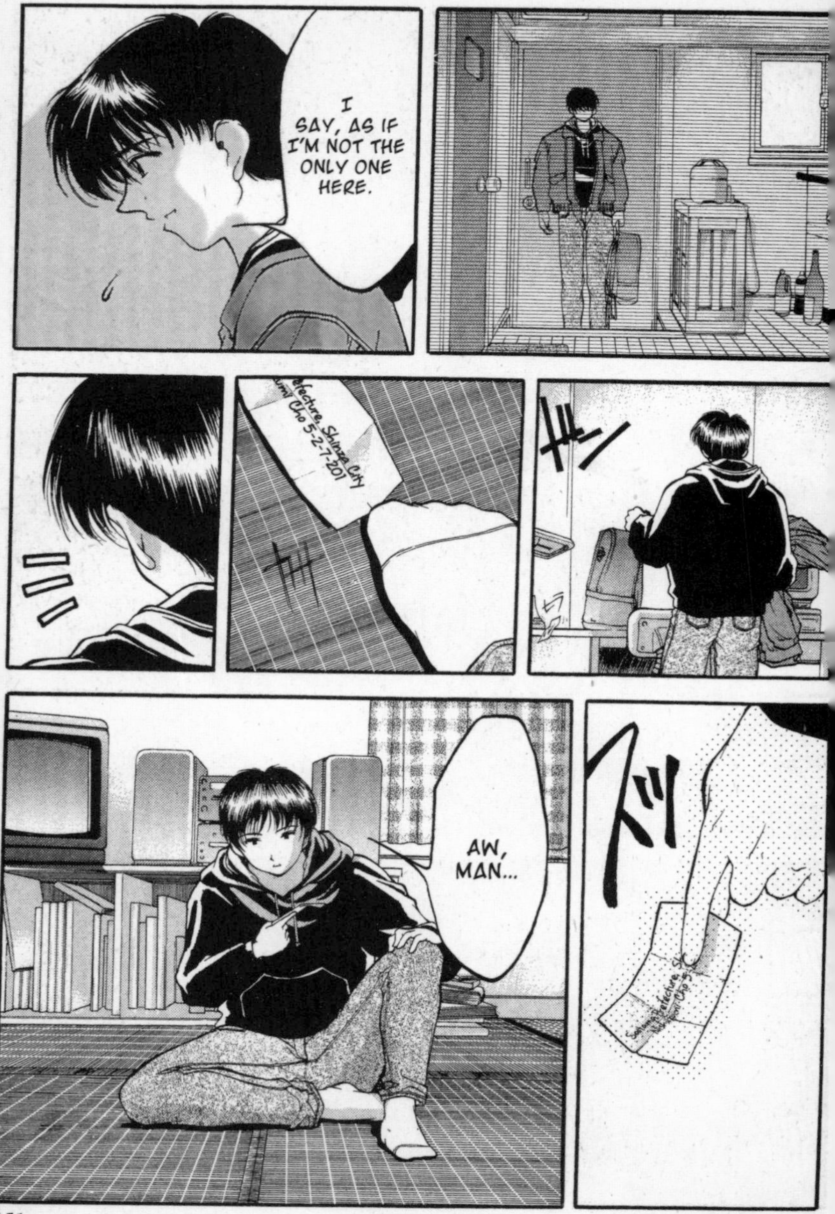
I SAY, AS IF I'M NOT THE ONLY ONE HERE.
efecture, Shinza City
umi Cho 5-2-7-201
AW, MAN...

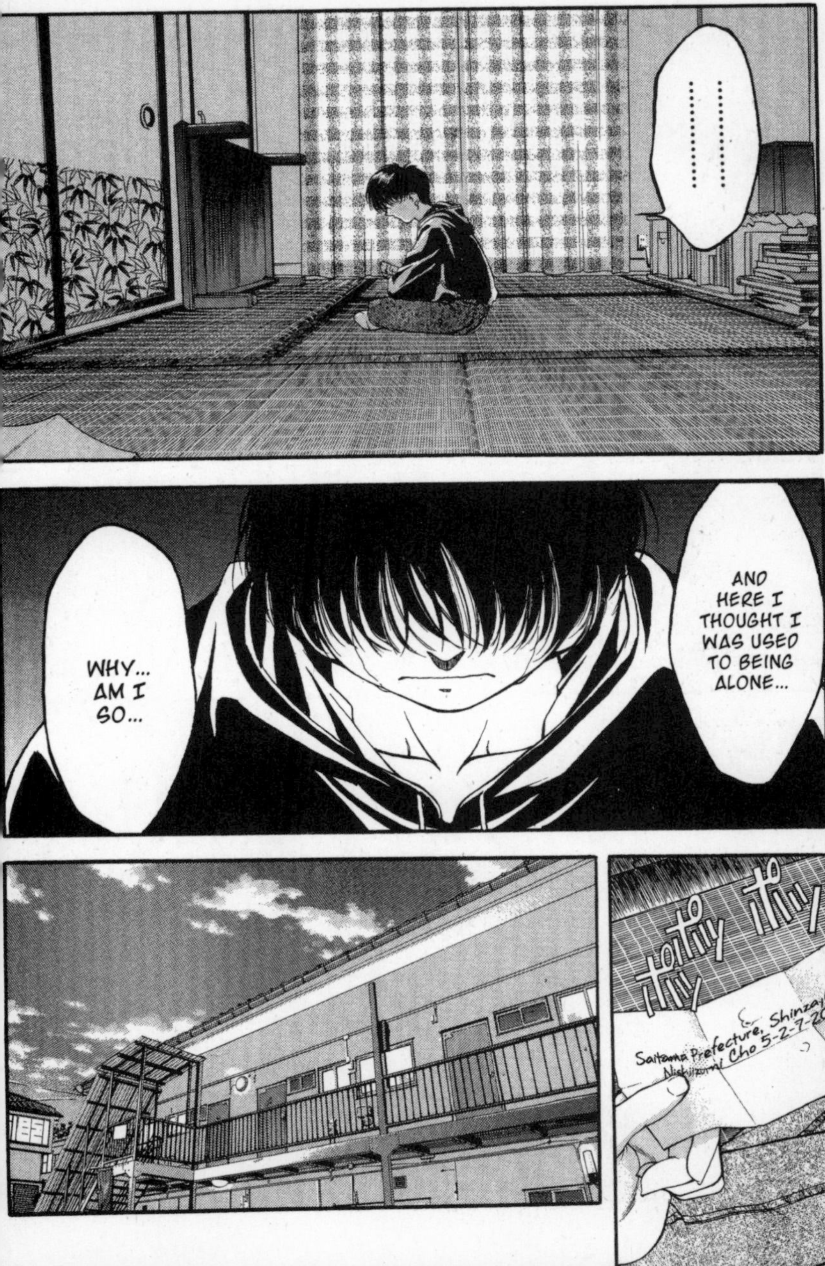
......
AND HERE I THOUGHT I WAS USED TO BEING ALONE...
WHY... AM I SO...
ポツ ポツ ポツ
Saitama Prefecture, Shinza
Nishiizumi Cho 5-2-7-20

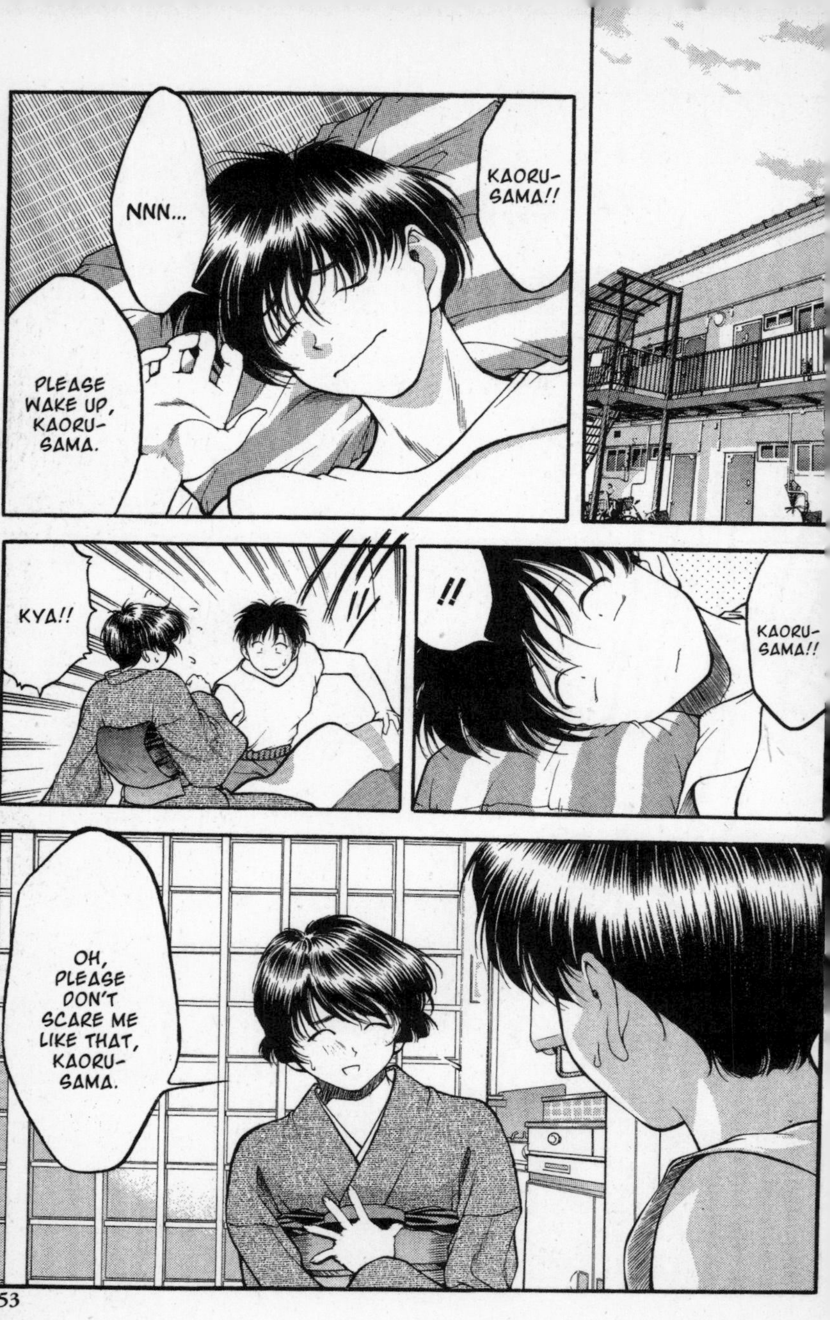
KAORU-SAMA!!
NNN...
PLEASE WAKE UP, KAORU-SAMA.
KAORU-SAMA!!
!!
KYA!!
OH, PLEASE DON'T SCARE ME LIKE THAT, KAORU-SAMA.

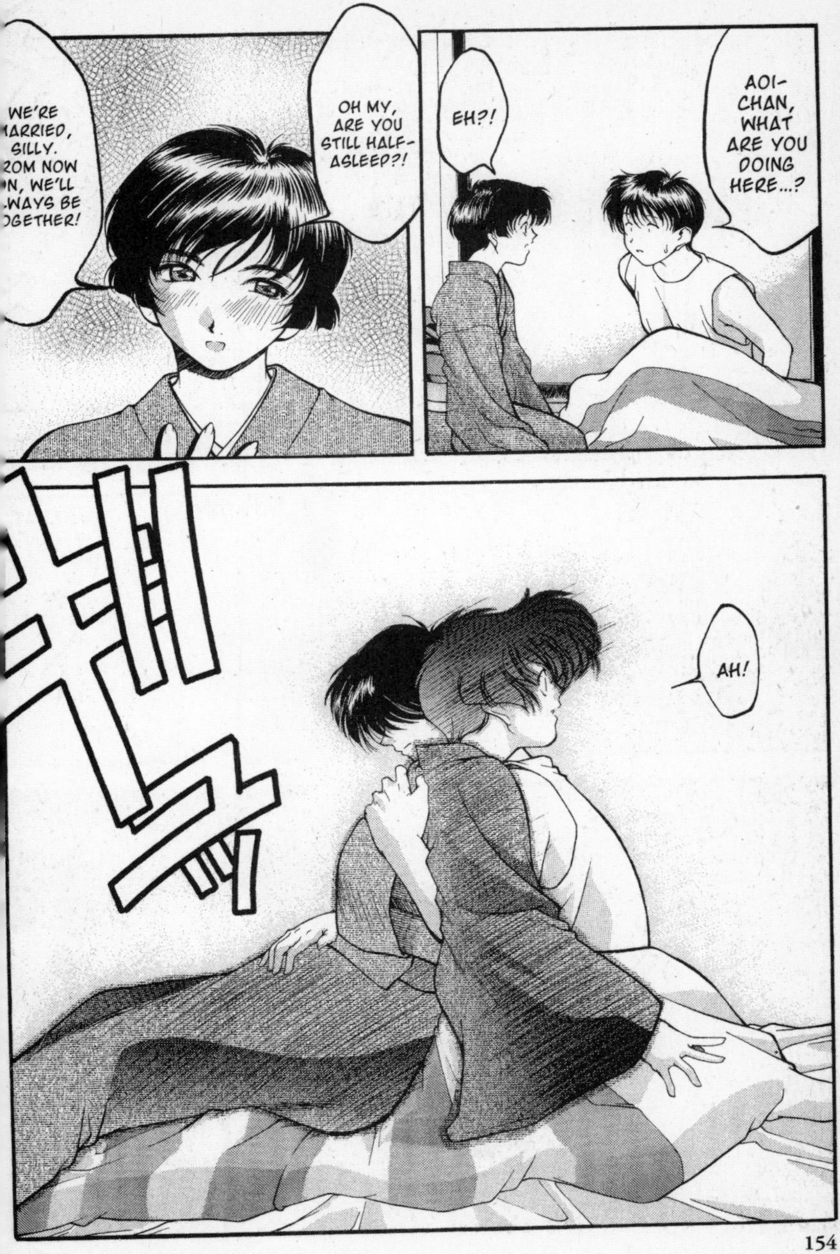
AOI-CHAN, WHAT ARE YOU DOING HERE...?
EH?!
OH MY, ARE YOU STILL HALF-ASLEEP?!
WE'RE ARRIED, SILLY. ROM NOW N, WE'LL -WAYS BE OGETHER!
AH!

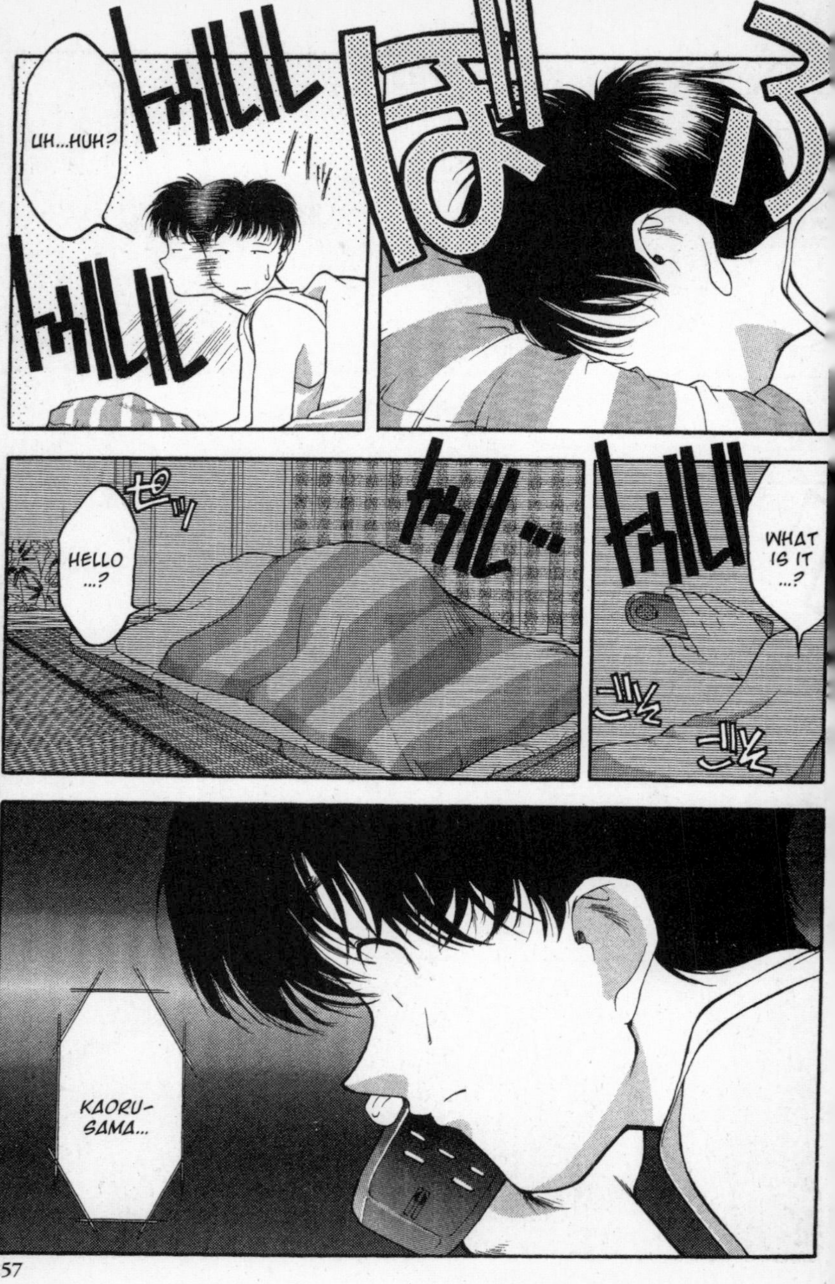
UH...HUH?
WHAT IS IT ...?
HELLO ...?
KAORU-SAMA...

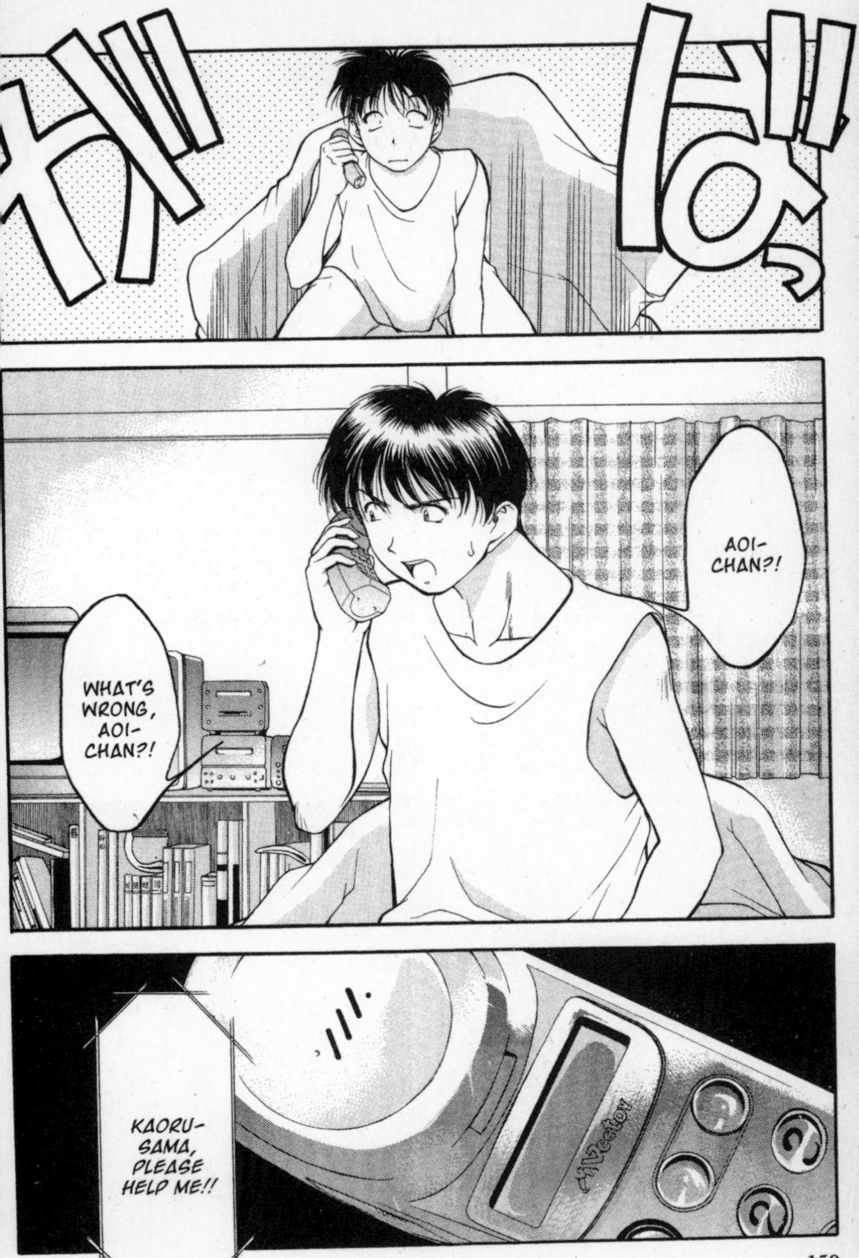
ばっ
ガ
AOI-CHAN?!
WHAT'S WRONG, AOI-CHAN?!
KAORU-SAMA, PLEASE HELP ME!!

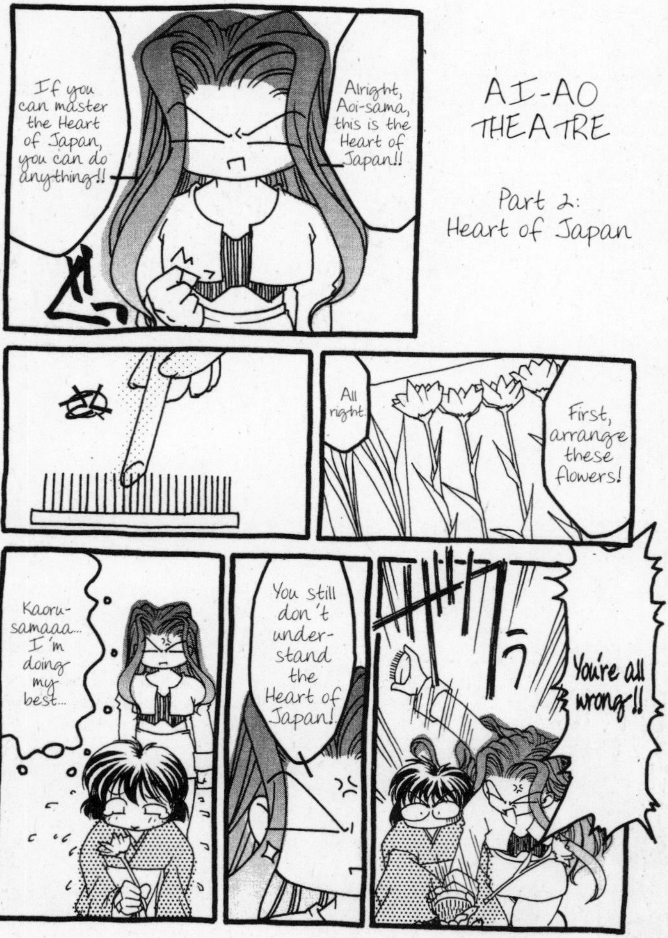
AI-AO THEATRE
Part 2: Heart of Japan
Alright, Aoi-sama, this is the Heart of Japan!!
If you can master the Heart of Japan, you can do anything!!
First, arrange these flowers!
All right.
You're all wrong!!
You still don't understand the Heart of Japan!
Kaoru-samaaa... I'm doing my best...

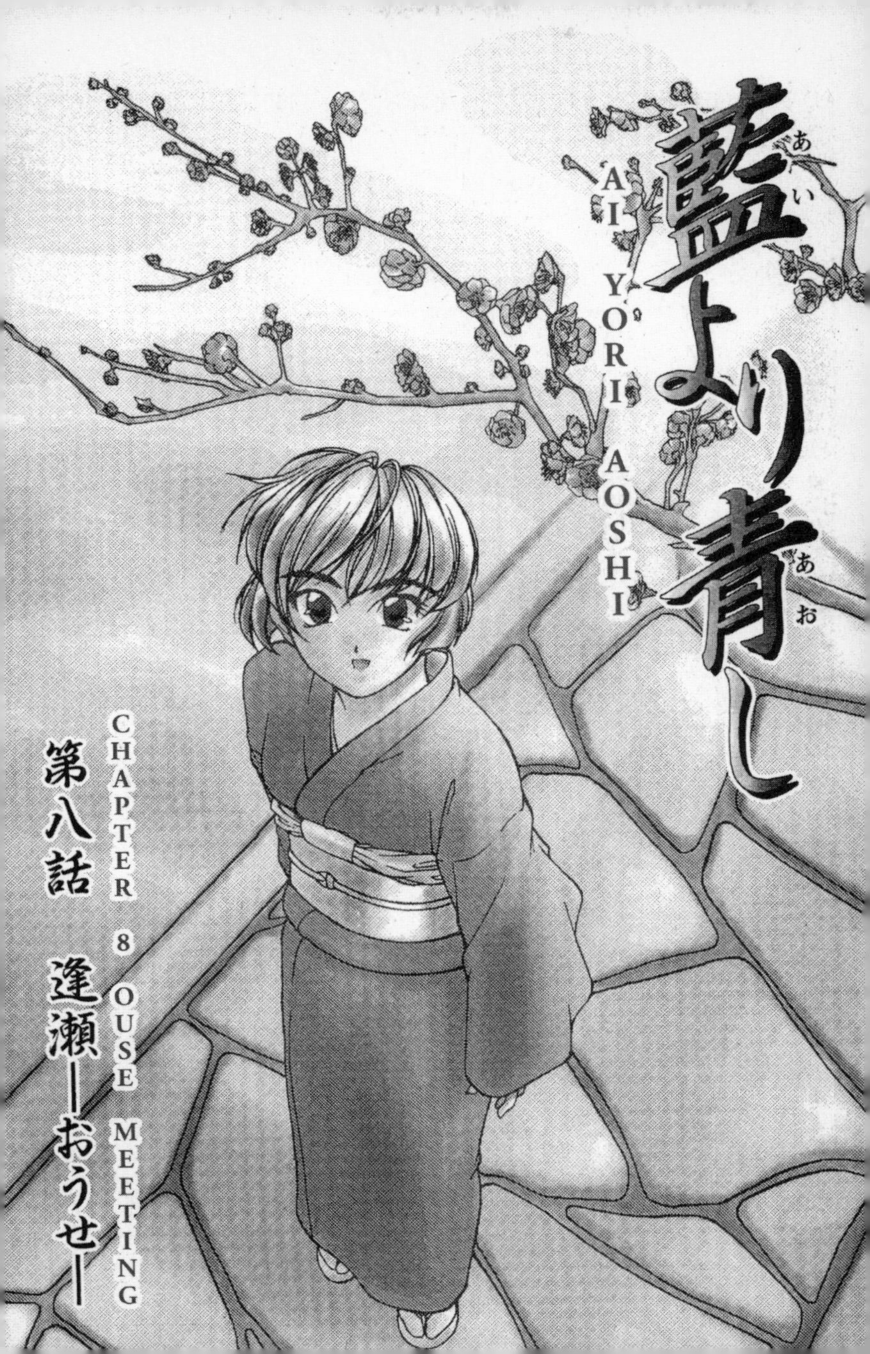
藍より青し
AI YORI AOSHI
CHAPTER 8 OUSE MEETING
第八話 逢瀬—おうせ—

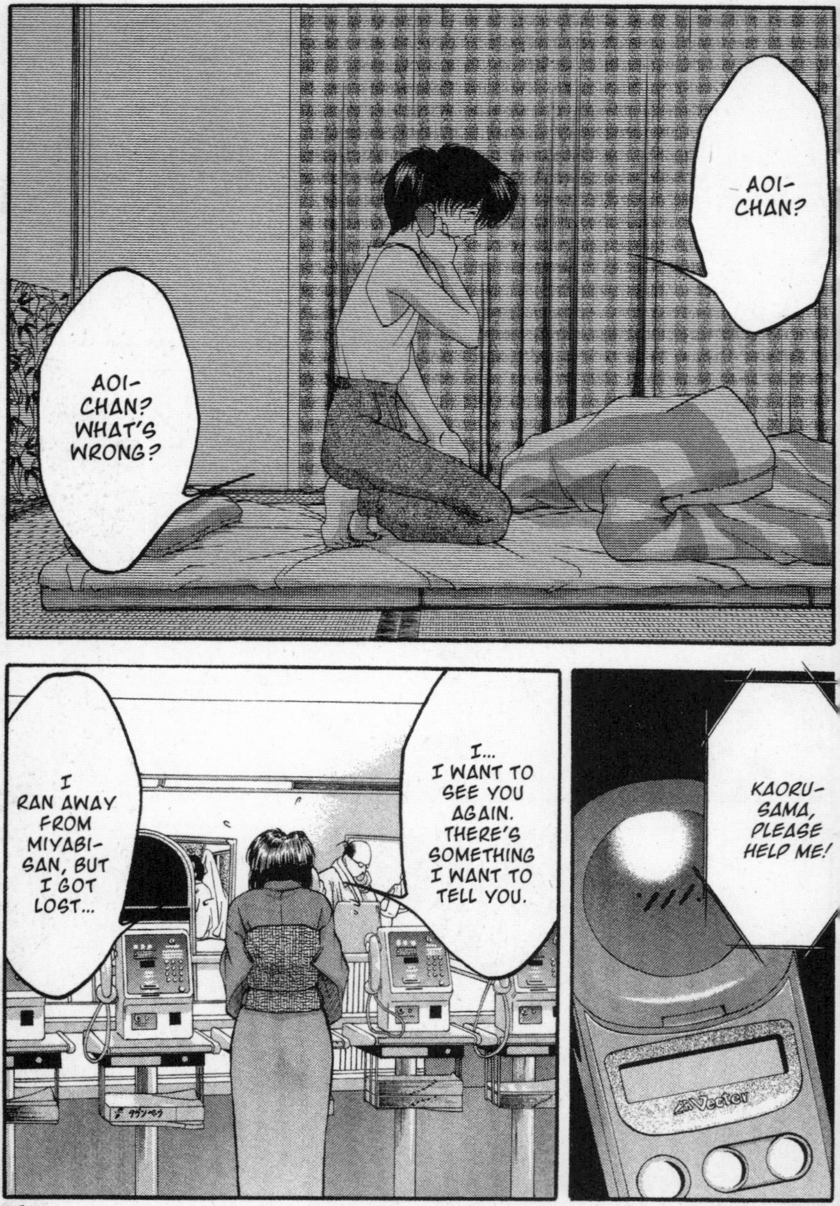
AOI-CHAN?
AOI-CHAN? WHAT'S WRONG?
KAORU-SAMA, PLEASE HELP ME!
I... I WANT TO SEE YOU AGAIN. THERE'S SOMETHING I WANT TO TELL YOU.
I RAN AWAY FROM MIYABI-SAN, BUT I GOT LOST...

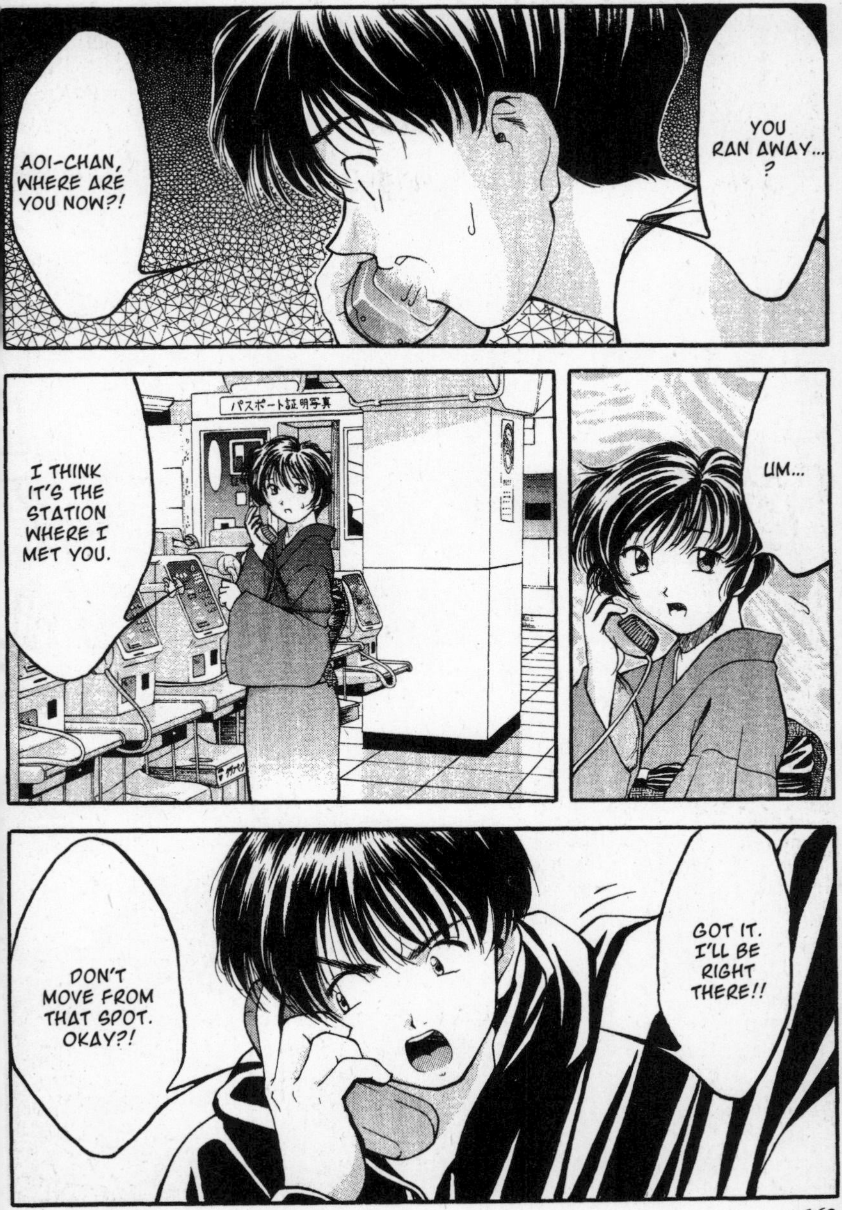
YOU RAN AWAY... ?
AOI-CHAN, WHERE ARE YOU NOW?!
UM...
I THINK IT'S THE STATION WHERE I MET YOU.
パスポート証明写真
GOT IT. I'LL BE RIGHT THERE!!
DON'T MOVE FROM THAT SPOT. OKAY?!

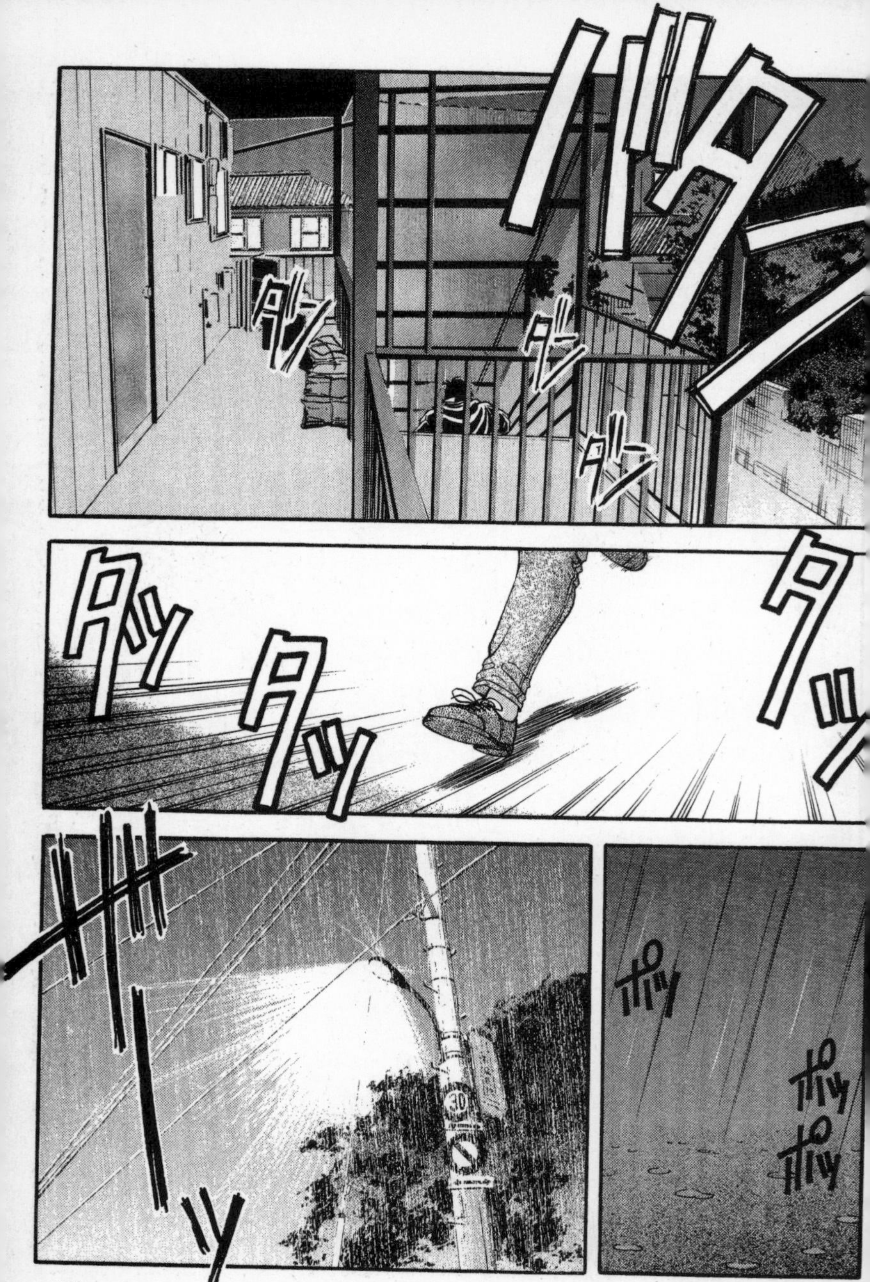
バタン
タッ
タッ
タッ
ポッ
ポッ
ポッ
ザーーッ

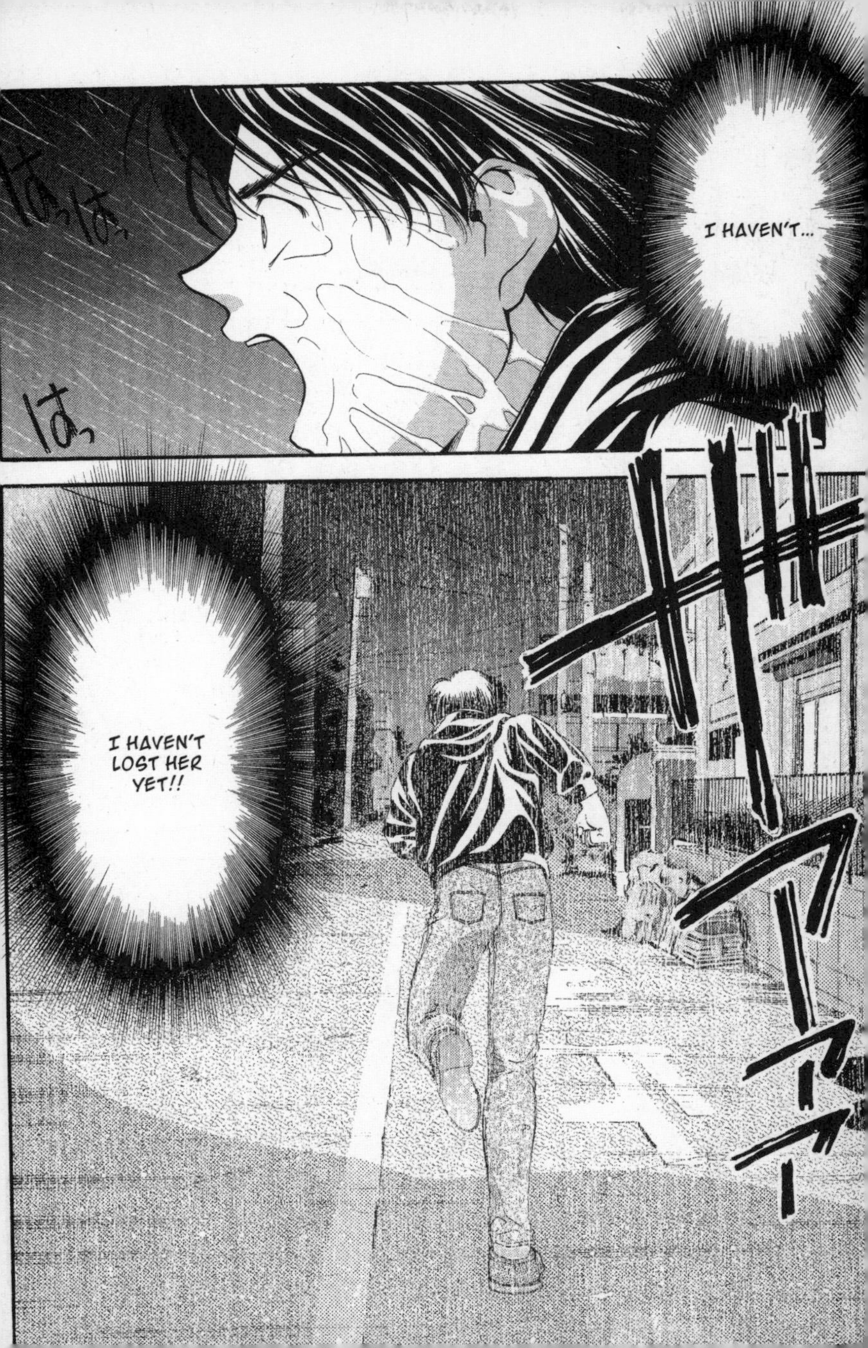
I HAVEN'T...
はっはっ
はっ
I HAVEN'T LOST HER YET!!

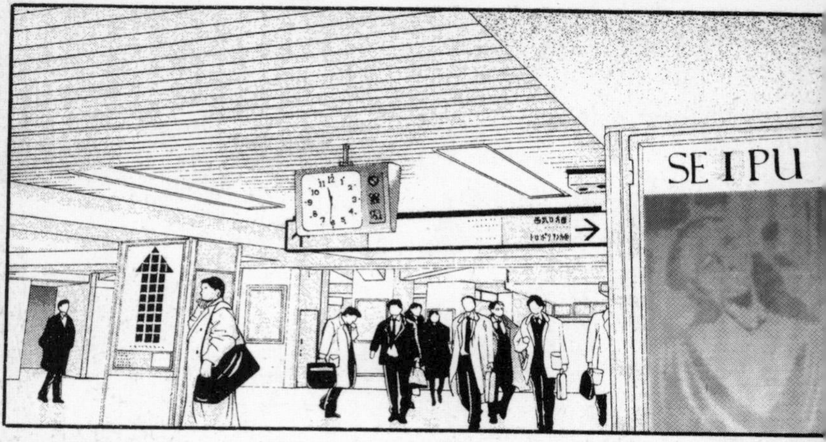
SE I PU
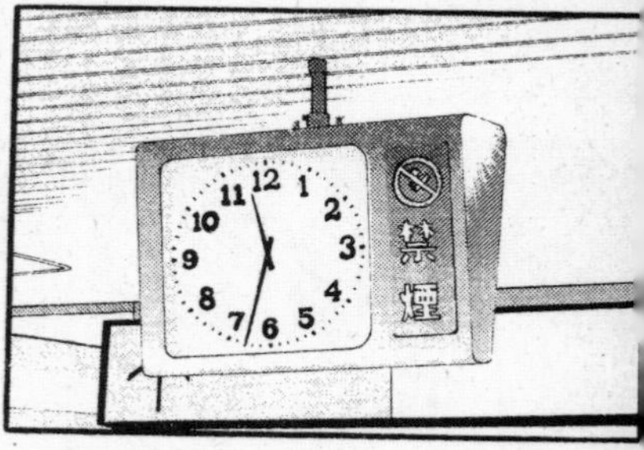
禁煙
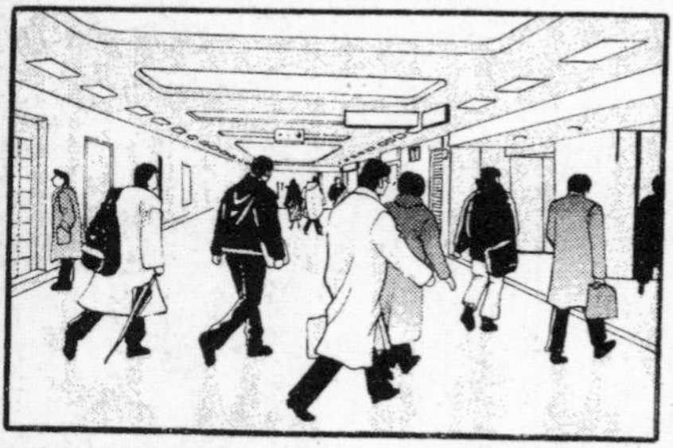
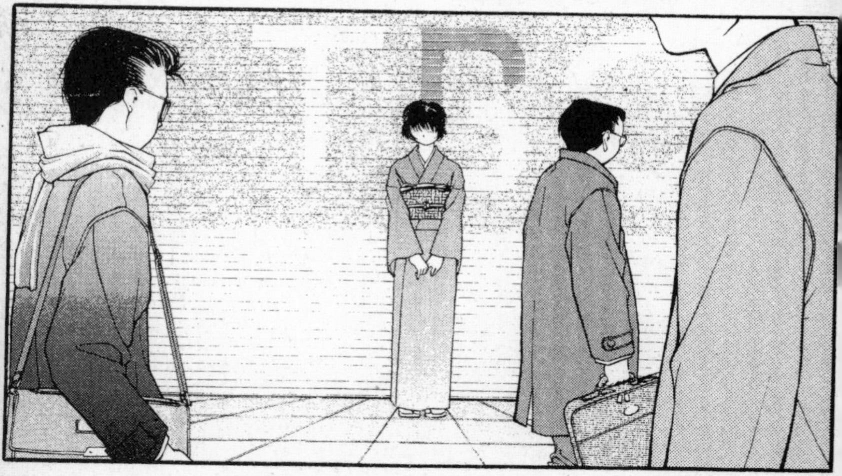

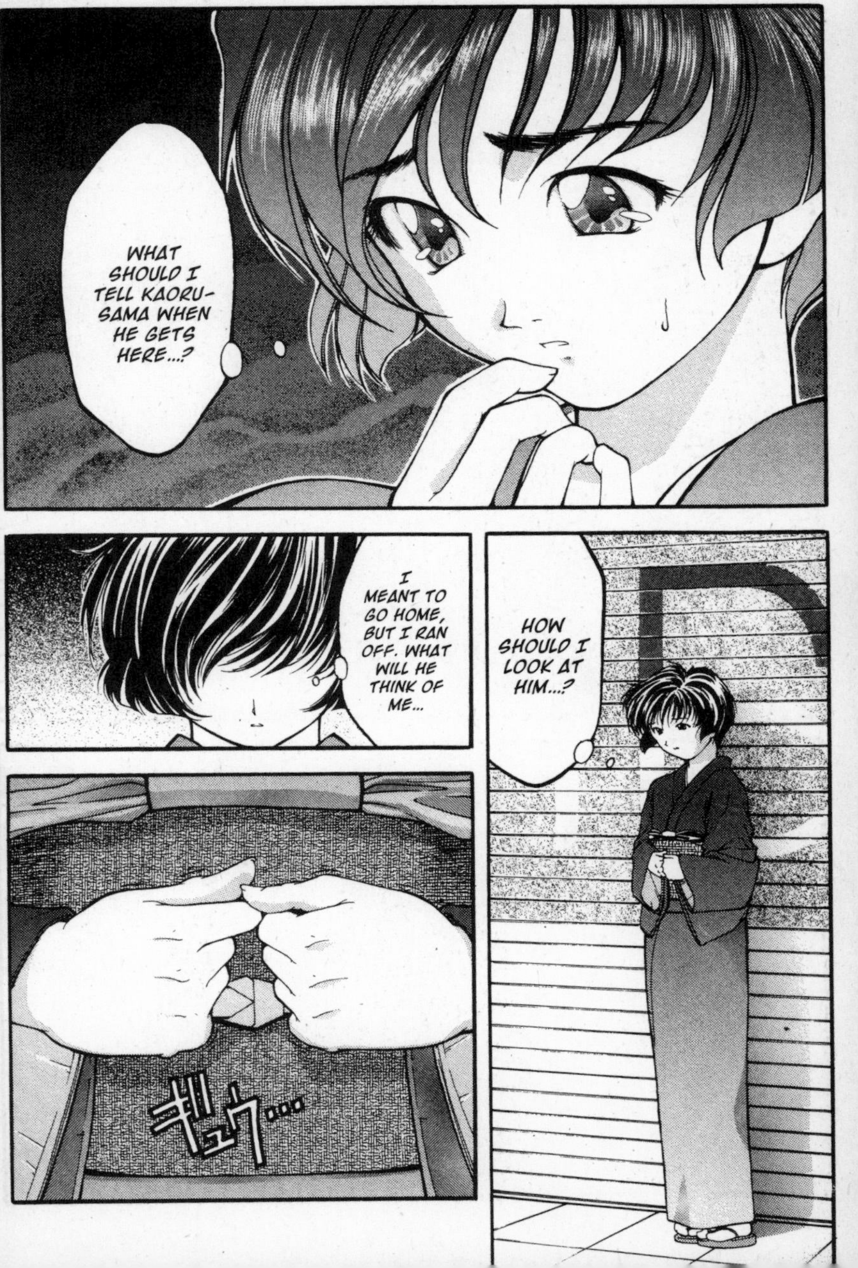
WHAT SHOULD I TELL KAORU-SAMA WHEN HE GETS HERE...?
HOW SHOULD I LOOK AT HIM...?
I MEANT TO GO HOME, BUT I RAN OFF. WHAT WILL HE THINK OF ME...
ギュウ...

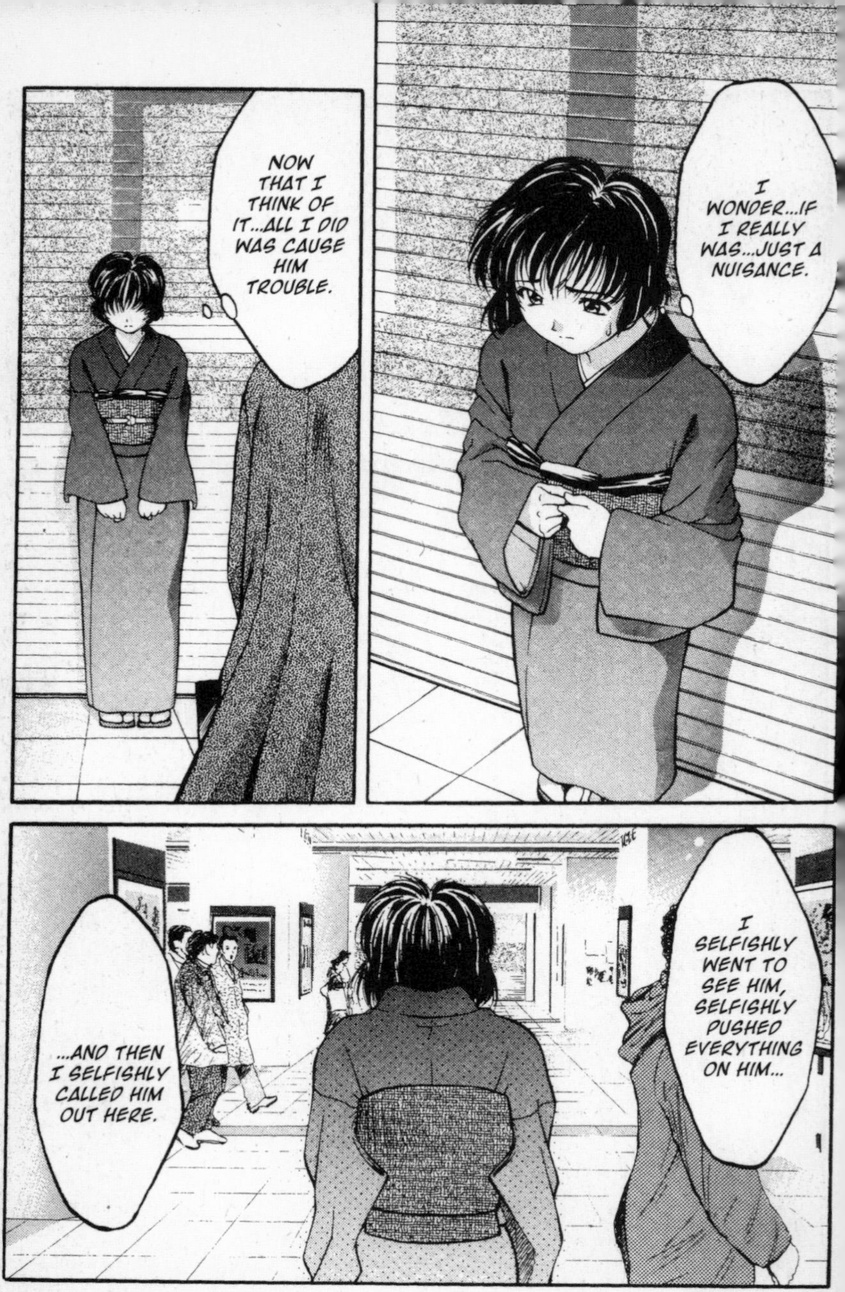
I WONDER...IF I REALLY WAS...JUST A NUISANCE.
NOW THAT I THINK OF IT...ALL I DID WAS CAUSE HIM TROUBLE.
I SELFISHLY WENT TO SEE HIM, SELFISHLY PUSHED EVERYTHING ON HIM...
...AND THEN I SELFISHLY CALLED HIM OUT HERE.

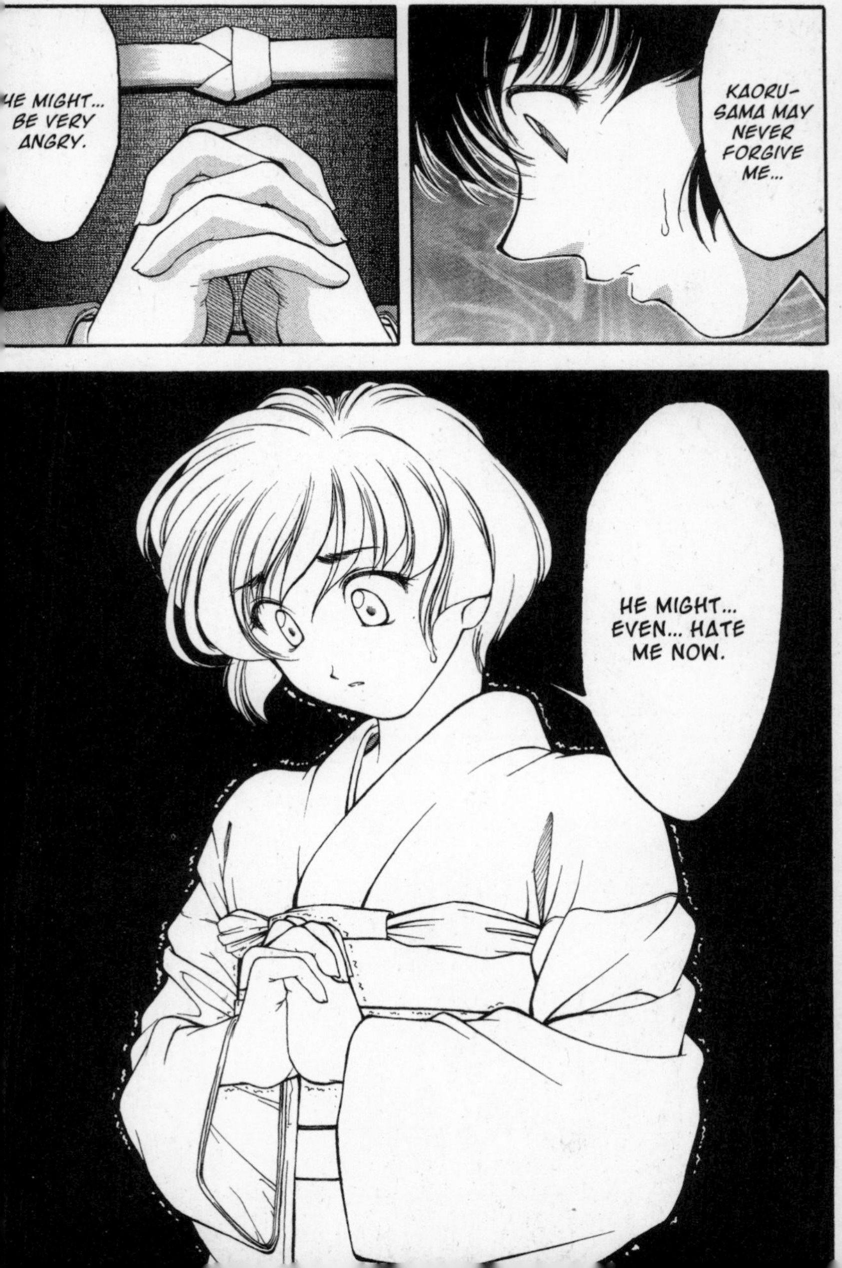
KAORU-SAMA MAY NEVER FORGIVE ME...
HE MIGHT... BE VERY ANGRY.
HE MIGHT... EVEN... HATE ME NOW.

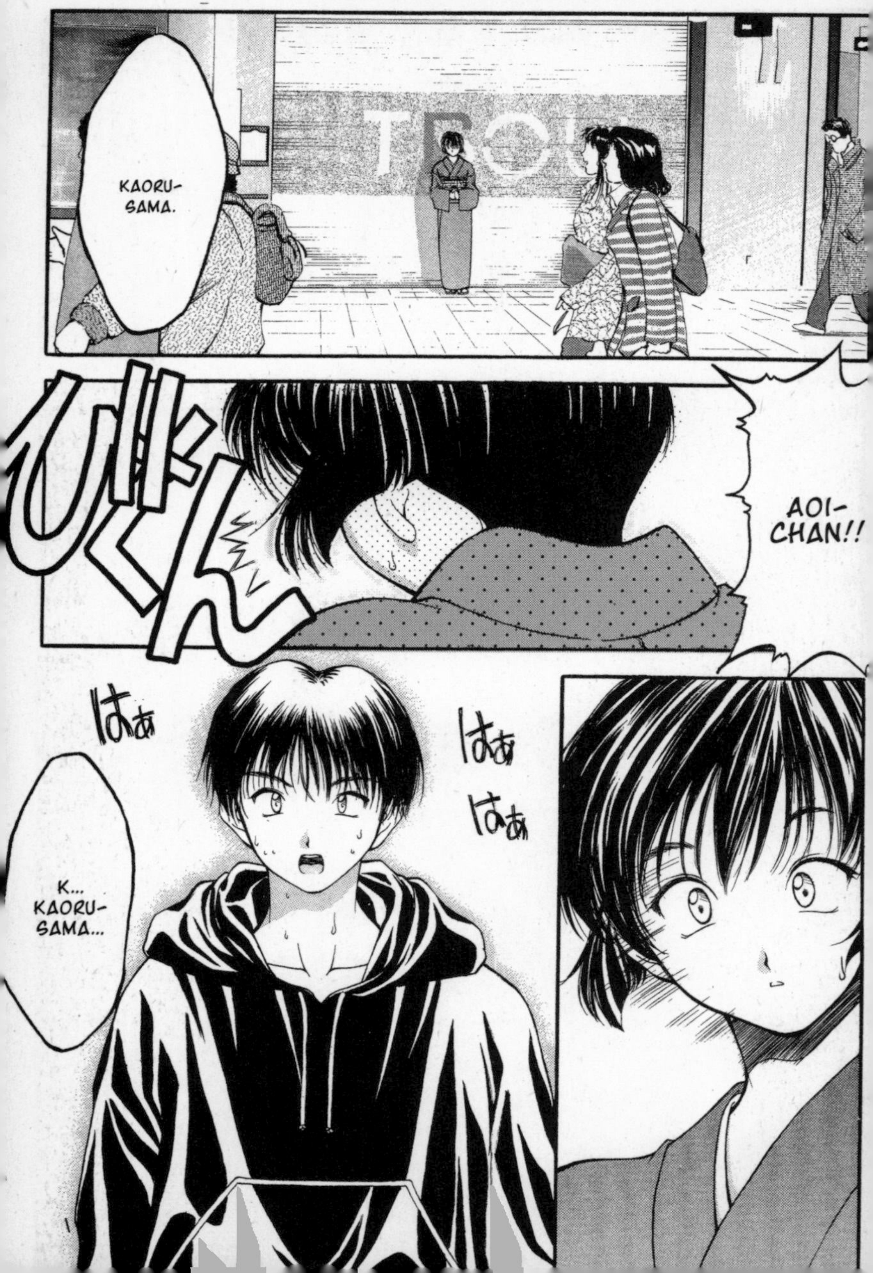
KAORU-SAMA.
AOI-CHAN!!
びくん
はぁ
はぁ
はぁ
K... KAORU-SAMA...

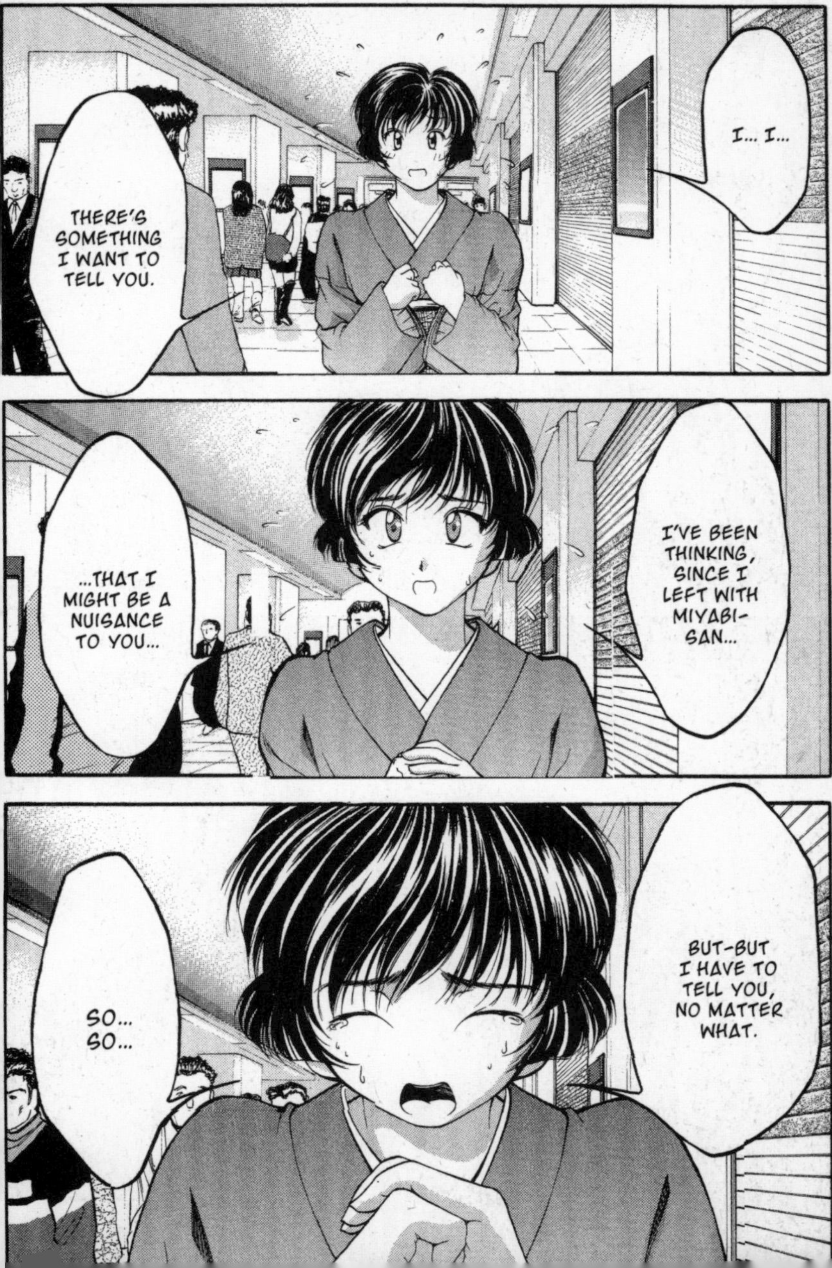
I... I...
THERE'S SOMETHING I WANT TO TELL YOU.
I'VE BEEN THINKING, SINCE I LEFT WITH MIYABI-SAN...
...THAT I MIGHT BE A NUISANCE TO YOU...
BUT-BUT I HAVE TO TELL YOU, NO MATTER WHAT.
SO... SO...

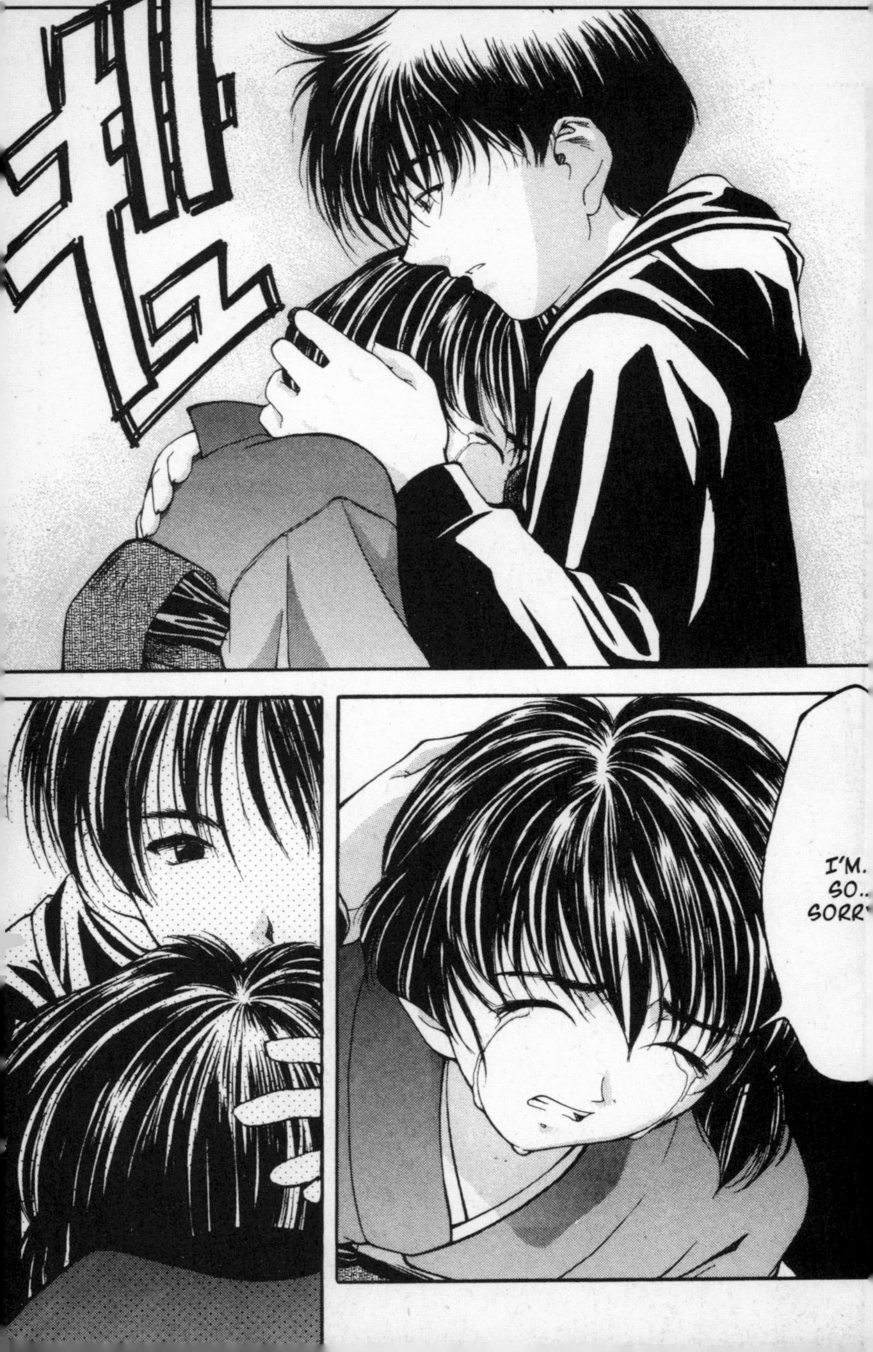
I'M.
SO..
SORR

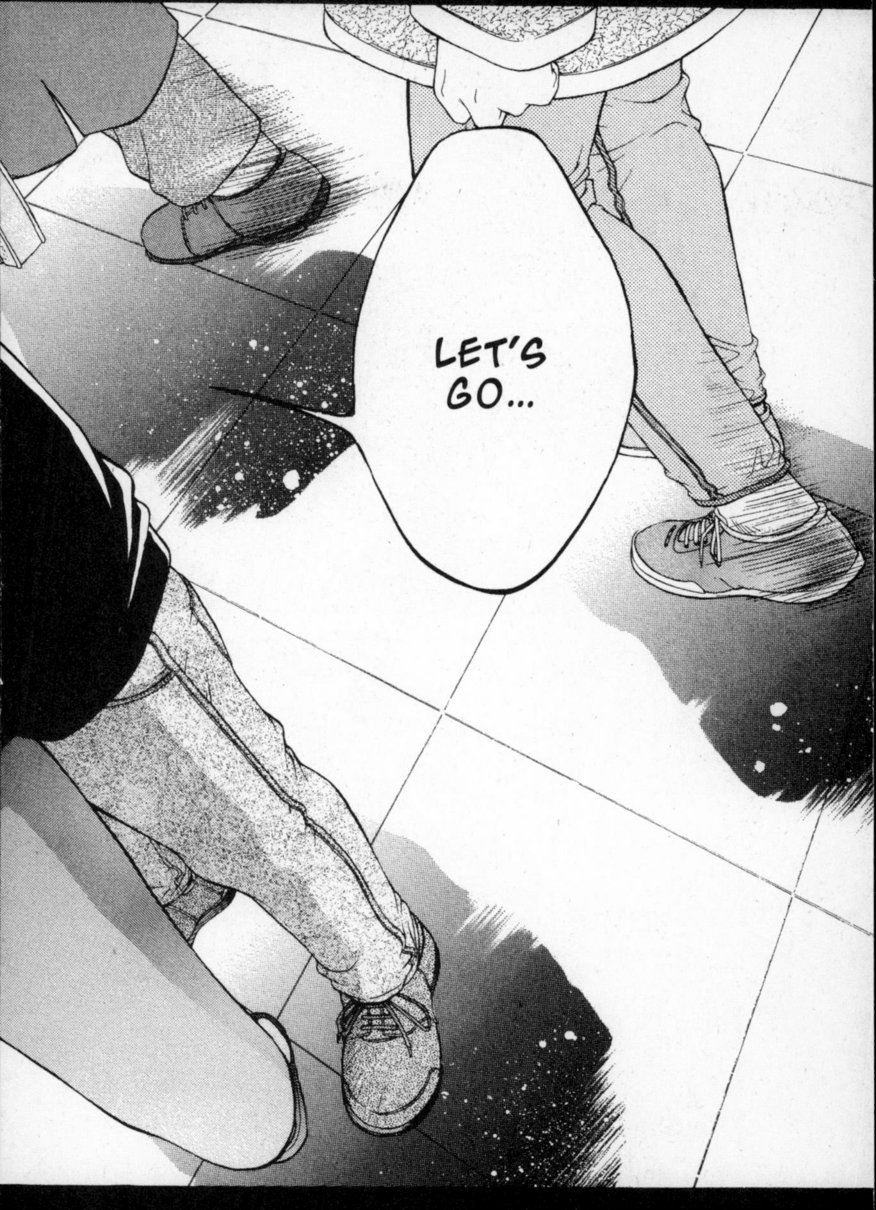
LET'S GO...

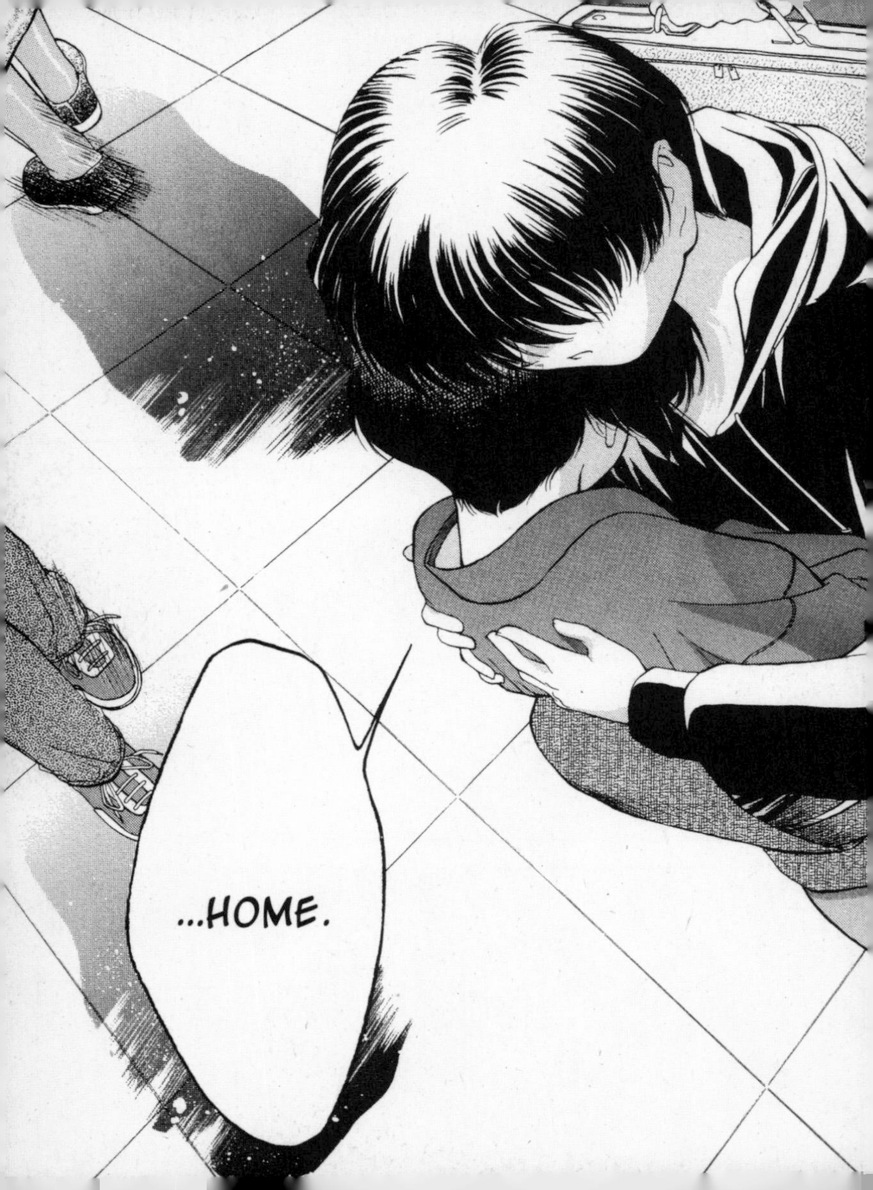
...HOME.

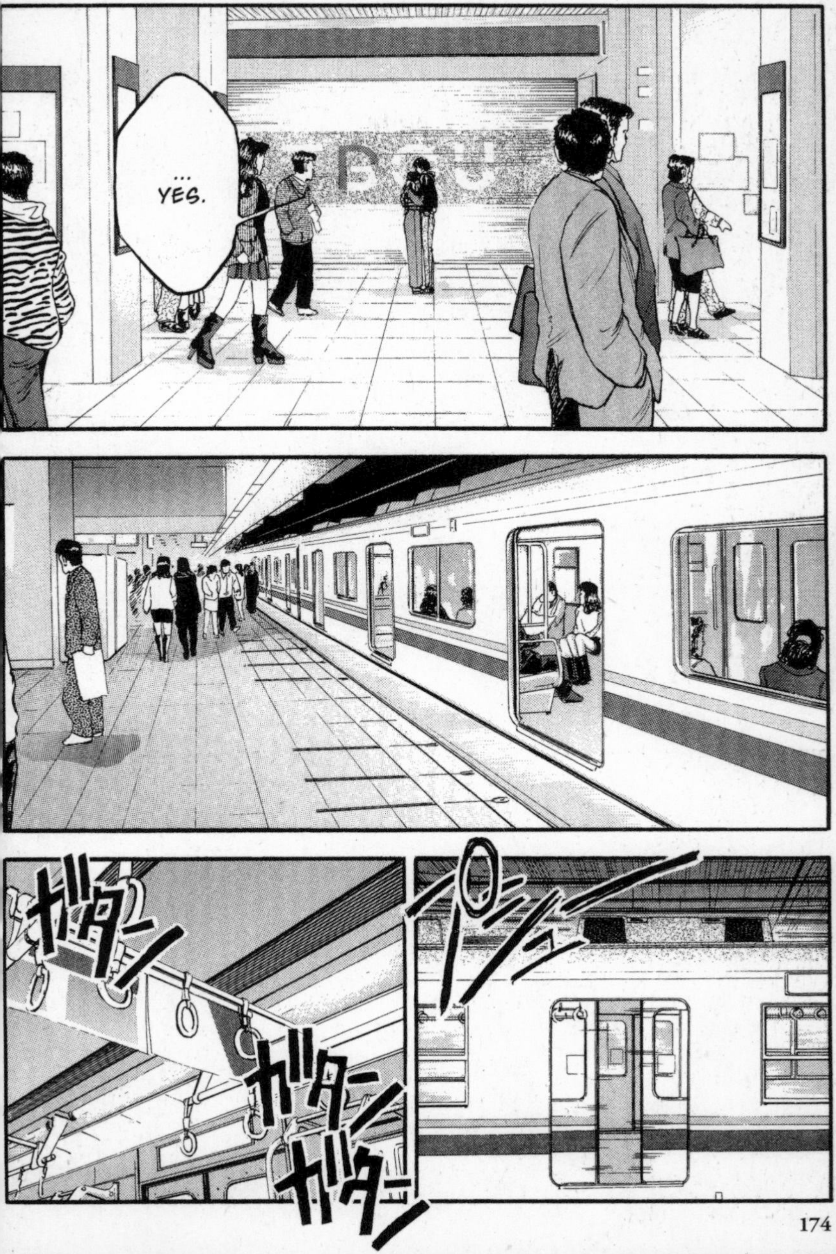
... YES.
プシュー
ガターン
ガターン
ガターン

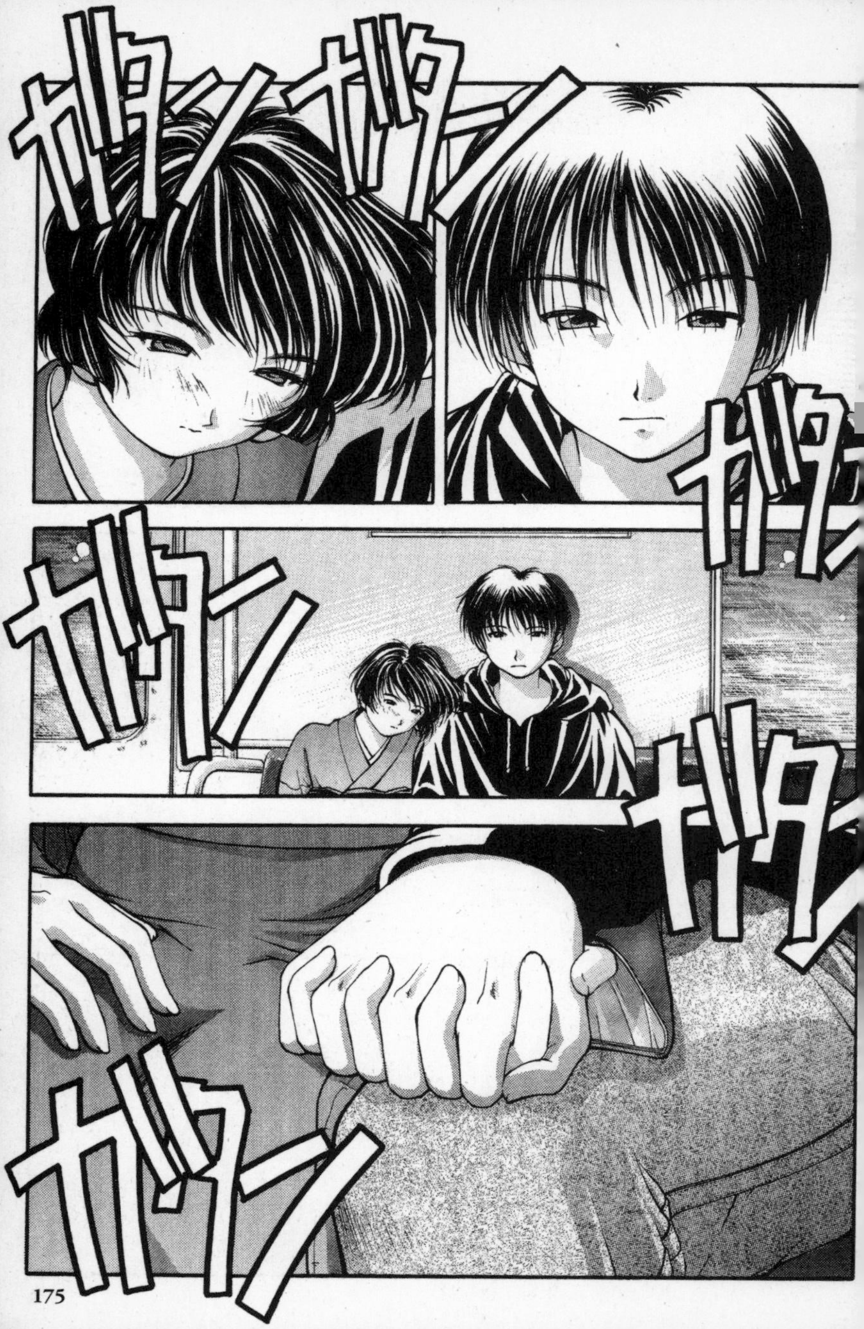
ガタン
ガタン
ガタン
ガタン
ガタン
ガタン
ガタン

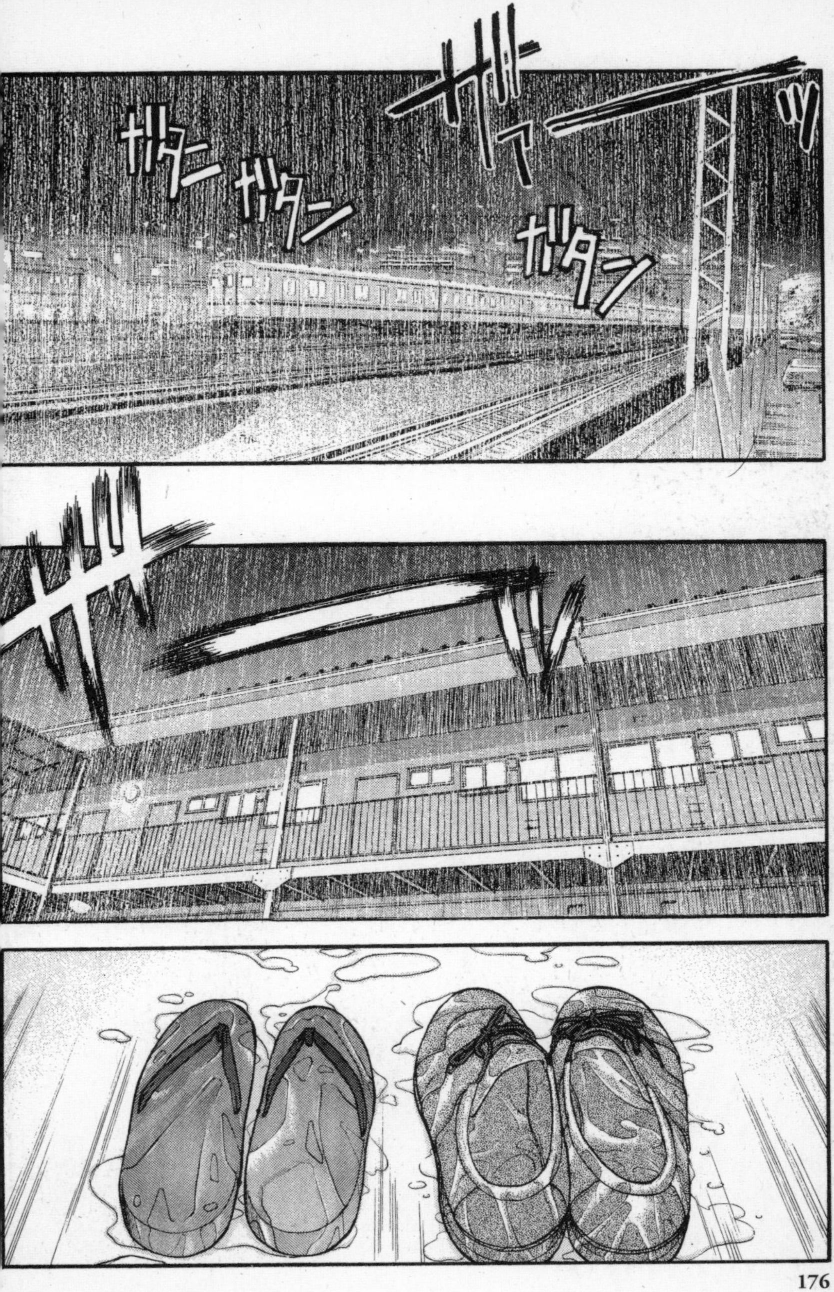
ザァーーッ
ガタン
ガタン
ガタン
ザザーーッ

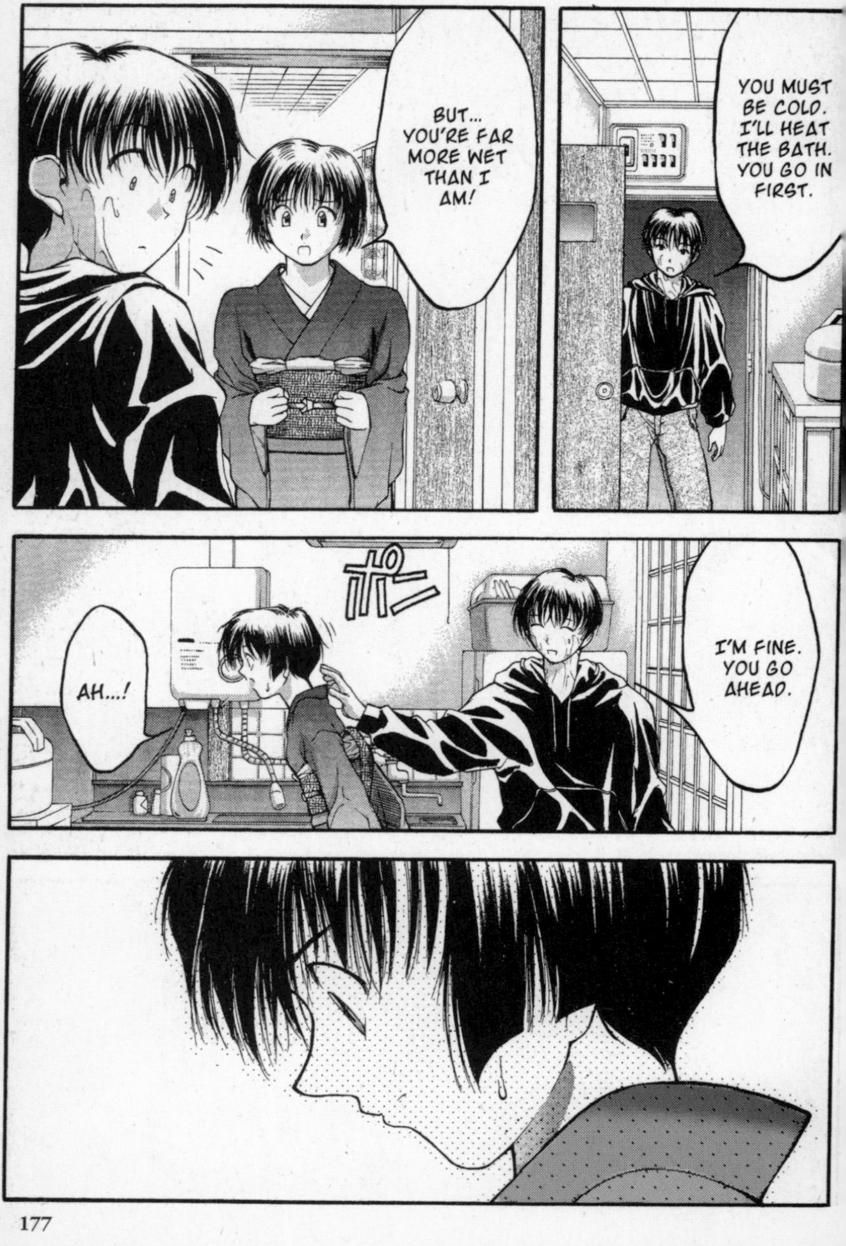
YOU MUST BE COLD. I'LL HEAT THE BATH. YOU GO IN FIRST.
BUT... YOU'RE FAR MORE WET THAN I AM!
I'M FINE. YOU GO AHEAD.
ポン
AH...!

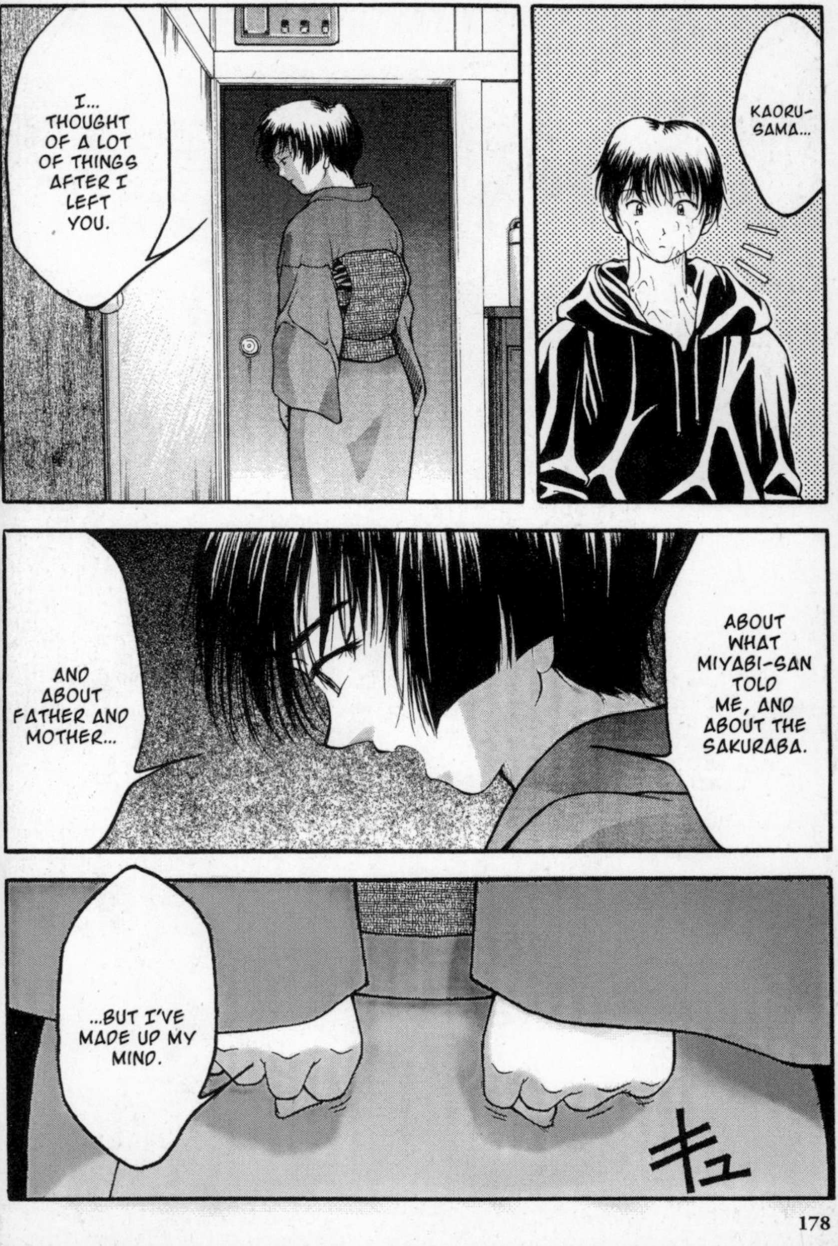
KAORU-SAMA...
I... THOUGHT OF A LOT OF THINGS AFTER I LEFT YOU.
ABOUT WHAT MIYABI-SAN TOLD ME, AND ABOUT THE SAKURABA.
AND ABOUT FATHER AND MOTHER...
...BUT I'VE MADE UP MY MIND.
キュ

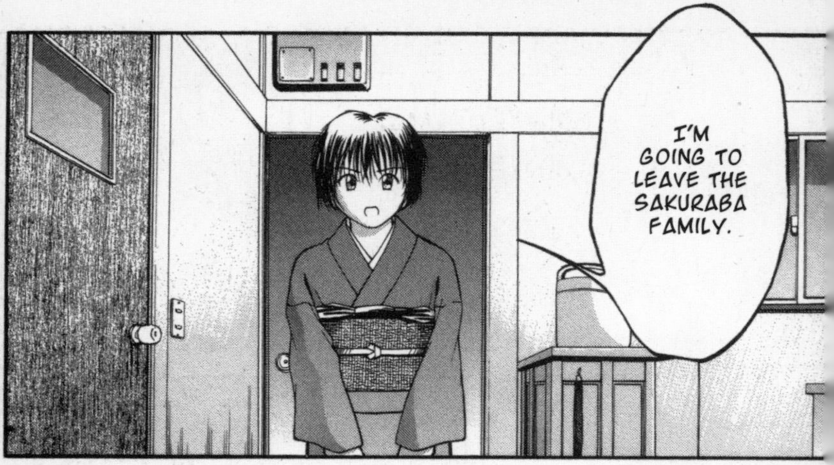
I'M GOING TO LEAVE THE SAKURABA FAMILY.
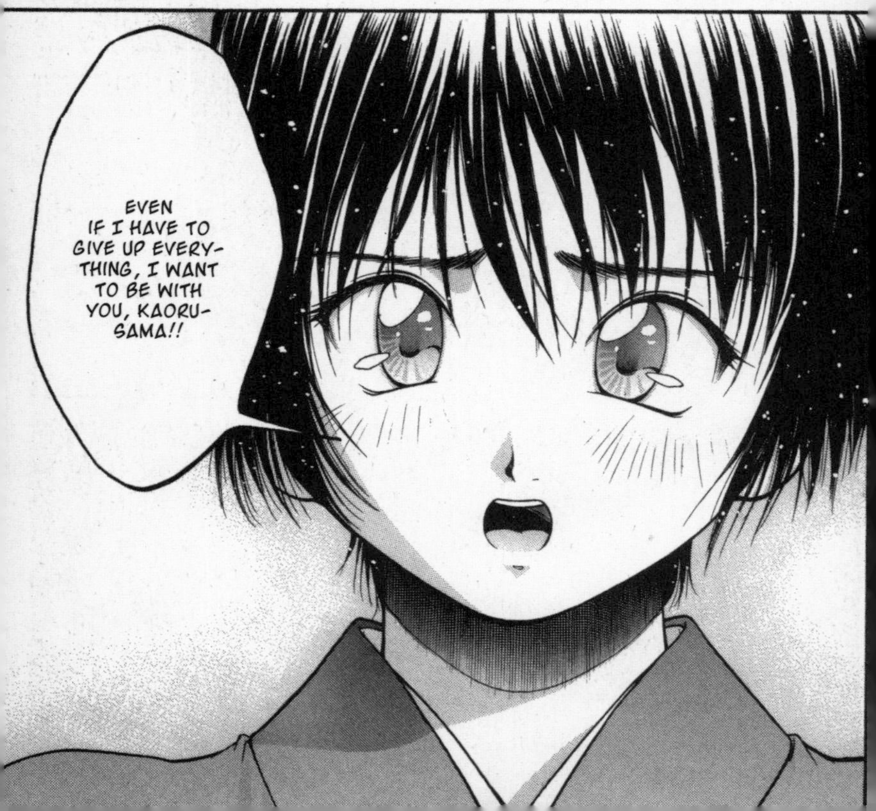
EVEN IF I HAVE TO GIVE UP EVERY-THING, I WANT TO BE WITH YOU, KAORU-SAMA!!

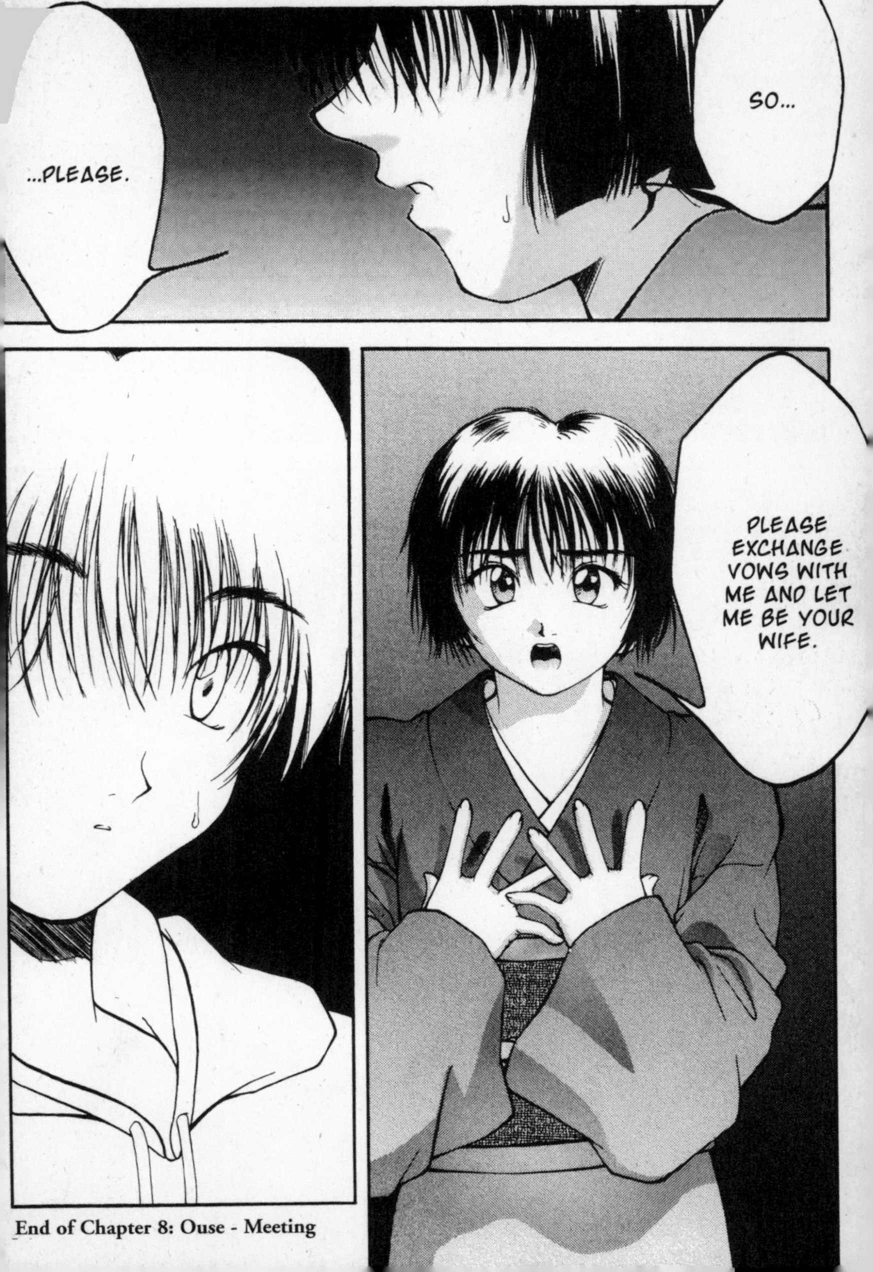
SO...
...PLEASE.
PLEASE EXCHANGE VOWS WITH ME AND LET ME BE YOUR WIFE.

End of Chapter 8: Ouse - Meeting

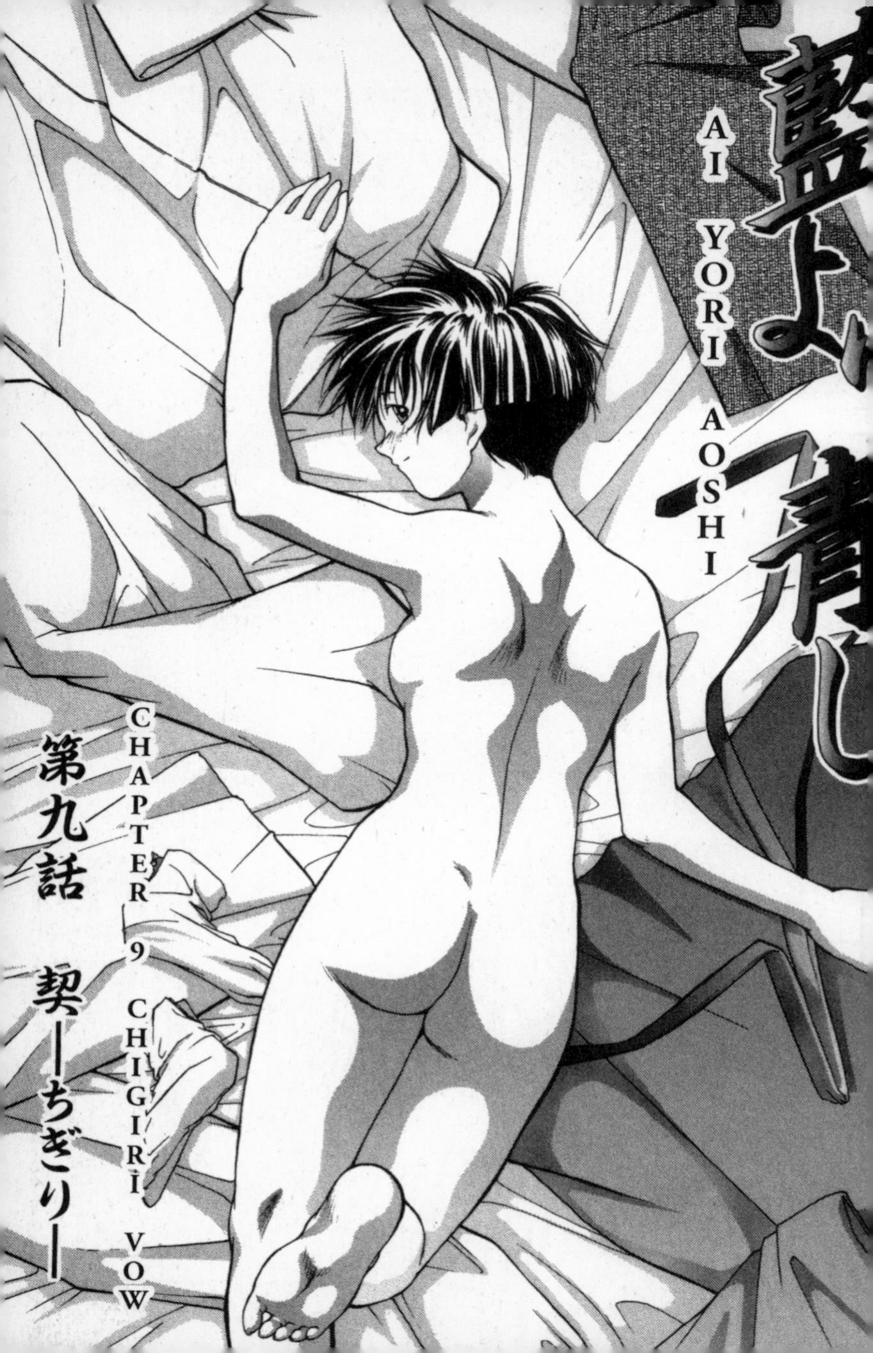
藍より青し
AI YORI AOSHI
第九話
CHAPTER 9
契—ちぎり—
CHIGIRI VOW

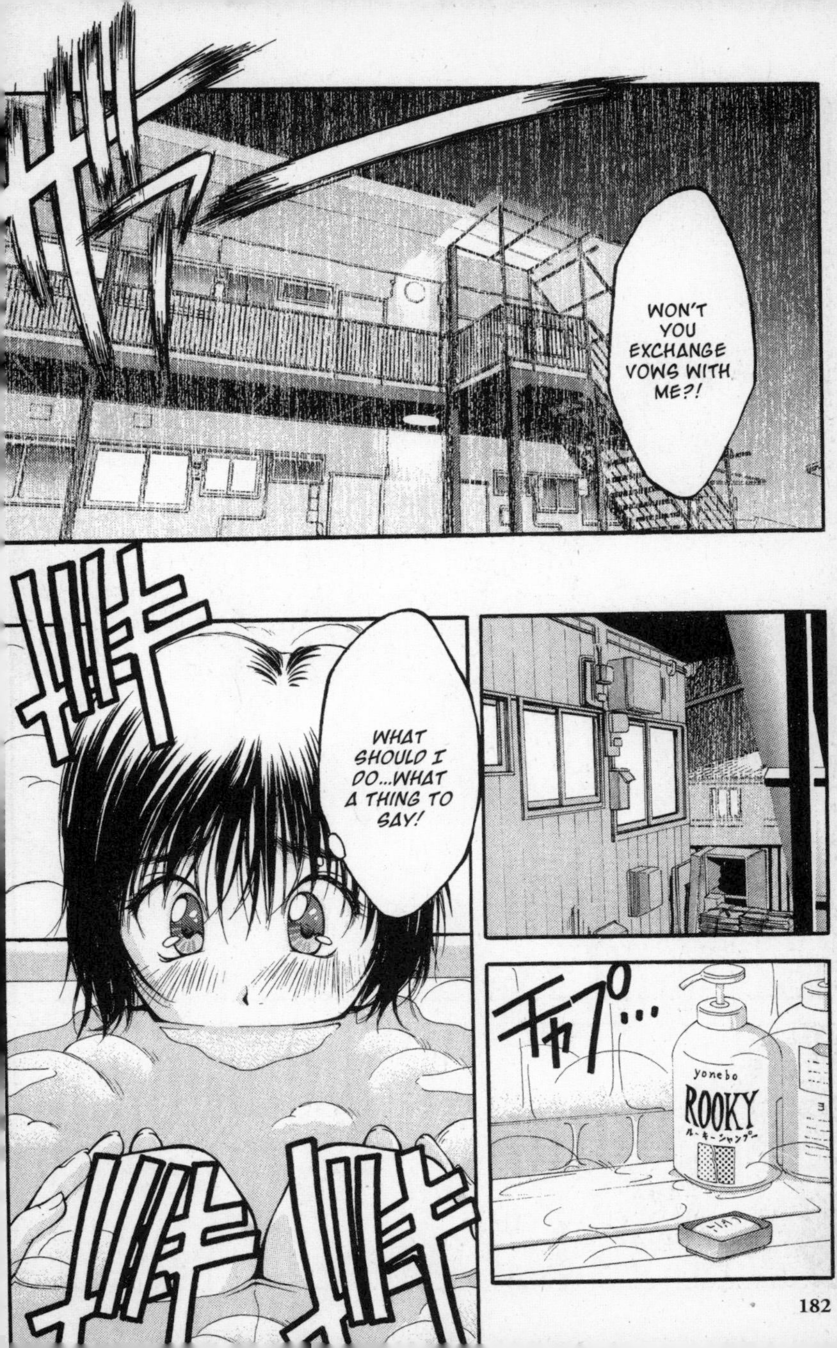
WON'T YOU EXCHANGE VOWS WITH ME?!
チャプ...
yonebo
ROOKY
ルーキーシャンプー
WHAT SHOULD I DO...WHAT A THING TO SAY!

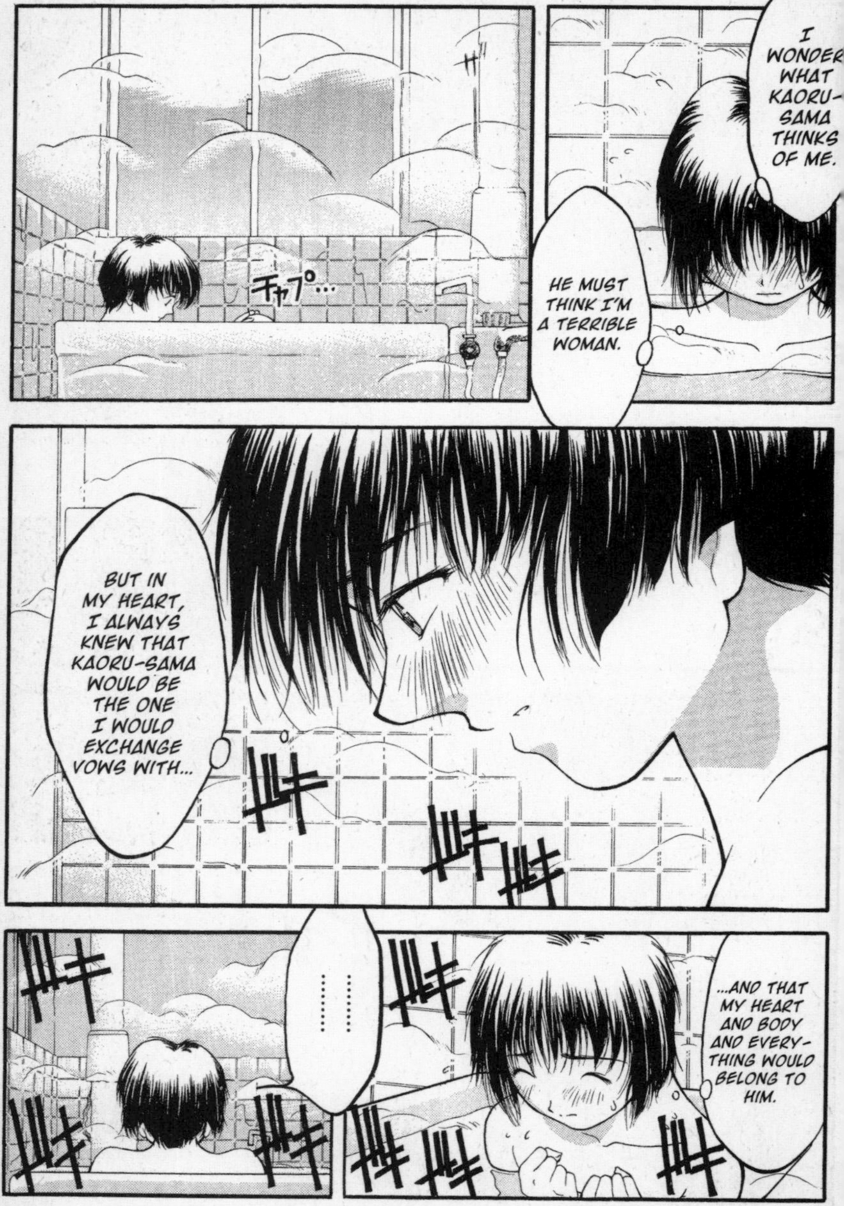
I WONDER WHAT KAORU-SAMA THINKS OF ME.
HE MUST THINK I'M A TERRIBLE WOMAN.
チャプ…
BUT IN MY HEART, I ALWAYS KNEW THAT KAORU-SAMA WOULD BE THE ONE I WOULD EXCHANGE VOWS WITH...
...AND THAT MY HEART AND BODY AND EVERY-THING WOULD BELONG TO HIM.
......

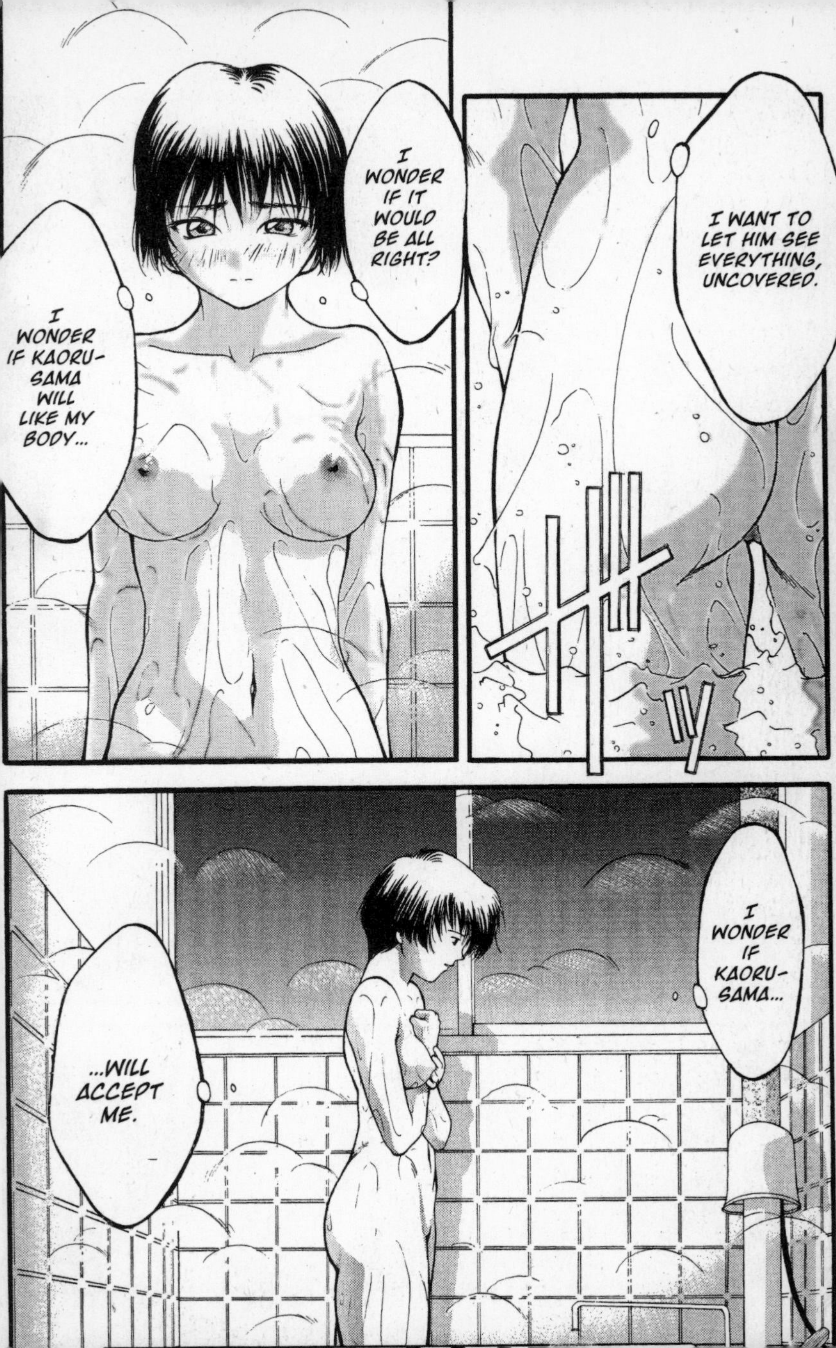
I WANT TO LET HIM SEE EVERYTHING, UNCOVERED.
I WONDER IF IT WOULD BE ALL RIGHT?
I WONDER IF KAORU-SAMA WILL LIKE MY BODY...
I WONDER IF KAORU-SAMA...
...WILL ACCEPT ME.

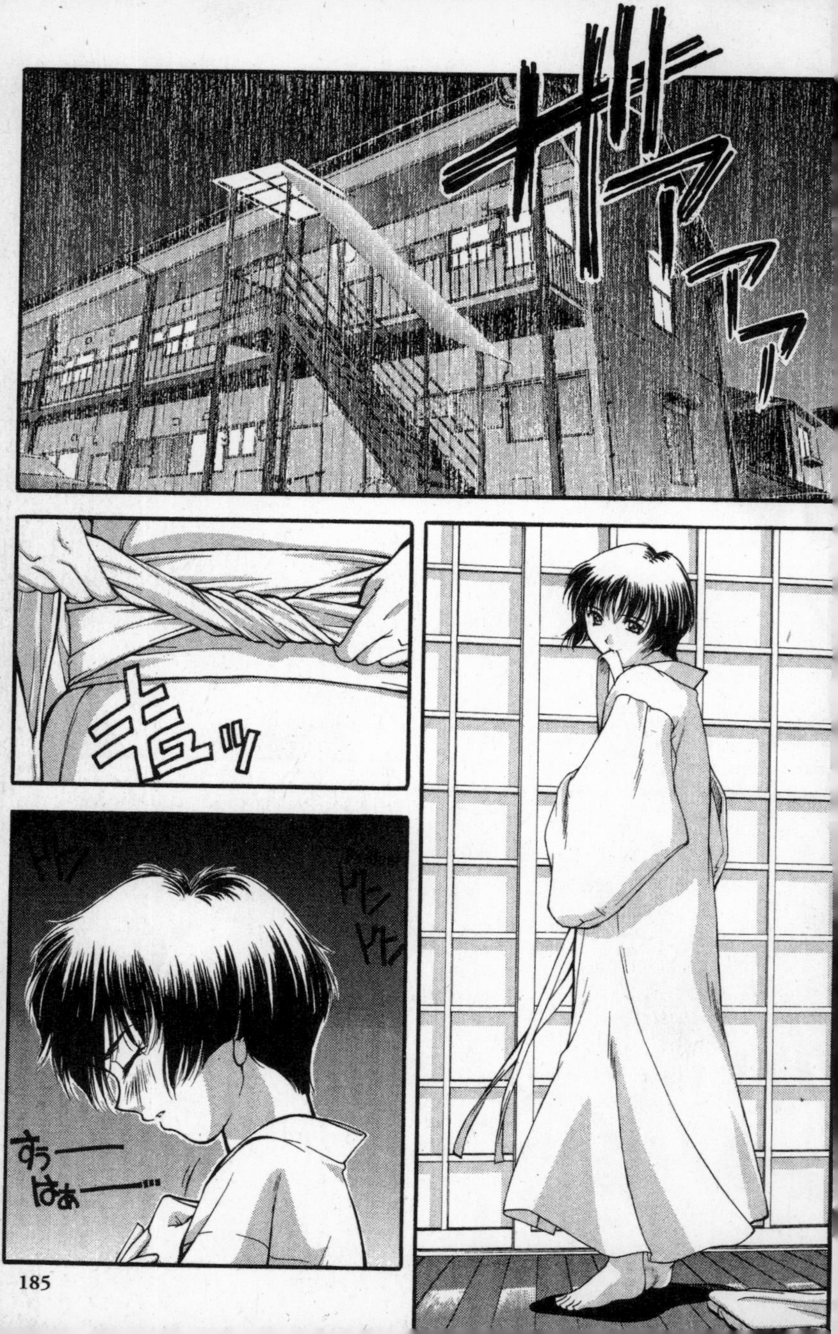
ザアアア
キュッ
ドキン
ドキン
ドキン
すぅーーー
はぁーーー…

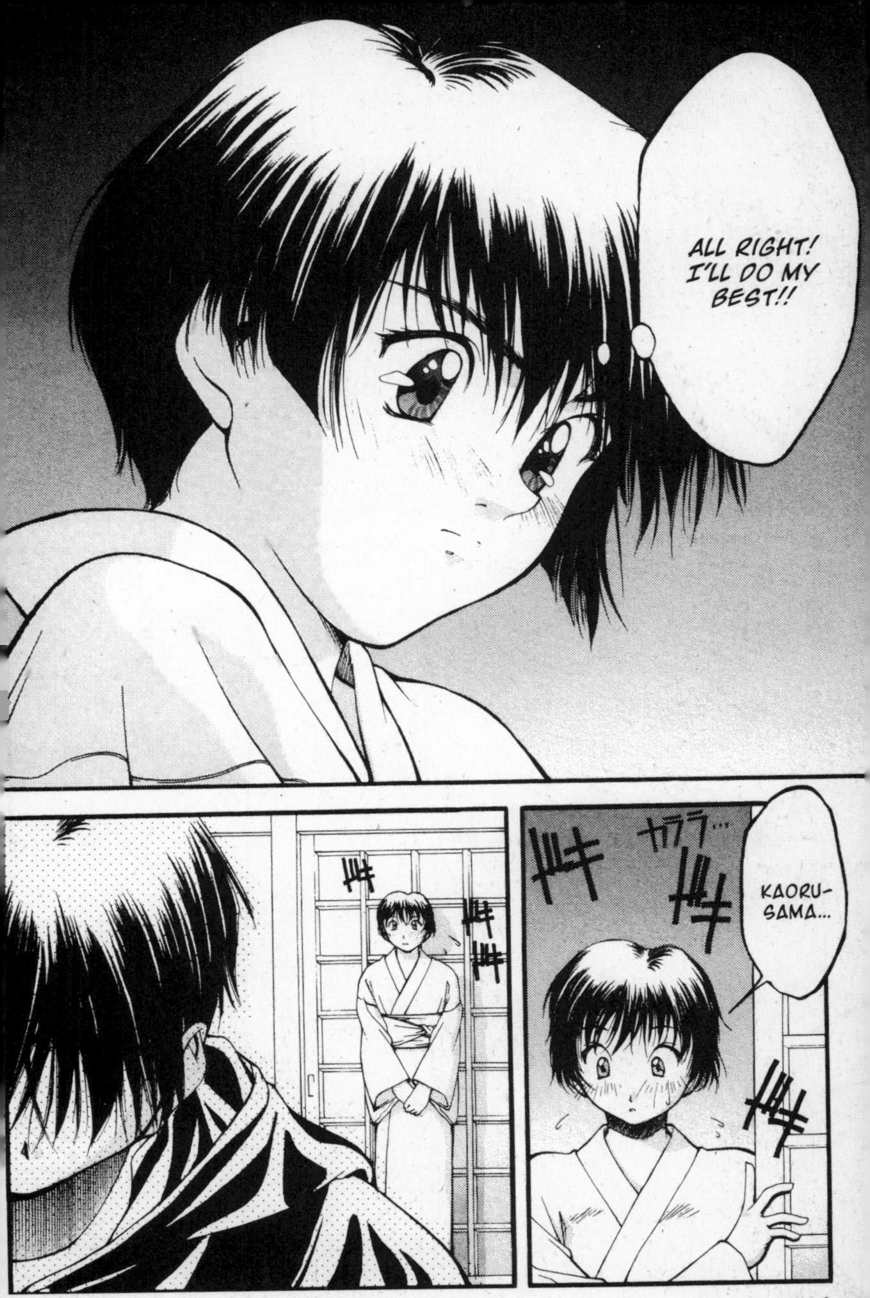
ALL RIGHT! I'LL DO MY BEST!!
ドキ
ガララ…
KAORU-SAMA...

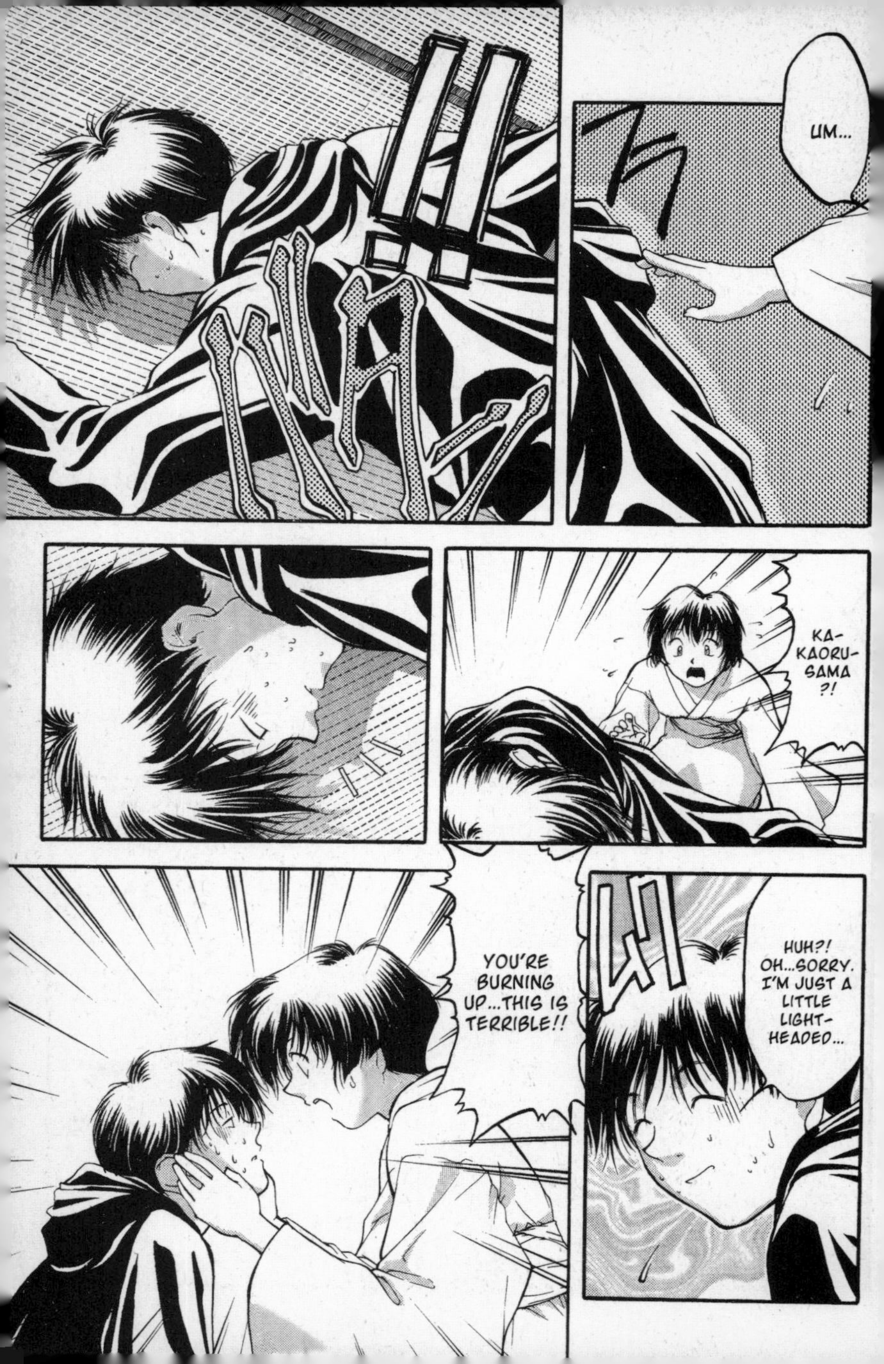
UM...
KA-KAORU-SAMA?!
HUH?! OH...SORRY. I'M JUST A LITTLE LIGHT-HEADED...
YOU'RE BURNING UP...THIS IS TERRIBLE!!

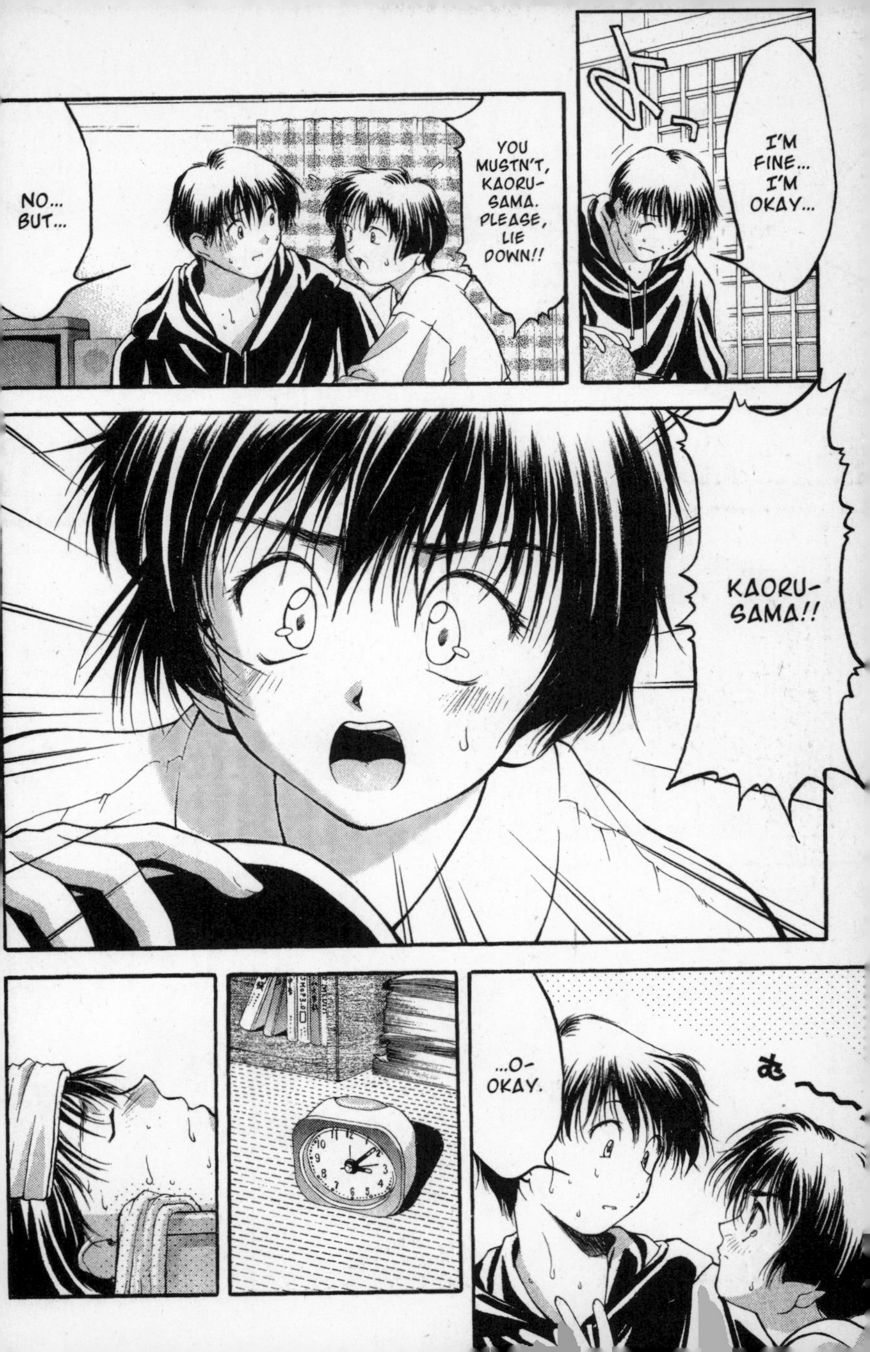
I'M FINE... I'M OKAY...
YOU MUSTN'T, KAORU-SAMA. PLEASE, LIE DOWN!!
NO... BUT...
KAORU-SAMA!!
...O-OKAY.

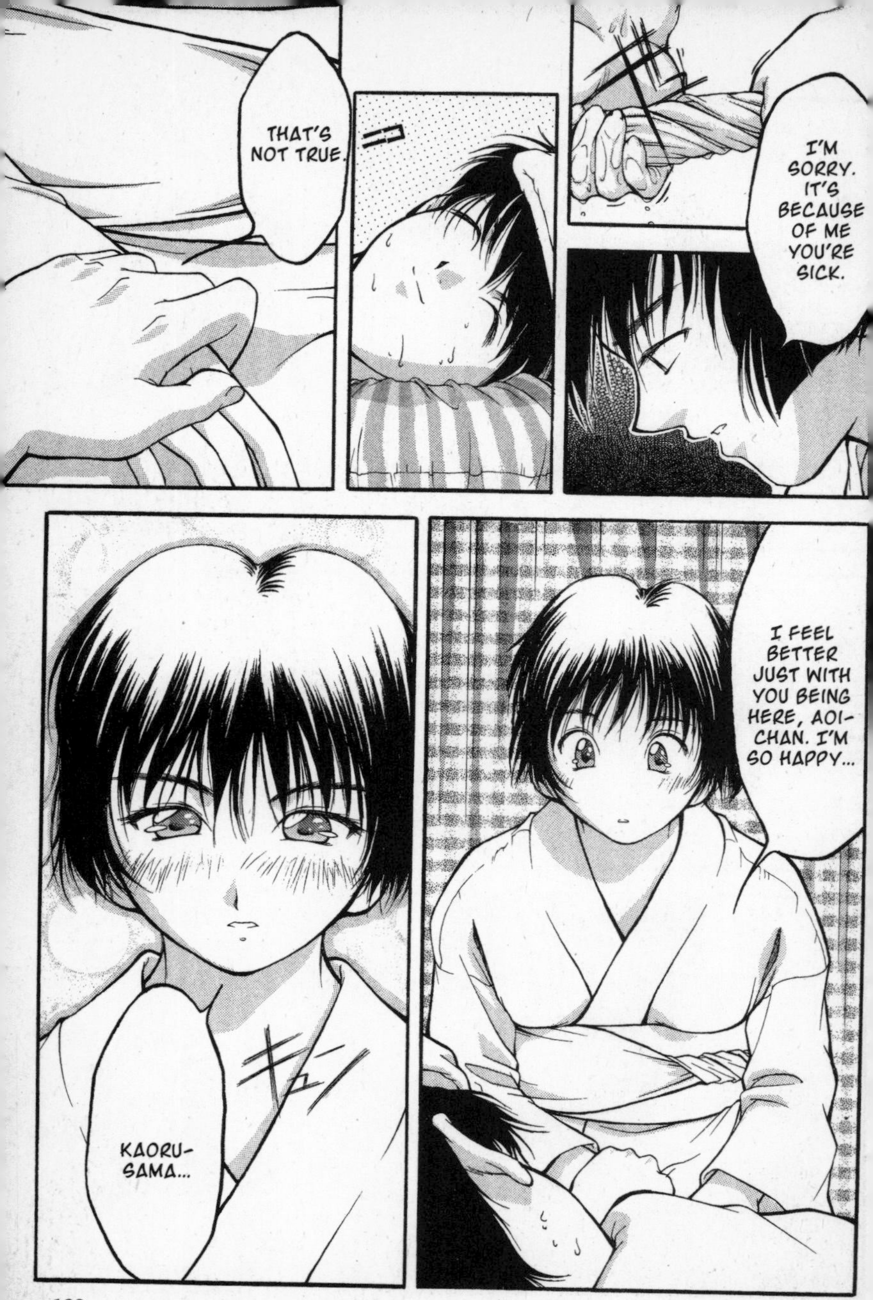
I'M SORRY. IT'S BECAUSE OF ME YOU'RE SICK.
THAT'S NOT TRUE.
I FEEL BETTER JUST WITH YOU BEING HERE, AOI-CHAN. I'M SO HAPPY...
KAORU-SAMA...

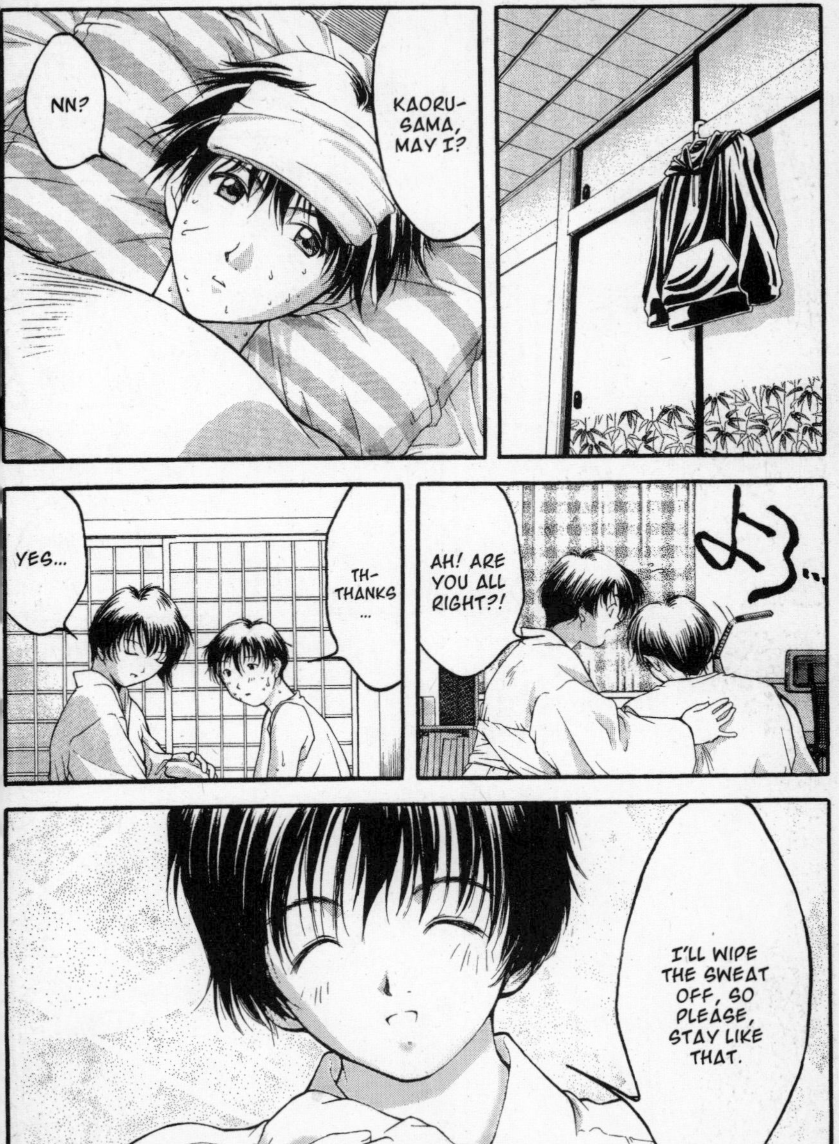
KAORU-SAMA, MAY I?
NN?
AH! ARE YOU ALL RIGHT?!
TH-THANKS...
YES...
I'LL WIPE THE SWEAT OFF, SO PLEASE, STAY LIKE THAT.

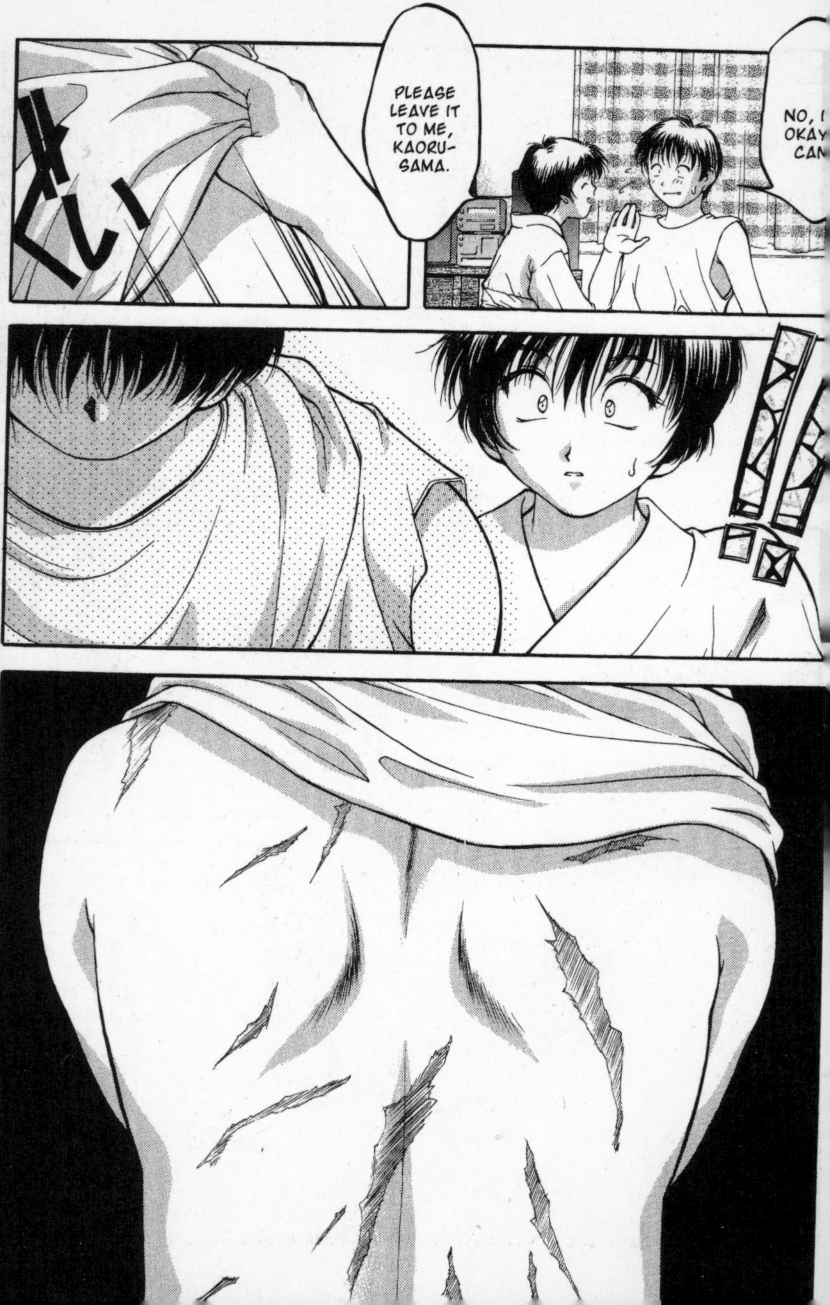
NO, I OKAY CAN
PLEASE LEAVE IT TO ME, KAORU-SAMA.

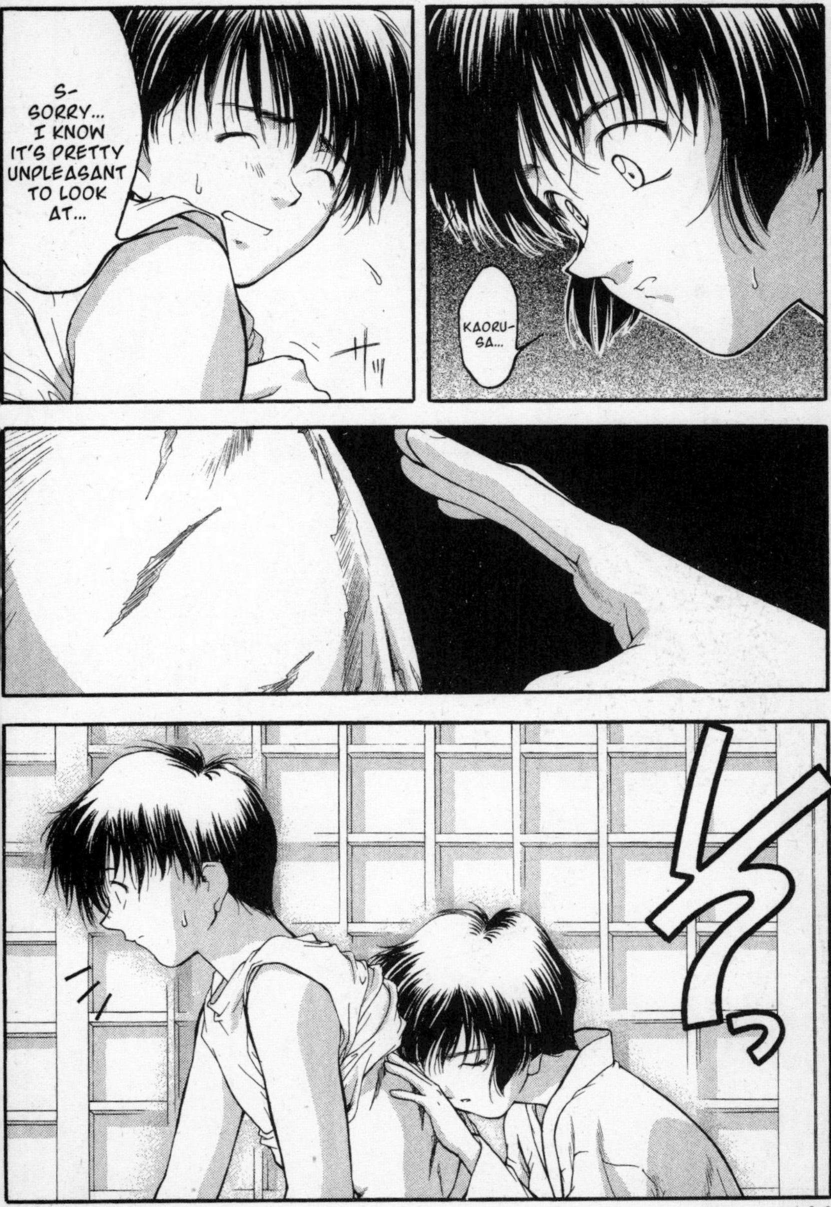
KAORU-SA...
S-SORRY... I KNOW IT'S PRETTY UNPLEASANT TO LOOK AT...
ザッ

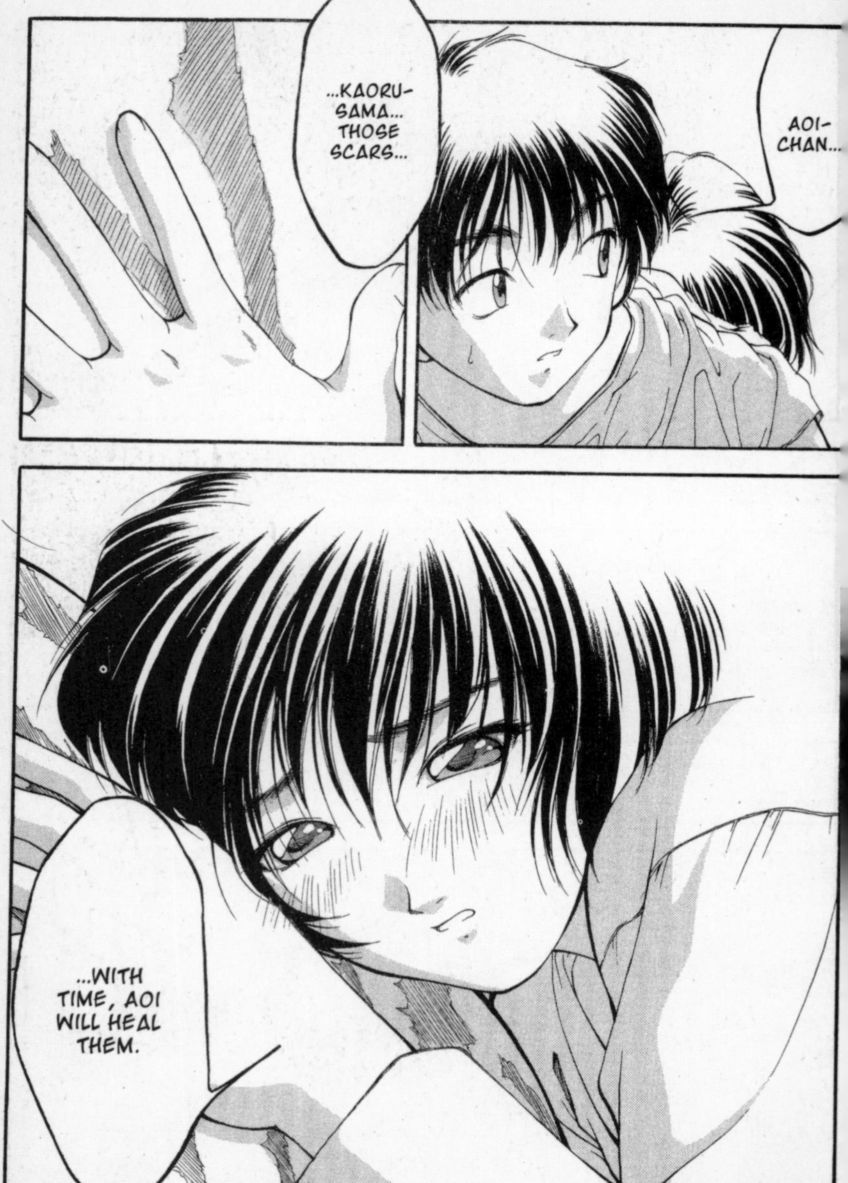
AOI-CHAN...
...KAORU-SAMA... THOSE SCARS...
...WITH TIME, AOI WILL HEAL THEM.

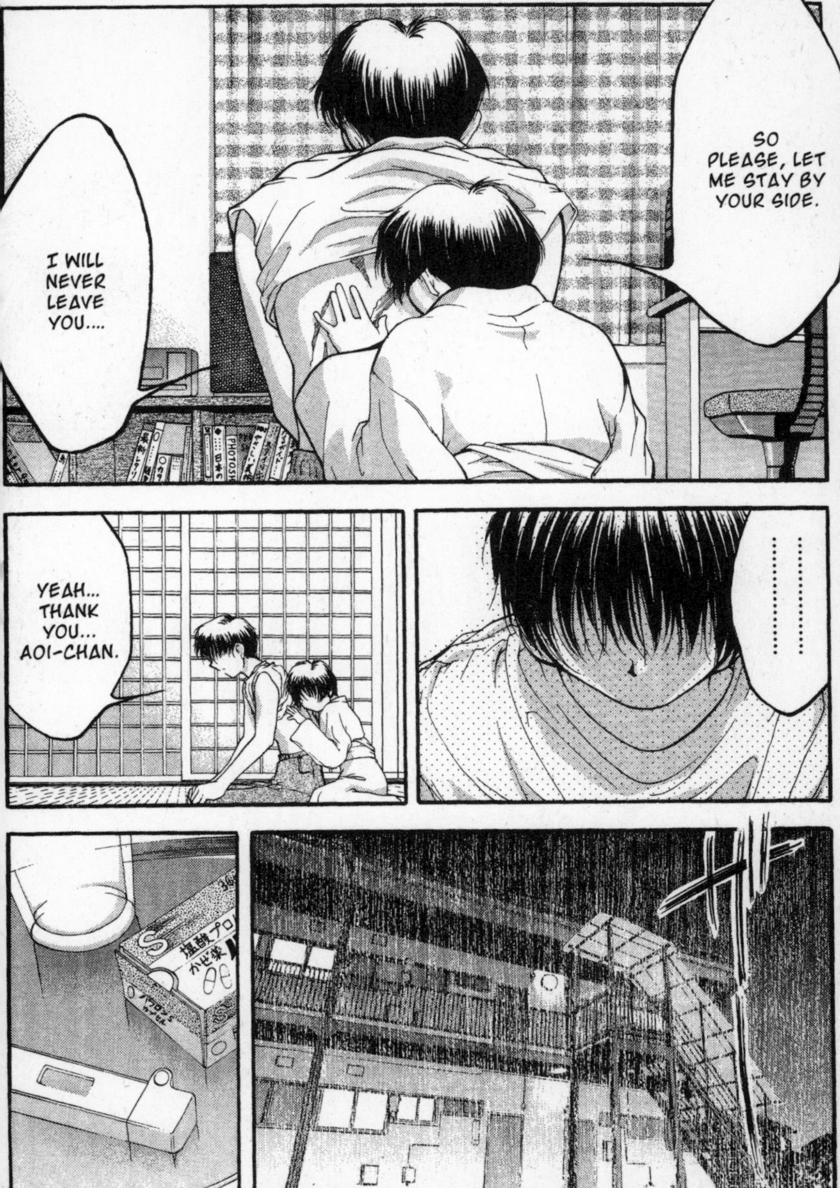
SO PLEASE, LET ME STAY BY YOUR SIDE.
I WILL NEVER LEAVE YOU....
......
YEAH... THANK YOU... AOI-CHAN.
かぜ薬

*cold medicine

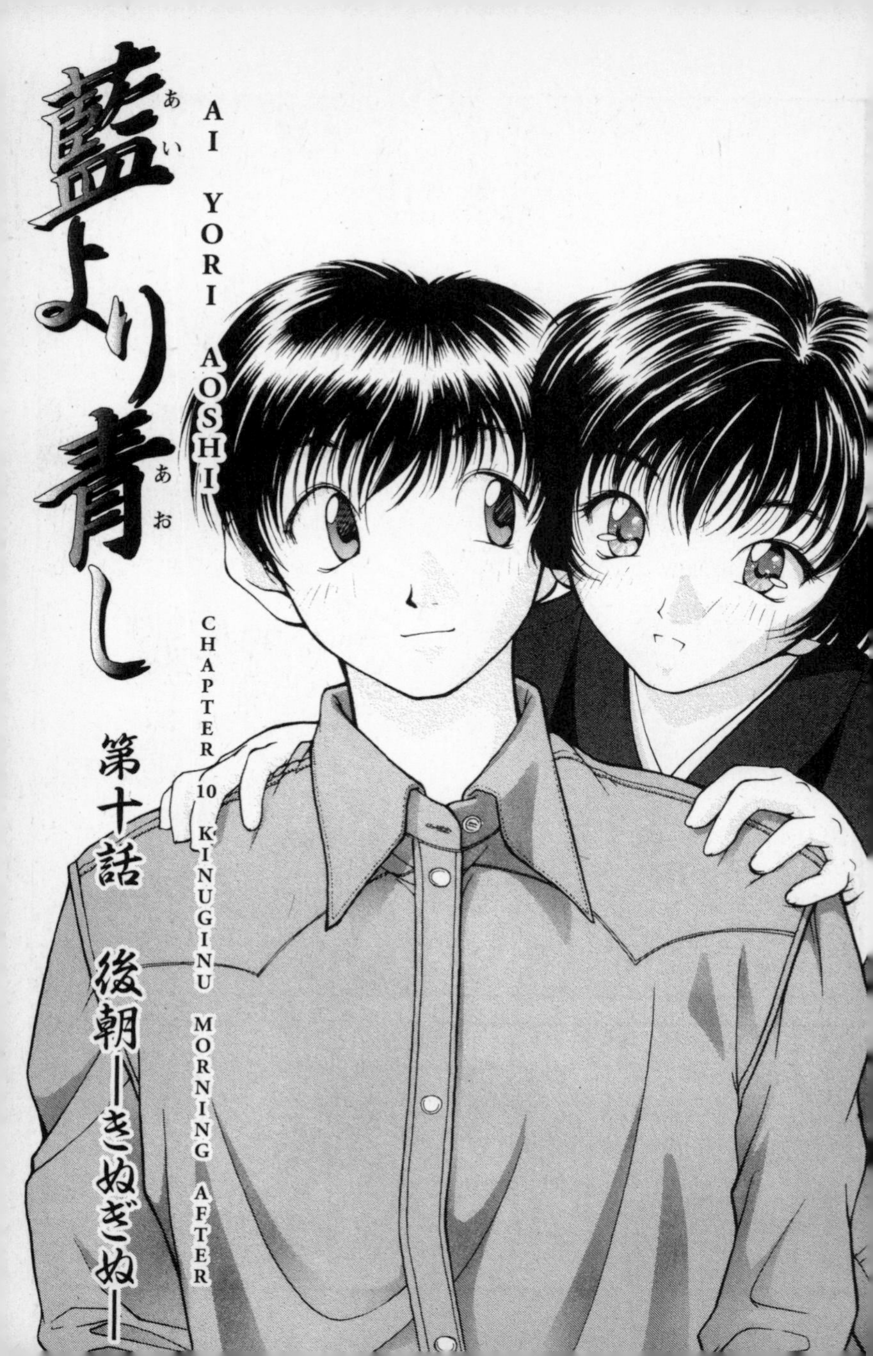
藍(あい)より青(あお)し
AI YORI AOSHI
CHAPTER 10 KINUGINU MORNING AFTER
第十話 後朝—きぬぎぬ—

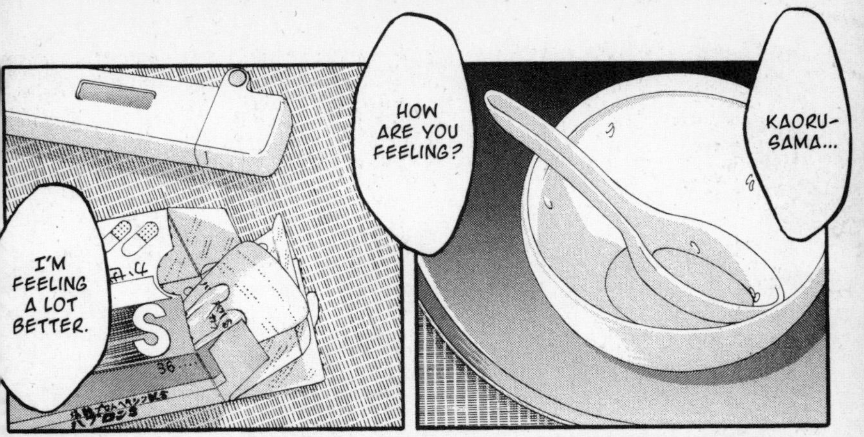
KAORU-SAMA...
HOW ARE YOU FEELING?
I'M FEELING A LOT BETTER.

*cold medicine

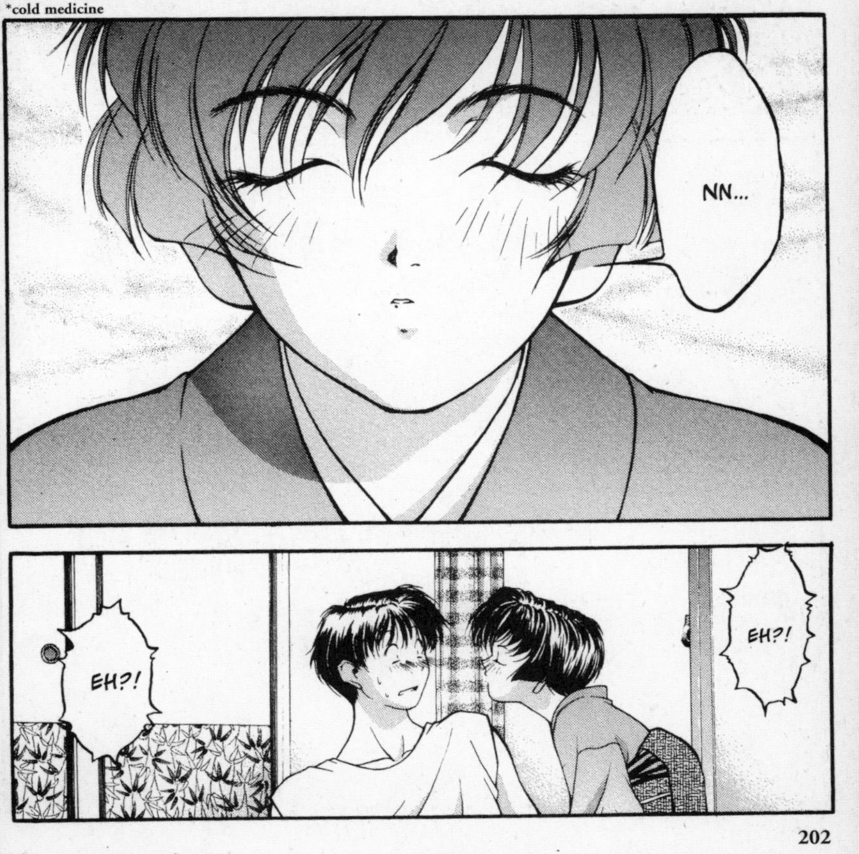
NN...
EH?!
EH?!

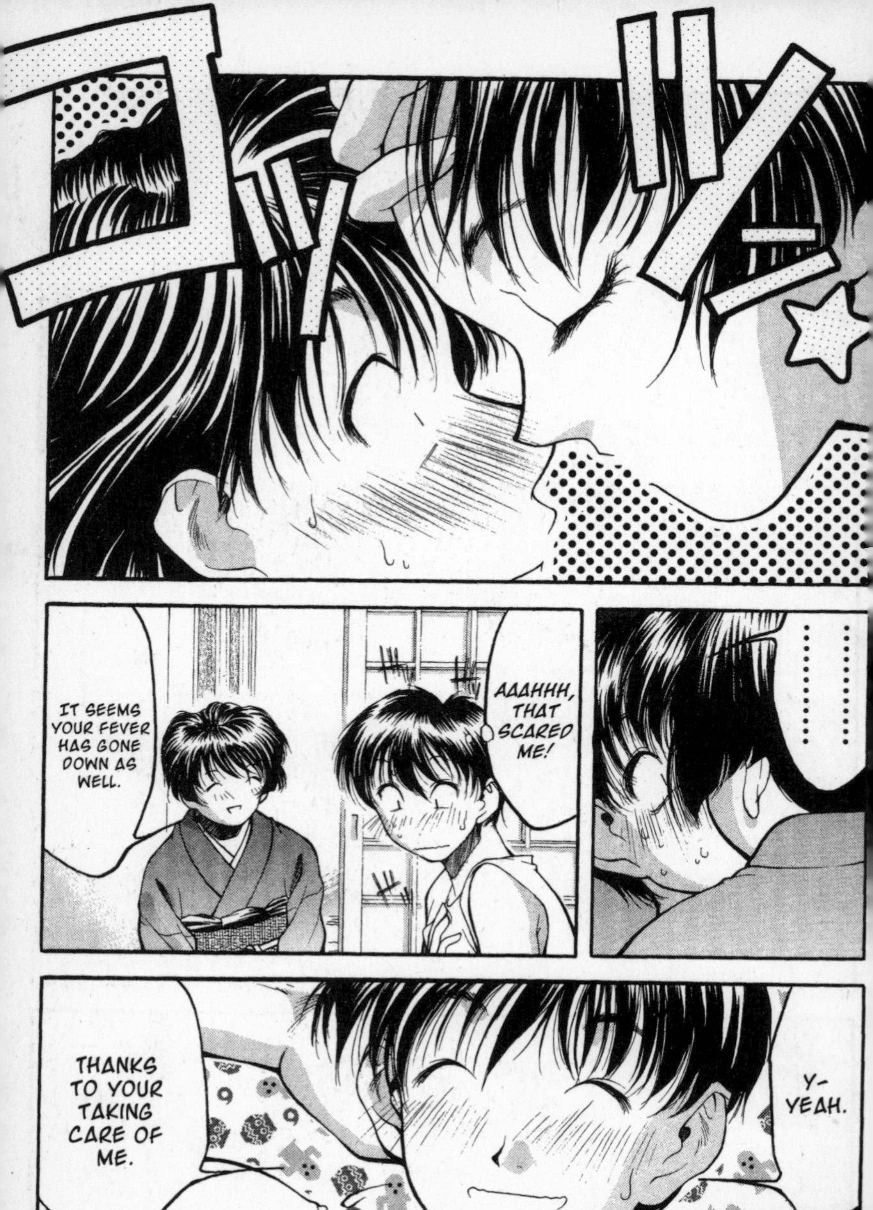
AAAHHH, THAT SCARED ME!
IT SEEMS YOUR FEVER HAS GONE DOWN AS WELL.
......
Y-YEAH.
THANKS TO YOUR TAKING CARE OF ME.

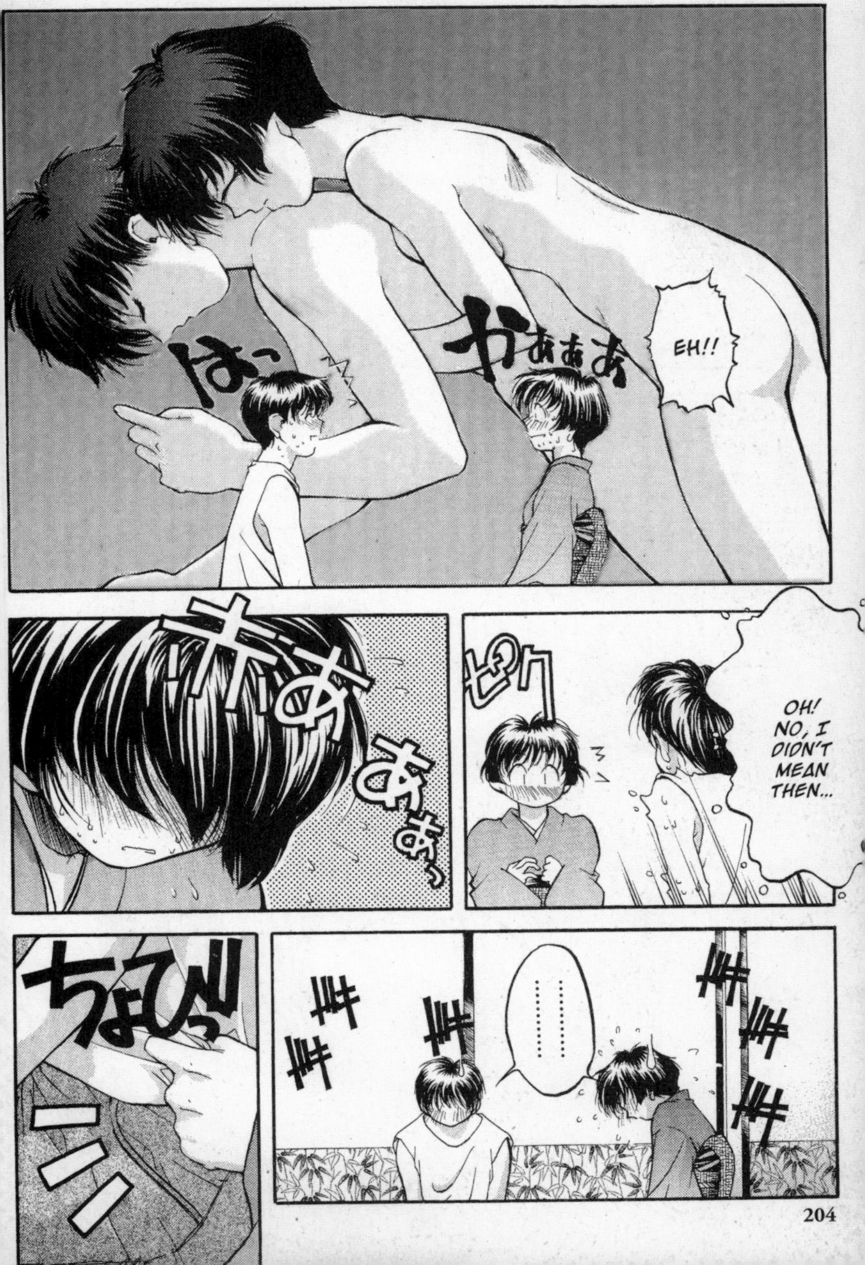
はっ
やぁぁぁ
EH!!
赤ぁぁぁっ
ビクッ
OH! NO, I DIDN'T MEAN THEN...
ちょいっ!!
......

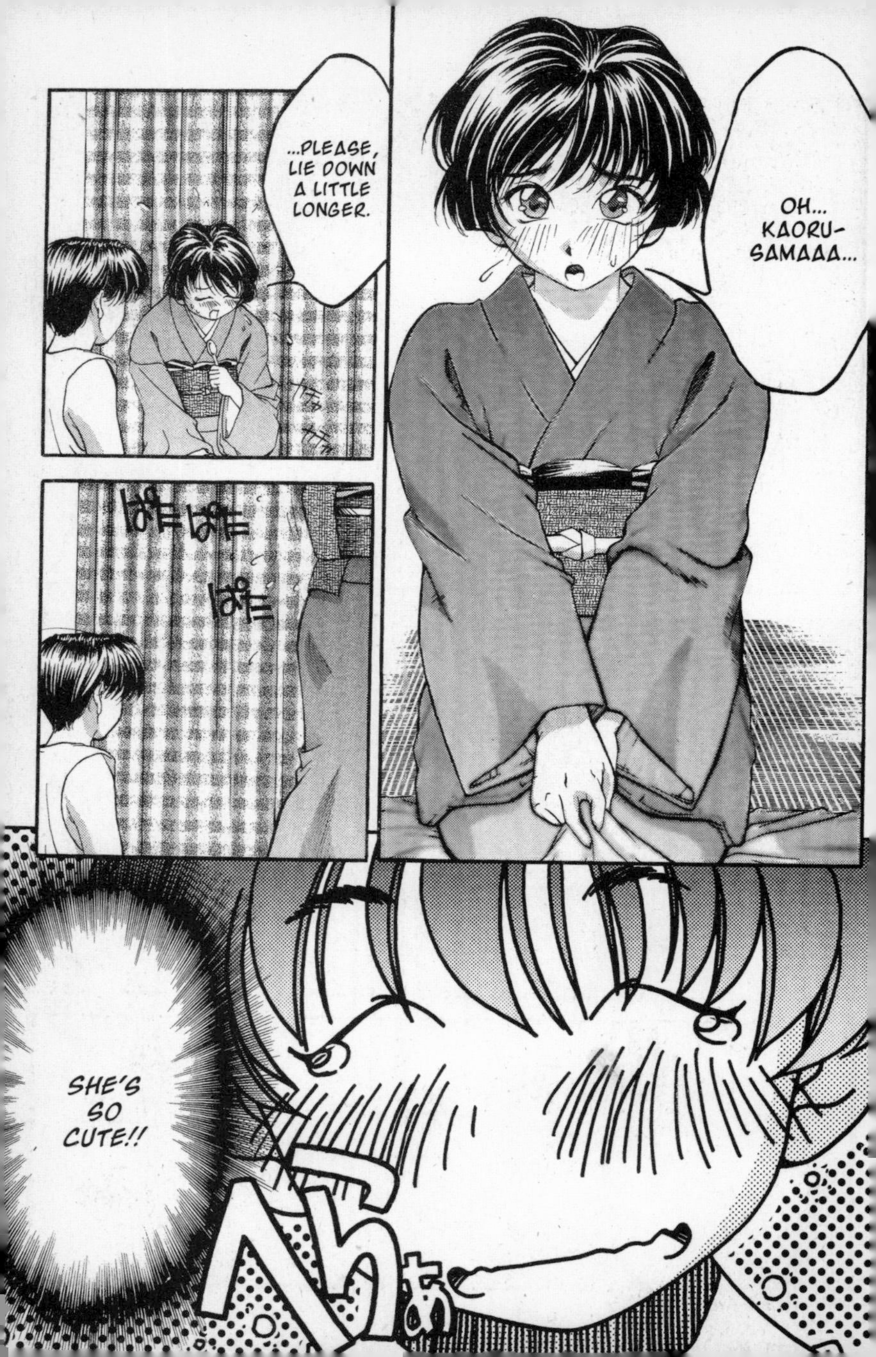

OH... KAORU-SAMAAA...
...PLEASE, LIE DOWN A LITTLE LONGER.
ぱたぱた
ぱた
SHE'S SO CUTE!!
へらぁ

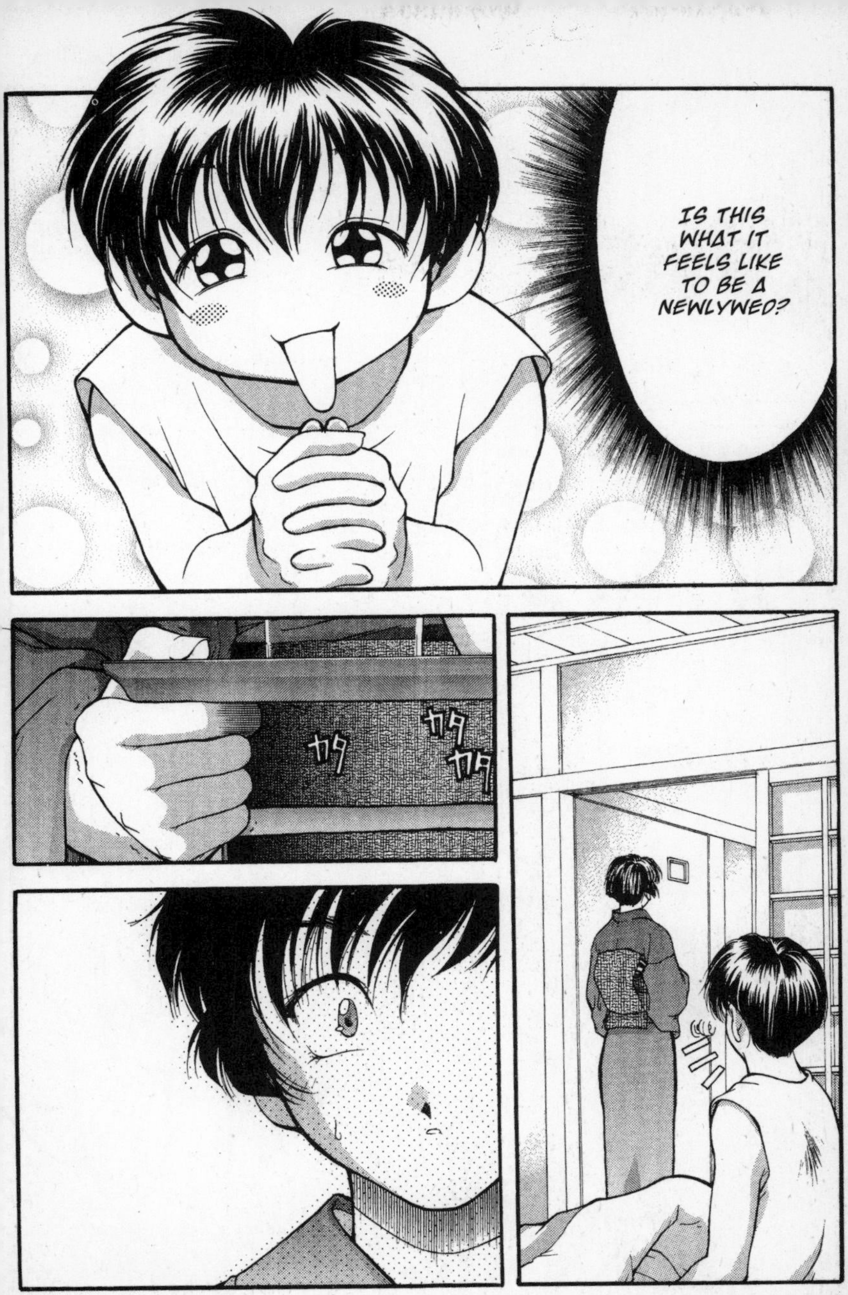
IS THIS WHAT IT FEELS LIKE TO BE A NEWLYWED?
カタ
カタ
カタ

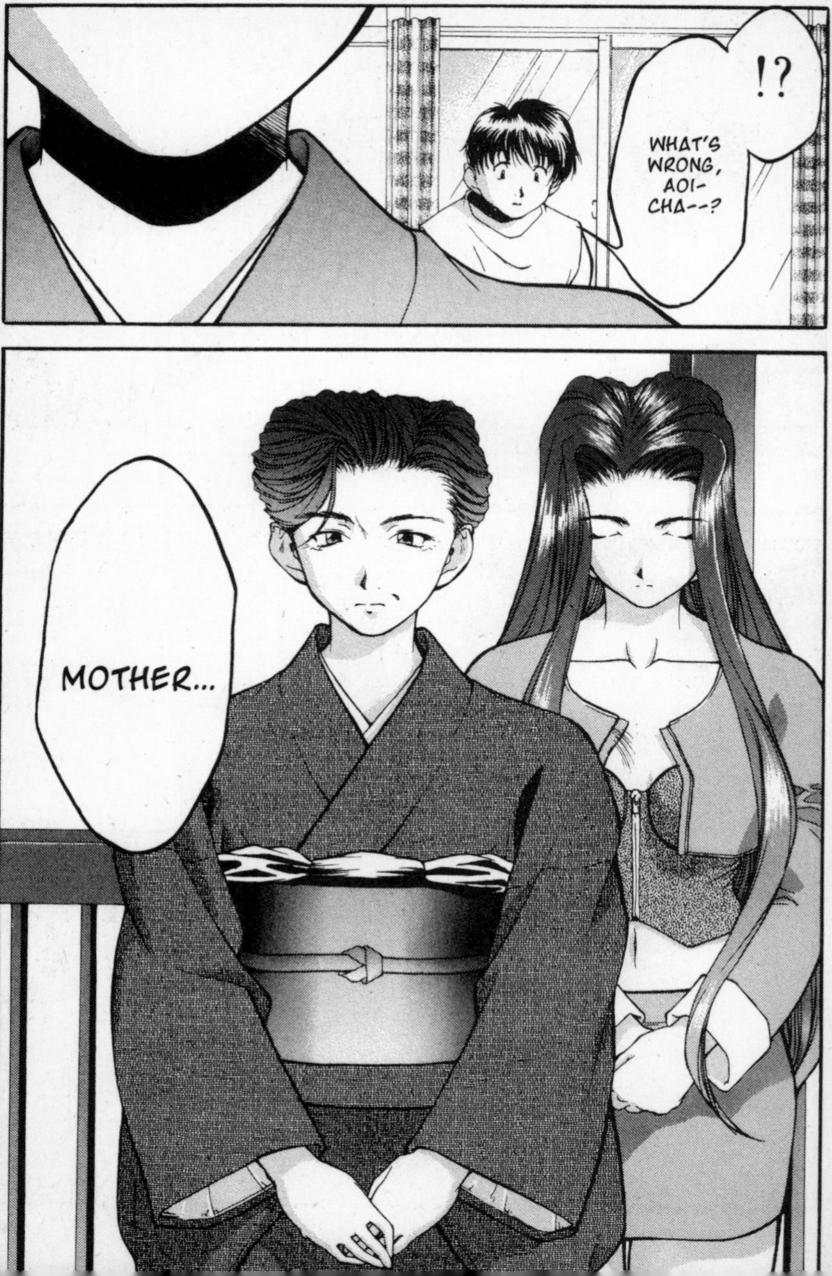
!?
WHAT'S WRONG, AOI-CHA--?
MOTHER...

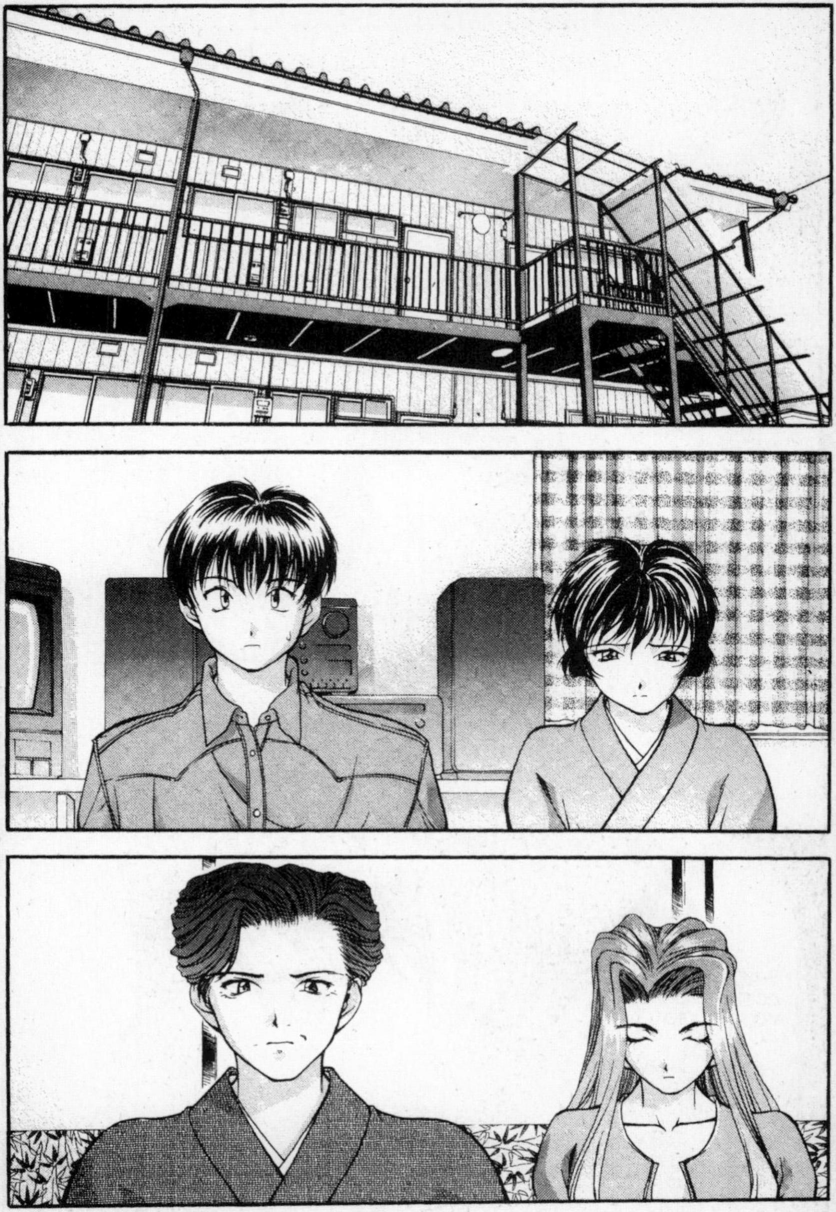

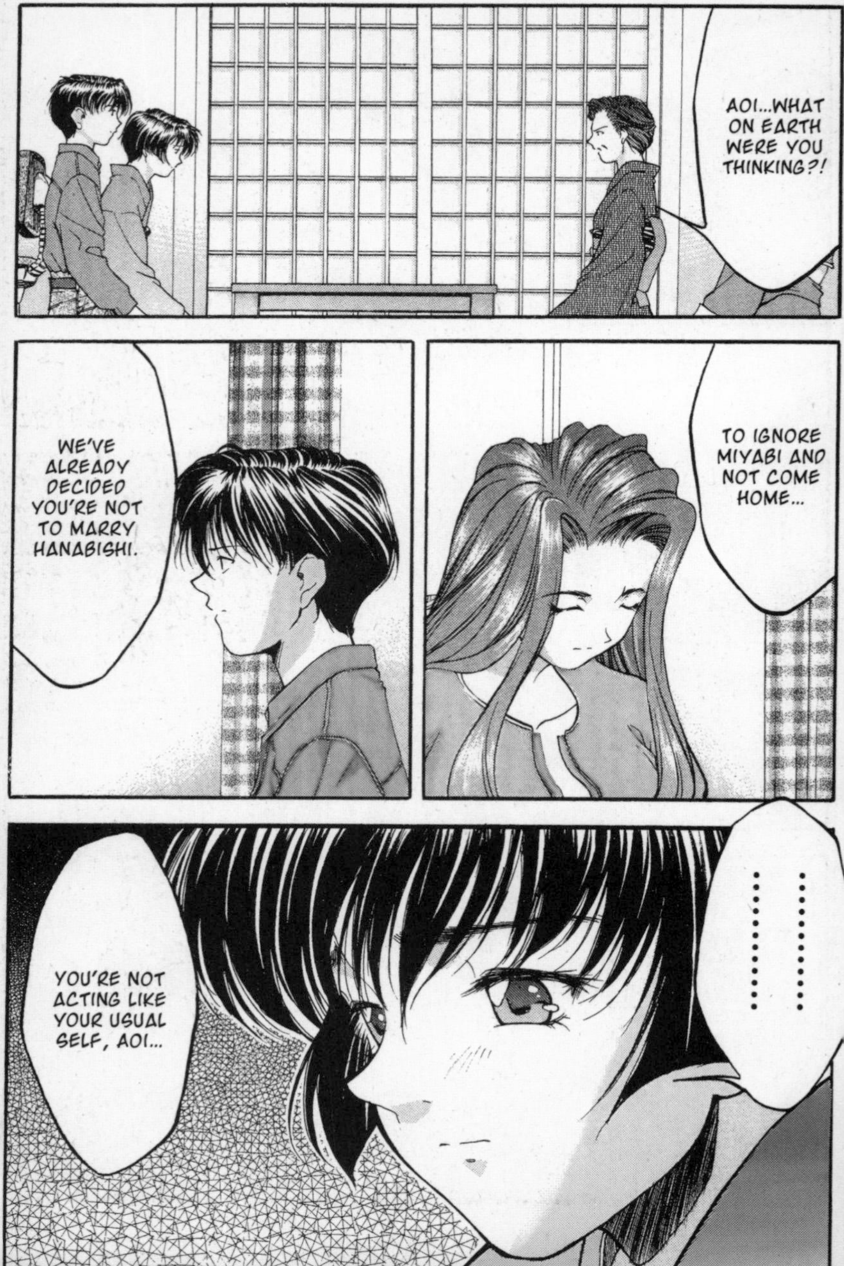
AOI...WHAT ON EARTH WERE YOU THINKING?!
TO IGNORE MIYABI AND NOT COME HOME...
WE'VE ALREADY DECIDED YOU'RE NOT TO MARRY HANABISHI.
......
YOU'RE NOT ACTING LIKE YOUR USUAL SELF, AOI...

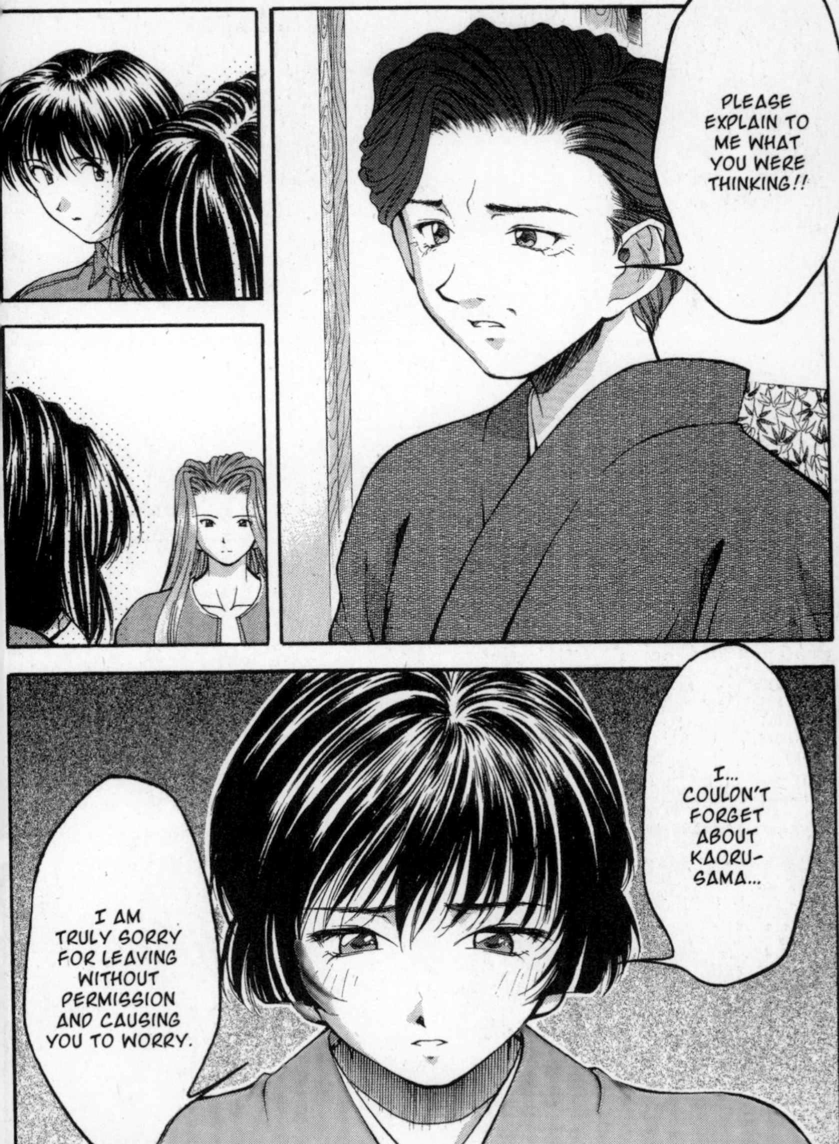
PLEASE EXPLAIN TO ME WHAT YOU WERE THINKING!!
I... COULDN'T FORGET ABOUT KAORU-SAMA...
I AM TRULY SORRY FOR LEAVING WITHOUT PERMISSION AND CAUSING YOU TO WORRY.

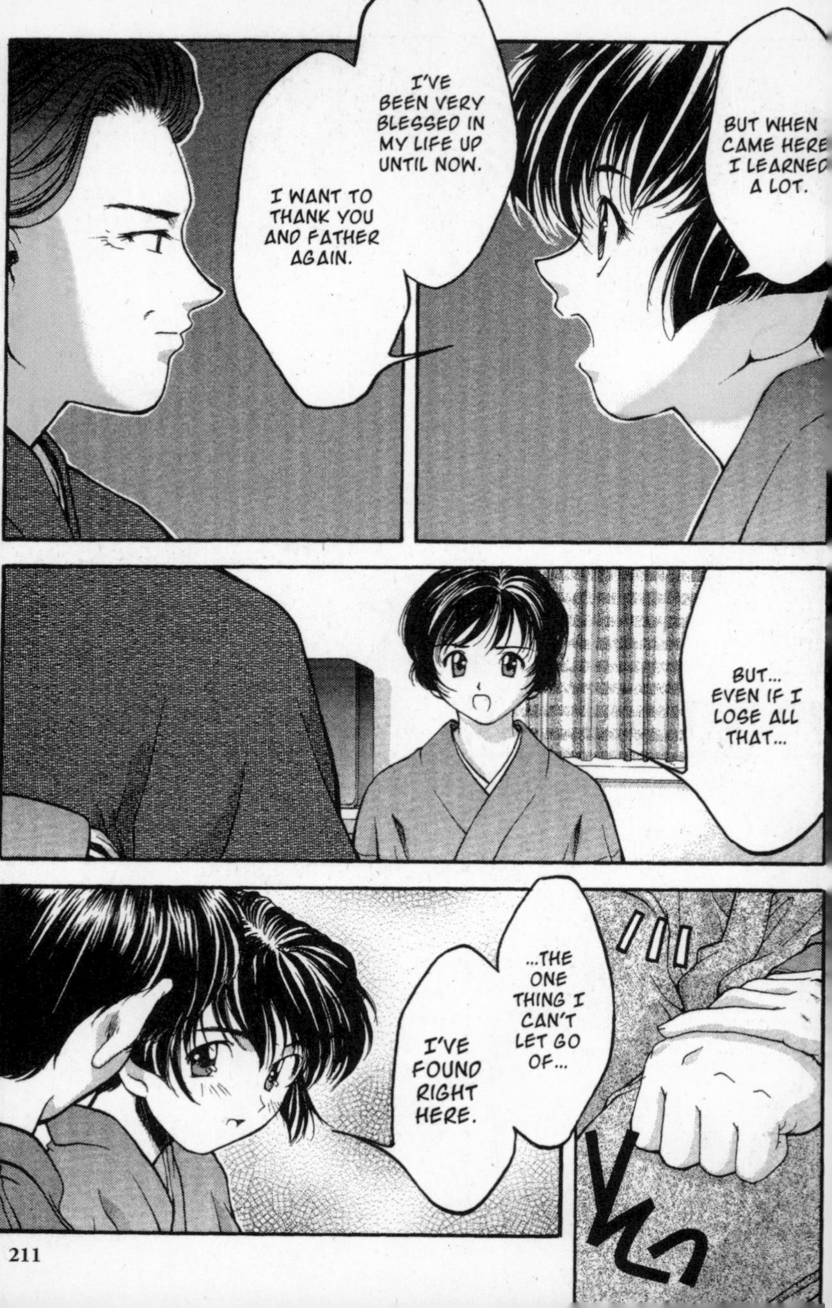
BUT WHEN CAME HERE I LEARNED A LOT.
I'VE BEEN VERY BLESSED IN MY LIFE UP UNTIL NOW.
I WANT TO THANK YOU AND FATHER AGAIN.
BUT... EVEN IF I LOSE ALL THAT...
...THE ONE THING I CAN'T LET GO OF...
I'VE FOUND RIGHT HERE.

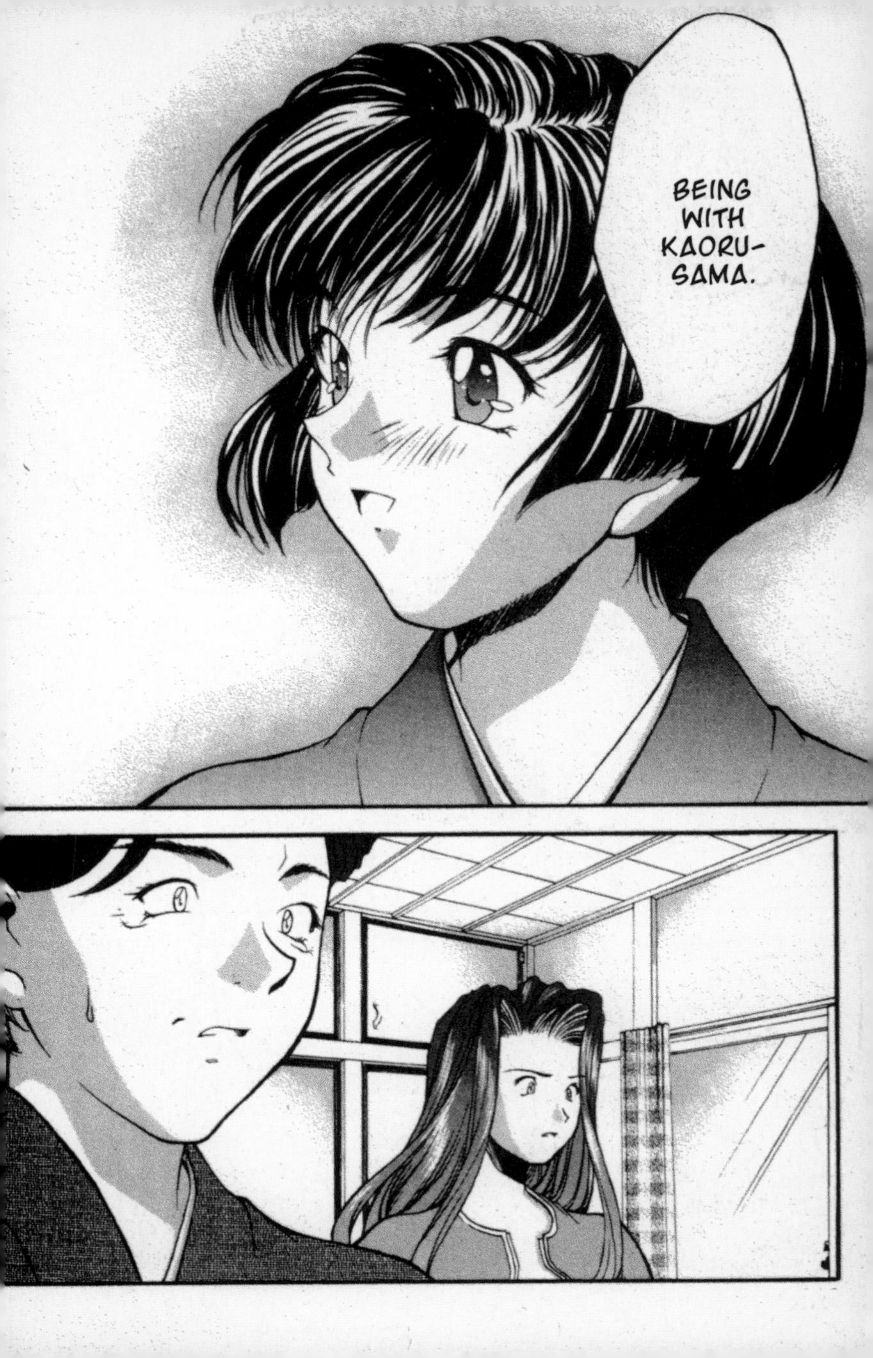
BEING WITH KAORU-SAMA.

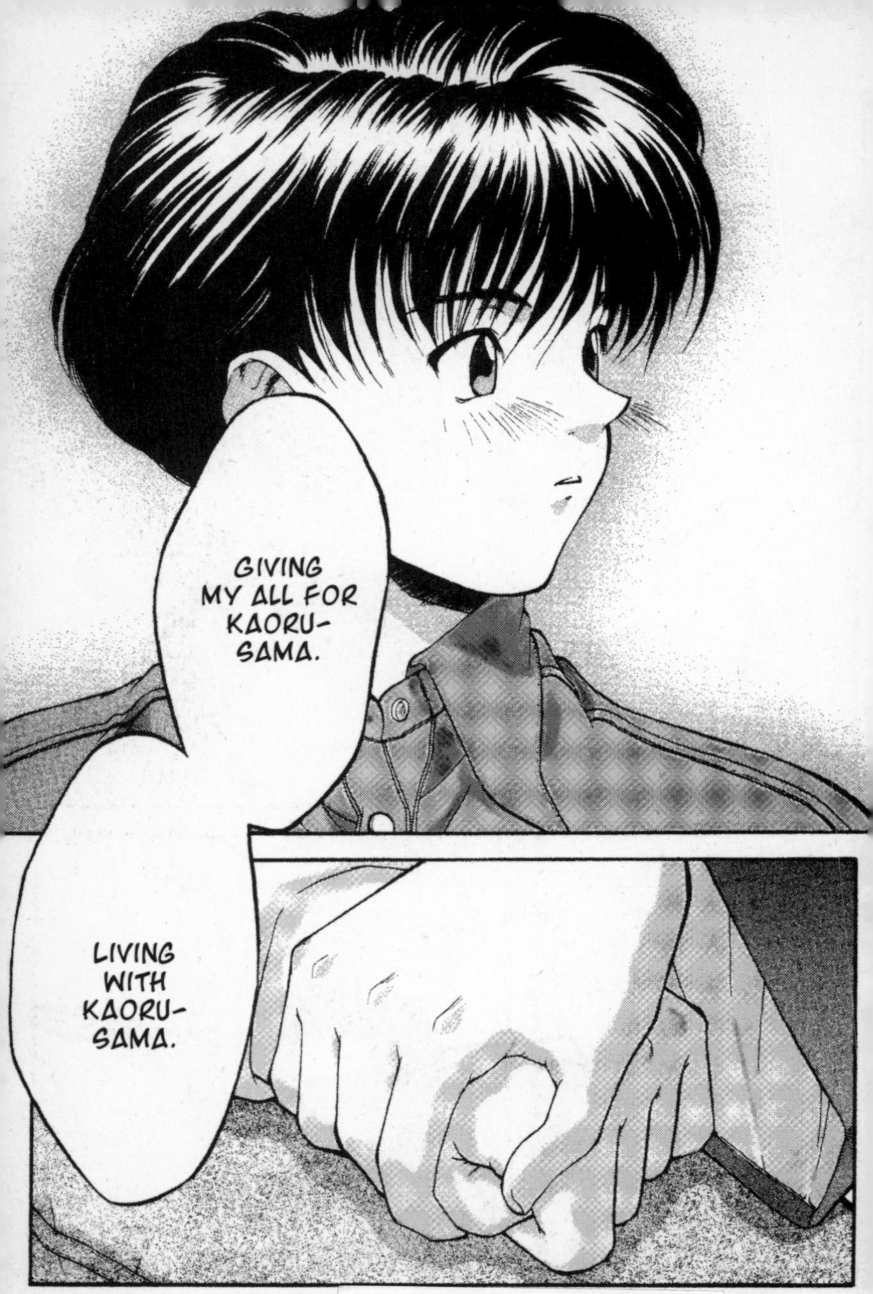
GIVING MY ALL FOR KAORU-SAMA.
LIVING WITH KAORU-SAMA.

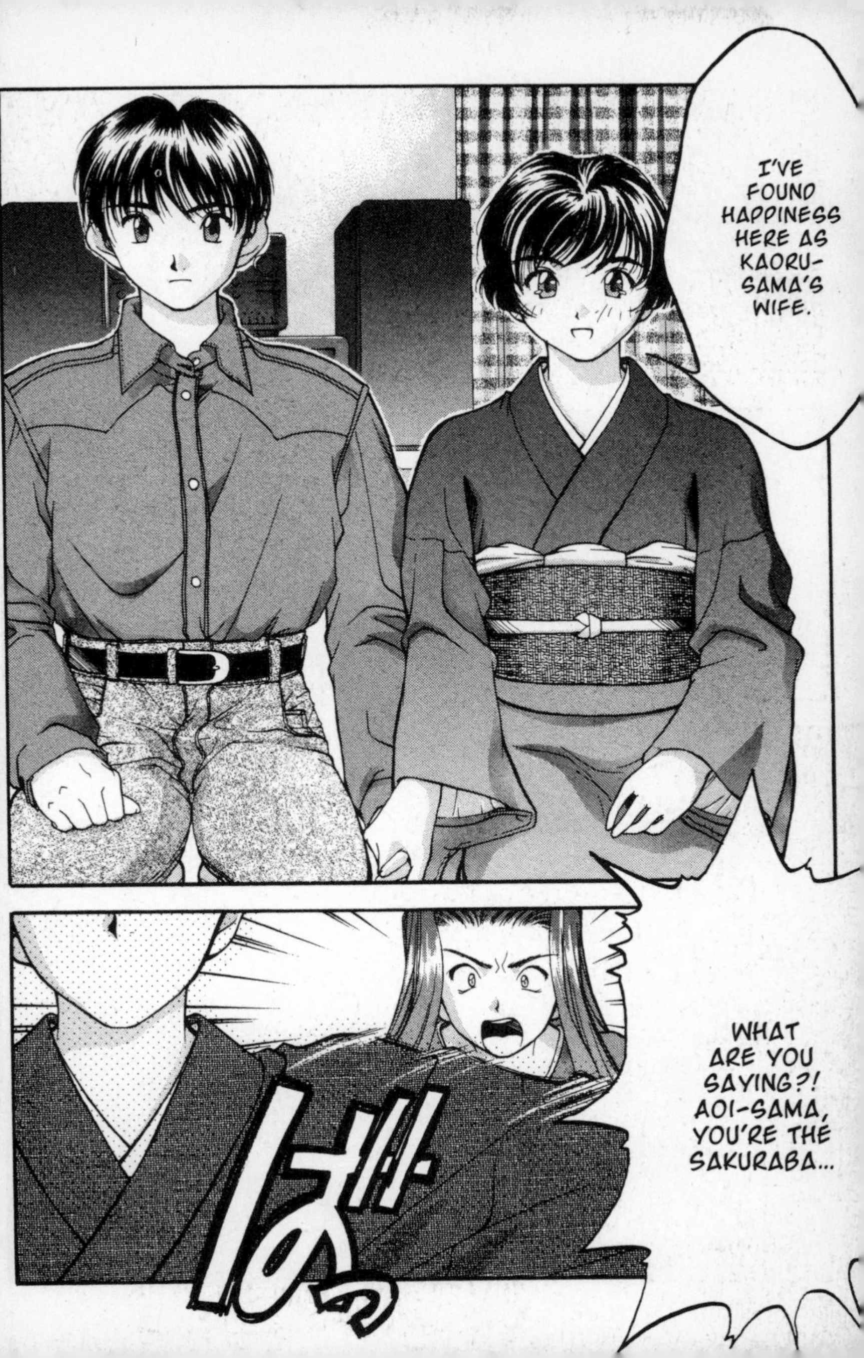
I'VE FOUND HAPPINESS HERE AS KAORU-SAMA'S WIFE.
WHAT ARE YOU SAYING?! AOI-SAMA, YOU'RE THE SAKURABA...
はっ

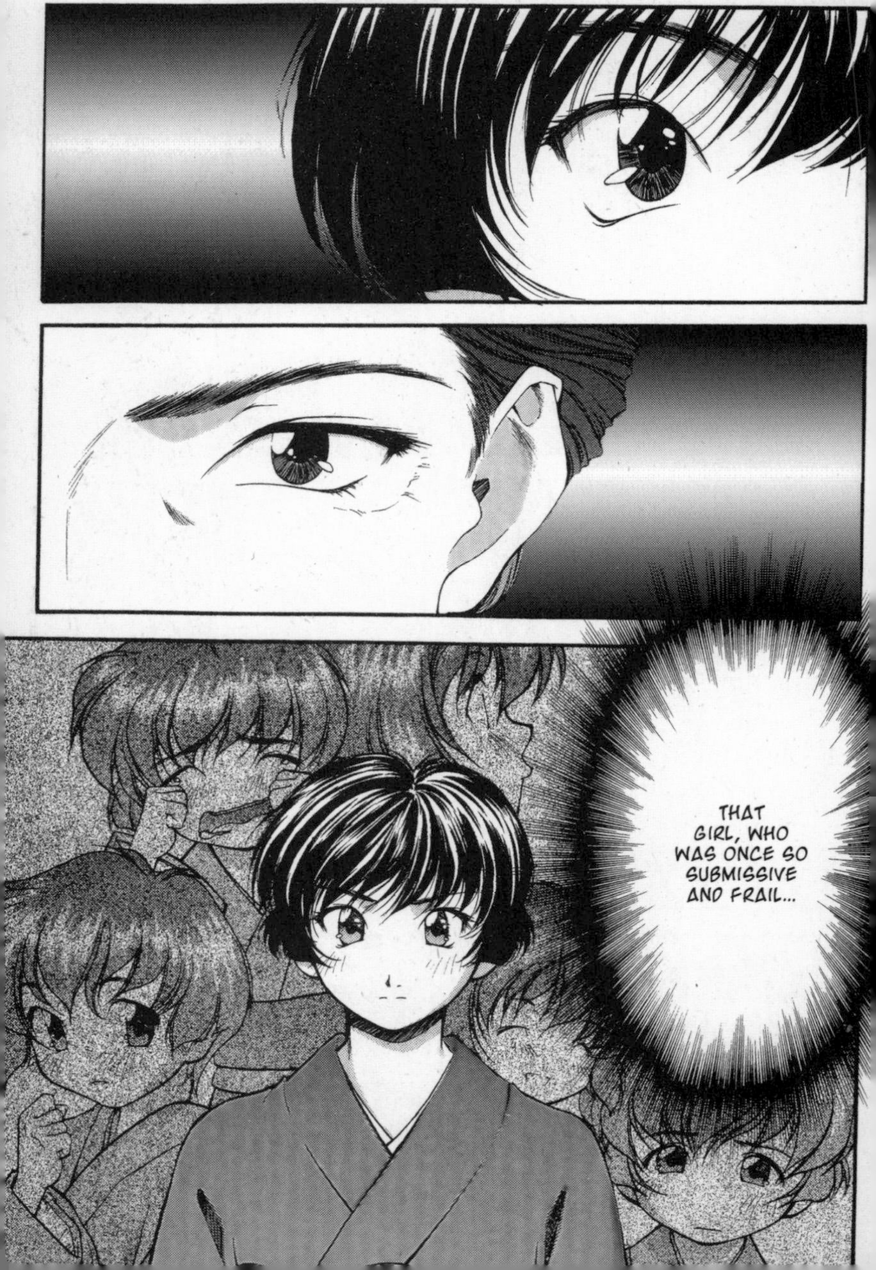
THAT GIRL, WHO WAS ONCE SO SUBMISSIVE AND FRAIL...

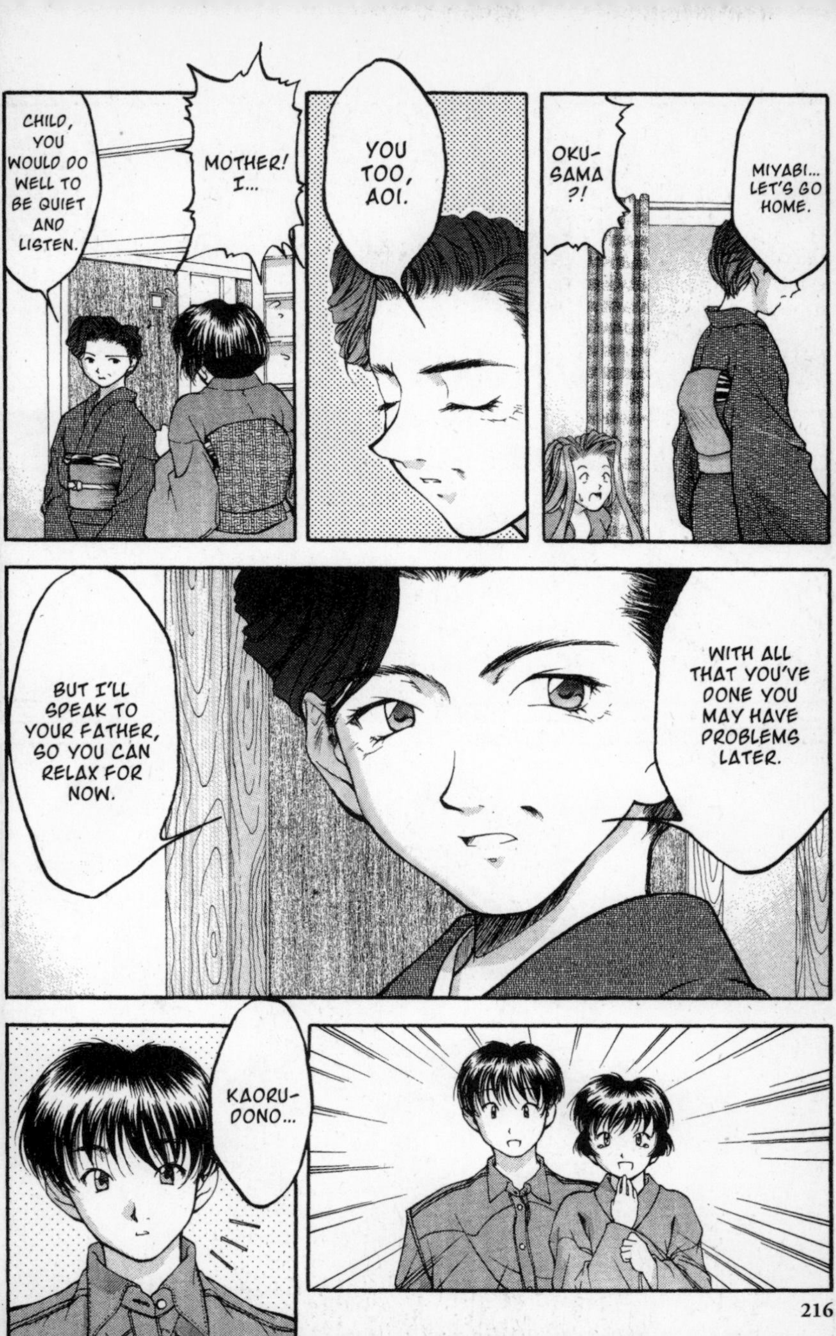
MIYABI... LET'S GO HOME.
OKU-SAMA ?!
YOU TOO, AOI.
MOTHER! I...
CHILD, YOU WOULD DO WELL TO BE QUIET AND LISTEN.
WITH ALL THAT YOU'VE DONE YOU MAY HAVE PROBLEMS LATER.
BUT I'LL SPEAK TO YOUR FATHER, SO YOU CAN RELAX FOR NOW.
KAORU-DONO...

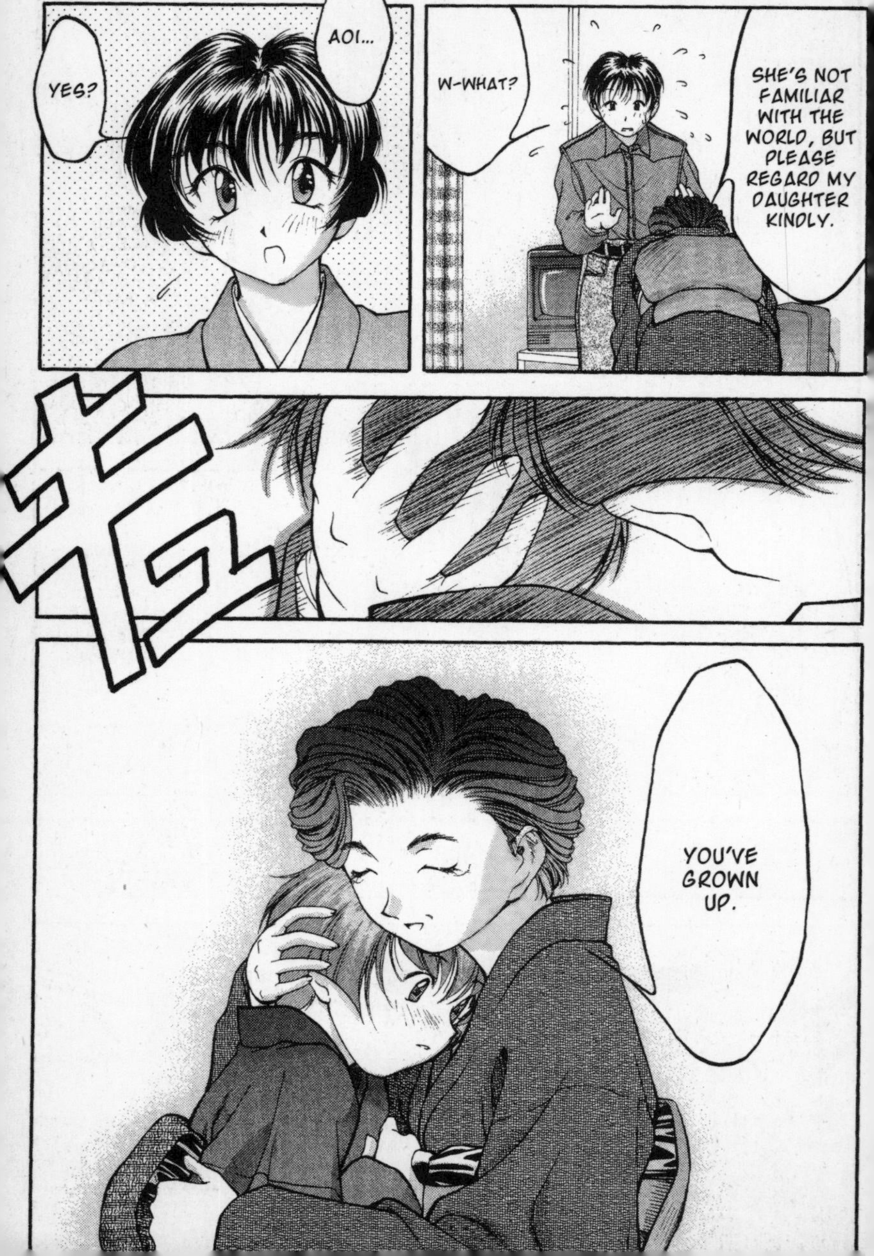
SHE'S NOT FAMILIAR WITH THE WORLD, BUT PLEASE REGARD MY DAUGHTER KINDLY.
W-WHAT?
AOI...
YES?
ギュ
YOU'VE GROWN UP.

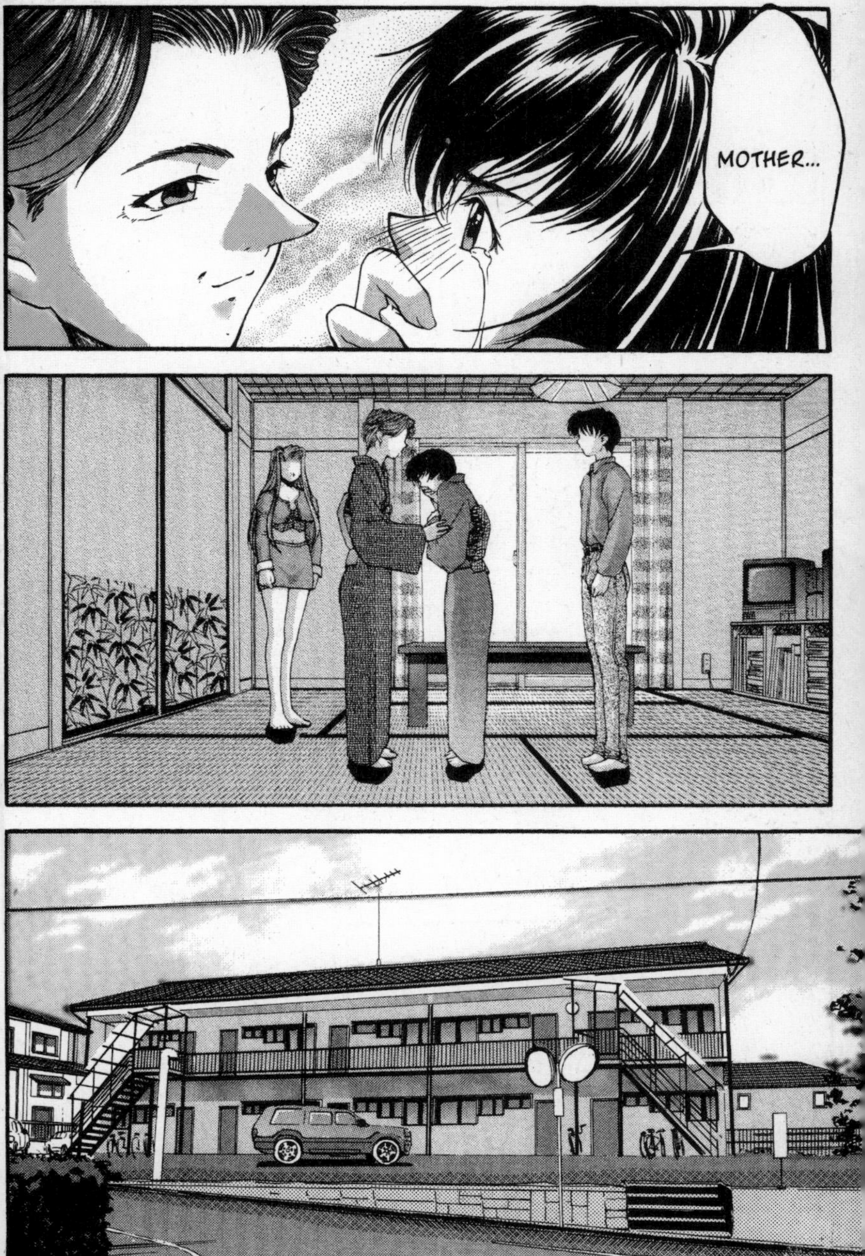
MOTHER...

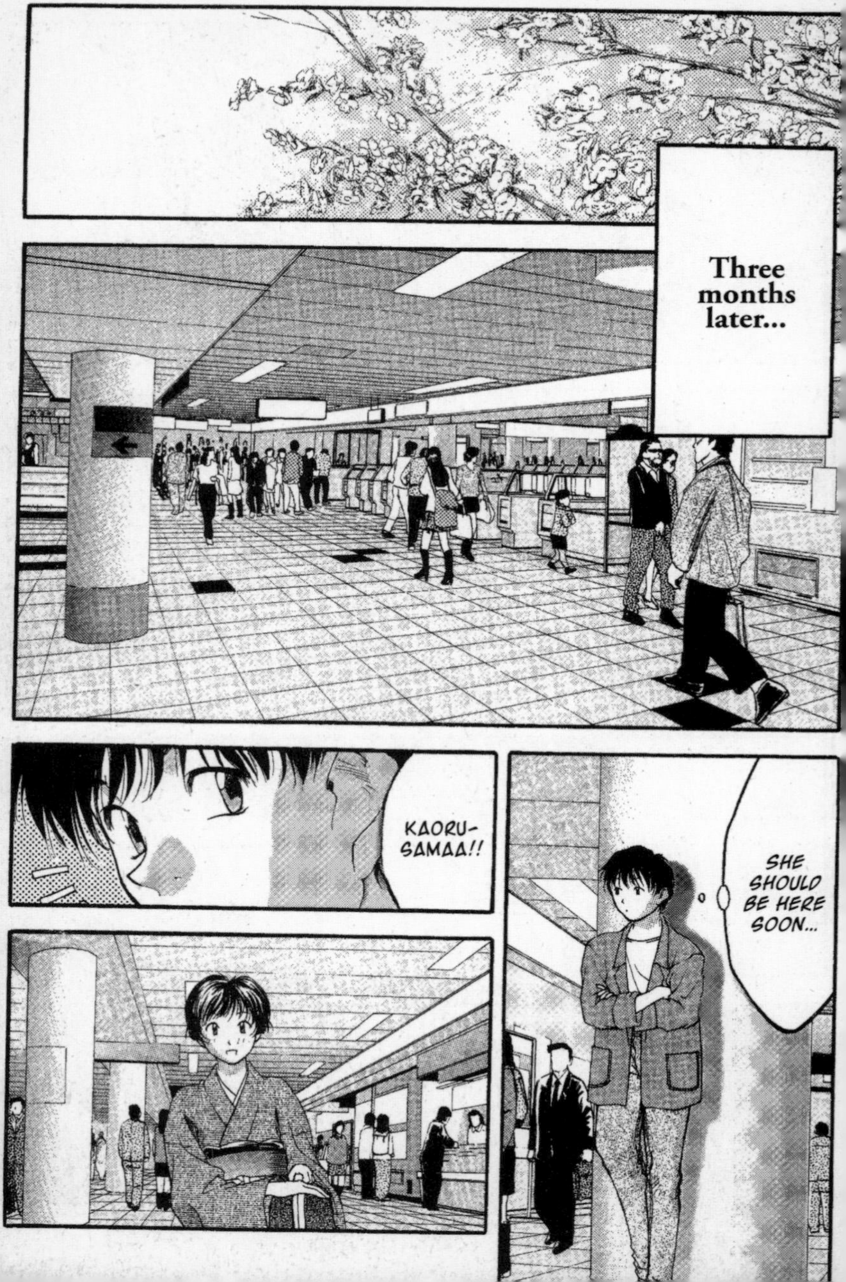
Three months later...
SHE SHOULD BE HERE SOON...
KAORU-SAMAA!!

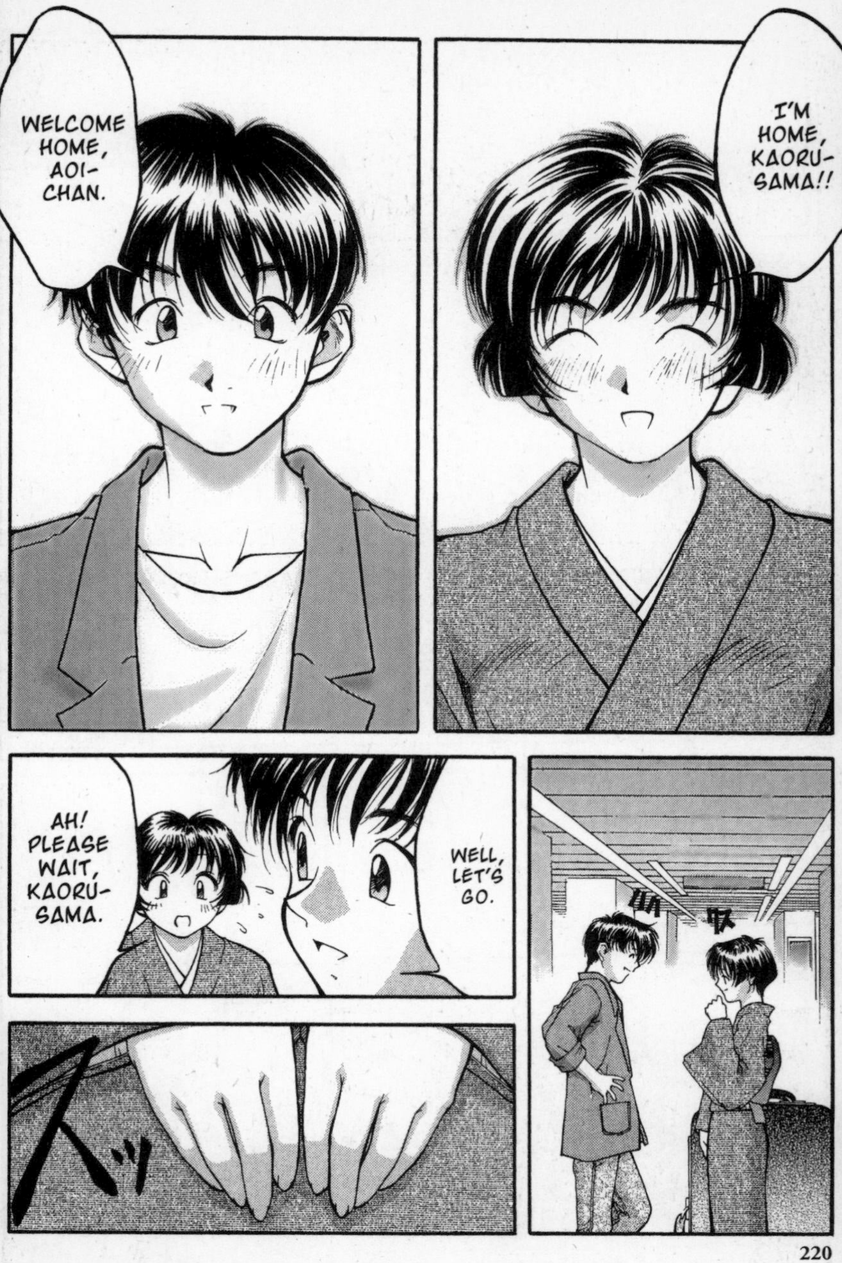
I'M HOME, KAORU-SAMA!!
WELCOME HOME, AOI-CHAN.
WELL, LET'S GO.
AH! PLEASE WAIT, KAORU-SAMA.

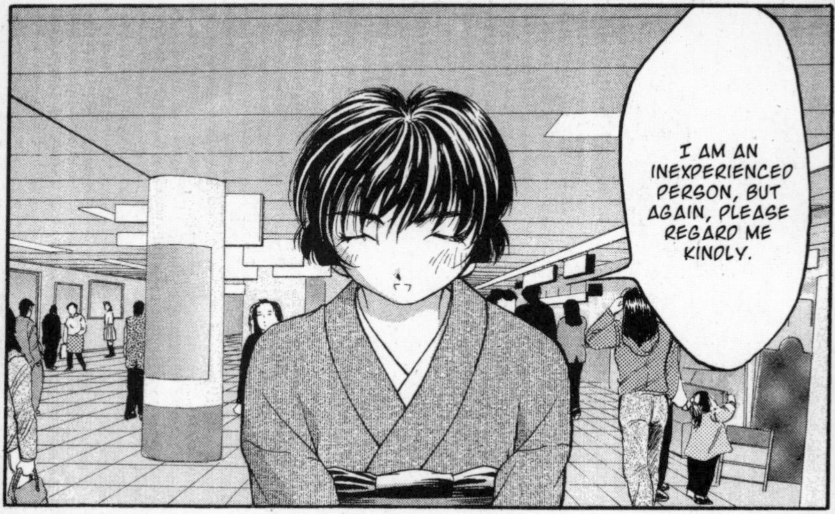
I AM AN INEXPERIENCED PERSON, BUT AGAIN, PLEASE REGARD ME KINDLY.

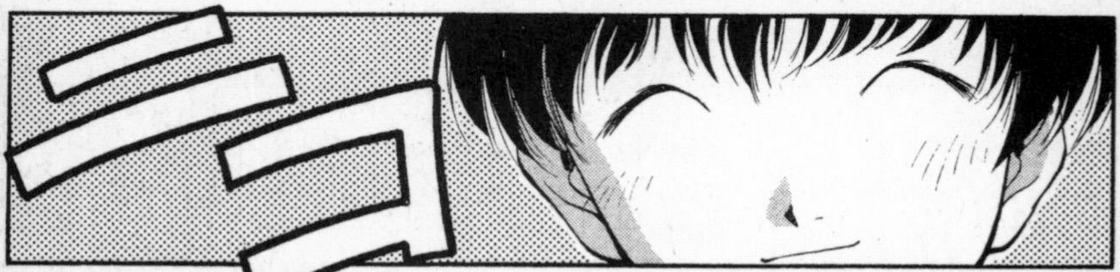

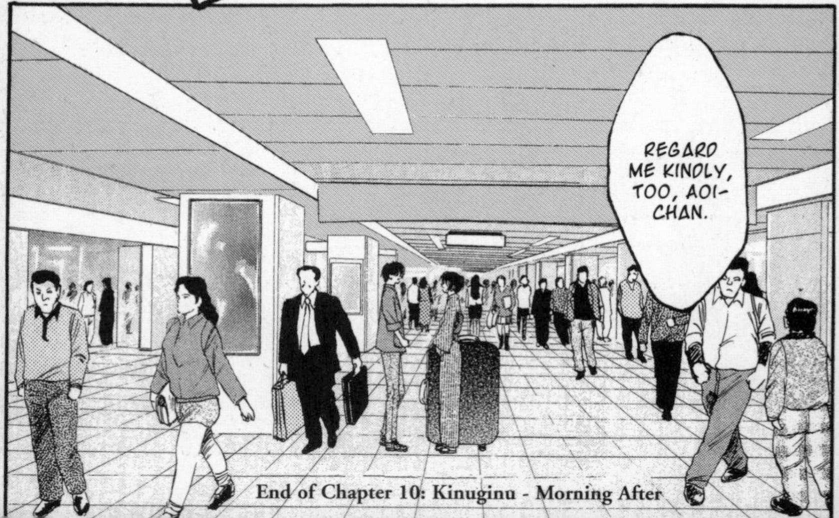
REGARD ME KINDLY, TOO, AOI-CHAN.

End of Chapter 10: Kinuginu - Morning After

# STAFF

## JAPAN STAFF

**ASSISTANTS**
Asahi Katuomaki
Hiroaki Satou
Kazuhiko Haru
Kazukata Maekawa
Keizou Isikawa

Makoto Takano
Makoto Nanase
Mitukage Syoutengai
Miyuki Nara
Satosi Kituyama
Victor U-5

**EDITOR**
Shouichi Nakazawa

**PRODUCTION**
Studio Little Cotton
Kou Fumizuki

## TOKYOPOP® STAFF

**TRANSLATION**
Alethea Nibley
Athena Nibley
w/ Jamie Rich

**EDITOR**
Jake Forbes

**DESIGN**
Aaron Suhr

**PRODUCTION**
Jennifer Miller
Tony DePietro
Eddie Ramirez
James Dashiell
Deron Bennett
James Lee

**VP PRODUCTION**
Ron Klamert

**PRESIDENT & C.O.O.**
John Parker

**PUBLISHER & C.E.O**
Stuart Levy

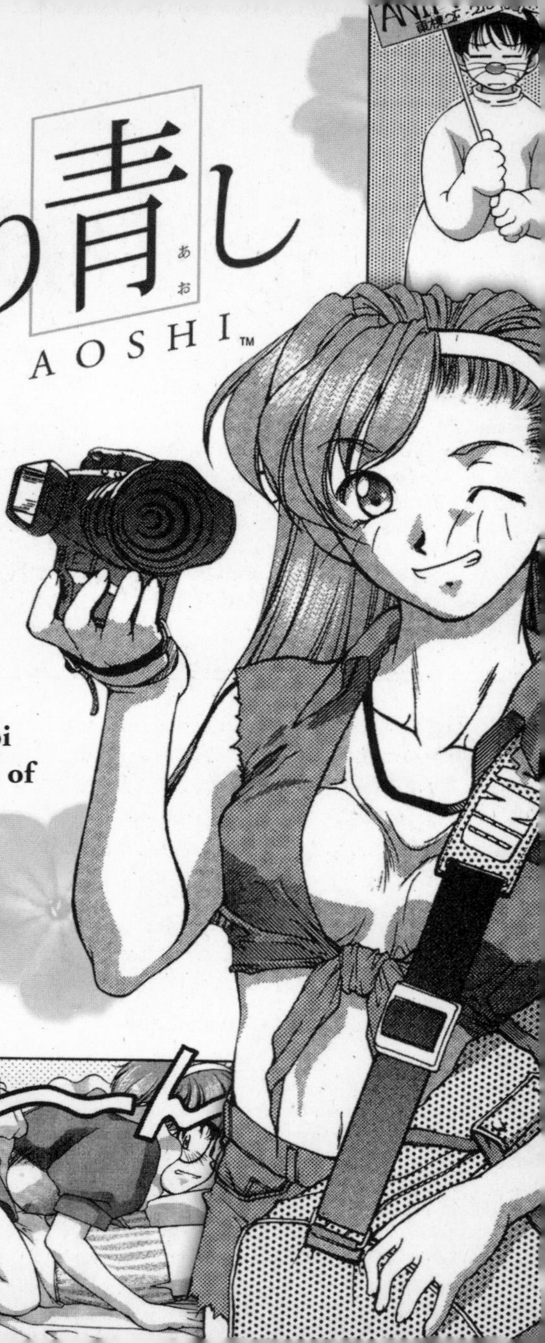

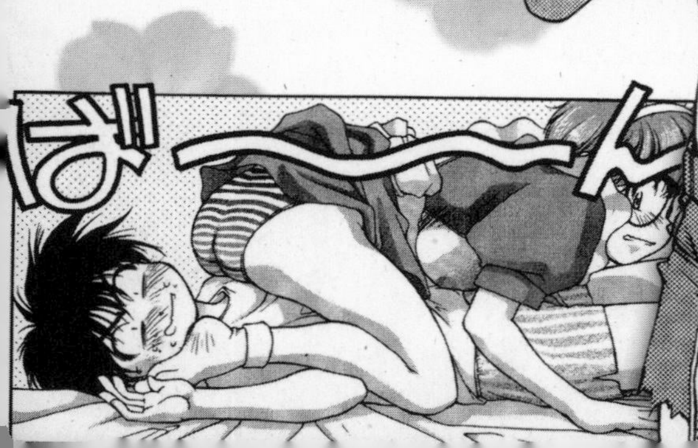

# GLOSSARY

藍より青し

AI YORI AOSHI™

**Charms:**
Many types of charms are sold at Buddhist Temples and Shinto Shrines all over Japan. Charms can be bought for oneself for luck, protection or good fortune, or given to others. A charm from a loved one is a very special gift. Even though organized religion as it is known in the West is not as prevalent in Japanese society, traditions and superstitions such as this are an important part of daily life for many Japanese.

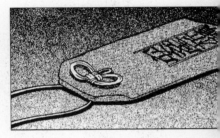

**Koizumi Studybook:**
(Seen on Pg. 55) A five volume manga series by Mari Koizumi that ran in *Young Animal* from 1998-2001. In this series, Mari-sensei and his assistant Nanako Kitoh provide lessons on various sexual/perverted subjects. It is a parody of the immensely popular (in Japan) manga series *Futari Ecchi*, a series about a pair of newlyweds who encounter problems in their marriage and sex lives.

**Zaibatsu:**
The name for the great family-controlled Banking/Industrial/Business combines which dominated Japan's economy in the 20th Century. Following World War II, many great zaibatsu networked together to form keiretsu, helping Japan to become the world economic power that it is today. The top zaibatsu are Mitsui, Mitsubishi, Dai Ichi Kangyo, Sumitomo, Sanwa and Fuyo. Zaibatsu are comparable to the "Barons of Industry" in early 20th Century America.

# Wafuku: Traditional Japanese Clothes

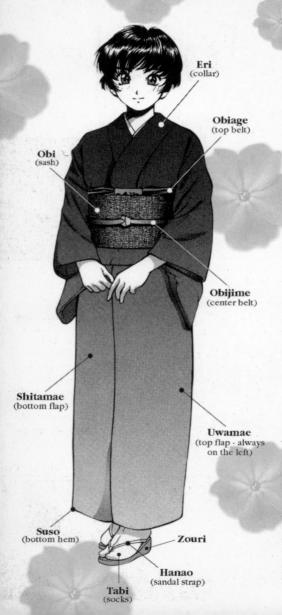

**Eri**
(collar)

**Obiage**
(top belt)

**Obi**
(sash)

**Obijime**
(center belt)

**Shitamae**
(bottom flap)

**Uwamae**
(top flap - always
on the left)

**Suso**
(bottom hem)

**Zouri**

**Hanao**
(sandal strap)

**Tabi**
(socks)

## Kimono:

Kimono, a word originally referring to any form of clothing, today refers specifically to traditional Japanese dress. Kimono as we know them today came into fashion during Japan's Heian period (794 to 1192), the height of Japan's imperial court when the capital moved to Kyoto. In the court society of the Heian period, female kimono were worn in many layers, with great importance placed upon the color used in each layer, which changed depending upon the season. Traditional kimono have many layers which cannot be seen once the dressing is complete. Kimono as they are commonly known in the Western World today, are less elaborate by comparison, often worn in a single layer, but that in no way diminishes their beauty and the care taken in making them. A crucial part of the kimono is the *Obi,* or sash, which is both beautiful and crucial for holding the kimono together. Today, most Japanese don't wear formal kimono as everyday attire, but reserve them for special occasions such as weddings, holidays and festivals. Aoi, being raised in a traditional manner by a very traditional family, is an exception to this.

## Sandals:

Japanese sandals come in two main types: *Geta* and *Zouri;* worn by men and women with kimono. Geta have wooden slats jutting out separately underneath the plane of the sandal that produce a clacking sound. Aoi's sandals are zouri, flat-bottomed sandals that are noticeably quieter. An important part of either form of sandal is the *Hanao,* the thong that holds the sandal to the foot. Hanao come in various colors and can even be patterned after kimono designs for the perfect match.

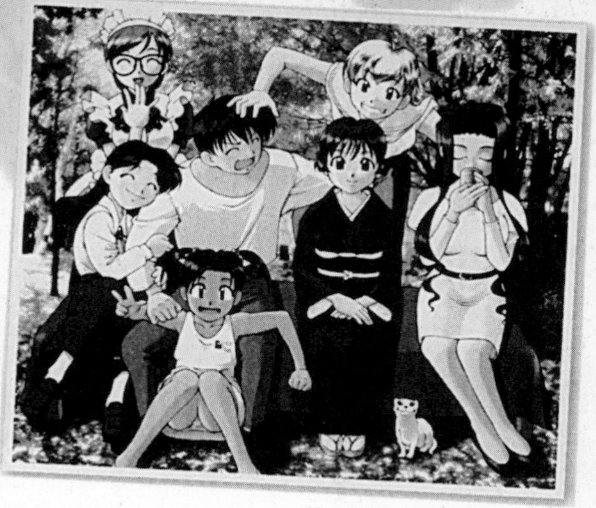

JAPANESE WEBSITE
WWW.AIYORIAOSHI.COM

ENGLISH WEBSITE
WWW.TOKYOPOP.COM

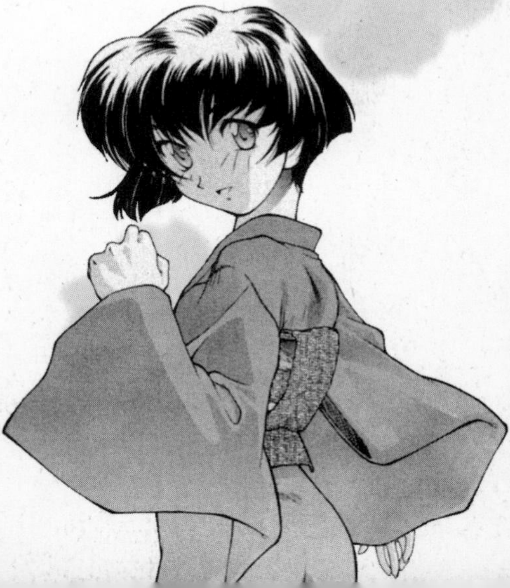

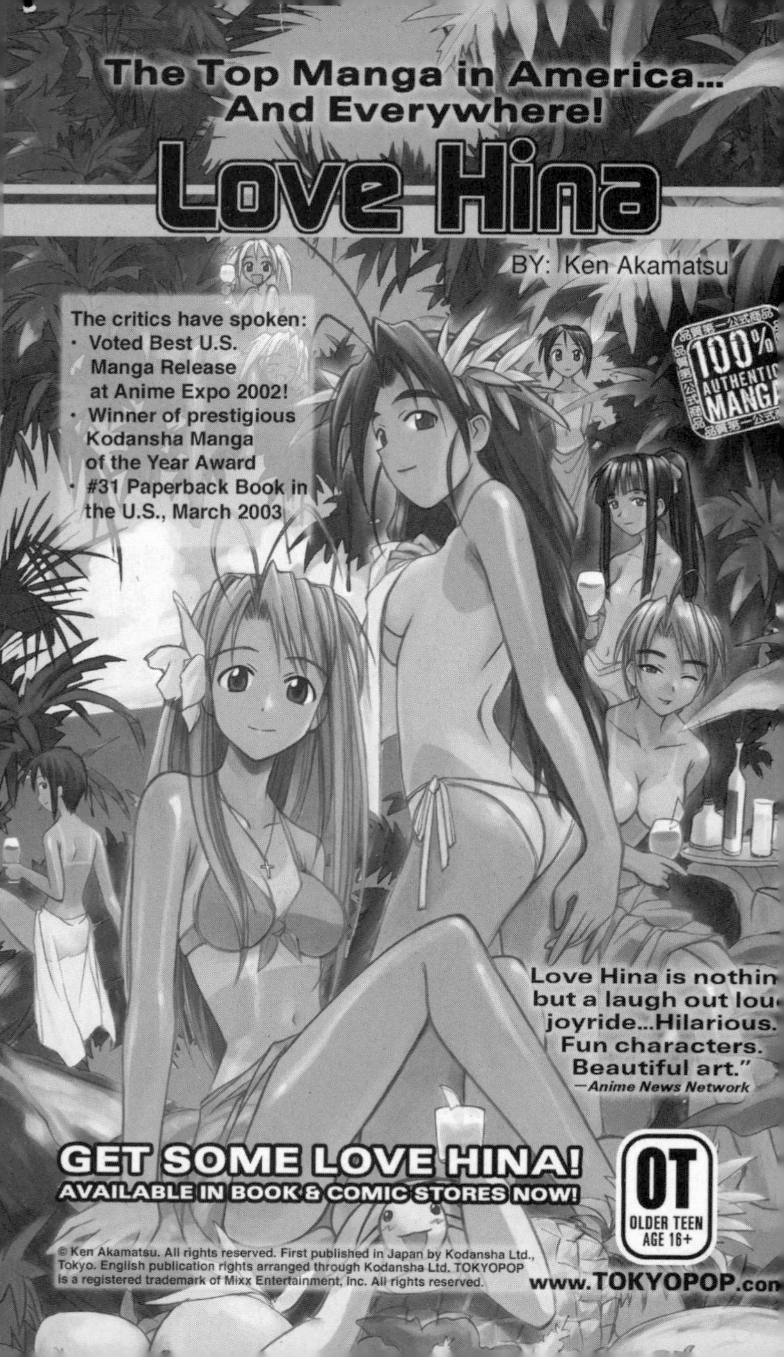

The Top Manga in America...
And Everywhere!
Love Hina
BY: Ken Akamatsu
The critics have spoken:
• Voted Best U.S. Manga Release at Anime Expo 2002!
• Winner of prestigious Kodansha Manga of the Year Award
• #31 Paperback Book in the U.S., March 2003
100% AUTHENTIC MANGA
Love Hina is nothin
but a laugh out lou
joyride...Hilarious.
Fun characters.
Beautiful art."
—Anime News Network
GET SOME LOVE HINA!
AVAILABLE IN BOOK & COMIC STORES NOW!
OT
OLDER TEEN AGE 16+
© Ken Akamatsu. All rights reserved. First published in Japan by Kodansha Ltd., Tokyo. English publication rights arranged through Kodansha Ltd. TOKYOPOP is a registered trademark of Mixx Entertainment, Inc. All rights reserved.
www.TOKYOPOP.com

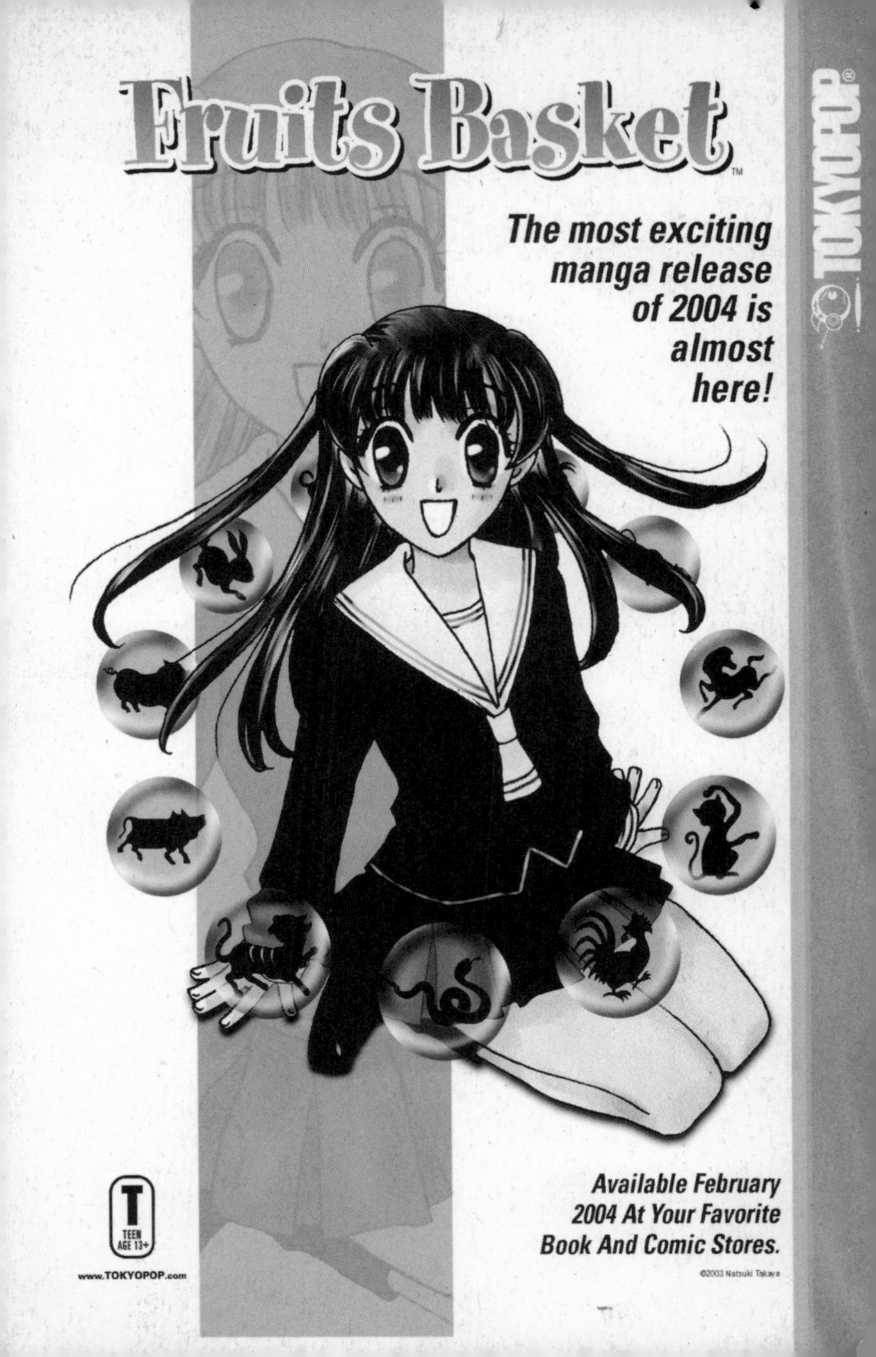

TOKYOPOP®
Fruits Basket™
The most exciting manga release of 2004 is almost here!
T
TEEN AGE 13+
www.TOKYOPOP.com
Available February 2004 At Your Favorite Book And Comic Stores.
©2003 Natsuki Takaya

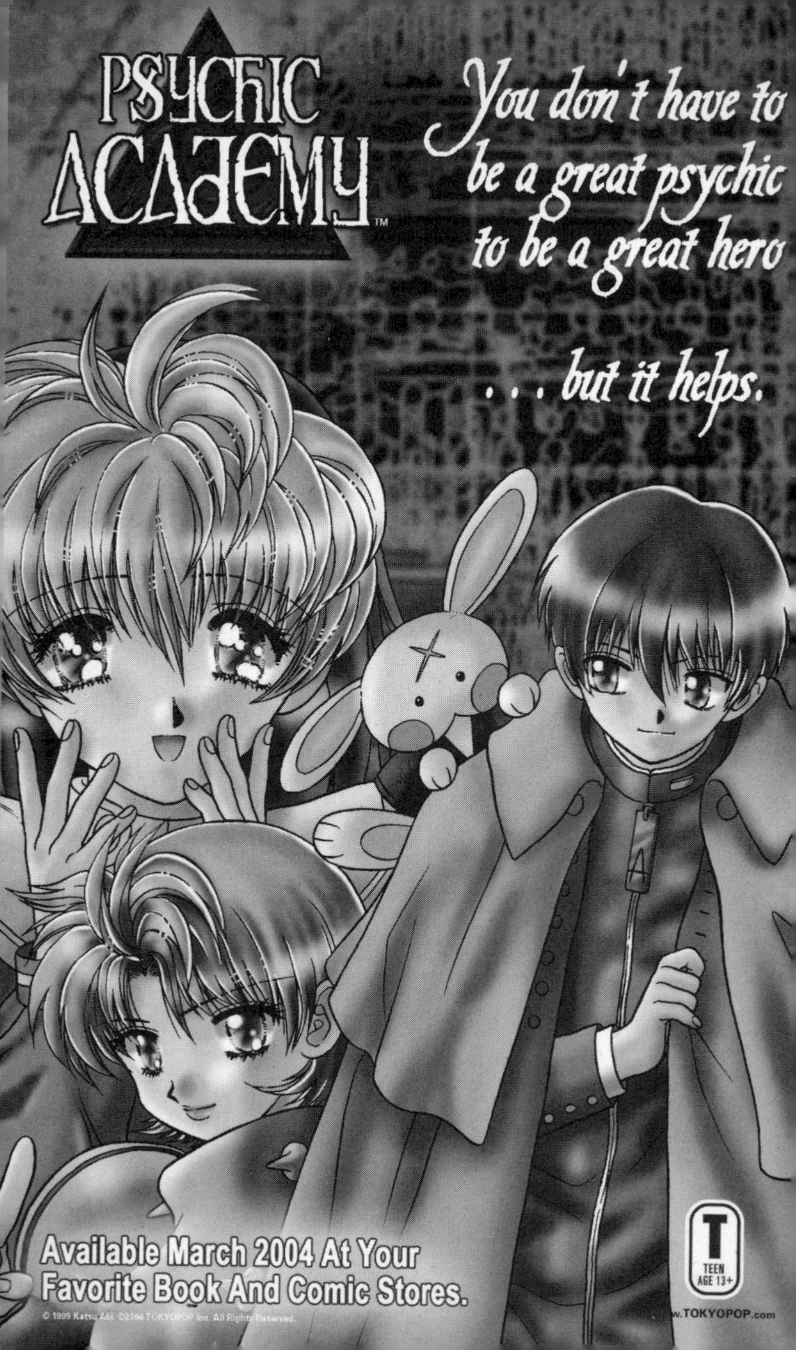
PSYCHIC ACADEMY™
You don't have to be a great psychic to be a great hero
. . . but it helps.
Available March 2004 At Your Favorite Book And Comic Stores.
T TEEN AGE 13+
© 1999 Katsu Aki. ©2004 TOKYOPOP Inc. All Rights Reserved.
w.TOKYOPOP.com

## MANGA

.HACK//LEGEND OF THE TWILIGHT
@LARGE
A.I. LOVE YOU February 2004
AI YORI AOSHI
ANGELIC LAYER
BABY BIRTH
BATTLE ROYALE
BATTLE VIXENS April 2004
BIRTH May 2004
BRAIN POWERED
BRIGADOON
B'TX January 2004
CARDCAPTOR SAKURA
CARDCAPTOR SAKURA: MASTER OF THE CLOW
CARDCAPTOR SAKURA: BOXED SET COLLECTION 1
CARDCAPTOR SAKURA: BOXED SET COLLECTION 2
  March 2004
CHOBITS
CHRONICLES OF THE CURSED SWORD
CLAMP SCHOOL DETECTIVES
CLOVER
COMIC PARTY  June 2004
CONFIDENTIAL CONFESSIONS
CORRECTOR YUI
COWBOY BEBOP: BOXED SET THE COMPLETE
  COLLECTION
CRESCENT MOON May 2004
CREST OF THE STARS  June 2004
CYBORG 009
DEMON DIARY
DIGIMON
DIGIMON SERIES 3 April 2004
DIGIMON ZERO TWO  February 2004
DNANGEL  April 2004
DOLL May 2004
DRAGON HUNTER
DRAGON KNIGHTS
DUKLYON: CLAMP SCHOOL DEFENDERS
DV June 2004
ERICA SAKURAZAWA
FAERIES' LANDING
FAKE
FLCL
FORBIDDEN DANCE
FRUITS BASKET February 2004
G GUNDAM
GATEKEEPERS
GETBACKERS February 2004
GHOST!  March 2004
GIRL GOT GAME
GRAVITATION
GTO

GUNDAM WING
GUNDAM WING: BATTLEFIELD OF PACIFISTS
GUNDAM WING: ENDLESS WALTZ
GUNDAM WING: THE LAST OUTPOST
HAPPY MANIA
HARLEM BEAT
I.N.V.U.
INITIAL D
ISLAND
JING: KING OF BANDITS
JULINE
JUROR 13 March 2004
KARE KANO
KILL ME, KISS ME February 2004
KINDAICHI CASE FILES, THE
KING OF HELL
KODOCHA: SANA'S STAGE
LAMENT OF THE LAMB May 2004
LES BIJOUX February 2004
LIZZIE MCGUIRE
LOVE HINA
LUPIN III
LUPIN III SERIES 2
MAGIC KNIGHT RAYEARTH I
MAGIC KNIGHT RAYEARTH II February 2004
MAHOROMATIC: AUTOMATIC MAIDEN May 2004
MAN OF MANY FACES
MARMALADE BOY
MARS
METEOR METHUSELA June 2004
METROID June 2004
MINK April 2004
MIRACLE GIRLS
MIYUKI-CHAN IN WONDERLAND
MODEL May 2004
NELLY MUSIC MANGA  April 2004
ONE April 2004
PARADISE KISS
PARASYTE
PEACH GIRL
PEACH GIRL CHANGE OF HEART
PEACH GIRL RELAUNCH BOX SET
PET SHOP OF HORRORS
PITA-TEN January 2004
PLANET LADDER February 2004
PLANETES
PRIEST
PRINCESS AI April 2004
PSYCHIC ACADEMY March 2004
RAGNAROK
RAGNAROK: BOXED SET COLLECTION 1
RAVE MASTER
RAVE MASTER: BOXED SET March 2004

# STOP!

Sumimasen! In your haste, you have opened to the back of the book. It would be most unfortunate if you were to start reading from this point. Perhaps you are new to TOKYOPOP's 100% authentic format? You see, in Japan, pages and panels read from right-to-left, and in respect for the manga-ka, TOKYOPOP keeps this format intact in its translated manga. At first it might feel bizarre reading like this, but we assure you that it will be second nature in no time! Please, so that you may properly enjoy this manga, turn the book over and begin reading from the other side. Arigatou gozaimasu!

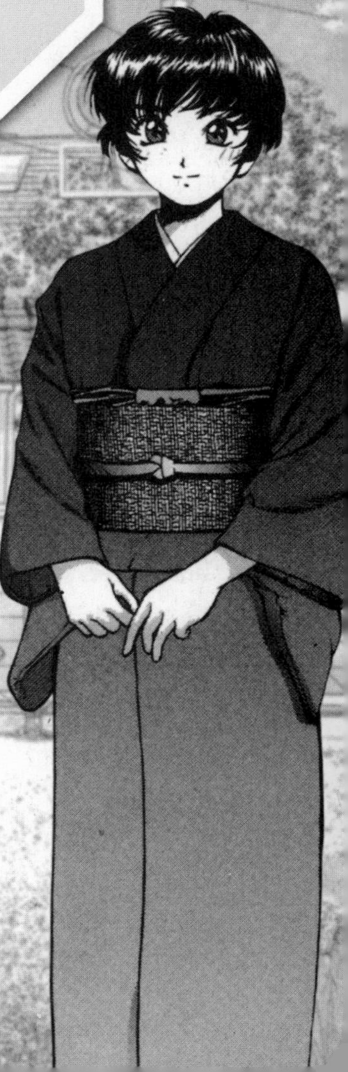

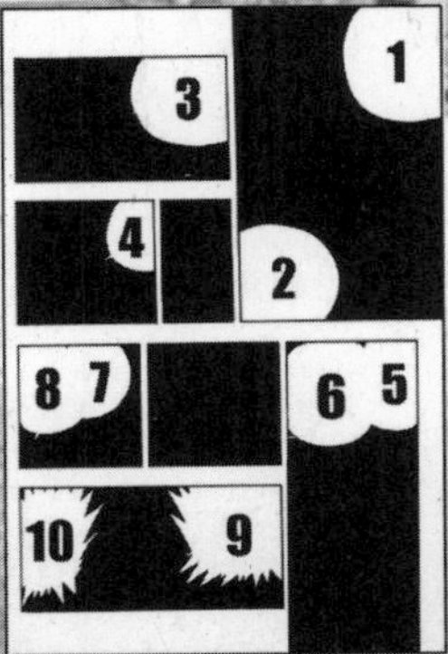
1
2
3
4
5
6
7
8
9
10